INCEST IN SWEDEN, 1680–1940

LUND
UNIVERSITY
PRESS

Incest in Sweden, 1680–1940

A history of forbidden relations

BONNIE CLEMENTSSON

Translation: Lena Olsson

Lund University Press

Lund University Press

The Joint Faculties of Humanities and Theology

LUND UNIVERSITY

LUND
UNIVERSITY
PRESS

P.O. Box 117
SE-221 00 LUND
Sweden
http://lunduniversitypress.lu.se

Lund University Press books are published in collaboration with Manchester University Press.

British Library Cataloguing-in-Publication Data
A catalogue record for this book is available from the British Library

ISBN 978-91-984699-0-5 hardback
ISBN 978-91-984699-1-2 open access

First published 2020

Lund University Press gratefully acknowledges publication assistance from the Thora Ohlsson Foundation (*Thora Ohlssons Stiftelse*)

Typeset
by New Best-set Typesetters Ltd

Contents

List of illustrations *page* viii
List of tables xi
List of graphs xiii
Abbreviations xiv

Introduction 1
The origin of incest prohibitions 2
Aim of the present study 6
Interaction, the creation of norms, and social control 8
Material and methodology 12
Laws and parliamentary material 12
Judgement-book material 14
Applications for dispensation 17
Analysing the material 20
The complexity of incestuous relationships 21
Research on incest 23
Outline 30

1 **Background and context** 32
The early modern judicial system 32
The secular judicial structure 32
The ecclesiastical structure 34
The Christian incest prohibition in a historical perspective 34

2 **Incest: a religious crime, 1680–1750** 46
Applications for dispensation 46
Marriage: an alliance based on feelings and reason 46
The prohibitions are challenged 49
Relationship categories 50

Virtuous or depraved love 51
Balancing between the legal and the illegal 57
Additional uncertain definitions 65
Criminal cases 69
The punishments 69
The court: a flexible practice 73
The statistics of the crime 77
Accusation and confession 80
Mitigating and aggravating circumstances 84
Violence and exploitation 89
Love and passion 98
Kinship 107
The local community 118
In preparation for the Civil Code of 1734 130
Partial summary and overview, 1680–1750 133

3 **Incest: a moral crime, 1750–1840** **136**
In the Age of Enlightenment 136
The development of jurisprudence 137
Applications for dispensation 139
An increase in the number of applications for marriage 139
Economic and cultural transformations in society 142
The applicants' arguments 146
The authorities' response 151
Challenges to the generational order 158
Criminal cases 166
Fewer criminal cases and milder punishments 166
Fewer convictions 170
Love: a mitigating circumstance 175
Violence and coercion 181
Incest: a moral crime 183
Incest prohibitions in public hearings 188
For protection against immorality 190
In support of healthy family relationships 194
Economic concerns and demands for justice 200
Partial summary and overview, 1740–1840 203

4 **Incest: a crime of violence, 1840–1940** **207**
An intermediate period, 1840–72 209
The Penal Act of 1864 209
Applications for dispensation 213
Criminal cases 216

The turn-of-the-century world of ideas, 1872–1940 225
The Marriage Act of 1915 228
Applications for dispensation 230
Criminal cases 253
Partial summary and overview, 1840–1940 264

The phenomenon of incest in Sweden over 250 years: a summary discussion 267
Continuity and change 270
Incest crimes: from religious crimes to moral crimes to crimes of violence 270
Economic circumstances 271
The institution of marriage 272
Views on love and passion 273
Kinship: from extended households to nuclear families 275
Kinship: family hierarchies 277
Kinship: from family position to age relationship 279
Incest offenders: from perpetrators to victims 281
And then what? 283

Appendix: Tables 287
Bibliography 300
Index 326

Illustrations

1 Hundred-court judgment book from the eighteenth century. Photo: VLA 11
2 In February 1730, the two cousins Nils Arvidsson and Ingeborg Bengtsdotter applied for permission to marry. Judiciary Inspection, draft, 1730, 3 June, Nils Arvidsson, Ingeborg Bengtsdotter. Photo: RA 18
3 The hundred-court judge led the hearing of criminal cases at the local courts. Drawing by Göte Göransson (1921–2015), by permission of his family 30
4 Johan Stiernhöök (1596–1675). Stiernhöök was elevated to the nobility in 1649 and has been called 'the father of Swedish jurisprudence'. Unknown painter from second half of the seventeenth century. Legal Department, Uppsala University 43
5 Flogging in the town square was a public event. Drawing by Göte Göransson (1921–2015), by permission of his family 68
6 The women wore 'whipping bodices' that left their backs bare when they were birched. Drawing by Göte Göransson (1921–2015), by permission of his family 71
7 The Göta Court of Appeal was established in 1634 in Jönköping. Its jurisdiction included the southern parts of the Swedish mainland (Götaland and Värmland and, after 1658, also Skåne, Blekinge, and Halland). *Ny illustrerad tidning*, 1866:27 76
8 A peasant couple from the eighteenth century. *En karl med lja och en quinna med härf* [A man with a scythe and a woman with a rake] by Pehr Hilleström (1732–1816). The Nordic Museum 99

9 The authorities were apprised of several crimes via gossip and curious neighbours, but people from the local community could also make an investigation more difficult by withholding information or providing refuge for a fugitive. The image shows Swedish folk costumes from different parts of the country. The use of folk costumes decreased in the nineteenth century when factory-made clothes became more common. Lithograph by H. Jensen. Uppsala University Library, ID 14141 117
10 For centuries, regular church attendance was an important feature in the lives of Swedes. *Ny illustrerad tidning*, 1866:9 135
11 The 'Haustafel' was a section in Luther's Small Catechism, where the duties of the individual towards his or her fellow human beings were clarified on the basis of the person's position in society. Luther, Martin, *Doktor Martin Luthers Lilla Katekes med kort utveckling*, Lund, 1914 154
12 The county sheriff announces a royal proclamation. Drawing by C. J. Ljunggren (1790–1852). Uppsala University Library, ID 1068 166
13 A romantic encounter. Drawing by Peter Georg Sundius (1823–1900). Uppsala University Library, ID 7709 176
14 A discussion in the Council of the State. *Ny illustrerad tidning*, 1888:7 188
15 Negotiations in the Second Chamber of the Riksdag. *Ny illustrerad tidning*, 1867:9 212
16 In the nineteenth century, the hundred court was still led by the hundred-court judge and the co-opted lay judges. *Vårt folk*, Iduns tryckeri, Stockholm, 1894, p. 125 216
17 In connection with the Industrial Revolution the population in Swedish cities increased greatly, creating a need for altered urban environments. During the late nineteenth century, many old city blocks were torn down and replaced with large, modern stone buildings. This picture shows the Swedish capital, Stockholm, at the end of the nineteenth century. Drawing by H. Feychting (1865–1901). Uppsala University Library, ID 2075 225

18 Olof Kinberg (1873–1960), physician, psychiatrist, and co-author of *Incestproblemet i Sverige* ('The incest problem in Sweden'), which was published in 1943. Photo: Jan de Meyere. Stockholm City Museum 254
19 After the turn of the century in 1900, the majority of incest crimes discovered were committed in families from the lowest social strata. Incest hence came to be defined as a lower-class problem. *Ny illustrerad tidning*, 1871:10 257

Tables

1 Investigated criminal cases 15
2 Family relationships 23
3 Incest prohibitions and punishments according to Leviticus 36
4 Applications for dispensation directed to the Skara Cathedral Chapter, 1710–34 52
5 Incest prohibitions and punishments in Sweden c. 1700 70
6 Incest cases from GHA, 1694–1716, number of cases and relationships 78–79
7 Incest cases from GHA 1694–1716, the reciprocity of relationships 97
8 Incest cases from GHA 1694–1716, number of pregnancies 124
9 Incest cases at GHA 1694–1716, 1783–1800, 1810 167
10 Incest prohibitions and punishments in accordance with the Civil Code of 1734 169
11 Incest prohibitions and punishments in accordance with the Penal Act of 1864 211
12 Applications for dispensation directed to the Ministry of Justice, 1915–20 232

Appendix 1 Numbers of applications for dispensation directed to the Judiciary Inspection for the specified years 288–289
Appendix 2 Numbers of applications for dispensation directed to the Skara Cathedral Chapter for the specified years 290–291
Appendix 3 Incest cases within the jurisdiction of the Göta Court of Appeal, 1694–1716, 1783–1800, 1810, 1840–58 292

Appendix 4	Incest prohibitions and punishments in Sweden 1500–2000, a schematic overview	293–295
Appendix 5	People executed for incest in Sweden 1749–1802	296–297
Appendix 6	Established punishments for incest criminals who risked the death penalty	298–299

Graphs

Graph 1 Applications for dispensation directed to the Judiciary Inspection, 1730–1815 140
Graph 2 Applications for dispensation directed to the Judiciary Inspection, 1780–1870, selected categories 214

Abbreviations

A.K.	Parliamentary records of the Second Chamber (*Andra kammarens riksdagsprotokoll*)
Bd	Parliamentary records of the peasant estate
Bo	Parliamentary records of the burgher estate
BoA	Appellate and application cases
BrB	Penal Code
D	Diary of the Judiciary Inspection (*Justitierevisionens diarium*)
dr	Thaler
F.K.	Parliamentary records of the First Chamber (*Första kammarens riksdagsprotokoll*)
GB	Marriage Code
GHA	Archives of the Göta Court of Appeal
GLA	The Regional State Archives in Gothenburg
hd	Hundred/hundred court
HSoB	The Scania and Blekinge Court of Appeal
JD	Ministry of Justice
JR	Judiciary Inspection
K	Draft (*Koncept*)
K.B.	Letters patent (*Kungligt brev*)
K.F.	Royal regulation (*Kunglig förordning*)
K.R.	Royal ordinance (*Kunglig resolution*)
LLA	The Regional State Archives in Lund
Pr	Parliamentary records of the clerical estate
R	Records of the Council of the Realm/Council of the State
RA	The Swedish National Archives
RoA	Parliamentary records of the knights and the nobility
SD	The Skara Cathedral Chapter
smt	in silver (coin)
SOU	Official Government Reports Series (*Statens offentliga utredningar*)
StD	The Strängnäs Cathedral Chapter
VLA	The Regional State Archives in Vadstena

Introduction

On 23 June 1702, a soldier named Jon Larsson and his wife's half-sister Karin Jönsdotter were brought before a local court in central Sweden where they tearfully confessed their sins. A few weeks before Christmas of the previous year they had engaged in sexual intercourse on one occasion, following which Karin had become pregnant.[1]

Their actions were in stark violation of the norms of the time regarding sexual relationships. Not only was Jon a married man and their relationship thus regarded as adulterous, but their sexual interaction was also defined as incestuous because Karin was the half-sister of Jon's wife. During the early modern age, the concept of incest included many more kinship categories than today, and any offences involving the closest degrees of kinship, of which this was an example, were equated with infanticide, heresy, and bestiality – crimes that were all defined as crimes against the state (*högmålsbrott* in Swedish), which, according to the legal opinion of the day should be punishable by the death of the guilty parties.

Jon and Karin insisted before the local court that they had never before been guilty of a similar sin and humbly begged for mercy. Jon's wife and Karin's mother pleaded with the court 'with weeping and howling' for the lives of the couple to be spared, and the farmers of the parish sent a joint application for mercy to the king on behalf of the defendants.[2] The case was referred to the court of appeal and from there on to the Crown. The answer was implacable. As a 'well-deserved' punishment for their crime, Jon and Karin were to be executed by beheading.[3]

1 Kåkind Hundred, AIa:38, 1702, 23 June.
2 Ibid.
3 GHA, BIIA:22, 1702, no. 96.

In addition to illustrating the extremely severe penalties meted out to sexual offenders in Sweden during the early modern period, this example demonstrates that the actual concept of incest included completely different kinship categories from the ones it covers in our own time. Several sexual relationships which were then defined as prohibited and which would, if discovered, be punished by death are completely legal today. Social attitudes to these relationships have thus undoubtedly changed from one extreme to another. Moreover, Sweden stands out in this respect in comparison to other countries. During the early modern period, Swedish law – and case-law – was one of the strictest in Europe, whereas in modern times it has become one of the most liberal.

How does such a transformation happen? How are people's attitudes to what is right and wrong formed and changed? How does official law interact with unofficial norms? Who in a society decides which laws and regulations should exist, and what has propelled the radical changes that have occurred over time? These are some of the questions that form the point of departure for my investigation and that I attempt to answer in this book. My analysis covers a period of over 250 years: from the late seventeenth century, when the law was especially severe, up through the first decades of the twentieth century, when legislation had approached today's more liberal levels.

For many people, the word *incest* has a peculiarly unfavourable ring to it. The concept is associated with violence, abuse, and the exploitation of minors; but the same concept also includes voluntary sexual relationships between related adults. Up until the late nineteenth century, incest crimes in Sweden were completely dominated by voluntary relationships. For that reason, such relationships are at the centre of this investigation.

The origin of incest prohibitions

Before presenting my study in greater detail, I wish to stop for a moment to discuss the origin of the prohibitions themselves. How exactly did incest prohibitions come about? This issue has long perplexed Western researchers. The question has been posed as to whether the discomfort that most of us experience at the thought of sexual contact between certain relatives arises in biology, in the environment, or in culture. Incest prohibitions are implicitly or explicitly represented in all societies, the prohibition against sexual relations within the nuclear family appearing to be all but universal.[4] This leads to the conclusion that an aversion to incestuous interactions is likely to be something inherently human, a biological truth, if you will. Nevertheless, in most societies, laws have been developed regulating which relationships should be allowed or forbidden. The form and content of these laws have varied depending on location and culture.[5] For instance, in northern India marriage between relatives has been strictly limited because of cultural taboos, whereas marriage between cousins or an uncle and a niece has been actively encouraged in southern India. In the Middle East, marriages between cousins whose fathers were brothers have been considered especially advantageous, while marriages between cousins in China and Korea have only been permitted if the parents were *not* brothers (i.e., if the parents were brother and sister or two sisters).[6]

If the phenomenon of incest had really been natural behaviour for humans, its limitations ought to have been the same everywhere, and there would have been no need to construct laws surrounding it. This argues against a biological explanation for incest.

At the beginning of the twentieth century, it was assumed in natural-science circles that incest prohibitions formed the starting-point of modern civilisation. Through socially constructed prohibitions, humans had distanced themselves from their animal origins.[7] Psychoanalyst Sigmund Freud contended that humans were born with a *natural longing for incestuous relationships*, but that, with the aid of cultural laws, they learned to suppress their forbidden desires. Freud named the inner conflict that resulted from this the Oedipus complex.[8]

A view diametrically opposed to Freud's was introduced by Finnish sociologist and philosopher Edvard Westermarck. Inspired

4 Turner and Maryanski 2005, p. 2; Herlihy 1995, p. 97. Ancient Egypt and Persia are perhaps the best-known exceptions to this rule, because these cultures permitted marriages between members of the nuclear family. Similar customs have been identified within various royal dynasties in other parts of the world as well, and these are usually explained by the necessity for keeping the 'royal blood' pure in order to legitimise the rule of those in power. But in a broader perspective, these cultures appear simply to be exceptions to an almost universal phenomenon of regulation in some form. Mitterauer 1994, pp. 233–6. Strong 2005; Frandsen 2009.

5 Serrano and Gunzburger 1983; Bittles 2012, pp. 13–28.

6 Bittles 2012, pp. 22–7, 37. For historical examples of incest regulation in different cultures, see also Mitterauer 1994.

7 Wolf 2004, p. 6.

8 Erickson 2004, p. 162.

by Darwin's theory of evolution, he claimed that natural selection in all probability brought with it a *natural moral aversion* to sexual relations between close relatives. According to Westermarck, the biologically conditioned aversion formed the basis of the socially constructed laws that had developed in different societies.[9] Initially, Westermarck's theories had very little impact. Most researchers viewed incest taboos as exclusively social constructions; and in order to explain why the prohibitions had emerged at all, various structural phenomena that could benefit the family and the group socially and economically were suggested, primarily by anthropologists.[10]

In the 1960s, the image of incest prohibitions changed when it could be shown on the basis of empirical studies that there is a close connection between those human relations that a child experiences while growing up and a later sexual aversion against the same people when the child reaches sexual maturity. Today, this phenomenon is considered empirically proven, and it is accepted by most researchers as an environmental imprinting which is not, however, affected by biological kinship ties.[11] On the other hand, opinions differ when it comes to what conclusions can be drawn from this phenomenon. Even if the environmental imprinting can explain why most people themselves avoid sexual relations with people to whom they have been close during their childhood and adolescence, it does not explain why there is a need for making laws about the behaviour of other people.[12]

In past ages, the existence of incest prohibitions was primarily legitimised by religious values. Today the prohibitions are largely explained by medical or genetic notions. According to current

---

9 Arnhart 2004, p. 199. For a more detailed analysis of the early debate and the differences between sociological and psychoanalytical viewpoints, see e.g. Pulman 2012.

10 One such explanatory model (called 'the alliance theory') described how groups could benefit from marrying their children to people from outside groups and in this way acquire a network of loyal allies within a larger area (exogamy, as opposed to endogamy when marriages were arranged within a person's own group). Claude Lévi-Strauss and Robin Fox are examples of two well-known anthropologists who have advocated this theory. Wolf 2004; Turner and Maryanski 2005, p. 44. The theories of Lévi-Strauss have been further developed by Françoise Héritier, as described in Frandsen.

11 Wolf and Durham 2004; Mitterauer 1994, pp. 233f, 245.

12 Durham 2004, pp. 126–30. For a more detailed survey primarily of anthropological and sociological research, see Frandsen 2009, pp. 21–32.

Swedish law, sexual relations are prohibited between members of the same nuclear family (between a parent and a child, or a grandparent and a grandchild, or between full siblings), and the prohibitions are justified by medical arguments but also by ethical reasons.[13] It is true that the risk of any children suffering serious genetic damage increases when the parents are closely related, and this may at first sight seem a logical reason for the formulation of the law; but in fact the risk is rather small. At the same time, there are other situations where there is a comparable risk of hereditary damage but where the state does not interfere. Single individuals may carry a predisposition for a hereditary disease that risks being transmitted to the next generation regardless of the partner chosen by such a person, but in such cases there are no legal restrictions to consider before choosing to have children.[14] Similarly, the risk of foetal injury rises rather dramatically when a prospective mother grows older, but no laws limit her ability to have children after a certain age.[15] Another medical inconsistency in modern Swedish law is the fact that a man and his niece are allowed to marry without restrictions while half-siblings must apply for a dispensation for marriage, although the genetic closeness, and thus the risk of foetal abnormalities, is exactly the same in both cases.[16] In other words, modern legislation is not entirely consistent, which is a sign of the topicality of the issue and at the same time of its complexity.

It is obvious that ideas surrounding incest and incest prohibitions have been affected by religious and medical values in society. It is also clear that both of these influences can be linked to specific periods of time. This book examines what other influences, in addition

---

13 BrB (Swedish Penal Code), Chapter 6, Section 7; *SOU* 2010:71, p. 338; Semmler 2003, p. 22. There have been proposals advocating a complete repeal of the prohibitions, made by those who do not believe that a genetic justification is a sufficiently strong foundation upon which to base a law. Report of the Committee on Justice, 1977/78:26, pp. 5f; Karlsson 2010.

14 *SOU* 2001:14, pp. 693f.

15 If the parents are cousins, the risk of foetal defects increases by about 3.3%. The risk of a child dying between twenty-eight weeks and ten to twelve years of age increases by about 3.7%. A forty-five-year-old woman runs a 3.3% higher risk of giving birth to a child with Down's syndrome compared to a twenty-year-old woman. If the woman is forty-nine years old, the risk increases to about 10%. Bittles 2012, pp. 226–8.

16 Tottie 1974, p. 36.

to religious and medical ones, have affected the changes mentioned above.

Aim of the present study

Regardless of the origin of incest prohibitions, their respective formulations have varied radically both *among* different cultures and *within* one and the same culture over time. With respect to Sweden, there was a radical and completely revolutionary shift in the sense that an act which is not even defined as illegal today was punishable by death around the turn of the century in 1700. Jon and Karin were executed for having had sexual intercourse with each other. Today, a similar relationship would not arouse any interest whatsoever from the authorities. The fact that the formulation of incest prohibitions has varied so significantly over time and space suggests that the prohibitions are, to some extent, social constructions. In other words, they are affected by values and ideas in society.

The aim of my investigation is to analyse the norms and culturally dependent values that have formed the basis of the theoretical regulation and the practical handling of incest cases in Swedish society from the late seventeenth century up until around 1940, and to situate this development in a wider European context. Consequently, I examine how ideas surrounding incest can be related to normative changes in society. The aim of the analysis is not simply to describe the radical change that took place, but also to explain how interest in incestuous relationships could be so strong and pervasive during the seventeenth century, whereas it came to be a more peripheral phenomenon later on.

Previous research has shown that sexual crimes were very severely punished in Protestant areas during the early modern period. However, many sexual crimes that in theory were to be punished by death were more leniently dealt with in practice.[17] Even so, Sweden and the Nordic countries stood out among Protestant countries when it comes to severity in connection with incest crimes. Icelandic historian Már Jónsson, who has studied criminal incest in Iceland, claims that the explanation for that severity is found in the concept of heresy. Originally, heresy meant *deviation from the Christian faith*; but in the Nordic countries it also came to be used synonymously

17 For instance, Hull 1996; Rublack 1999; Thunander 1993; Gunnlaugsson 1994.

with *blodskam* (literally 'blood shame'), the old Swedish word for incest.[18] Heresy was equated with bestiality and other 'sodomitic' sins which were defined as crimes against 'God's law'. This gave religious authorities a prominent role in the interpretation of the criminal nature of the acts. The actual legislation may thus be regarded as a consequence of both ecclesiastical and secular legal claims.

But the religious legitimisation of incest prohibitions cannot in itself explain how Jon and Karin ended up in court. The couple were defended by several people from their immediate surroundings, and the case still ended with a death sentence. This raises questions as to just how firmly anchored the strict law actually was among the general public. In order to understand how the law was enforced, social practices must be studied in some detail. Norms and attitudes do not necessarily adhere to official legislation. Rather, they may be seen as the result of an interaction between legislators and the general public. In order to understand what norms dominated a society during a specific period of time, one must investigate how the theoretical legislation was in fact implemented in that society.

On a comprehensive level, my investigation aims to shed light on how the sexuality of individuals has been restricted by different norms and values in society. By using historical examples and long timelines, I want to show what a revolutionary change the theoretical legislation, as well as the practical application of the incest prohibitions, has undergone, and how this development can be linked to prevailing norms and values throughout the entire studied period. Sometimes these norms have been specific to Sweden; but Swedish developments may often be linked to cultural ideas that have existed in parallel in various European countries. Previous research has touched on different aspects of the prohibited relationships during different times and in different countries. However, no one has studied the processes underlying the judicial involvement and its long-term changes. The question is how the extreme shifts of direction in the Swedish circumstances can be accounted for. The answer to this question will also open up new perspectives on and insights into our current norms and values in this field.

18 Jónsson 1998, p. 4. Similar arguments are discussed by David Gaunt in Gaunt 1996, p. 229. In the judgement books from the turn of the century around 1700, it was common for the crime of incest to be designated 'heresy'. See, e.g., the registers in GHA, BIIA:3; GHA, BIIA:8. See also Korpiola 2005, p. 109.

Interaction, the creation of norms, and social control

Ultimately, my study is about how norms are created in a society and how they change, and, more specifically, about defining the boundary between permitted and prohibited sexuality, with a focus on kinship ties. During most of the period investigated, the normative order of society was based on the idea that sexuality should only be practised within marriage and for the purpose of procreation. For several centuries, all extramarital sexual activity was thus defined as prohibited. Incest was only one of many forbidden sexual acts. In modern times, the definition of prohibited sexual activity has changed, as has the meaning of the concept of incest. As was pointed out above, relationships that were once utterly forbidden are regarded as entirely legal today. Conceptions as to what is right and wrong have changed, and new norms surrounding sexuality have evolved. But how are such norms created, and how do they change?

Scholars have long debated the relationship between actor and structure as a theoretical dilemma. While some researchers emphasise the significance of an actor's free will, others instead foreground social structures as limitations on the ability of an individual to think and act independently. However, few scholars imagine this issue as an either/or question, positioning themselves somewhere between the two extremes.[19] In sociology the structural restrictions that society indirectly sets up for an individual are often emphasised, which engenders a somewhat deterministic basic view of human development. The individual is born into a society with a specific social and cultural framework and taught to accept the prevailing normative order. The individual's scope for action is connected to the different positions or stereotypical roles that he or she is given in this society and to the expectations that the people around him or her have regarding that particular position (e.g., as a man, woman, student, grandmother, shoe salesman, athlete, Christian, academic, etc.).[20] According to this way of looking at things, the structural framework will ultimately shape everything, from identity and thought patterns to emotional life.

On this issue, I position myself relatively close to those researchers who emphasise the free will of actors and their opportunities for influencing the people around them. Although the structures mentioned above no doubt impose certain limitations on an actor's

19 Giddens and Sutton 2014, pp. 64–8.
20 Charon 2007, pp. 18–20.

freedom of action, I believe that there are a number of different ways in which an individual may relate to his or her surroundings, and that this creates a potential for change in society which is anything but predictable.

My line of reasoning has, in part, been inspired by *symbolic interactionism* as presented by American sociologist Joel M. Charon. This theoretical perspective may be said to be a subdivision or further development of more traditional sociology. Above all, it emphasises an individual's scope for action within the structural framework.[21] Proponents of this theory distance themselves from the determinism which characterises studies that proceed from more structuralist perspectives; instead, they stress the significance of *interaction* for the development of an individual. In this context, the individual is described not as a passive recipient of social influences but as an actor who actively processes input data, and who *interprets* each specific situation and thereafter *chooses* to act in accordance with his or her own aims and interests. The whole thing is seen as an ongoing process where the actor continuously receives new information and is able to modify his or her goals and actions.[22]

According to this theoretical perspective, all human communication is carried out through *symbols*, language being the most obvious example. But interpersonal interaction is also carried out with the aid of gestures, facial expressions, texts, or images, all of which have symbolic meanings. Because communication is carried out via symbols, a message is always interpreted before its recipient reacts to it.[23]

Through interactions with other people, individuals define and evaluate both themselves and the people around them. The evaluation of various objects, events, or attitudes is partly based on how other people judge the same thing. However, an individual does not slavishly follow the judgement of other people, but always makes a personal interpretation. The freedom of an individual lies in the interpretation. Here is an opportunity to depart from other people's assessments of the same situation. The key point of symbolic interactionism is thus that individuals act *in interaction with* those around them.

---

21 George Herbert Mead (1863–1931) is regarded as having laid the foundation for symbolic interactionism, but the expression itself was coined by Herbert Blumer in the 1930s. Giddens and Sutton 2014, p. 62; Blumer 1969, p. 1.

22 Charon 2007, pp. 25, 41.

23 Charon 2007, pp. 131–8.

Social interaction not only determines the values and actions of individual actors; it also gives rise to shared social norms. Charon defines a society as a group of people interacting and cooperating with one another. This cooperation creates shared perspectives which form the basis of the culture of the society. The culture may be said to comprise general 'agreements' on norms and values, on formal and informal rules and on traditions and morals. These common values are *used* by an individual as benchmarks in order to evaluate his/her own actions and the actions of other people. But interaction and cooperation do not mean that there is consensus within the group or society. On the contrary, Charon emphasises that a continuous negotiation and adaptation of positions takes place over the course of interpersonal meetings. Ideas are challenged, defended, and reshaped into new variants that can then be questioned anew. The definition of norms and values is negotiated and renegotiated throughout this communication, and this creates a dynamic process that never comes to an end.[24]

A number of historians have chosen to view society and the social interactions of people in a similar way. One historian has described social norms as 'a regulatory system for how social life should be led'. Norms are *created* through the actions and statements of individual people, but at the same time they *govern* the actions of those same individuals.[25] Historian Karin Hassan Jansson, who has studied rape cases in early modern Sweden, views the construction of gender in a society as a 'contentious process'. Each prevailing norm in society was, she says, preceded by a struggle, and the same norm runs a constant risk of being challenged anew. Jansson calls this process, which leads up to the common formation of norms in a society, a 'struggle for definitions'.[26]

Prevailing social norms and ideals are defended through resistance to divergent norms and behaviour. This resistance has been referred to as *social control*. Social control may be divided into different levels of *formal* and *informal control*, formal control being linked to laws and regulations or ecclesiastical provisions while informal control describes the control individuals have over one another's

---

24 Charon 2007, pp. 153, 159, 162f, 166f.

25 Hansen 2006, p. 27.

26 Jansson 2000, pp. 157, 162–5; quotation on pp. 164f. See a similar line of reasoning in Marklund 2000, p. 182.

1 Hundred-court judgement book from the eighteenth century.

behaviour.[27] Cultural ideas often corresponded on different levels, but they could also be in conflict with one another. Attitudes concerning right and wrong could, for instance, vary among different social groups (e.g., the nobility and the peasantry); but tensions and challenges could also emerge within one and the same group. In such situations an opportunity would arise for renegotiation and change of the content of the norm.

With the aid of these input values, it is possible to define the scope of the present investigation. My point of departure is thus that official norms and attitudes are the result of continuous negotiations at the level of individual actors. Individuals who attempted to improve their own positions in connection with various conflicts simultaneously challenged or reinforced common values in society. It was not until the rules were challenged that a phase of negotiation was initiated, where both challengers and defenders of certain values were forced to articulate their arguments in order to gain legitimacy

27 For different interpretations of *social control*, see, e.g., Hansen 2006, pp. 27f; Lindstedt Cronberg 1997, pp. 16f; Liliequist 1992, pp. 19f; Österberg, Lennartsson, and Naess 2000, p. 241.

for their respective points of view. In my view, it is in such negotiations that the underlying causes of the shifts in norms that have occurred over time become visible. By constantly focusing on the definition of boundaries, it is possible to reveal the grey area where dissimilar opinions intersected with or overlapped one another, where norms were in conflict, and where negotiations geared towards establishing new shared values became necessary.

Material and methodology

The aim of my study is to investigate how norms surrounding incest have changed in Sweden from the end of the seventeenth century up until 1940. I wish to do this by drawing attention to values that have been brought to the fore when the boundaries of prohibitions have been challenged in different social arenas. For this reason, I have sought out source material that variously reflects the process of negotiation that followed upon such challenges. This material falls into four separate categories: 1) laws and preparatory legislative documents; 2) parliamentary records and reports from government-initiated investigations; 3) judgement-book material on the court-of-appeal and hundred-court levels; and 4) applications for dispensation. I have endeavoured to read as much as possible within all these categories in order to develop an idea of quantitative facts, general phenomena, and recurring discussions and arguments. In order to cover as lengthy a period of time as possible, I have sampled the criminal-case material at predetermined points in time. The location of those points in time has been governed by the availability of searchable records in combination with an attempt to create regular intervals over time. Taken altogether, the material became quite extensive. I have gone through approximately 230 criminal cases, of which roughly every fourth case was followed up at the hundred level, and, in addition to this, 200 applications for dispensation. This is the equivalent of over 4500 handwritten pages from more than 300 different volumes taken from four different regional archives. To this should be added all the printed source material.

Laws and parliamentary material

The two first categories of material reproduce debates engaged in by the educated elite in society, such as theologians, lawyers, and politicians. The laws in a society can be said to make up a stylised or generalised ideal which reflects the values that have acquired the highest degree of support in the negotiation process among legal scholars at a specific point in time. But the ideals embodied in law have always been preceded by negotiations that show which competing values and points of view were put forward in the debate. In the course of the negotiations, opinions were aired which – for different reasons – never gained the approval of the majority, and which are hence not visible in the legislation. In order to understand the range of ideas that has existed in society at different points in time, preparatory legislative material and parliamentary records are thus an important source for analysis.

The Swedish book of statutes was redrafted in 1734 and 1864. In addition, the Marriage Code was revised in 1915. All changes to the laws were preceded by various preparatory legislative inquiries and by discussions that would sometimes go on for decades. In addition to laws and preparatory legislative material, I have gone through all the letters patent and royal ordinances I was able to find via registers where the Crown clarified what positions cathedral chapters and courts of appeal should assume with respect to different relationships within the prohibited degrees of kinship. For the more recent period, there are also government-initiated investigations – the Official Government Reports Series (*SOU*) – that may present lines of argument developed at the highest level.

During the first half of the nineteenth century, the issue of incest was the subject of animated debate in the Swedish parliament, the *Riksdag*. Every parliamentary debate was initiated by a proposal for a legislative amendment. The bills and the discussions that followed within the different estates[28] have been preserved in printed form, material that reveals how different opinions were justified, defended, and questioned. During the nineteenth century, the question of the formulation of incest prohibitions was raised in twelve parliaments, all of which are included in the basis for my study: 1809/10, 1823, 1828, 1834, 1840, 1844, 1847, 1859/60, 1862/63, 1868, 1870, and 1871. This material thus contains all the debates, official letters, appendices, opinions, and decisions preserved in written form from the four estates, the Committee on Legal Affairs, and the Crown.

In addition to this material I have used an academic dissertation on this topic, published in 1813, and a commentary to this dissertation, as well as two major scholarly studies of incest crimes and

28 The four estates of the realm in pre-1866 Sweden were the nobility, the clergy, the burghers, and the peasantry.

incest criminals in Sweden that were conducted during the interwar years.[29] I have used these last-mentioned studies as a source of statistical information regarding the prevalence of the crime of incest during the decades after 1900; at the same time, they make up a part of the source material for ideas concerning the crime of incest during the 1930s.[30]

The origin and purpose of incest prohibitions were debated in all these arenas, along with proposals for changes and the consequences that such changes were expected to entail. There is thus a wealth of source material in which incest prohibitions were debated, both by legal scholars and by politicians and theologians, and, towards the end of the investigated period, also by representatives of the medical profession.

Judgement-book material

The two other categories of material, judgement books and applications for dispensation, have been used to compare the theoretical debate to the practical handling of various incest cases. This source material can also be expected to reflect attitudes at a more popular and general level, because it was primarily people from the broader social groups that were prosecuted for incest crimes: freeholders and farmers, craftsmen and soldiers, the occasional burgher, millers, saltpetre-boilers, boatswains, and innkeepers. Women were primarily referred to by their civil status: spinster, wife, or widow, sometimes by the patronising noun *kvinnsperson* ('female').

The judgement-book material is primarily taken from the Göta Court of Appeal, which was one of four courts of appeal in Sweden at the beginning of the investigated period. In broad terms, its jurisdiction covered the southern part of Sweden as defined by its current national boundaries.[31] The reviewed criminal-case material was divided into three investigative periods in accordance with Table 1.

From 1689, a royal decree prescribed that all cases regarding crimes against the prohibited degrees of kinship in the first and

29 Schlyter 1813. Anonymous 1831/32; Kinberg, Inghe, and Riemer 1943; *SOU* 1935:68.

30 Kinberg, Inghe, and Riemer 1943; *SOU* 1935:68.

31 The other courts of appeal were the Svea Court of Appeal (Northern Sweden), the Åbo (Turku) Court of Appeal (present-day Finland), and the Dorpat (Tartu) Court of Appeal (present-day Estonia). Inger 2011, p. 81.

Table 1. Investigated criminal cases

Period[32]	Number of appellate court cases	Of which include records from the hundred court[33]
1694–1716	131	15
1783–1800, 1810	51	21
1840–58	50	22
Total	232	58

second degrees should be submitted and then verified by a court of appeal before the final judgement was confirmed.[34] Using the material from the courts of appeal as a basis, it is thus possible to capture all incest crimes that were tried in the hundreds of southern Sweden during the selected periods. The decision of the court of appeal relied to a large extent on the court records of the hundred courts. In case of doubt, complementary material was requested from the lower courts, and in exceptional cases the defendants were summoned for personal hearings by the court of appeal, although usually the judgements were based exclusively on the minutes submitted from the hundred courts.[35]

32 The division into periods has been governed by the periods from which there are surviving records (1694–1716 and 1783–1858). The material from 1715 is, however, missing. The second period (1783–1800) is complemented with a year out of sequence (1810), because a new law came into force in this year, and I wanted to find out whether this left an impression on the criminal-case material.

33 Approximately 25% of the appellate court cases have been complemented with minutes from the hundred courts – somewhat fewer from the first period and somewhat more from the latter periods. The records of the hundred courts have been found by searching in several different record series (e.g., ECII AABA: *renoveringar* (transcripts), EVAC: *handlingar för underställda brottmål* (documents for referred criminal cases), microfiches and local judgement books for ordinary or extraordinary court sessions). The cases from the earlier period are sometimes damaged or missing. From the end of the eighteenth century, the supply of material becomes more reliable while at the same time the volume swells to what can be over a hundred handwritten pages for one single case. For this reason, I have prioritised looking for cases that were particularly interesting from the perspective of my research questions.

34 K.B. (letters patent) 1689, 25 April.

35 Thunander 1993, pp. 40, 48f. One example of defendants being summoned to a personal hearing is GHA, BIIA:8, 1698, no. 180.

So, what can be learned from these documents? The established model of the court-of-appeal records always included the current date, the names of the defendants, and the names of the associate judges present. The family relationship between the defendants was carefully noted, as was the previous judicial decision of the lower court.

Often certain circumstances with respect to the crime are mentioned: whether a child had been conceived, whether the defendants had confessed or denied committing the crime, how long the sexual relationship had continued, whether the crime had been committed while under the influence of alcohol, whether one of the parties (the woman) had been 'enticed' or 'lured', whether the defendants showed any remorse or contrition, whether their general conduct was good or not, whether they had the support of their families or the local community, and so on. All this information can be found in this material, but it is not consistently stated, which creates uncertainty regarding the circumstances in which the alleged crimes were committed. The information mentioned in the records must therefore be seen as an absolute minimum, and it is not possible to draw general conclusions about a course of events based on what is not mentioned. But because the main function of the records was to justify a judicial decision, it seems reasonable to assume that the circumstances documented were those that were perceived to be relevant for the judgement.[36]

The local hundred trials at the beginning of the investigated period were held in public, before the family, friends, and neighbours of the defendants. These persons could also actively intervene in the proceedings by taking a stand for or against the accused. For this reason, early modern Swedish local-court sessions have been likened to the activities of a social arena for conflict resolution.[37] The records from the hundred courts are, as a general rule, comparatively detailed, with more space devoted to statements from

---

36 The documentation from the work of the court of appeal is divided among a number of different record series which have been reviewed in order to find the series that provide relevant information. For this reason, my investigation has focused on the following series: BIIA: *Brottmålsutslag* (Criminal-case judgements), EIAC: *Kungliga brev och resolutioner i kriminalmål* (Letters patent and royal ordinances in criminal cases) and, to a certain extent, AII: *Brottmålsprotokoll* ('Records from criminal cases'). Series that turned out to contain little or nothing of value to this investigation are, e.g., BIII: *Öppna utslag och resolutioner* (Open findings and decisions), EIAA: *Kungliga brev och resolutioner* (Letters patent and royal ordinances).

37 For instance, Österberg, Lennartsson, and Naess 2000.

the accused and from any witnesses in comparison to the more summary notes kept by the courts of appeal.

Whenever someone was accused of a crime against the prohibited degrees of kinship, the regulatory framework was challenged; and in the trial that followed, any alternative assessments of the crime that might have existed in society became visible. Using the terminology of Karin Hassan Jansson, one may call this a *struggle for the definition* of a shared norm, where the defendants, the judges, and any witnesses were negotiating with one another.

An analysis of the judgement-book material entails certain risks that must be borne in mind. The negotiations in the courtroom were not conducted among equals. During the greater part of the investigated period, the structure of society was pronouncedly hierarchical. Thus, the words of the authorities obviously carried more weight than those of the peasantry, and it was the representatives of the educated elite who conducted the trials. They were the ones who decided which questions to pose, which investigations were relevant, what was worth writing down, and how the case was to be described for the next court instance. In addition, the scope for interpretation by single individuals has also varied considerably depending on the age, sex, and social position of the person in question within the respective group. In spite of these objections, there is no doubt that this material is able to provide important information about where the regulatory framework was challenged, which kinship categories were valued differently by different groups or by different actors, and what arguments were used in order to legitimise a specific viewpoint.

Applications for dispensation

An application for dispensation was a request to enter into matrimony with a person whom the law actually forbade the applicant to marry. Kinship within the prohibited degrees was only one of several obstacles for which the Crown could grant dispensations.[38] The

38 For example, people applied for a dispensation for marriage in order to marry 1) in spite of not having reached the correct age for marriage; 2) in spite of the period of mourning from a previous marriage not having been completed; 3) in spite of not being able to read or having insufficient knowledge about Christianity; 4) when a spouse had been missing for a long period of time without having been declared dead (often pertaining to the wives of soldiers whose husbands had been away for several years); or 5) when a noble applied for permission to marry a commoner without losing his or her privileges.

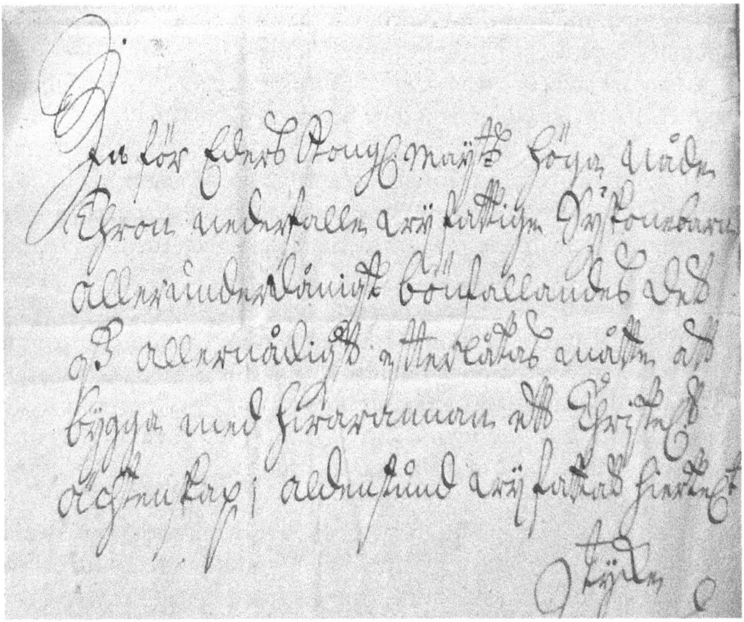

2 In February 1730, the two cousins Nils Arvidsson and Ingeborg Bengtsdotter applied for permission to marry.

originals of the applications for dispensation are preserved in the Judiciary Inspection archives in the National Archives in Stockholm. Applications were drawn up according to strict rules – the tone in the applications was always extremely humble and subservient – but could in spite of this convey a surprising degree of obstinacy.[39]

Even though most applications for dispensation were probably written by a third party, they will have been read out to and approved by the applicants before being sent in; and if one looks beyond the genre-based expressions, these official letters often mention some circumstance explaining *why* it was believed that the prohibition could be circumvented. By analysing the encounter between the applicants from the general public on the one hand and the decision-making authority on the other (who and how many people applied

39 During the eighteenth and nineteenth centuries, several special letter-writing guides were printed, where rules of etiquette for letter-writing were set down. The style recommended in one of the best-known letter-writing guides was adopted in most applications for dispensation. Biurman 1767 [1729], pp. 9–11, 60f.

for permission to marry, what arguments the applicants employed, the authority's assessment, etc.), it is possible to show how various incestuous relationships were defined and evaluated – by single individuals, or by whole groups in the society of the time. In this way, the applications for dispensation may be seen to convey the attitudes that existed among common folk during the period in question.

Despite the fact that it was only the Crown that had the authority to grant dispensations for marriage, the cathedral chapters also received queries regarding marriage. Usually there are no searchable registers for such documents, but the Skara Cathedral Chapter is an exception, which is why I have been able to complement my collection of materials with dispensation requests that were submitted to Skara between the years 1710–34 and 1776–1806.[40] However, these documents consist of notes in the cathedral chapter's record book rather than the actual official letters of the applicants.

The upper social orders, with titles such as Lieutenant, Colonel, Major, Knight, Hundred Court Judge, Burgher, or Merchant, are overrepresented in the applications for dispensation. In these cases, women were given the titles *jungfru* (Maid), *fröken* (Miss), or *välborne fröken* (Honourable Miss). However, applications from ordinary farmers and craftsmen were also common. Thus, virtually all social groups are represented in this material, albeit not in correct proportion to their respective percentages of the population.[41]

In order to acquire basic quantitative knowledge about the number of applications for dispensation pertaining to various kinship categories, I have counted the number of applications for individual years in the registration diary of the archive. I then requested and read more than 200 separate cases in order to make a qualitative assessment of the arguments in the applications and in the decisions.

---

40 The number of applications for dispensation that were received by the Skara Cathedral Chapter was 76 for the first period and 39 for the second. See Appendix 2. I am particularly grateful to Professor Göran Malmstedt, who made me aware of the existence of this register.

41 The percentage of nobles, priests, and high-ranking commoners (*ofrälse ståndspersoner*) was around 5% of the Swedish population until the mid-nineteenth century. Carlsson 1977, p. 18. In my material, where the applications for dispensation have been divided according to kinship category, the more exalted titles account for around 50%. Because references are often made only to 'the widower', 'the maid-servant', or 'the farmhand' in the judgement-book material, as well as in the applications for dispensation, I have chosen not to draw up exact statistics for titles and social groups.

These cases were selected on the basis of kinship category in order to obtain a sufficient number of documents for different relationships. The cases were handled in more or less standardised ways for long periods of time, and I have prioritised looking for critical junctures for new routines, i.e., cases that became precedential for future cases. This explains why I collected a particularly large number of cases from the decades around the turn of the century in 1800, a period which – as I will demonstrate – emerges as a clear turning-point for social attitudes to incest and incest prohibitions.[42]

Like the judgement-book material, the applications for dispensation show where the definitions of boundaries for incest prohibitions were not fully accepted by the entire population. It can of course be said that an application for dispensation was in itself a sign of the legislation being respected by the applicants, but at the same time an application involved a strain on the regulatory framework.[43] After all, the purpose of the application was to circumvent the established rules and to obtain a legal exemption from the official prohibitions. Consequently, the applications indirectly undermined the legitimacy of the law. For this reason, the applications for dispensation may be said to have represented a threat against the prevailing definition of boundaries, and every time a person applied for a dispensation the decision-makers were obliged to take up a position with regard to how the relationship should be assessed. In this way, the applications came to initiate repeated negotiations concerning the definitions of boundaries for incest prohibitions.

Analysing the material

I have used a few quantitative operations in order to create a general picture of the framing of incest cases. This gave me an overview of how many applications for dispensation and incest cases I was dealing with, which relationships are represented in which material, and which assessments were usually employed in different incest cases. By reviewing a sizeable source material, I hence acquired a

42 The archived documents are divided into 1) application documents = *utslagshandlingar* (findings); 2) discussions in the Council = *rådsprotokoll* (Council records); and 3) decisions = *koncept* (transcripts). I have read 161 findings, 51 Council records, and 139 transcripts.

43 In spite of the applications being subject to a charge, the authorities regarded the processing of the applications as a burden on social resources, not as a welcome source of income. See p. 200.

stable basic understanding of the prevalence of the phenomenon, recurring lines of argument, and expected results in different situations. With the aid of this quantitative review, it was possible to identify patterns in the material – patterns which, in the next stage of analysis, I was able to connect to specific factors such as kinship category, sex, age, or social position.

In order to explain the identified patterns, the quantitative method was complemented by qualitative analyses. The detailed, qualitative analyses draw attention to specific arguments that were presented in different contexts, making it possible to reconstruct the norms that were brought to the fore when different incest cases were debated. It is thus primarily with the aid of the qualitative analysis of norms and attitudes that I have been able to explain patterns – and deviations – in the material.

The complexity of incestuous relationships

During the early modern period, a distinction was made between relationships through blood, consanguinity (*skyldskap* in Swedish), and affinity in the sense of relationships through marriage (*svågerskap* in Swedish). Consanguinity thus referred to a biological relationship, i.e., relatives who shared the same blood ties. Affinity referred instead to the relationship established between spouses. Through marriage, new family ties were created between the husband and the wife's entire family and vice versa. However, the affinity bond did not come into existence in connection with the marriage ceremony itself, but in connection with the sexual contact between the parties.[44] If a man had a sexual relationship with two sisters, one after the other without being married to either, this, too, was defined as incest. What applied to the man applied in equal measure to the woman.[45]

The difference between consanguinity and affinity relationships was not per definition a difference in the closeness of kinship ties. Closeness was instead measured in different degrees on the basis of how many generations there were between the persons in question and their most recent common ancestor. One can imagine a family tree where each step vertically or horizontally represents one degree

44 Nehrman 1729, pp. 178, 182; Nehrman 1747, p. 14.

45 Consequently, a woman's sexual relationship with two brothers or with a father and son was also regarded as incestuous, and so on. On the great significance of sexual intercourse for marriage ties, see Marklund 2004, pp. 168f; Sandén 2005, pp. 190–2; Lennartsson 1999, p. 160.

of kinship. According to this classification, a man was related to his mother in the *first lineal degree* and his grandmother in the *second lineal degree*. Collaterally, the man's family relationship with his sister was regarded as the *first collateral degree* and with his cousin as the *second collateral degree*. The corresponding affinity relationships referred, lineally, to a man's relationship to his *wife's mother* or his *wife's grandmother* and collaterally to his *wife's sister* or his *wife's cousin*.

The second affinity degree also included kinship ties created via *two* marriages. For instance, a man was considered to be related to his *wife's stepmother* in the second affinity degree (the family tie was created through the man's marriage to his wife *and* through his wife's father's marriage to his wife's stepmother).

This classification could become incredibly complex, in particular when the family relationships were complicated by various diagonal kinship ties, by stepfamily relationships, or by half-biological kinship ties. However, in the absence of a better or clearer system of classification, I have decided to use the already existing basic structure with one addition. In order to reduce complexity as far as possible, I have chosen to use the man as the point of departure when calculating which family relationships different people had to one another. Between a man and his *uncle's widow* there is, for instance, the same family relationship as between a woman and her *deceased husband's nephew*, but in my view it is unnecessarily confusing to use both. Table 2 presents the most common relationships according to the principles of classification used during the early modern period, and that outline will be followed throughout this book.[46]

At the beginning of the investigated period, the most common Swedish term for incest crimes of both consanguinity and affinity was *blodskam* (literally 'blood-shame', from the German *Blutschande*) or *kätteri* (heresy). The crime of incest could also be called *frändsämjospjäll* (lit. 'kindred-friendship-spoiling') in the more distant degrees. Paraphrases such as *olovlig beblandelse* (illegal intercourse) or *köttslig beblandelse i förbjudet led* (carnal intercourse in a prohibited degree) were also common ways of describing this crime in the context of court proceedings. The word *incest* comes originally from Latin and consists of two parts, *in-castus*, which means 'unclean'. Incest as a concept was primarily used in its original Latin form by lawyers when different degrees of closeness were to be

46 In the source material there are a number of older family terms, but I have chosen to use modern terminology, except in direct quotations.

Table 2. Family relationships

Closeness	Relationship, a man and (his) ...	
	Consanguinity	Affinity
First lineal degree	mother, daughter	stepmother, stepdaughter, mother-in-law, daughter-in-law, a mother and her daughter
Second lineal degree	grandmother, grand-daughter	wife's grandmother, wife's granddaughter, grandfather's widow
First collateral degree	sister	stepsister, wife's sister, brother's widow, two sisters
Diagonally	aunt/niece and wife's niece	wife's aunt, wife's niece, uncle's widow
Second degree	cousin	wife's cousin, wife's stepmother, wife's brother's widow

calculated, but sometimes the word was also used synonymously with *blodskam*.

Research on incest

A study focusing on incest in a longer perspective cannot avoid touching on several different fields of historical research, such as jurisprudence, sexuality, religion, medicine, and family history, to mention just a few of the most obvious areas. In other words, the very breadth of this topic risks causing the investigation to lose focus. Another difficulty has to do with the fact that incest – and thus also incest prohibition – has been defined in dissimilar ways in different societies at different points in time. As pointed out by the Austrian historian Michael Mitterauer, an understanding of the incest phenomenon itself is made more difficult by the bluntness of the concept. Above all, it is problematic that several kinship categories are lumped together in different contexts, because this reduces the chance of discovering different explanatory models for different prohibitions. It also makes comparisons between different studies more difficult.[47] From a research perspective, the complexity of the

47 Mitterauer 1994, pp. 243–5. Basic problems with the definition of the concept of incest and other research dilemmas are also presented in Frandsen 2009, pp. 17–20.

topic thus entails significant challenges; but at the same time, it is perhaps this very complexity that is the topic's main attraction.

Comparatively few historical studies focus on the phenomenon of incest. In investigations dealing with crime in general or with morality, incest is often mentioned as a crime among others without distinguishing or problematising the different relationship categories, which renders comparisons more or less meaningless.[48] In other investigations, the phenomenon of incest is only partially touched upon. Some have focused on criminal cases, thereby excluding couples who applied for permission to marry in spite of being related to one another.[49] Conversely, other researchers have focused solely on marriage patterns between related individuals, an approach which excluded all criminal cases from the investigation.[50] However, a few researchers who have made the incest phenomenon their main object of investigation should be mentioned.

German historian Claudia Jarzebowski has made a detailed study of the crime of incest in eighteenth-century Germany. As religion lost its explanatory power, the meaning of the concept of incest was renegotiated in society. Jarzebowski raises the question of what significance ideas about sexuality, family, and violence had in these negotiations.[51] During the first half of the eighteenth century, the function of the prohibitions was mainly to protect the institution of marriage by defining boundaries between legal and illegal relationships. During the latter part of the eighteenth century, the focus became the incestuous act in itself. Intrafamilial sexual acts threatened the stability of the family and thus of society as a whole. The purpose of the prohibitions now became to defend society itself. When mothers and daughters at the end of the eighteenth century claimed that the husband or father had forced them to perform sexual acts, lawyers were less inclined to take them at their word than they had been at the beginning of the century. Jarzebowski believes that this change can be tied to the new bourgeois family ideals that were spreading in society. In other words, the family ideal was protected at the expense of the individual.[52]

Jarzebowski points out that women's chances of receiving milder punishments decreased during the eighteenth century; but

48 Thunander 1993; Sundin 1992; Hull 1996; Terjesen 1994.
49 E.g., Lindstedt Cronberg 2002; Terjesen 1994.
50 Kuper 2009; Göransson 1990.
51 Jarzebowski 2006, pp. 9f, 41.
52 Jarzebowski 2006, pp. 261–5.

her colleague Ulinka Rublack argues that women who claimed to have been forced to commit incestuous acts did not find a sympathetic audience for their versions of events during the sixteenth and seventeenth centuries either.[53] Both of these researchers have chosen to foreground cultural beliefs as influential factors in the handling and assessment of incest, which makes it interesting to compare their results to the findings of my study.

Dutch historian Florike Egmond has studied the handling of incest crimes in Holland from 1585 to 1810. In contradistinction to the German scholars, Egmond describes a relatively mild attitude toward women who had been forced to take part in an incestuous act. They were punished, to be sure; but the punishment was often mitigated.[54]

Seth J. Denbo, a British historian, has studied ideas surrounding incest in England in the eighteenth century as a method for gaining a deeper understanding of the importance of family life. Using law texts, criminal cases, and contemporary popular literature, he arrives at the conclusion that incest was, above all, discussed on the basis of the expected behaviour among family members and the different hierarchical structures within the family, but also on the basis of economic incentives.[55] Although England went through a Protestant Reformation in the sixteenth century, the handling of incest crimes was not transferred from the ecclesiastical to the secular judicial apparatus, as was the case in most of the other Protestant countries. As a consequence, incest crimes were, in accordance with ecclesiastical traditions, treated with a significantly greater degree of leniency here than in other Protestant countries during the centuries following the Reformation.[56] Incest crimes were only heard by a secular court when the case in question involved rape.

During the whole of the eighteenth century, prohibited relationships between related individuals – sometimes even marriage – occurred without the authorities displaying any significant degree of interest in the matter. If the relationship was reported to the ecclesiastical authorities, the marriage was annulled, which meant that any children

53 Rublack 1999, p. 239.

54 Egmond 2001, p. 24.

55 Denbo 2001, pp. 19f, 241.

56 For a brief period in the mid-seventeenth century, the death penalty was introduced for incest, but these laws were rarely respected and they were repealed after approximately a decade. Not until the beginning of the twentieth century did incest become a formal crime in accordance with secular law. Kuper 2009, pp. 52–5, 63; Denbo 2001, pp. 22f.

were considered illegitimate and lost their right of inheritance.[57] American historian Polly Morris's investigation of incestuous relationships in Somerset from 1730 to 1835 showed similar results. Incestuous marriages were rarely called into question, and if they ended up in court they were dealt with in the same manner as was ordinary infidelity. Only in isolated cases were the people involved excommunicated or ordered to undergo penance.[58] The attitude to incest prohibitions and the handling of incest crimes were thus very special in England, since developments there differed from the ones in both Catholic and Protestant areas.

While England was the Protestant country where incest crimes were given the most lenient treatment, similar breaches of the law were punished all the more severely in the Nordic countries. Two Norwegian historians have dealt with the crime of incest in Norway during the seventeenth century. In her study, Harriet Marie Terjesen demonstrates that the practical assessment of criminal cases often adhered to the severe legislation, with crimes involving the closest degrees of kinship carrying the death penalty. However, a majority (60%) of the convicted criminals managed to escape before the punishment could be implemented.[59] Kari Telste notes a reduction in the number of incest cases in the judgement-book material towards the end of the seventeenth century. She attributes this change to a discrepancy between popular norms and legal practice. People simply avoided reporting the crimes because the punishments were considered undeservedly harsh.[60] Finally, Torleif Hansen has also studied criminal cases regarding incest in Norway. His investigation deals with the first decades of the eighteenth century in the town of Bergen. Hansen's study includes almost forty cases where the most frequently occurring relationship categories were between a man and his *stepdaughter*, his *niece*, and his *sister-in-law*, which were the same relationship categories that occurred in German-speaking areas. While people in the first category were

57 Denbo 2001, pp. 195–8, 182–7.

58 Morris 1992, pp. 143, 152–7. In 1835, a controversial law, 'Lord Lyndhurst's Act', was passed. This law prescribed that marriages entered into before 1835 between individuals who were related within the prohibited degrees were to be considered valid. However, the law led to protests and increased control rather than to a liberalisation of the relationships in question. Morris 1992, pp. 140f; Kuper 2002, p. 163.

59 Terjesen 1994, pp. 105, 139f, 146f, 164.

60 Telste 1993, p. 226.

sentenced to death, people in the latter two categories were usually pardoned.[61]

In addition, Tyge Krogh has studied Danish incest crimes, while Icelandic conditions have been investigated by Már Jónsson. Both present accounts of a similarly strict legislation where several incestuous relationships were punishable by death. In Denmark, the practical handling of incest crimes became somewhat more lenient after 1683, when it became more common for the king to commute death sentences to life imprisonment. A few decades later, the same development occurred in Iceland.[62]

With the exception of England, the available research describes a generally strict punishment policy throughout the Protestant part of the world with respect to crimes against the prohibited degrees. In theory, crimes against the closest kinship degrees were to be punished by death. On the other hand, the practical application of the legislation could vary somewhat among countries. The Nordic countries, and Sweden in particular, stood out in this context because the strict theoretical legislation was followed up by an unusually severe application of the laws.

As in England, developments in France were somewhat atypical. During the eighteenth century, incest was defined as a crime that resulted in severe punishment; but in connection with the French Revolution, incest prohibitions were declared to be empty religious rhetoric that had been foisted on the people, whereafter the prohibitions were completely abolished in 1791. To be sure, abuse and exploitation of a relative who was a minor might be prosecuted under other criminal classifications, but the French scholar Fabienne Giuliani demonstrates that the phenomenon of incest became all but completely suppressed during the first half of the nineteenth century. Nevertheless, although incest was no longer a crime against the law, incestuous acts never ceased to be considered moral crimes. Towards the end of the nineteenth century, when the medical debate had continued for a few decades, incest was increasingly often described as unnatural acts perpetrated by monsters.[63]

Apart from the criminal-case studies, something should be said about research that has dealt with incest prohibitions from a

61 Hansen 1993, pp. 180f.

62 Krogh 2000, pp. 158–90; Jónsson 2003; Jónsson 1998.

63 Giuliani 2009a; Giuliani, 2009b, Giuliani 2014. For ideas about incest in eighteenth-century France, see Chammas 2011.

completely different point of view, namely how possibilities for dispensation have been used by different social groups.

An interdisciplinary anthology containing contributions from seven countries presents a theory on the significance of kinship and marriage patterns in Europe from the Middle Ages to the modern period. The authors demonstrate that Europe has gone through two structural changes with respect to attitudes to and applications of kinship. At the transition from the late medieval to the early modern period, the emphasis on *vertical* kinship ties is said to have increased. To a greater extent than before, property came to be transferred in its entirety from father to eldest son while daughters and younger sons were relegated to the background. Also, privileges and political offices were transferred in accordance with vertical systems; and within the business world, various patron–client relationships dominated.

During the eighteenth century, however, this pattern was gradually exchanged for a more *horizontal* structure as lateral networks were established. Appointments were awarded on the basis of an individual's personal network of contacts and friendships, rather than on the basis of his lineage. Childhood friends jointly collected investment capital and became equal partners. Contacts and networks thus became more important in the struggle for offices and privileges than descent and family ancestry. In connection with these changes, marriage patterns were also affected. From the second half of the eighteenth century and for another 150 years thereafter, endogamous marriages became especially advantageous, and marriages between cousins became very popular.[64] In other words, cultural shifts in marriage patterns coincided with changes in the economic conditions in society.

Unlike most other European countries, Catholic as well as Protestant, England allowed cousin marriages from the sixteenth century.[65] Adam Kuper, who has investigated some of the most prominent bourgeois families in nineteenth-century England, believes that cousin marriages were regarded as both unproblematic and

64 Sabean, Teuscher, and Mathieu 2007a; see also Johnson and Sabean 2011; Sabean 2011a.

65 Henry VIII used incest prohibitions and possibilities for dispensation on a number of occasions in his marital affairs. In connection with his fifth marriage, he wanted to marry the cousin of his previous wife, Anne Boleyn, which is why he pushed through a legislative amendment that legalised cousin marriages. Kuper 2009, pp. 60f.

advantageous in certain social groups, especially among the middle classes. Entire networks of family alliances were created, which gave an individual's own group advantages in the general competition for capital and appointments.[66] According to Kuper, there was also a good deal of tolerance with respect to relationships between a man and the sister of his deceased wife, even though that relationship was prohibited. This might be a consequence of the theoretical incest prohibition not being as strongly upheld in practice in England as it was in other countries. Perpetrators of incest crimes who were discovered were sentenced to relatively mild punishments, which signalled that the crime was, after all, not regarded as a particularly serious one. [67]

Although cousin marriages were prohibited in the rest of Europe, the nobility in several countries had, with the aid of the system of dispensations, practised similar strategies since the Middle Ages. During the nineteenth century, the same tendencies in marriage patterns became increasingly common in bourgeois groups in several European countries, including France, Germany, Italy, Switzerland, and Austria.[68] Swedish historian Anita Göransson has pointed to the existence of similar strategies within the Swedish bourgeoisie.[69]

In summary, that scholars who have studied incest crimes have often concentrated on the period between 1550 and 1750, which was the period during which the punishment for such crimes was at its most severe in the Protestant areas of Europe. Researchers who have instead focused on voluntary incestuous relationships, conducting studies of different marriage patterns within different groups, have usually focused their investigations on the period between 1750 and 1900, when marriages between relatives were most common. My study differs from previous research, because I use both the criminal-case material and applications for dispensation. In addition, my investigation covers the age of Lutheran orthodoxy, the nineteenth century with its liberal reform activities, and a part of the twentieth century. I view the incest prohibitions and the practical handling of incest cases as expressions of different social norms, and the long period under investigation becomes necessary in order to survey and

---

66 Kuper 2009, pp. 134, 158, 197f.

67 Kuper 2009, pp. 66–82.

68 Kuper 2009, p. 243; Johnson 2011; Sabean 2011a; Lanzinger 2015; Saurer 1997.

69 Göransson 1990.

foreground the changes that occurred and to find reasonable explanations for them.

Outline

In order to elucidate and explain the changes that have occurred over time with respect to the social position and significance of incest prohibitions, the investigation has been divided into three parts which, very roughly, take their respective point of departure in the three turns of the century in 1700, 1800, and 1900. Norms and ideas are often enduring structures in society and difficult to make visible; but by locating samples a hundred years apart, differences between the periods can be made to stand out. Even so, each sample represents ideas that were articulated several decades before and after the actual turn of the century, and even though I use exact years to divide the periods in my presentation, the boundaries should be regarded as fluid.

Naturally enough, the two first samples are given somewhat more space than the final one. This is because I deal with the entire eighteenth and nineteenth centuries but only with the first half of the twentieth century. During the earlier periods, incest prohibitions were a highly contentious issue which was the subject of animated

3 The hundred-court judge led the hearing of criminal cases at the local courts.

debate in society. As ideas regarding incest changed, the number of cases was reduced, as was the number of fiery contributions to the debate.

The first part of the empirical investigation is preceded by a background chapter where I describe the jurisprudential context at the beginning of the period investigated, while at the same time early modern Swedish society is put in relation to a broader European context. Brief updates of social and jurisprudential developments recur at the beginning of each subchapter. Within each empirical section, the dispensation material and the criminal-case material are presented separately, and after that the overall values which emerged in both collections of material are highlighted and compared to the European context in a partial summary. In the final part of the book, I discuss the general results of the investigation on the basis of terms relating to continuity and change from a long-term perspective.

1

Background and context

The early modern judicial system

The secular judicial structure

In comparison to many European countries, the Swedish judicial system was organised in an unusually uniform manner during the early modern period. In broad outline, it consisted of three secular judicial bodies.

The first body was the local court, *tinget* (the *Thing*), also called *häradsrätten* (the hundred court) in the countryside or *rådhusrätten* (the municipal court) in the towns. The *häradshövding* (hundred-court judge), who acted as the judge for the local court sessions, summoned the court sessions three times a year: winter, summer, and autumn. If a serious crime was discovered in between the regular court sessions, an extra session was summoned, a so-called *urtima ting* (extraordinary court session).[1] In addition to the hundred-court judge, trusted farmers from the local community functioned as judges. In ancient times, the Things were highly public events that were attended by ordinary people from the local community. Many of these individuals also participated in the actual trial process as witnesses or plaintiffs.

Hovrätten (the court of appeal), which was the second body in the judicial system, was established in the seventeenth century for the purpose of relieving pressure on the Crown. Above all, the court of appeal was intended to ensure uniformity in the administration of justice by overseeing the work of the lower courts. Each year the lower courts were obliged to send in a transcript of their judgement books, a *renovering*, to the court of appeal, so that the appellate court could make ex-post-facto assessments of judicial decisions.

1 Sundin 1992, pp. 60–70.

Serious crimes, however – that is, crimes where the defendant risked the death penalty – along with all cases regarding crimes against the prohibited degrees in the first and second degree were to be assessed by the court of appeal before a final judgement was handed down, which is why the records were sent to the court of appeal immediately after the local court sessions.[2] The courts of appeal also served in an advisory function for the lower courts when any doubts arose regarding the nature of the law, but defendants themselves had no right to appeal to the next instance.

The court of appeal was made up of a president and fourteen members, or, as they were called, *assessorer* (associate judges), half of whom were noblemen, half commoners. They would often have a basic education in civil or criminal law and their periods of service usually lasted for more than ten years, sometimes upwards of 25–30 years. The combined experience of judicial work in the group was thus generally significant. A large majority of the criminal cases were settled exclusively on the basis of the records sent in by the lower courts. If there was a lack of agreement regarding individual judicial decisions, the case was settled by means of a vote. The members of the court of appeal had the authority to deviate from a prescribed punishment when this was considered appropriate. They could *arbitrera* (mitigate) a punishment or *leuterera* (pardon) a person if there were especially extenuating circumstances. These decisions were not entirely arbitrary but were to a large extent governed by earlier cases, and new decisions also became precedential for future ones. If a criminal risked the death penalty, the court of appeal had to apply to the Crown for permission to issue a pardon. They could also consult the Crown if they were unsure of the proper meaning of the law in a particular case.[3]

The third and final body was *Kungl. Maj:t* (the Crown). It was thus the king who had the supreme judiciary power in the country, although he acted in consultation with *rikets råd* (the Council of the State). The Council of the State consisted of around twenty ecclesiastical and secular men of great power, men whose education varied a good deal. In the absence of the monarch, decisions could be made by the Council alone. If the Crown received a question from a cathedral chapter or a court of appeal, the monarch often answered

2 Thunander 1993, p. 14; K.B. (letters patent) 1689, 25 April.

3 Thunander 1993, pp. 12, 221–5. For more detailed information on the composition of the court and the educational level of the members, see Thunander 1993, pp. 27–40.

by way of an official letter or a regulation that laid down how he wished similar cases to be dealt with in all judicial bodies in the future. These regulations were given the status of official laws, and the courts of appeal adhered to them in future judicial decisions.[4]

The ecclesiastical structure

In premodern society, the secular judicial structure had an ecclesiastical counterpart. On the local level, the vicar (*kyrkoherde* in Swedish) acted as the leader of his parish. He was, above all, responsible for the spiritual welfare of his parishioners. Via sermons, teaching the catechism, and catechetical examinations in the parishioners' homes (*husförhör*), he functioned both as a teacher and as an examiner of the scriptural knowledge of the peasantry. The vicar usually chaired the parish meetings, where minor infractions against prevailing norms were tried and judged. He often had an assistant in the form of a curate (*adjunkt*), an assistant vicar (*kaplan*), a perpetual curate (*komminister*), or a parish clerk (*klockare*).

The dean (*prost*) was responsible for a deanery (*kontrakt*) which could include several cures (*pastorat*). He acted as a supervisor of and advisor to the vicar. Above him, the dean had a bishop who managed the regional cathedral chapter. During earlier periods the cathedral chapter, or the 'consistory' as it was also called, had had significant judiciary power in society; but around the turn of the century in 1700, the hearing of most criminal cases had been transferred to the secular courts. At the beginning of the investigated period, the cathedral chapters were primarily responsible for the education of the country's priests, but their purpose was also to pass judgement in certain religious and marital cases.[5]

The Christian incest prohibition in a historical perspective

All the major world religions, including Christianity, Judaism, Islam, Buddhism, and Hinduism, have regulated sexual relations between relatives in some way.[6] But the prohibitions developed in the

4 From 1789 judiciary power was taken over by *Högsta Domstolen* (the Supreme Court). Thunander 1993, pp. 183f.

5 Lennartsson 1999, pp. 32–40; Marklund 2004, p. 19.

6 Bittles 2012, Chapter 2. The different forms of incest prohibitions in relation to different cultures and times are presented in great detail by Michael Mitterauer in Mitterauer 1994.

Christian world appear exceptional in scope. The Catholic Church based its prohibitions on the Bible; but the text was vaguely worded, making alternative interpretations possible. The Catholic Church chose to interpret the text so that the number of prohibited degrees was extended far beyond the wording of the Bible. From the year 1215, incest prohibitions included both consanguinity and affinity relationships up to the fourth degree.[7] In other words, a man and a woman were prohibited from marrying if they had one common relative four generations earlier. With respect to affinity relationships, a widower was forbidden to marry anyone who had been similarly related to his deceased wife. The rules necessitated an exogamous marriage pattern; that is to say, marriages had to be contracted outside a person's own kinship sphere.[8] In addition to the above prohibitions, there were also regulations governing so-called 'spiritual kinship' (e.g., *godparenthood*) and 'legal kinship' (e.g., *adoption*).[9]

In Sweden, the marital laws of the Catholic Church were applied from the twelfth century onwards, which is when Christianity began to permeate the country's judicial system in earnest.[10] The incest prohibitions are mentioned in the earliest laws from the thirteenth century, where relationships in the first and second degree were equated to manslaughter of a close relative.[11] In the eyes of the church and the law incest was a most reprehensible sin; but the punishments were usually limited to fines, even though the Old Testament text recommended capital punishment.[12] Table 3 presents the prohibitions that are enumerated in the Bible.

---

7 Prior to the year 1215, the prohibition was extended all the way up to the seventh degree. Donahue 2016, p. 35; Christensen-Nugues 2004, p. 313; Gaunt 1996, pp. 226f.

8 Gaunt 1996, pp. 219f; Christensen-Nugues 2004, p. 313. Scholars have pointed out that from a financial perspective, these extended prohibitions had positive consequences for the Church, because the rules minimised the risk of the formation of smaller and stronger family alliances that could compete with the Church for influence in society. Herlihy 1995, pp. 103f. Regarding the earliest formulations of the prohibitions, see also Ubl 2008.

9 Salonen 2001, pp. 105–8; Herlihy 1995, pp. 96f; Jarzebowski 2006, pp. 41–9.

10 Christensen-Nugues 2004, p. 309. It is likely that there were some kinds of restrictions for marriages between relatives even before this, but the first written evidence can be found in the Swedish *landskapslagar* (provincial law-rolls). Inger 2011, pp. 28–30.

11 Christensen-Nugues 2004, p. 314.

12 For a more detailed presentation of the punishments in early Swedish legislation, see Almquist 1961, pp. 31f.

Table 3. Incest prohibitions and punishments according to Leviticus

Relationship	Closeness	Relationship, a man and (his) ...	Punishment
Consanguinity	First/second lineal degree	*mother*, *granddaughter*	–
	First collateral degree	sister, half-sister	death
	Diagonally	aunt	'impure'
Affinity	First/second lineal degree	stepmother, stepdaughter, a mother and her daughter, *wife's granddaughter*	death
	First collateral degree	brother's wife, *stepsister*, *wife's sister*	'impure'
	Diagonally	uncle's wife	death

Source: Leviticus: Prohibitions: Chapter 18, verses 7–18; Punishments: Chapter 20, verses 11–21.
Note: Italicised relationships are mentioned only in Chapter 18, not in Chapter 20.

From the table, it appears that the biblical text was unclear with respect to certain points. For instance, there was no explicit prohibition against a man marrying his own *daughter*. Neither was the relationship between a man and his *niece* mentioned, nor the one between a man and his *cousin*. However, these were kinship ties that were forbidden according to older customs in several countries. In addition, the prohibitions were listed in Chapter 18 of Leviticus, whereas the punishments were stated in Chapter 20; but not all relationships mentioned in the former chapter are referred to in the latter. The question was how these relationships should be punished. Furthermore, the interpretation was made even more difficult by the fact that several of the relationships prohibited in Leviticus occurred in other biblical stories without the relationship being condemned.[13] It was therefore very difficult, not to say impossible, to establish an exact regulatory system exclusively based on the text of the Bible.

13 Genesis (20:12 and 29:9–30) tells the story of Abraham, who was married to his half-sister, and of Jacob, who was married to two sisters who were also his cousins. In Exodus (6:20) there is a man who was married to his aunt. For a more detailed analysis of the biblical vagueness and for possible explanations of this, see Carmichael 1997, Chapter 1.

When the Catholic Church prohibited relationships between relatives up to the fourth degree, the freedom to choose marriage partners was limited to a far greater extent than what is stated in the Bible. As has been pointed out by Jarzebowski, the prohibitions thus also came to regulate the social order in society.[14]

In parallel to the prohibitions, there was the possibility of applying for a dispensation from the Pope for marriages in the kinship degrees prohibited according to canon law but not mentioned in the Bible.[15] During the Middle Ages, this possibility was almost exclusively used by members of the nobility.[16] In addition, people from the very top of society – both abroad and in Sweden – used the same regulatory framework in order to wriggle out of an unwanted marriage after the event.[17]

After the Reformation, the right to grant dispensations for marriages between relatives was transferred to the Swedish monarch; but the tradition according to which the Church was the first place to turn to survived until the turn of the century in 1800.[18]

The European context

In Catholic Europe, the extended interpretation of prohibited family relationships up to the fourth degree prevailed during the greater part of the Middle Ages. In the fifteenth century this changed as a result of the papal right to give dispensations being questioned in the contemporary theological debate. The discussion intensified in connection with the Reformation and then continued off and on for several centuries. Martin Luther recommended the Bible

14 Jarzebowski 2012, pp. 10, 13.

15 In practice, however, this authority was delegated to an administrative unit in Rome, the so-called Apostolic Penitentiary. Salonen 2001, pp. 67f. During the later Middle Ages, some dispensations could be handled within the Nordic countries without being sent to Rome; Gaunt 1996, p. 222.

16 Salonen 2001, p. 266; Gaunt 1996, p. 224.

17 Salonen 2001, p. 114; Jarzebowski 2006, p. 45; Hehenberger 2003, p. 195. Christensen-Nugues 2004, pp. 313–15.

18 For the transition from ecclesiastical to secular law, see Korpiola 2006. At the beginning of the eighteenth century, the number of applications regarding marriage received by the cathedral chapters was still far greater than those directed directly to the king, while the relationship was the opposite towards the end of the same century. Compare Tables 4 and 5 in the Appendix. Catholic leaders sometimes also attempted to nationalise the handling of applications for dispensation. Lanzinger 2015, pp. 155–7.

as a guiding principle. Only the degrees of kinship enumerated in Holy Writ should be prohibited and the Pope had, according to Luther, no right of dispensation whatsoever.[19] In spite of this authoritative clarification, opinions among Lutheran theologians and lawyers continued to diverge. Everyone agreed that the boundaries of the prohibitions as defined by the Catholic Church should be circumscribed in order to better agree with the Bible, but the question was by how much. On the one hand it was argued that the Bible should be interpreted literally, on the other hand that one should try to find an underlying principle that still adhered to the logic of the text.

During the seventeenth century, most Lutheran theologians came to advocate a limited, but still generalising, interpretation of the prohibited degrees.[20] At the same time, punishments were recommended that corresponded better with the message of the Bible. In other words, *fewer prohibitions* but *more severe punishments* were required. Introducing a new, but at the same time uniform, punishment system was nevertheless problematic, especially in geographical areas where the administration of justice was divided into smaller regional units (e.g., German and Dutch areas).[21] In countries where Protestantism had been introduced, the handling of incestuous crimes was usually transferred from ecclesiastical to secular courts, while at the same time the penalties were made more severe.[22] England was an exception to this rule, however, because there incestuous crimes continued to be tried by the ecclesiastical courts after the Reformation with relatively mild punishments as a consequence.[23]

Above all, the academic debate surrounding the prohibited degrees, their boundaries and penalties had to do with the question of *which* relationships were in fact prohibited by God. Clear answers were sought, but there was only a vaguely worded biblical text as a foundation for forming an opinion. Because there were no firm guidelines, the theoretical discussions continued for centuries.

19 Jónsson 1994, p. 856.
20 Jónsson 1994, p. 858.
21 Egmond 2001, p. 24; Jarzebowski 2006, pp. 57f.
22 Jónsson 1998, p. 4; Egmond 2001, p. 22; Hastrup 1990, pp. 154–60; Rublack 1999, pp. 233f; Hull 1996, pp. 16, 26, 61f. In Sweden, the handling of certain crimes against the state, among these incest in the closest degrees, had already been transferred to the secular courts before the Reformation. Korpiola 2005.
23 Egmond 2001, p. 23; Morris 1992, p. 139; Kuper 2002, pp. 158, 160.

The Swedish context

After the Reformation, the attitude to crimes against morality hardened in Sweden as well. The Catholic Church had considered all sexuality to be more or less sinful. Although marriage was considered a sacrament, sexuality was primarily seen as a necessary evil and a concession to human frailty. With the Protestant Reformation, especially in its Lutheran guise, sexuality within marriage was upgraded. Sexuality in its proper element was regarded as something that contributed to a good marriage, which in its turn was the foundation of a good household and, ultimately, of a good society. Conversely, all forms of extramarital sexuality were seen as offences against God's commandments, transgressions which contributed to the corruption of society and to the threat of God's wrath striking everyone in the form of war, pestilence, crop failure, or other disasters. This provided a link between morality and social development that could justify severe sexual legislation even when punishing crimes that did not really have an actual plaintiff, e.g., with respect to fornication.[24] The policymakers of the sixteenth century endeavoured to increase the correspondence between the biblical message and its practical application.[25] With regard to the regulation of incestuous relationships, this meant that the number of prohibitions decreased in comparison to the number during the Catholic period, but that the punishments became harsher for those prohibitions that remained. In connection with *Västerås riksdag* (the parliamentary session at Västerås) in 1528, it was established that 'heresy' with a person's mother, sister, or stepmother, with a mother and daughter, or with two sisters and 'such', was prohibited by God and thus regarded as an *eldsak* (a crime punishable by burning at the stake).[26] This confusion between the concepts of incest and heresy also occurred in the other Nordic countries and goes some way towards explaining why attitudes toward the crime of incest were especially strict in this region.[27] Several letters patent from the

24 The Reformers were critical of several parts of the matrimonial legislation in canon law. For a more detailed survey of the Reformers' criticism and the changes made to matrimonial legislation after the Reformation, see Donahue 2016, pp. 40–55; Witte 2002, pp. 199–255.

25 Thunander 1993, p. 93.

26 *Kongl. stadgar, förordningar, bref och resolutioner* (Royal statutes, royal regulations, letters patent, and royal ordinances), p. 5.

27 Jónsson 1998, p. 4; Gaunt 1996, p. 229. In the judgement books from the turn of the century around 1700, it was still common for this crime to be designated 'heresy'. See, e.g., the registers in GHA, BIIA:3; GHA, BIIA:8.

second half of the sixteenth century reiterate and emphasise that these crimes could only be atoned for by death, not by means of the payment of a fine.[28]

Sveriges Rikes Lag (*The Statute Book of Sweden*) was published in print form for the first time in 1608. For want of an official church code, the Swedish king had parts of Leviticus added as an appendix to the law. The severe biblical text thus became part of the legislation, which explains why the seventeenth century became the strictest orthodox period in the history of the country.[29]

As in other countries, however, Swedish theologians and lawyers continued to be unsure of how to assess different incestuous relationships. The discrepancy between the degrees mentioned in the Bible and the degrees that were prohibited in practice was never properly clarified.[30] It was also felt that contradictory decisions had been made in different cases.[31]

In connection with a preparatory legislative document from the end of the seventeenth century, Swedish lawyer Johan Stiernhöök presented a proposal for a new marriage code where he commented on the prohibited degrees. He concluded that there was no written

28 See, e.g., Erik XIV's proclamation of 1563 on capital criminal cases, Johan II's official letter of 1578, and the parliamentary decision of 1604. *Kongl. stadgar, förordningar, bref och resolutioner*, pp. 48f, 68f, and 119. However, the fact that there was a need for reiteration indicates that the more severe punishments were not applied immediately and that people who violated these laws could initially buy themselves free. Almquist 1961, pp. 34, 39f.

29 Inger 2011, pp. 87f, 146f.

30 During most of the seventeenth century, the Swedish Church Ordinance of 1571 was in force, which prohibited marriages to the fifth degree. Before the Swedish Church Law of 1686, individual dioceses could also create local regulations. The definition of prohibited degrees thus diverged between the *Statute Book* and the Church Ordinance. Lennartsson 1999, pp. 40f, 87, 111.

31 The law-drafting committee of 1642 was summoned because 'diverse appeals and complaints' were received on an almost daily basis from subjects regarding the administration of justice. Both with respect to decisions and procedure there was 'a great deal of confusion and disorder'. *Åtgärder för lagförbättring 1633–1665* ('Measures for the improvement of the laws', 1633–1665), p. 33. The task of the law-drafting committee in 1643 was, among other things, to establish what position to take with respect to the king's previous 'contrary resolutions regarding *gradib(us) prohibitis*' (the prohibited degrees). *Åtgärder för lagförbättring 1633–1665*, p. 36. Later regulations and resolutions also refer to the earlier 'disorder'. See, e.g., K.B. (letters patent) 1678, 1 March, and K.F. (royal ordinance) 1680, 3 December.

law to comply with. In other Protestant countries, the laws had gone through an official adaptation since these countries had 'thrown off the papal yoke'. But the appendix to the *Statute Book* that had been introduced in Sweden in 1608 had not been interpreted or commented on by trained lawyers, which is why Stiernhöök believed it was necessary to untangle this matter.[32] According to Stiernhöök, the prohibitions should be based on 'the word of God and secular law and the practice that has been customary among us'.[33] He divided the prohibited degrees into three categories: first, the relationships explicitly prohibited in the Bible; second, the relationships that ought to be forbidden as a logical consequence of God's prohibitions. The third and final of Stiernhöök's categories concerned the relationships that were not prohibited by God or the Bible but only by ancient custom or habit, and consequently he categorised these prohibitions as secular – not divine.[34] Furthermore, Stiernhöök observed that practice had differed greatly with respect to all of these relationships. In Rome, as in England and in Poland, dispensations were granted for marriages in the first collateral affinity degree (*wife's sister*): the Austrian king had married his *niece*, the Swedish king Gustavus Vasa had, in his third marriage, married his deceased *wife's niece*, and there were also the example of a nobleman in Sweden marrying his *wife's sister* without a dispensation.

Stiernhöök believed that no dispensation from God's own prohibitions could be given, either by kings or by popes. On the other hand, the handling of degrees of kinship not explicitly mentioned in the Bible could be discussed. He argued that it was reasonable to punish sexual congress in the closest degrees by death, because here God's prohibitions corresponded to 'moral law' and 'natural law' and because other Reformed leaders in Germany, Prussia, and Denmark did the same.[35] Relationships between cousins were not

32 *Förarbeten till Sveriges Rikes Lag 1666–1686* (Preparatory legislative documents for *The Statute Book of Sweden*, 1666–1686), pp. 108f; quotation on p. 109.

33 *Förarbeten till Sveriges Rikes Lag 1666–1686*, p. 116. Similar formulations were also used in connection with other preparatory legislative texts. In 1643 the law-drafting committee made their decisions, in their own words, 'in accordance with God's law, other secular laws, and the best interest of one's conscience' (*Åtgärder för lagförbättring 1633–1665*, p. 61).

34 *Förarbeten till Sveriges Rikes Lag 1666–1686*, pp. 109f.

35 Stiernhöök referred to Germany in spite of the country's not being unified until 200 years later. He presumably referred to certain German-speaking Protestant areas. *Förarbeten till Sveriges Rikes Lag 1666–1686*, pp. 111–13.

mentioned in the Bible but were forbidden in both Catholic and Protestant countries (even if dispensations were often granted for the elite), so Sweden should also require dispensations for such relationships, according to Stiernhöök. However, marriages in the second affinity degree (*wife's stepmother*, *wife's brother's widow*) could be allowed.[36]

In contradistinction, diagonal affinity relationships (*aunt/niece*) were problematic. A man's kinship with his *aunt* was, logically speaking, as close as his kinship with his *niece*, but only the former relationship was prohibited in the Bible. In this case Stiernhöök relied on written statements from Hugo Grotius, Moses Maimonides, and Martin Luther, all of whom differentiated between these relationships, among other things with the justification that an aunt was in the position of a parent to a man; consequently, he was obliged to show her due respect and deference.[37] Conversely, when the relationship concerned a man's *niece* it was the niece who should show respect for the man.

Stiernhöök's argumentation shows that although incest prohibitions were primarily based on religious arguments, there was a parallel, active idea to the effect that cultural ideas and local customs should also be considered before official rules could be established. With respect to the closest relationship categories, Stiernhöök was of the opinion that God's law, moral law, and natural law agreed with one another. In other words, he described what he regarded as a self-evident norm in society.

He also admitted that the assessment of some kinship categories (e.g., *niece*, *cousin*) was not obvious and that it was possible to hold different and conflicting opinions. Whether these relationships should be defined as prohibited or allowed was hence a matter of negotiation. In active negotiation Stiernhöök drew on contemporary ideas surrounding the interrelationships among different family members, which explains why the kinship between a man and his *aunt* could be differentiated from his kinship to his *niece*, even though the degree of closeness of these relationships was in fact the same. The difference lay in the duties that followed from a certain position in the family.

---

36 *Förarbeten till Sveriges Rikes Lag 1666–1686*, pp. 114f.

37 Moses Maimonides (1135–1204) was a well-known Jewish philosopher whose writings were still considered important in the seventeenth century. Hugo Grotius (1583–1645) was a Dutch scholar, theologian, and lawyer. He was known for his views regarding jurisprudence and natural law and has been referred to as 'the father of international law'.

4 Johan Stiernhöök (1596–1675). Stiernhöök was elevated to the nobility in 1649 and has been called 'the father of Swedish jurisprudence'.

Filial deference, or the respect that children were expected to feel for their parents, was of fundamental significance in early modern society. The entire social structure rested on hierarchies, and its stability depended on people's respect for all authorities. The first authority an individual encountered was his or her parents, and to fail in respect for them would be tantamount to rejecting the hierarchical order. Because the relationship between a parent and a child was likened to that between a ruler and a subject, such impertinence could disturb the balance throughout society.[38] Indeed, filial deference was regarded as the foundation of a stable society, and even adult children who did not show proper respect for their parents could be prosecuted.[39] Because the man was considered the dominant party in a marriage relationship, his duties would be downright contradictory if he were in a subordinate filial role to his wife while at the same time he was expected to dominate her in his role as a husband. These reasons were not viewed as an impediment in the same way for a relationship between a man and his niece, because the father's position of authority was similar to that of a husband. According to Stiernhöök, it was up to the respective secular leader to decide whether a secular prohibition should apply in such cases.

That there was great uncertainty regarding some relationships during the early modern period is also clear from other records from the preparative legislative material. From the mid-seventeenth century up to *1734 års lag* (the Civil Code of 1734), there were various suggestions concerning what consequences should follow a man's possible relationship with his own *niece*, his *wife's niece*, or his *wife's sister*. It was admitted that practice had varied and that legal scholars disagreed on what penal consequences were reasonable.[40] The concrete legislative proposals prescribed, by turns, fines, banishment, and death. On one occasion a harsher punishment was recommended for one of these relationships compared to the others, but on another occasion the situation might be reversed.[41] It is obvious that a man's relationship with his *niece* or with his *wife's sister* were regarded as relationships that were particularly difficult to assess. There was no obvious set of values, no common norm, on which agreement in the assessment of these offences might have been based. The inconsistency indicated by the legislative

38 Hammar 2012, pp. 111–13.

39 The same rules applied to, for instance, parents-in-law and spouses who had married into a family. Odén 1991, pp. 90–2; Odén 2001.

40 *Åtgärder för lagförbättring 1633–1665*, p. 227; *Förarbeten till Sveriges Rikes Lag 1666–1686*, p. 116.

41 *Åtgärder för lagförbättring 1633–1665*, pp. 62, 152, 227; *Förarbeten till Sveriges Rikes Lag 1686–1736*, Volume 7, pp. 353, 442.

proposals suggests that there was active negotiation in respect of how these relationships should be regarded and assessed.

In summary, there was uncertainty when it came to determining the boundaries of incest prohibitions and the criminal consequences of certain relationships; and although the debate rested on a religious foundation, it is clear that the argumentation of the legal scholars also comprised secular elements. The question is what consequences this had for the practical handling of incest matters, criminal cases as well as applications for dispensations.

2

Incest: a religious crime, 1680–1750

Applications for dispensation

Marriage: an alliance based on feelings and reason

Today, the choice of a marriage partner may primarily be based on the feelings that the presumptive spouses have for each other. But from a historical perspective, marriage has been closely connected to both political and economic agreements, on a social as well as on an individual level.[1] Marriage not only connected two individuals; their respective families were also united through new bonds of loyalty and friendship. In this context it has been pointed out that marriage has been the foremost form for building alliances throughout history.[2] The structural regulation of property and property transfer has had a great influence on the marriage system, because it has indirectly determined which alliances were advantageous in different situations. When choosing a marriage partner, individuals – regardless of their positions in society – have assessed their own and their families' future opportunities for supporting themselves in various ways. It was often the case that this decision was not made by the individual in question but by his or her family. According to American historian Stephanie Coontz, the importance of the economic and strategic decisions before a marriage was so commonly accepted

1 For instance, Melby et al. 2006, p. 15. A discussion on the transfer of property can be found in Lindstedt Cronberg 1997, pp. 185f. The importance of a dowry in various cultures and eras is discussed in Goody 1983, pp. 216–40.

2 E.g., Coontz 2005, p. 53. Augustine is said to have seen incest prohibitions as a means of *increasing the bonds of friendship between different family groups*. Herlihy 1995, p. 102. Gaunt, too, argues that this was a conscious aim on the part of the Catholic Church. Gaunt 1996, pp. 221–4.

that individuals did not expect their personal feelings to play any part in deciding on a marriage partner.[3]

However, research has shown that the view of the ideal marriage changed during the latter part of the eighteenth century. This transformation apparently occurred at slightly different times in the entire Western world, including North America. From the late eighteenth century onwards, love and personal desires were given a different weight in the marriage market.[4] According to German sociologist Niklas Luhmann, the codes for intimacy changed during this period. Previously, love had rested on ideals such as social hierarchy and solidarity within the family. Love between spouses had been seen as something of a social duty, but now it came to be understood more as a shared emotional partnership.[5]

According to the above line of reasoning, the ideal marriage was, until the late eighteenth century, primarily a practical transaction between families, while after this time love was seen as the very basis for an ideal marriage. This does not imply a denial of the fact that people fell in love with each other before the breakthrough of the 'love match' ideal, only that expectations for the marital relationship changed.[6] Nor did it mean that emotions and personal taste were of no importance in earlier periods. On the contrary, several historians have pointed out that the feelings of presumptive spouses were considered long before the cultural change described above. Similarly, economic circumstances continued to play a role in later matrimonial transactions as well. Not least in wealthier social groups did the future maintenance of the couple continue to be a decisive factor in many marital alliances throughout the nineteenth century.[7]

3 Coontz 2005, pp. 5–7. See also Sjöberg 2001, pp. 134–63; Ambjörnsson 1978, p. 159; Matović 1984, pp. 84–6; Hansen 2010, p. 50.

4 Coontz 2005, pp. 5, 306; Davidson 2012, p. 24; Bjurman 1998, pp. 14f, 23; Marklund 2004, pp. 230–4; Telste 1999, pp. 278f; Ambjörnsson 1978, pp. 158, 165. According to Seth J. Denbo, there was an ongoing conflict between the parents' right to arrange their children's marriages and the children's right to be involved in the decision-making. Another contentious issue was the importance of emotional ties between spouses throughout the eighteenth century in England. Denbo 2001, pp. 201–3.

5 Luhmann 2003, pp. 31, 61–5, 118f. See also von Braun 1989, p. 87; Ambjörnsson 1978, p. 165.

6 Coontz 2005, p. 7.

7 Kuper 2009, pp. 24–8, 243; Davidoff & Hall 1987, p. 221; Matović 1984, pp. 190f; Göransson 1992, p. 534; Rundquist 1989, p. 44.

In other words, we are talking about a gradual shift of conjugal ideals from the practical to the emotional.

British historian Catherine Frances emphasises that young people of marriageable age and their families have always had a joint interest in the success of any matrimonial union, from an economic as well as an emotional perspective. Both factors were important, and no one stood to gain from alliances that lacked either ingredient for future happiness.[8] It is thus reasonable to assume that economic factors *interacted* with personal taste when a marriage partner was to be chosen, both before and after the emergence of the new romantic ideal.

Investigations conducted on the basis of the potential of marriages for forming alliances often describe two different strategies for optimising the economic and social position of a person's own family. One has to do with marrying of young people to individuals outside one's own family in order to increase one's network of loyal allies. The other strategy focuses on preserving property and capital within one's own group through strategic marriages within the family.[9] The latter strategy has often been linked to social groups with major property holdings; for instance, the nobility or, during later periods, the emerging middle classes. Within anthropology, such marriage patterns are referred to as 'exogamous' and 'endogamous', respectively, and they have often been seen as relevant to how incest prohibitions have developed in different cultures.[10]

The fact that the nobility allowed itself to be governed by economic incentives when arranging marriages for the next generation may not seem surprising, considering the extent of their economic assets, but similar arrangements could also be found in lower social circles, as may be demonstrated by an example from the Strängnäs Cathedral Chapter. In 1680, Johan Persson applied for a dispensation to marry his second cousin on his mother's side of the family. The argument used in favour of the acceptance of the application was expressly that the couple wanted to marry 'for the sake of a freehold that both of them were due to inherit'. This confirms that economic and

8 Frances 2005, p. 40. For similar lines of reasoning, see also Davidson 2012, pp. 25, 30; Lennartsson 2012, p. 115; Jarzebowski 2014, p. 170 and the literature referred to therein.

9 E.g., Kuper 2009; Göransson 1992, p. 109.

10 E.g., Turner and Maryanski 2005, pp. 35–44.

practical circumstances functioned as incentives for marriage alliances among the lower social orders as well.[11]

The prohibitions are challenged

As we have seen, the possibility of applying an endogamous marriage strategy was severely limited by the extended interpretation of the incest provisions by the Catholic Church throughout the Middle Ages. Even marriages between comparatively distant relatives were quite simply forbidden. However, after the Reformation the rules began to be questioned by the group that possessed the greatest assets in Sweden – the nobility.

During the sixteenth and seventeenth centuries the prohibition against cousin marriages was fiercely criticised by the Swedish aristocracy, and it is likely that it was economic interests that motivated their engagement with this issue, in spite of the debate being conducted on theological grounds.[12] Nevertheless, resistance was strong among legal scholars, which is why the debate continued. On 1 March 1678, the Swedish king decided that marriages between cousins should be completely forbidden. A mere two years later, however, the decision was repealed, and instead an opportunity for any person to apply for dispensation to marry a cousin was formally introduced.[13] From 1680 onward, it was thus permitted to apply for dispensation for cousin marriages. In other words, the pressures exerted and the opposition to the prohibition resulted in some relaxation of the regulatory framework.[14] But this did not mean that the national debate on cousin marriages fell silent. The priesthood in particular continued to argue against such alliances. According to the reasoning of the clergy, God's meaning may be ambiguously worded; but the relationships were nevertheless clearly unsound, and for this reason it was recommended that the prohibition should be retained, if for no other reason than as a precaution.[15]

11 StD, AI:9, 1679, 3 December, no. 4, p. 6. See also Gaunt 1996, p. 234.

12 Winberg 1985, pp. 40f; Lennartsson 1999, pp. 120, 152; Gaunt 1996, pp. 231–3.

13 K.B. 1678, 1 March and K.F. 1680, 3 December.

14 Winberg 1985, p. 41, and the literature referred to therein; Gaunt 1996, p. 233; Inger 2011, p. 109.

15 The lack of clarity in the biblical text was partly due to certain generally worded prohibitions – for instance, the prohibition against a man being together with a person who was 'of his flesh', which was said to refer to

In spite of the resistance of the clergy, cultural acceptance of cousin marriages appears to have been significant at the beginning of the period investigated, both within and outside of noble circles. In the parliamentary records of the clergy from 1723, Bishop David Lund claimed that if the prohibition against cousin marriages was removed, 'herds' of 'common men' would attempt such marriages.[16] In other words, Lund describes cousin marriages as particularly popular among the peasantry, and there are examples from the dispensations that support his view.[17]

Keeping in mind the debate engendered by cousin marriages, it is interesting to note that the relationship between a man and his *niece* did not elicit as strong a reaction in the social debate. Neither prohibition was explicitly mentioned in the biblical text, but unlike the prohibition against cousin marriages, the prohibition against marriages between uncles and nieces was not at all questioned to the same extent. Nor have I found any applications for dispensation regarding such marriages from the first half of the eighteenth century. This prohibition hence appears to have been accepted in spite of the impossibility of justifying it from a religious point of view.

Relationship categories

Since the beginning of the Reformation, it was only the Crown that had the power to accept or reject an application for marriage; but the habit of primarily turning to the Church in such matters continued until the beginning of the nineteenth century. During the early eighteenth century, the numbers were comparatively modest: a handful of cases per year and instance.[18] The procedure entailed certain

---

cousins – and partly due to an element of uncertainty in the translation from Hebrew. In addition, the logic of God's wanting to forbid the relationship between a man and his *aunt* but not between a man and his *aunt's daughter*, who was of the same flesh as her mother, was questioned. The same line of reasoning applied to an *uncle's wife* and an *uncle's daughter*. *Pr. 1686*, IV, pp. 313–16.

16 *Pr. 1723*, p. 542.

17 See, e.g., a case from Strängnäs Cathedral Chapter, where a father opposes his son's intended marriage because of the woman's personal qualities rather than the fact that she was his son's cousin. StD, AI:10, 1681, 17 October, no. 1.

18 More applications for marriages were received by the cathedral chapters than by the Judiciary Inspection (*justitierevisionen*) at the beginning of the century, while these proportions were reversed by the end of the same century.

costs, which made it easier for individuals with means to complete the application procedure.[19]

In these cases, the cathedral chapter functioned mainly as an information point. They could often – but not always – answer the question of whether a relationship was permitted or not, but they did not have the authority to approve an application if the relationship was included in the prohibited degrees. In order to legalise the relationship, it was necessary to have a royal dispensation. Sometimes the cathedral chapter acted as a mediator by drawing up an application to the Crown, but applicants were also at liberty to have a document written and despatched in some other manner.

Between 1710 and 1734, seventy-six applications for dispensation were received by the Skara Cathedral Chapter. Out of these, eight were cases that involved biological cousins, whereas twice as many concerned various cousins through affinity (*wife's cousin*, *cousin's widow*, *two cousins*, *wife's cousin's widow*). See Table 4.

Virtuous or depraved love

As is clear from Table 4, the different cousin relationships by consanguinity or affinity (*cousin*, *wife's cousin*, *cousin's widow*, *two cousins*) were among the most commonly occurring grounds for applications with respect to separate categories at this time. The authorities' assessment of these applications was comparatively free of conflict. The applications did not cause any discussions among the members of the cathedral chapter, and the results were the same irrespective of whether a case dealt with consanguinity or affinity relationships, full or half relations. Requests were routinely sent on to the Crown, and almost without exception returned with a favourable answer.[20]

19 The application had to be written on a purchased, stamped sheet of paper. The cost of the paper was rated according to the titles of the applicants, and in 1736 cost between sixteen öre and two thalers in silver. K.F. 1736, 23 September. A housemaid earned around three thalers a week. Lagerqvist and Nathorst-Böös 1999, p. 78.

20 See, e.g., SD, AI:31, 1722, 10 January, no. 7, p. 328; SD, AI:32, 1724, 8 July, no. 2, p. 1; SD, AI:32, 1725, 19 July, no. 19, p. 133. Examples of couples referred to the Crown: SD, AI:30, 1711, 13 June, no. 2, p. 79. Including a favourable answer: SD, A1:34, 1732, 12 January, no. 1, p. 363; SD, AI:34, 1731, 24 November, no. 1, p. 347; SD, AI:34, 1734, 16 January, no. 3, p. 668. See also JR, K, 1730, 20 March, Rasmus Olofsson, Karin Mårtensdotter; JR, K, 1730, 9 June, Christian Månsson, Boel Svensdotter; JR, K, 1730, 26 November, Per Persson, Elin Andersdotter.

Table 4. Applications for dispensation directed to the Skara Cathedral Chapter, 1710–34

Relationship	Closeness	Relationship, a man and (his)...	1710–34
Consanguinity	Second degree	cousin	8
	Diagonally (2+3)	parent's cousin	8
		first cousin once removed	10
	Total		26
Affinity	Diagonally (1+2)	wife's niece/wife's niece's daughter	6
		sibling's stepdaughter	3
		son-in-law's/daughter-in-law's sister	2
		step-parent's sister	2
	≥ Second degree	wife's cousin	7
		cousin's widow	5
		two cousins	2
		stepfather's niece	1
		wife's brother's widow, wife's former husband's sister	6
		father-in-law's widow	1
		step-grandfather's widow	3
		wife's cousin's widow	2
		wife's nephew's stepdaughter	1
		wife's nephew's widow	1
		wife's uncle's widow	1
		uncle's widow's daughter	1
		aunt's husband's widow	3
		grandmother's brother's widow	1
		a woman and her uncle's widow	1
		wife's step-granddaughter	1
	Total		50

Source: SD, series AI.
Note: Including half-family and mirror relationships (maternal/paternal relatives).

The applications often presented the relationship in brief terms, whereupon the question about marriage was posed.[21] In isolated cases it is clear that there were warm feelings between the applicants. The two cousins Nils Arvidsson and Ingeborg Bengtsdotter, for example, wanted to form 'a Christian marriage union' with each other because they had 'taken a heartfelt liking to each other' and wanted to 'love each other with a decent and virtuous love'.[22] But it was unusual to talk about personal feelings and mutual love in this manner. This fact does not exclude the possibility that other couples applying were indeed in love, but the absence of descriptions of love in the application documents testifies to the fact that these arguments were not considered important or legitimate when an application for dispensation was to be justified. By contrast, it was often pointed out that the relationship was a *virtuous* one. The applicants' good name and virtue were also sometimes certified by a clergyman or a vicar in a separate testimonial.[23] In addition, the importance of virtue was confirmed in the decisions of the authority. In a royal decision from 1730, it was noted that the couple 'have formed their marriage union in propriety and virtue, so we will also give our gracious approval to its consummation'.[24] In other words, the moral status of the relationship was a more important factor in the assessment than any feelings the applicants may have had. Because similar moral values were reproduced both in the application documents and in the decisions, these norms appear to have had strong support throughout society.

This agrees well with the research that places the cultural breakthrough of the love match in the late eighteenth century. At the beginning of the eighteenth century, emotions and personal inclinations were not considered convincing arguments for pushing through a request for dispensation. It is true that love between spouses was defined as a positive quality because it contributed to *a good marriage*, which in its turn promoted a stable society; but love could also be dangerous. The early modern concept of love has been described as dichotomous, both favourable and unfavourable. The dividing line was drawn between marital and extramarital

---

21 For instance, JR, BoA, 1720, 25 April, Carl Christiernum, Agneta von Hyltén.

22 JR, K, 1730, 3 June, Nils Arvidsson, Ingeborg Bengtsdotter.

23 For instance, JR, BoA, 1730, 20 March, Rasmus Olofsson, Karin Mårtensdotter.

24 JR, K, 1730, 26 November, Per Persson, Elin Andersdotter.

love.[25] As was pointed out above, virtuous love promoted harmony between the spouses, which led to individual happiness, a well-functioning household, and social stability. Conversely, extramarital love risked leading individuals astray, causing them to make short-sighted choices which might ultimately lead to misfortune and penury for the individual and to encumbrances for society (for instance, through illegitimate children who were not provided for). By taking legal measures against extramarital sexuality, the institution of marriage was protected, and through it the entire social order.

For this reason, virtue became more important than personal expressions of sentiment in the assessment of applications for dispensation. It was virtue that defined the relationship as legitimate while a lack of virtue consequently posed a problem. While cousins in virtuous – meaning chaste – relationships were routinely given permission to marry, couples that had offended against the norms of morality found it more difficult to follow through on their marriage plans.

For almost ten years, Cavalry Captain Johan Kempe repeatedly applied for permission for his daughter to marry her cousin, by whom she had had a child.[26] Bengt Månsson and his cousin Margareta Andersdotter applied to the Skara Cathedral Chapter for permission to 'enter into marriage after having had illicit intercourse with each other', but because the couple had 'not commenced their intended marriage in decent and virtuous love but in dissoluteness', the consistory did not wish to forward their application to the Crown.[27] Jon Jonsson from Råttekullan also asked the Skara Cathedral Chapter for help in forwarding an application for marriage to the Crown in order to marry his cousin. The couple had had sexual relations for several years, but applied for dispensation only after she became pregnant. Jon's otherwise good conduct and name were certified in separate testimonials by the local clergyman and by other parishioners, but the cathedral chapter refused to help him.[28]

25 On the significance of marital love for society, see Stadin 2005, pp. 400f. On the dual meaning of love, see Nilsson [Hammar] 2012, pp. 117, 123; Jarzebowski 2014, p. 174.

26 SD AI:30, 1711, 1 March, no. 10, p. 89; SD AI:30, 1712, 21 May, no. 1, p. 241; SD AI:30, 1713, 18 March, no. 20, p. 343; SD AI:30, 1713, 28 October, no. 14, pp. 419f; AI:31, 1714, 5 October, no. 12, p. 43; SD, AI:31, 1714, 26 October, no. 9, p. 51; SD, AI:31, 1717, 8 July, no. 10, p. 219. Outcome unknown.

27 SD AI:34, 1731, 13 January, no. 40, p. 242.

28 SD, AI:30, 1711, 11 January, no. 10, p. 79. See also SD, AI:31, 1720, 3 March, no. 7, p. 241.

In these cases, the behaviour of the couples was apparently governed by older popular ideas on how a marriage could be entered into. In the middle of the seventeenth century, it was the promise of marriage together with the sexual act that legalised the relationship. The sexual act confirmed the marriage and made it legally binding. When a man and a woman agreed to marry in future, they could have sex with each other without violating the informal norms.[29] Their relationship was not necessarily considered blameworthy, although their sexual relations preceded the official marriage ceremony, as long as they were prepared to finalise the marriage vows later. However, this custom went against the ideas of the Church on how marriages should be entered into, ideas which emphasised that the official marriage ceremony established the validity of the marriage. Around the turn of the century in 1700, both these ideas coexisted in Sweden, but in time there was a shift away from the popular norms.[30]

The family relationship between the couples in the cases described does not seem to have been perceived as a major obstacle on the part of the applicants. Some even claimed to believe that the prohibition had been rescinded. The two cousins Sven Johansson and Johanna Persdotter were another couple who applied for permission to marry only after having had a child together. In their defence, they claimed that they had been deceived by a rumour according to which the requirement for dispensation for cousin marriages had been removed.[31]

The authorities knew about these parallel values in the peasant population and worried that the possibility of dispensation would be misused in order to legalise illegal relationships. In August 1729, the Bishop of Skara wrote to the king and said that the regulations were used to make 'general adaptations after the fact' in the diocese.[32] People simply initiated sexual relationships and applied for permission to marry only after the woman had become pregnant. In order to put a stop to such loose behaviour among the peasantry, several letters patent were published during the early eighteenth century

29 For a discussion about legitimate/illegitimate acts in relation to legal/illegal acts, see Jansson 2010, pp. 29–32. See also Lennartsson 1999, p. 121; Lindstedt Cronberg 1997, pp. 114f; Taussi Sjöberg 1996, p. 142. Similar customs existed in both Norway and in German-speaking areas. Telste 1999, pp. 94f; Rublack 1999, pp. 135f.

30 Lennartsson 1999, pp. 156–61.

31 SD, AI:34, 1729, 25 June, no. 4, p. 42; JR, BoA, 1730, 11 March, Sven Johansson, Johanna Persdotter.

32 JR, BoA, 1730, 11 March, Sven Johansson, Johanna Persdotter.

where it was established that only couples who felt 'virtuous love' for each other could expect to have their applications for marriage approved. If the relationship had been begun 'in depravity', they could instead expect to be tried in the local court and fined in accordance with the applicable law.[33] The letters patent were proclaimed to the people in connection with the weekly sermon.

It is obvious that virtue was an important criterion that at least in theory had to be fulfilled in order for an application for marriage to be approved. Illicit love could never be rendered acceptable by marrying after the fact. However, the real world worked differently. In reality, several couples had their applications approved in spite of their having violated the norms of morality. Among others, Sven Johansson and Johanna Persdotter as well as Jon Jonsson from Råttekullan, all mentioned above, were able to obtain official permission to marry.[34] In a similar manner, Anders Persson was allowed to marry his deceased wife's cousin although they had had sexual intercourse.[35] Another case tells the story of the physician Petter Blekander, who had a sexual relationship with his cousin, Helen Hultman. When she became pregnant, they married *without* having acquired a royal dispensation for the marriage. The official application was only sent in a month after the wedding but was rejected. The couple continued to live as 'husband and wife' and had another child together. When the cathedral chapter in Skara found out about the situation a year later, they commenced an investigation of the case. Four years later, the final outcome was that the couple was after all given formal permission to continue their hitherto illegal marriage.[36]

In all these cases, a directly contradictory message was conveyed from the highest decision-making instance in the country. At a formal

33 K.B. 1725, 22 June; K.B. 1725, 26 June; K.B. 1733, 6 October.

34 SD, AI:30, 1711, 8 February, no. 2, p. 81; SD, AI:34, 1730, 8 April, no. 4, p. 141.

35 SD, AI:31, 1722, 10 January, no. 7, p. 328.

36 In the investigation, the officials were primarily interested in how the clergyman who married the couple had been able to conduct an illegal marriage ceremony, but because he had died there was no one to punish. The couple was sentenced to pay a fine of fifty thalers in silver to the hospital. SD, AI:30, 1714, 27 February, no. 2, p. 450; SD, AI:30, 1714, 14 March, no. 3, p. 453; SD, AI:31, 1714, 26 October, no. 9, p. 51; SD, AI:31, 1714, 21 December, no. 2, p. 76; SD, AI:31, 1715, 12 January, no. 5, p. 77; SD, AI:31, 1715, 16 February, no. 12, p. 83; SD, AI:31, 1719, 22 April, no. 1, p. 209.

level, it was proclaimed that no one who had offended against the norms of morality would be granted dispensation for marriage after the fact. At the same time, marriage applications from several couples who were cousins, and who had violated the norms in precisely this manner, were, in practice, approved. However, both the normative ideal and the contradictory practical procedure aimed to promote and defend the institution of marriage. In this context, the family relationship was felt to be less significant than the unchaste behaviour.

Balancing between the legal and the illegal

Even though the cousin relationships dominated as separate categories among all the applications for dispensation, they were in the minority when considering the total number of applications that reached the cathedral chapter. According to Table 4 on p. 52, 54 out of 76 cases were applications from people in other family relationships. The second largest category (18) of the applications was from people who were related in the second and third consanguinity degrees (*parent's cousin*, *cousin's daughter*). These degrees fell outside the boundary of the prohibitions, and the applications were in most cases approved immediately or with some hesitation.[37] Diagonal affinity relationships (*wife's niece*) caused greater problems, as did affinity relationships in the second collateral degree (*wife's cousin*, *wife's brother's widow*). These relationship categories were comparatively common, which proves that marriage alliances of this kind were accepted by portions of the peasant population.[38] Leaseholder Jöns Andersson was one of these. He was eager to marry his *wife's brother's widow*, Ingeborg Andersdotter. Jöns asked his local vicar for help. The vicar wrote to the consistory in Linköping, which in its turn referred the matter to the king. It becomes clear that the leaseholder had 'urgently' asked permission for this marriage; and although both the vicar and the consistory tried to prevent it because of the 'close family relationship', it had not been possible to 'dissuade' the couple from their plans, since they were 'unwilling

37 In occasional cases the rules regarding the family relationship were investigated in greater detail because there was contradictory information. See SD, A1:31, 1722, 31 January, no. 1, p. 339 (*parent's cousin*); SD, A1:34, 1730, 22 July, no. 21, p. 172 (*parent's cousin*).

38 Up to thirteen cases in a diagonal degree and seven in a collateral degree, when affinity cousins are disregarded.

to give up this application for marriage'.[39] The couple's persistence paid off, and they had their application approved by the Crown.[40]

Judging from the number of applications for dispensation, relationships in the diagonal affinity degree and in the second collateral affinity degree were almost as frequent as cousin relationships and were thus equally acceptable to the general public. The attitude of the authorities was more sceptical, though, as was illustrated by the above example. Several applications were met with uncertainty or direct hostility, and in certain cases the cathedral chapter acted in direct opposition to the legislation.

Applications from a man and his *wife's niece* could be rejected with a simple observation that such marriages could not be allowed.[41] When Lars Olofsson asked to marry his deceased *wife's brother's daughter by the latter's concubine*, the consistory pointed out that God's law did not differentiate between affinity and consanguinity relationships and rejected the application.[42] In some applications it was emphasised that the woman was only the child of the man's wife's *half*-sibling, but after having noted that full and half relations were considered to be the same, the consistory rejected these cases as well.[43] Nor was an application for dispensation approved from a man and his *wife's nephew's widow*.[44] In one case the cathedral chapter ventured to forward an application for marriage between a man and his deceased *wife's sibling's granddaughter* to the Crown, but the answer was definite: the relationship was 'quite prohibited' and the question 'inappropriate'.[45] The attitude to these relationship categories was thus generally unfavourable on the part of the authorities. At the same time, an application from a *sibling's stepdaughter* and a *step-parent's sister* would be approved, kinship ties that in theory are exactly as close as those mentioned above.[46]

39 JR, BoA, 1730, 21 April, Jöns Andersson, Ingeborg Olsdotter.
40 JR, K, 1730, 3 June, Jöns Andersson, Ingeborg Olsdotter.
41 SD, AI:33, 1727, 9 October, no. 11, p. 296.
42 SD, AI:31, 1716, 15 February, no. 11, p. 155.
43 SD, AI:30, 1710, 30 July, no. 3, p. 24; SD, AI:33, 1728, 11 December, no. 34, p. 334; SD, AI:34, 1734, 6 March, no. 12, p. 688.
44 SD, AI:31, 1714, 5 October, no. 18, p. 44; SD, AI:31, 1714, 27 October, no. 14, p. 58.
45 SD, AI:30, 1713, 24 February, no. 4, p. 332.
46 SD, AI:31, 1723, 8 May, no. 22, p. 410; SD, AI:33, 1727, 30 August, no. 15, p. 69; SD, AI:31, 1720, 21 December, no. 6, p. 273; SD, AI:33, 1727, 19 July, no. 6, p. 48.

The status of these kinship categories thus seems to have been vague and uncertain.

When there was a biological family relationship, there was no doubt that relationships up to and including the second degree (*cousin*) were forbidden, even though this prohibition was not mentioned in the Bible. Because consanguinity and affinity relationships, according to the rhetoric of the time, should be equated, all affinity relationships in the second degree should also be forbidden; but in this case there was great disagreement and uncertainty, at least when the kinship tie in question was collateral. In March 1727, the incest prohibition between a man and his *wife's cousin* was rescinded by the Crown on the grounds that such applications for dispensation were very common and that they were usually not rejected.[47] Because the kinship between a man and his *wife's brother's widow* was equally close, the royal ordinance should have applied to this relationship category as well.[48]

However, opinions as to whether these relationships should in fact be allowed were divided among the authorities in the country. As late as 1700, both the hundred court and the court of appeal had sentenced a man and his *wife's brother's widow* to death for having committed single adultery. The death sentence was reversed by the Crown, which declared that the family relationship of the couple could not form the basis for the death penalty, but it is noteworthy that both the hundred court and the court of appeal were prepared to sentence the couple to death.[49] In 1720, the status of this relationship was debated within the clerical estate in a parliament where it was stipulated after a general discussion that marriages between a man and his *wife's brother's widow* should not be permitted.[50] The leaseholder Jöns Andersson, who applied for marriage three years after the prohibition had been rescinded, also encountered fierce resistance from the Linköping Cathedral Chapter before his application was forwarded to and approved by the Crown. In general,

47 K.F. 1727, 3 March.

48 Before the change to the law, persons with similar relationships were denied permission to marry, but after the change to the law these were approved. SD, AI:30, 1713, 18 June, no. 3, p. 370; SD, AI:31, 1719, 11 November, no. 7, p. 229; SD, AI:33, 1727, 11 December, no. 2, p. 312; SD, AI:34, 1732, 27 October, no. 9, p. 488; SD, AI:34, 1733, 28 February, no. 1, p. 524.

49 K.B. 1700, 28 March.

50 *Pr. 1719*, vol. 1, p. 110.

priests and lawyers thus seem to have been unfavourably disposed towards marriages in the second affinity degree.

But in two other cases where the family relationships of applicants were similar, the Skara Cathedral Chapter chose to approve the application without obtaining the Crown's official permission. The first case had to do with a man and his deceased *wife's former husband's sister*. According to the records, this couple were not 'so closely related by marriage that the match' could be prevented.[51] The second case had to do with a man who wanted to marry his deceased *wife's half-brother's concubine*. The approval was justified simply by noting that the application was considered 'reasonable'.[52]

According to the ideas of the time, a family relationship was formed as a consequence of the sexual act, and no differentiation was made as to whether the people were full or half relatives. Indeed, this was specifically emphasised in other cases, as we have seen. It follows that both of these relationships should have been defined as incestuous in the second collateral affinity degree, just like the relationship to a *wife's brother's widow*. But the cathedral chapter denied permission to marry a *wife's brother's widow* while permitting a marriage between a man and his *wife's half-brother's concubine* and his *wife's former husband's sister*, even though all these cases were examples of the same degree of kinship. How should one understand this lack of logic and consistency on the part of the members of the cathedral chapter?

Because the various relationships were not expressly defined in exact degrees, it is possible that the deviations were not entirely deliberate. Common relationship categories, such as *wife's niece* or *wife's brother's widow*, were well known and assessed in accordance with previous procedures; but the relationship between, for instance, a man and his *wife's former husband's widow* was less common and perhaps not directly associated with the earlier relationship. In addition, it is likely that the decision-makers in these situations subconsciously allowed themselves to be affected by their own subjective values regarding the definition of a family relationship.

There are many indications that the basic values of the educated elite differed from the formal rules in two particulars. First, some lawyers opposed the practice of completely equating full relatives with half-relatives.[53] Second, several lawyers are on record as thinking

51 SD, AI:31, 1719, 8 July, no. 7, p. 219.
52 SD, AI:30, 1711, 30 August, no. 17, p. 164.
53 Thunander 1993, pp. 105, 110–13.

that crimes of incest *in combination* with adultery should be rated as worse than crimes of incest alone. A proposal for legislation from 1696 suggested that the death penalty in the first collateral affinity degree should be replaced by a fine for a *deceased wife's sister* and *two sisters*. In these cases neither of the parties was married and the offence was therefore less serious, according to a majority of the trusted lawyers who had been given the task of drawing up the proposal for legislation.[54] However, this proposed legislation never became legally valid, and it was firmly rejected in a royal regulation from 1699. Instead, this regulation emphasised that *anyone* who committed adultery *or* fornication in the first affinity degree should be sentenced to death.[55] The material thus shows that there was an informal norm among the educated elite that was in opposition to the formal rules, both when it came to full relatives versus half-relatives and when the crime of incest was combined with adultery. It is likely that the assessments made by the members of the cathedral chapter were affected by these informal values when the applications dealt with relatively infrequent relationship categories, such as, for instance, *wife's half-brother's concubine*, since the verdicts diverged from the routines.

On other occasions, the members of the cathedral chapter consciously used their positions to affect the outcome of individual cases in direct opposition to the boundaries drawn up in law. They did this by trying to prevent marriages between people whose family relationship did *not* pose a legal obstacle. Nils Jönsson wanted to marry his deceased *aunt's husband's widow*, Elin Persdotter, and turned to his local vicar, who forwarded his request to the cathedral chapter. The cathedral chapter called on the vicar to dissuade the couple from their plans, although the family relationship did not pose any formal obstacle to marriage. Two months later, Nils appeared before the members of the cathedral chapter in order to repeat his request in person, but he was denied permission to go through with the marriage on this occasion as well. An additional week later, Nils appeared before the same consistory again, this time together with his intended bride Elin; together, they pleaded

54 *Förarbeten till Sveriges Rikes Lag 1686–1736*, IV, p. 442. See also the discussion between the associate judges of the Göta Court of Appeal regarding a crime of incest between a man and his *deceased wife's unmarried half-sister*. GHA, AII:10, 1715, 21 October, pp. 714–21.

55 K.F. 1699, 10 October. This ordinance would often be referred to in subsequent judicial decisions.

for formal permission to marry. Again, the cathedral chapter attempted to dissuade them from their intended marriage, partly because of the difference in age between them (not specified), partly because of their family relationship. But Nils and Elin did not back down; and as their family relationship was not prohibited 'either in the word of God or in secular law', the cathedral chapter finally reluctantly agreed to the marriage.[56]

According to the cathedral chapter's own words, there was thus no formal prohibition against Nils and Elin's marriage. In spite of this, the couple had to put up quite a fight in order to have their wish granted, as their relationship was evidently considered inappropriate by the priesthood. Two other couples in the same relationship category had their marriage plans questioned in a similar manner by the cathedral chapter.[57] Another man was dissuaded from marrying his *stepmother's aunt*, although this family relationship was not formally forbidden either. The cathedral chapter commented that 'such a marriage neither can nor should be allowed'. Five years later a new request was submitted, probably from the same couple, but the cathedral chapter did not grant the request this time either. It was noted that the relationship was not prohibited in the law of God, but 'those who are so closely related, and want to marry, should be dissuaded from it'.[58] In this case, the aversion of the orthodox Church against marriages between related individuals was of such magnitude that it reached beyond both the words in the Bible and the letter of the law.

---

56 SD, AI:34, 1733, 7 November, no. 3, p. 649; SD, AI:34, 1734, 16 January, no. 6, p. 668; SD, AI:34, 1734, 23 January, no. 3, p. 672. On the first occasion, Nils and Elin are not mentioned by name, but the request concerns the same kinship degree and comes from the same parish, which makes it likely that the three cases concern the same couple. See also SD, AI:34, 1734, 23 January, no. 2, p. 672; SD, AI:34, 1734, no. 6, p. 680. The cathedral chapter here reluctantly permitted the marriage between a man and his *daughter-in-law's sister*, who in spite of active dissuasion 'did not want to refrain from their intended marriage'.

57 SD, AI:32, 1725, 24 February, no. 29; SD, AI:34, 1733, 7 November, no. 3.

58 SD, AI:32, 1724, 8 July, no. 25; SD, AI:33, 1729, 16 April, no. 14. This and the previous case concerned the same family relationship. The names of the applicants are only mentioned on one occasion, but the two applications came from the same parish and the same priest. In the latter application the cathedral chapter is requested to reconsider its previous decision, which is why the two cases probably concern the same couple.

In 1703, a royal ordinance was published that forbade marriages between individuals related in direct linear affinity degrees (*stepfather's widow*, *stepmother's stepmother*).[59] The express aim of the prohibitions was to protect and promote respect between the generations. It is likely that the cathedral chapter opposed the above-mentioned relationships for similar reasons, and that they used their authority to influence applicants. But since the authorities did not have support for their opinion in the formal legislation, they had to give in when the applicants stood their ground.

If a relationship fell within the boundaries of the prohibitions, however, it did not matter how insistent and stubborn the applicants were. Anders Nilsson from Vilske Hundred in the county of Halland actively questioned the formulation of the prohibitions when he wanted to marry his deceased *wife's stepdaughter*. The local vicar refused to marry them. Anders then turned to the consistory in Gothenburg, but they too denied him permission to marry, whereupon Anders wrote directly to the king. With the 'utmost humility', he begged to be allowed to marry Ingeborg, because according to his assessment their family relationship could not be considered either a 'consanguinity or an affinity relationship'. Nor did he believe filial deference to be a factor to consider in their case. The request was denied. A few months later Anders repeated his request, but his application was not approved this time either.[60]

Anders's actions constituted an active challenge to the formulation of the prohibitions, and the assessment of the authorities raises some questions. Anders was denied marriage to his *wife's stepdaughter*, while other people were permitted to marry their *sibling's stepdaughter* (p. 58). The family relationship in the first case should be considered somewhat more distant, because here there were *two* marriages between the parties while in the second case there was only one. Nevertheless, it was the second relationship that was approved.

During this period, the common denominator for the relationships of which the Skara Cathedral Chapter did not approve is not completely clear from the dispensation material; but on the basis of knowledge regarding the reasoning of more recent times and the legal practice of the same period, my guess is that the respective position in the family of the people concerned played a decisive role for the assessment in each of the examples mentioned. For

59 K.R. 1703, 2 December.

60 JR, BoA, K, 1730, 3 June, Anders Nilsson, Ingeborg Olsdotter.

instance, the position in the family can explain why Anders was denied the marriage he desired. He wanted to marry his wife's stepdaughter. The stepdaughter's position was thus within the same household as himself, in the same family. In cases where a man wanted to marry his sister's or brother's stepdaughter, the woman came from a *different* household, *another* family. Historian David Herlihy has argued that the aim of the formulation of incest prohibitions was, among other things, to avoid marriages between individuals living within one and the same household, and that may explain the assessment of this case.[61] Whether the daughter actually lived in Anders's household was not investigated, though. The fact that Anders did not consider filial deference to be endangered can be interpreted as an indication that the couple were of the same age, but their respective ages were not explicitly stated. Individual circumstances concerning the type of accommodation or the relationship between the applicants' ages did not engender documented discussions or debates among the decision-makers, which indicates that these circumstances were not considered important for the outcome.

I will return later to the significance of the position in the family for the assessment of different incestuous relationships. Here, I will confine myself to noting that those prohibitions that were challenged usually involved the second consanguinity and affinity degrees (*cousin*, *wife's cousin*, *wife's brother's widow*) and the diagonal affinity degree (*wife's niece*). These relationships thus appear to have been accepted to a similar degree among the general public. On the part of the authorities, cousin relationships were treated routinely, and dispensations were handed out by rote on condition that the relationship in question was virtuous. If the couple had violated the norms of morality, the procedure was more difficult and more drawn-out; nevertheless, it frequently ended on a positive note.

Affinity relationships, collateral as well as diagonal ones, were dealt with in more ambiguous ways. *Wife's cousin*, *wife's brother's widow*, and *wife's niece* were defined as prohibited, while other relationships with the same degree of kinship were approved. Those whose task it was to defend and maintain the formal norms thus deviated from these norms in their assessments by approving some relationships that should have been included in the prohibitions (for instance, *sister's stepdaughter*, *wife's half-brother's concubine*).

61 Herlihy 1995, pp. 105f. The importance of family structure for the formulation of the incest prohibitions is also discussed in Mitterauer 1994, pp. 240f, and Jarzebowski 2014, p. 177.

At the same time, the cathedral chapter used its authority in order to prevent marriages between people whose family relationships did not pose a formal obstacle (*stepmother's aunt*). In 1727, the prohibition against marriages in the second collateral affinity degree (*wife's cousin, wife's brother's widow*) was abolished, which confirms that the assessment of these relationship categories changed at this time.

Additional uncertain definitions

As was clear from the previous section, the actions of the cathedral chapter indicate that there was general uncertainty as to whether certain relationship categories should be defined as legal or illegal. The same uncertainties are revealed by the kinds of cases that were submitted in the first place. Some applications were private initiatives from couples who wanted to marry, but it was more common for the communication to occur via the couple's local vicar. For this reason, it is especially interesting to note that the proportion of applications for non-prohibited relationships was as high as 40% (30 out of 76).[62] Not even theologically schooled vicars knew where to draw the line between permitted and prohibited family relationships. They had to consult a higher instance. Some relationships also caused consternation among the members of the cathedral chapter and had to be sent on to the king for clarification.[63]

The uncertainty regarding the definition of the status of relationships which is reflected in the applications for dispensation recurs in the judgement-book material. Here, two boundaries had to be defined: the boundary between legal and illegal family relationships, and the boundary between relationships that had to be punished by death and relationships that could be atoned for by a fine. Strictly speaking, only criminal cases where the defendants risked capital punishment should be referred to the court of appeal from the lower courts. This notwithstanding, a little over 20% of the incest cases in the Göta Court of Appeal between 1694 and 1716 concerned cases where the family relationship was not so close that the defendants risked capital punishment if they were convicted. These cases should never have been sent to the court of appeal in the first place;

62 See Table 4 on p. 52. Relationships beyond the second consanguinity or affinity degree were not forbidden.

63 See, e.g., SD, A1:31, 1722, 31 January, no. 1, p. 339 (*parent's cousin*); SD, A1:34, 1730, 22 July, no. 21, p. 172 (*parent's cousin*).

they ought to have been dealt with by the hundred court, the cathedral chapter, or the Crown, depending on the relationship category concerned. The fact that these cases exist reveals that the hundred-court judges were unsure of how to apply the legislation. In fact, the most common question from a lower court to the court of appeal during the seventeenth century concerned the prohibited degrees.[64] In their turn, the courts of appeal were in some cases also forced to consult the king before making a decision.[65]

In an attempt to introduce order among the concepts, official letters were sent from the Crown to all cathedral chapters and courts of appeal on a number of occasions. These letters announced the outcomes of different applications, based on the relationship concerned in each case. Usually a brief justification for the decision was added, presumably to create an increased uniformity of assessment for similar requests.[66]

All this reflects considerable uncertainty and confusion regarding the drawing of boundaries between legal and illegal matrimonial unions, both among lawyers and theologians. Keeping this in mind, it is not strange that the peasantry also made mistakes from time to time. In 1715, shoemaker Bengt Mattsson began a sexual relationship, under promise of marriage, with the widow Sissa Matsdotter. But when Sissa became pregnant and Bengt went to the clergyman to ask for the banns to be published, it transpired that their relationship was prohibited. The reason was that Bengt had made Sissa's stepdaughter, Hanna, pregnant on an earlier occasion. Bengt and Sissa themselves claimed that they had not realised that his previous relationship to Hanna posed an obstacle to their marriage plans, and a request for a dispensation for their marriage was sent to the Crown. The request was rejected, however, and the couple were sentenced to flogging and birching, respectively, for their crime.[67]

---

64 Thunander 1993, pp. 264f. Examples of relationships where the lower courts argued that there was no established law on which to base their decisions: *stepson's widow*, *half-sister's daughter*, GHA, BIIA:16, 1706, no. 74; GHA, BIIA:8, 1698, no. 71.

65 Thunander 1993, p. 102.

66 For instance K.B. 1738, 15 February; K.B. 1738, 23 November; K.B. 1741, 10 June; K.B. 1744, 12 June; K.B. 1744, 12 December; K.B. 1749, 22 February; K.B. 1752, 23 December; K.B. 1754, 7 November; K.B. 1761, 2 April; K.B. 1761, 16 April; K.B. 1761, 21 May; K.B. 1767, 2 June; K.B. 1768, 19 June; K.B. 1768, 22 June; K.B. 1769, 22 November; K.B. 1774, 8 August.

67 GHA, BIIA:25, 1716, no. 242; GHA AII:10, 1715, 14 December, pp. 814f.

Farmer Per Nilsson also found out about the prohibition only when he went to the clergyman to have the banns published for himself and his *daughter-in-law's niece*, who was now pregnant.[68] Similarly, Anders Andersson began a sexual relationship with his *uncle's concubine*, Elin Andersdotter. When she became pregnant he wanted to marry her, because 'in his simplicity, he could imagine nothing other than that he for this would have due leave and free permission'.[69] Another man first had sex with a woman, for which he was made to pay both 'spiritually and secularly'. Next, he made the same woman's niece (*concubine's niece*) pregnant and wanted to marry her. The niece was well aware of his previous relationship, but neither of them could have imagined that the earlier fornication could pose an obstacle to their plans.[70] The innkeeper and widow Brita Persdotter began a relationship with her deceased husband's half-brother's son (*half-uncle's widow*). Both claimed that they had acted in the 'hope and intention' of 'forming a marriage union' with each other. They had not understood that their family relationship was an obstacle to their desires.[71] Bengta Ingierdsdotter was even promised by her vicar that she could marry her deceased husband's half-sister's son (*half-aunt's husband's widow*). When a child was on its way and the couple wanted a formal blessing, they were nevertheless stopped outside the church door and were prosecuted in the local court instead.[72] Even so, it is unclear whether all these relationships were in fact included in the prohibitions because they were dealt with in dissimilar ways by the authorities.[73]

In all the cases outlined above, the couples had already begun a sexual relationship with the intention of marrying in due course, but instead ended up before a court accused of incest. The couples claimed that they had been completely unaware of the prohibitions,

---

68 GHA, BIIA:4, 1695, no. 129.

69 GHA, BIIA:12, 1702, no. 95.

70 GHA, BIIA:8, 1698, no. 155.

71 GHA, BIIA:16, 1706, no. 132.

72 GHA, BIIA:18, 1708, no. 85. Other relationships where people claimed to be ignorant about there being any prohibition at all against marriage were, for instance, *uncle's widow*, *stepson's concubine*, and *stepfather's widow*. In all these cases the defendants were sentenced to a fine or to corporal punishment.

73 It is true that the Skara Cathedral Chapter disliked the idea of a marriage between a man and his *aunt's husband's widow*, but nevertheless allowed such marriages because the family relationship was not defined as prohibited. See pp. 61f.

5 Flogging in the town square was a public event.

and through their actions (the sexual act in combination with the intention to legalise the relationship by marrying after the fact) they challenged the boundaries drawn by the authorities between legitimate and illegitimate relationships. The family relationships between these people (affinity relationships in the diagonal or second degree) were the same as the relationships between couples that usually applied for dispensation for marriage. These relationship categories were thus not considered offensive or inappropriate by the general public.

A similar uncertainty regarding the boundaries of the prohibitions appears to have been more or less general in Europe.[74] The confusion surrounding the drawing of boundaries was thus widespread around the turn of the century in 1700 and may be seen as a consequence of the imprecise formulations in the Bible. The lack of clarity gave rise to countless reinterpretations and discussions among learned men. Because the authorities could not agree on a common solid foundation on the basis of which the boundaries of incest prohibitions should be drawn, they could not convey a uniform norm to the

74 A lack of certainty regarding the boundaries of the prohibitions is described with respect to, e.g., Norway, Holland, Austria, and England in Terjesen 1994, pp. 140, 164; Egmond 2001, p. 25; Hehenberger 2003, pp. 197–201; Morris 1992, p. 165.

lower orders either. The uncertainty clearly shows that there were no firm rules for how certain relationship categories should be assessed, which provided scope for the assessments being influenced by other social values. In Sweden, virtue consequently became decisive for certain dispensation cases.

Criminal cases

The punishments

In spite of the repeated negotiations and discussions among lawyers and theologians regarding the formulation of incest prohibitions during the second half of the seventeenth century, no concrete changes to the law had been made in Sweden at the turn of the century in 1700. The incest prohibitions were defined and punished according to the appendix of 1608 as the primary policy document with the addition of certain letters patent, resolutions, and ordinances.[75] Together, these documents created formal legal standards that equated consanguinity with affinity relationships. See Table 5.

Table 5 thus shows the official legal standards that lawyers had to work with. These were also the penalties to which the members of the courts of appeal actively referred when they dealt with various incest cases. The applicable punishment for the relationship categories *niece*, *wife's niece* and *wife's sister* – the assessment of which, judging by the varying nature of the legal proposals, had been a cause of disagreement among lawyers – was fixed in the practical work of the courts, at least insofar as it was one and the same punishment that was referred to in the courtroom. How the law was applied in practice will be discussed later.

The legal position of women and men charged with crimes of incest was comparatively equal.[76] In cases where the death penalty was imposed, both women and men were executed by beheading and buried outside consecrated grounds. A regular funeral with all the appurtenant rituals – the ringing of church bells, the delivery of a sermon, handfuls of earth dropped on the coffin – was a token

75 Letters patent, ordinances, and statutes were often given legal status. Thunander 1995, p. 22. See, e.g., K.B. 1611, 1 October; K.B. 1678, 1 March; K.F. 1680, 3 December.

76 However, there were cases where the woman seems to have been exposed to coercion or pressure by the man, which in our eyes would give her the status of victim rather than criminal. These cases will be discussed later.

Table 5. Incest prohibitions and punishments in Sweden c. 1700

Relationship	**Closeness**	**Relationship, a man and (his) ...**	**Punishment**
Consanguinity	First lineal degree	mother, daughter	death
	Second lineal degree	grandmother, granddaughter	death
	First collateral degree	sister, half-sister	death
	Diagonally	aunt, niece	death
	Second collateral degree	cousin	fine
Affinity	First lineal degree	mother-in-law, daughter-in-law, stepmother, stepdaughter	death
	Second lineal degree	wife's grandmother, wife's granddaughter	death
	First collateral degree	wife's sister, brother's wife, two sisters	death
	Diagonally	uncle's wife, wife's niece	death
	Second degree	wife's stepdaughter, wife's brother's widow	fine

of respect both for the dead person and for his or her family. Denying the convicted criminal this final mark of respect was thus an active part of the punishment, and that part might be differentiated further still. Some people were buried quietly in a distant corner of the churchyard, others outside the consecrated grounds and still others, in the worst-case scenario, at the place of execution by the provost or the knacker. The more serious the crime, the further away from the churchyard would a person be buried.[77] In cases where the crime was perceived to be particularly reprehensible, a woman's body would be burned and a man's body broken on the wheel after the execution. Being broken on the wheel (*stegling*) meant that the body was dismembered and displayed in public – for the purpose of

77 Liliequist 1988, pp. 153f.

6 The women wore 'whipping bodices' that left their backs bare when they were birched.

degrading the offender's body and providing a deterrent for the community.[78]

In the rare cases where the accused were reprieved from the death penalty, they were sentenced to corporal punishment.[79] A woman was then birched outside the door of the local courthouse while a man was sentenced to either flogging or running the gauntlet. Corporal punishments were also rated according to how serious the crime in question was perceived to be. A woman was sentenced to a maximum of thirty pairs of birch rods and the man to forty pairs of switches or nine gauntlets.[80]

With respect to crimes in the more distant degrees, men and women were fined the same amount, i.e., eighty thalers in silver. In addition to this, a fine for adultery or fornication was added which, in the case of a married individual, would double the sum of the fine.[81] These sums were very high – the yearly salary for a farmhand was around ten thalers in silver.[82] If the convicted person could not

78 See, e.g., GHA, BIIA:20, 1710, no. 107; GHA, BIIA:15, 1705, no. 46. On the punishment of breaking on the wheel, see Thunander 1993, pp. 74f. It should be noted that breaking on the wheel in this Swedish sense is a punishment inflicted after death, not, as in other countries including Britain, before.

79 The man and the woman were pardoned simultaneously on only six out of sixty-three occasions.

80 The reason why rods were exchanged after two or three blows is that their strength was gradually reduced as the birching went on. The woman's punishment could be made harsher by sentencing her to, e.g., 'birching twice outside the door of the local courthouse with 14 days in between' or to be 'birched as much as she can take' or a 'harsh birching', i.e., the executioner held the birch rod. If a man was to be punished extra severely, he was sentenced to run six to nine gauntlets. Running the gauntlet was originally a military punishment. The punishment meant that the convicted person was forced to run between double rows of men (often fifty in number), each of them armed with a cane that was used to strike the convicted person as he passed between them. Thunander 1993, pp. 81–3.

81 A married party was sentenced to eighty thalers in silver while the fine for an unmarried party would be half as much. In total, 160 thalers in silver for him and 120 for her was common. *Åtgärder för lagförbättring 1633–1665*, p. 226. See, e.g., GHA, BIIA:24, 1714, no. 79.

82 The yearly salary of a farmhand is an estimation based on the following information: in 1665, a year's salary for a farmhand was five thalers. Thunander 1993, p. 79. In the 1720s, the yearly salary for farmhands was raised to twelve to fifteen thalers in silver. *Bd, 1723,* II, pp. 254f.

afford to pay, he or she was forced to undergo corporal punishment in the form of birching, running the gauntlet, or flogging.[83] Furthermore, everyone had to undergo an ecclesiastical punishment in addition to the secular one. They were sentenced to so-called public penance and absolution (*uppenbar kyrkoplikt och avlösning*). The public penance was a punishment involving public shaming where the criminal had to sit on a special stool in church during the sermon. After having confessed his or her crime before the entire congregation, the person in question was given absolution and could then be reintegrated into the Christian community. Originally the aim of public penance was forgiveness and reintegration after the commission of a crime, but it increasingly came to function as a distinct public-shaming punishment.[84] During the nineteenth century, public penance was replaced by more private variants where the guilty person was allowed to confess in the vestry before the church council or privately before the local clergyman.[85]

The court: a flexible practice

In the sixteenth century, the Swedish Reformer Olaus Petri drew up ethical guidelines for the judgeship. During the ensuing centuries, Swedish lawyers employed these *judge's rules* as guiding principles in parallel with the statute book. According to the judge's rules, no law could replace the judge's ability to apply discernment and personal good judgement. There were always individual cases that did not fit the legal text, and it was the task of the judge to decide whether the law was reasonable in each individual case. In parallel with the official regulatory framework, judges were thus also expected to make assessments of individual cases. They were to take account of 'old customs', or what they believed to be 'right and proper'. To a certain extent, judges were thus allowed to rule according to their own conscience. The right to deviate from the letter of the law was primarily reserved for the court of appeal – not the hundred court – and it came with certain limitations. Among other things, a judge was not permitted to reprieve a defendant from the death penalty without the king's approval when the guilt of the defendant was

83 See, e.g., GHA, BIIA:20, 1710, no. 18.
84 Lindstedt Cronberg 1997, p. 59.
85 The so-called 'shame stool', also referred to as 'the adulterer's stool' or 'the thief's stool', was abolished in 1855. Inger 2011, p. 298.

considered proven, although the system no doubt provided scope for a certain arbitrariness.[86]

Previous research has shown that several of the brutal capital punishments handed out on the hundred-court level for, among other things, sexual crimes and theft were routinely reduced to corporal punishment or fines by the court of appeal. In such cases, the legislation and the practical application were far apart. In addition, Swedish research has shown that the courts of appeal often used their ability to affect the outcome of the case in a direction that favoured the defendants; this contributed to a general humanisation of the application of punishments. However, the exception to this more lenient practice were crimes that were considered to have been committed against God's law, including crimes of incest.[87]

This conclusion is confirmed by my study with one exception. An incestuous relationship in the diagonal affinity degree (*wife's niece*, *uncle's widow*) should in theory lead to capital punishment; but in practice earlier precedents were invoked, whereupon the defendant in question had his or her sentence reduced to corporal punishment as a matter of course, unless there were particularly aggravating circumstances.[88] In these cases a more lenient practice was thus routinely applied, similar to that of the treatment of more common sexual crimes. In all other incest cases where the legislation prescribed the death penalty, the judgement was upheld in 70–75% of the cases, which far exceeds other categories of crimes.[89] Crimes

86 Thunander 1993, pp. 66f, 185, 194–97; Lindberg 1992, pp. 352–6. The possibility for flexible judgements has been shown to exist in other Protestant areas as well. See examples from German-speaking areas in Hull 1996, pp. 55f.

87 Thunander 1993, p. 179.

88 Out of the seventeen cases that led to a conviction (thirty-three defendants), one person was sentenced to death because the crime was aggravated by infanticide. The others were sentenced to fines or corporal punishment.

89 Between 1681 and 1699 the Göta Court of Appeal upheld approximately 15% of the capital punishments for all crimes of theft and all sexual crimes. Thunander 1993, pp. 109, 117. If one disregards affinity relationships in the diagonal degree, where all punishments were routinely reduced to fines, ninety-five prosecuted individuals risked the death penalty for crimes of incest, out of which sixty-five (twenty-five men and thirty-six women) were actually sentenced to death, which corresponds to a little under 70%. In addition, the men absconded on twenty-two occasions when faced with the threat of the death penalty and could thus not be tried for their crimes. Supposing that these twenty-two people would also have been sentenced to death, the proportion of death sentences ends up at around 75%. See Appendix Table 6.

of incest in close family relationships were thus equated with capital offences such as treason, murder, and bestiality, rather than with adultery or fornication, which negatively affected the chances of having the sentence reduced.

Sweden stood out with regard to severity in comparison to other Protestant countries. In German-speaking areas, certain consanguinity relationships were punished by death, while people who had violated an affinity prohibition were only sentenced to corporal punishment or banishment. In Holland, defendants were rarely sentenced to death at all unless the crime of incest was aggravated by other crimes, such as infanticide or rape.[90] In Sweden's neighbouring countries, Denmark and Norway, only vertical consanguinity and affinity relationships were punished by death; but according to Jónsson's research this was a more lenient practice that had been introduced during the late seventeenth century. Danish historian Tyge Krogh also provides examples of the somewhat more lenient case law in Denmark around the turn of the century in 1700. However, before 1683, harsher punishments for crimes of incest seem to have been applied in Norway, Denmark, and Iceland. In other words, all the Nordic countries practised a very severe sentencing policy with respect to incest during most of the seventeenth century. Towards the end of that century, the legal situation in Denmark and Norway, and somewhat later also in Iceland, was mitigated, whereas Swedish courts continued to sentence incest criminals in accordance with the strict wording of the Bible. Krogh points out that theology lost authority in Denmark in comparison to other branches of scholarship after the introduction of royal absolutism in 1660, which might explain the more lenient practice established in that kingdom. Henceforth, the vague punishments in the Bible were interpreted less strictly by Danish lawyers and theologians; consequently, incest criminals were more often sentenced to hard labour or banishment rather than death.[91]

In spite of Swedish courts standing out with respect to strictness, there was a tendency on the part of the courts to acquit rather than convict in uncertain cases according to the motto *the more severe*

---

90 Rublack 1999, p. 235; Hull 1996, p. 99; Hehenberger 2003, p. 192; Egmond 2001, p. 25.

91 Hard labour could in practice also mean a death sentence. Krogh 2000, pp. 111, 161f. Jónsson 1998, pp. 4, 7f. Terjesen, too, describes the strict case law of Norwegian courts during this period (1602–61). Terjesen 1994, p. 107.

7 The Göta Court of Appeal was established in 1634 in Jönköping. Its jurisdiction included the southern parts of the Swedish mainland (Götaland and Värmland and, after 1658, also Skåne, Blekinge, and Halland).

the crime, the more unambiguous the evidence must be.[92] The courts of appeal actively looked for mitigating circumstances that could justify a milder sentence, especially when there was a risk of capital punishment. If there was incontrovertible evidence of a crime that should lead to death, the court could not unilaterally reduce the

92 See similar formulations in, e.g., GHA, BIIA:8, 1698, no. 180; GHA, BIIA:12, 1702, no. 132.

sentence. They had to refer the case to the king or the Council of the State (*riksrådet*). In such official letters, the court of appeal summarised what they felt to be mitigating circumstances; but here they did not act entirely consistently. Mitigating circumstances that were emphasised in one case might be completely ignored in another, depending on which outcome the members of the court of appeal believed to be reasonable. The circumstances were thus actively put to use in order to strengthen the members' own assessment of the case.[93] Regardless of whether the petition for mercy from the court of appeal actually led to a reprieve, the material thus reveals the assessment made by the associate judges in individual cases.

The statistics of the crime

The relationship categories

During the seventeenth century, the number of sexual crimes tried in Swedish courts increased significantly. In research, this change is usually explained by assertions to the effect that legal control was stricter – not that there was an actual increase in the number of illicit sexual relations.[94] But how great a proportion of these crimes were incest cases?

Historians Jan Sundin and Rudolf Thunander have studied Swedish crime statistics on the hundred-court level and the court-of-appeal level, respectively. According to their calculations, crimes of incest made up approximately 30% of the sexual crimes that reached the court of appeal from the second half of the seventeenth century.[95] In actual numbers, this corresponded to around six cases per year with respect to the Göta Court of Appeal. Crimes of incest were thus not

93 See, e.g., GHA, BIIA:14, 1704, no. 123, where *the support of the family* is specifically emphasised, and GHA, BIIA:14, 1704, no. 4, where it is pointed out that the sin had only been committed on *one occasion*. These cases can be compared to another case where both of these circumstances were mentioned on the hundred-court level but completely ignored when the case was assessed in the court of appeal. Vista Hundred, Ala:12, 1694, 18 May; GHA, BIIA:3, 1694, no. 49.

94 For instance, Thunander 1993, p. 93.

95 Thunander's numbers are based on two samples, 1655–64 and 1681–99. Thunander 1993, pp. 104, 109. Sundin's investigation covers the entire eighteenth century, where the crime of incest remains at a comparatively constant level in comparison to other sexual crimes. Sundin 1992, p. 47, Table 3.

particularly common, but even so they occurred more frequently than, for instance, murder.[96] Between 1694 and 1716, just over 130 incest cases were tried at the Göta Court of Appeal. Table 6 shows the relationship categories involved in these criminal cases.

Out of all these incest cases, a clear majority, around 85%, were affinity relationships or sexual relationships among non-biological relatives.[97] In 107 cases, around 80%, the case ended in a conviction.[98] Three relationship categories were significantly more common than others. From the most common to the least, these cases concerned a man who had had sexual relations with his *wife's sister* (twenty-five cases), his *wife's niece* (twenty-two cases), and his *stepdaughter* (twenty-one cases). In fourth place came a man who had had sexual contact with *two sisters* (eleven cases).

Table 6. Incest cases from GHA, 1694–1716, number of cases and relationships

Family relationship	Closeness	Relationship, a man and (his) ...	Number of cases
Consanguinity	First, second lineal degree	daughter, granddaughter	2
	First collateral degree	sister	4
	Diagonally (1+2)	aunt	1
		niece	6
	Second collateral degree	cousin	4
	Diagonally (2+3)	cousin's daughter	1
	Sum total, consanguinity		**18**

96 According to Sundin's statistics, crimes of incest were around 30%, 50%, and 100% more common than murder at the beginning, middle, and end of the eighteenth century, respectively. Sundin 1992, p. 47, Table 3.

97 The number of criminal cases does not correspond to the number of relationships because the same relationship was sometimes tried in court on more than one occasion. The deviation as a percentage is marginal, though.

98 By this I mean a conviction for the crime of incest. In some cases, the defendant was acquitted of the crime of incest but sentenced for defamation or fornication with someone else.

Table 6. Incest cases from GHA, 1694–1716, number of cases and relationships (Continued)

Family relationship	Closeness	Relationship, a man and (his) ...	Number of cases
Affinity	First/second lineal degree	mother-in-law	1
		daughter-in-law	2
		stepmother	2
		stepdaughter/step-granddaughter	21
		a mother and her daughter/stepdaughter	2
		father and son with the same woman	3
	First collateral degree	wife's sister	25
		brother's wife/widow	4
		two sisters	11
		brother with the same woman	3
	Diagonally	wife's aunt	1
		wife's niece	22
		uncle's widow	6
		a woman and her niece	1
	≥ Second degree	wife's cousin	1
		two cousins	1
		stepson's/stepfather's widow	3
		wife's father's cousin	1
		mother-in-law's sister	1
		wife's brother's widow/concubine	2
		brother's daughter-in-law	1
		daughter-in-law's cousin	1
	Sum total, affinity		**115**

Source: GHA, series BIIA. The material for 1715 is missing. Two cases occur twice because the same case includes two different relationships.

The death penalty comprised all relationship categories in the first collateral or lineal degree and in the diagonal degree, regardless of whether the family relationship was consanguineal or affinal; but, as was pointed out above, in practice the sentences of couples in the diagonal affinity degree (*wife's niece*, *uncle's widow*) were routinely reduced.[99] Even so, the risk of being sentenced to death for those accused of crimes of incest in other relationship categories was quite apparent, since the sentence was upheld in around 70% of the cases. On the basis of a calculation of percentages, it is clear that there was a somewhat greater chance for women to escape capital punishment than for men.[100]

Accusation and confession

In the vast majority of cases – in particular when the family relationship was comparatively distant – the crime of incest was revealed only when a woman became pregnant. This pattern recurs in all criminal cases regarding extramarital sexuality during the same period, but it is especially apparent with respect to crimes of incest in the first lineal and collateral affinity degrees (e.g., *stepdaughter*, *daughter-in-law*, *mother and daughter*, *wife's sister*).[101]

Several of the women who were summoned to the local court because of a revealing pregnancy initially blamed the paternity on a man who was not in fact the father – often a man who was no longer in the neighbourhood and therefore could not be summoned and questioned by the court. Catharina Olufsdotter and Bärta Andersdotter both identified boatswains as the fathers of their children.[102] The widow Karin Jönsdotter claimed to have been 'bedded' by an army private, while Margaretha Hansdotter said that the father of her child was 'a man travelling on the highway'.[103] Maria Nilsdotter claimed that she had been together with a 'strange man with a black coat, a cane, and his own hair'.[104] The interrogations

99 See footnote 88.

100 Of the convicted men, 76% (twenty-nine out of thirty-eight), and of the convicted women 63% (thirty-six out of fifty-seven) were sentenced to death. See Appendix Table 6.

101 See Table 10 on p. 169.

102 GHA, BIIA:23, 1713, no. 36; GHA, BIIA:3, 1694, no. 43.

103 GHA, BIIA:4, 1695, no. 103; GHA, BIIA:11, 1701, no. 118. See also Lister Hundred, AIb:1, 1703, 15 April.

104 GHA, BIIA:24, 1714, no. 272. See also GHA, BIIA:9, 1699, no. 119, where the woman initially identified a farmhand, then a soldier, and finally her stepfather.

were, however, extremely detailed. The woman was questioned about the man's name and appearance and whence he came, and then careful investigations were conducted in order to find him, even when he was said to be elsewhere. The woman's position was often made more difficult by rumours that pointed to one of her relatives as the father of the child. After exhaustive interrogations and investigations, most people eventually confessed to their crimes.[105]

According to the *Roman-canon law of evidence*, the legal principle that was applied, it was necessary to have either a confession from the accused *or* the testimony of two witnesses that confirmed the crime if a conviction was to be attained.[106] However, in practice almost all cases were settled by way of a confession. It was uncommon for a person to be convicted in spite of pleading not guilty, and this was even more unlikely if the defendant risked being sentenced to death. Sentencing a person to death without a confession and absolution would be the same as sending this person to eternal damnation. The more serious the offence, the stronger evidence was required, and an aggravated capital offence 'should be based on obvious reasons and evidence and a free and unenforced confession'.[107]

Consequently, accusations alone were not enough to convict a person, and besides, an initial confession could be recanted at a later stage. This led to prosecuted individuals being acquitted owing to a lack of evidence if they stuck to their denials.[108] In spite of this, most people confessed their crimes and endured their punishments. Confessions were also common in connection with other sexual crimes, and it has been pointed out that the possibility of reintegration into society may have been a reason for the confession.[109] But after the crime of incest, a prosecuted individual could rarely

105 See, however, GHA, BIIA:25, 1716, no. 122.

106 The evidence was rated in three steps: circumstantial evidence, half-proof *(semiplena probatio)*, and full proof (*plena probatio*). An eyewitness was counted as half-proof and not enough to convict a person of a crime. Without eyewitnesses only circumstantial evidence remained, and that could not lead to a conviction. The Roman-canon law of evidence was introduced in the seventeenth century but was only officially adopted in connection with the Civil Code of 1734. Sundin 1992, p. 62; Taussi Sjöberg 1996, pp. 21–3. Inger 2011, p. 408.

107 A similar phrase is repeated by the court of appeal in several uncertain cases. E.g., GHA, BIIA:8, 1698, no. 180.

108 See, e.g., GHA, BIIA:6, 1696, no. 162; GHA, BIIA:12, 1702, no. 132; GHA, BIIA:3, 1694, no. 43; GHA, BIIA:20, 1710, no. 109; GHA, BIIA:8, 1698, no. 180.

109 Lindstedt Cronberg 1997, pp. 131f, 142f.

hope to be forgiven and reintegrated into society. It is conceivable that the confession reflected a desire on the sinner's part to atone for the crime and thus save his or her soul and be a part of God's community in Heaven. Jonas Liliequist, who has studied the crime of bestiality in Sweden, argues that the motivation for those who themselves reported their crimes was often a guilty conscience. Such confessions often concerned an undiscovered sin that had been committed in an individual's youth and over time increasingly weighed on his conscience, leading finally to self-incrimination. In these cases, those who had committed bestiality wanted to atone for their sins by enduring a secular punishment. Few asked for mercy.[110]

In my material, such self-incrimination is rare.[111] The confessions that were made were often a long time in coming, judging from expressions according to which the person in question had 'eventually confessed' or 'finally confessed after several exhortations'.[112] If there was aggravating circumstantial evidence but no confession, the accused was repeatedly urged to 'confess the truth' by both the clergy and the judges. Interrogations were lengthy and detailed. The man and the woman were questioned separately, whereupon their stories were compared. Any discrepancies in their statements were questioned. Sometimes the prosecuted individuals were confronted with the lie that the other person had already confessed to the crime and that the accused person might just as well confess too.[113] Torture was not allowed, but occasionally the accused were put in 'harsh' (*svårt*) or 'hard' (*hårt*) prison, which could mean that they were flogged, that handcuffs were screwed too tight, or that they were hung up against cold stone walls for long periods of time.[114] Although most prosecutions began with the suspects violently denying the charges, they almost always ended with confessions.[115] It is impossible to determine for certain whether this was because of

110 Liliequist 1992, p. 106. Liliequist discusses capital punishment specifically as a ritual of atonement in Liliequist 1988.

111 Nevertheless, see GHA, BIIA:23, 1713, no. 135; GHA, BIIA:11, 1701, no. 93.

112 For instance, GHA, BIIA:6, 1696, no. 35; GHA, BIIA:11, 1701, no. 118; GHA, BIIA:13, 1703, no. 62; GHA, BIIA:23, 1713, no. 126; GHA, BIIA:25, 1716, no. 162.

113 For instance, GHA, AII:10, 1714, 30 October, pp. 437, 458–64; GHA, BIIA:24, 1714, no. 232; Lister Hundred, AIb:1, 1703, 15 April.

114 Inger 2011, p. 194; Liliequist 1988, p. 147. Harsh prison is, for instance, mentioned in GHA, BIIA:8, 1698, no. 180.

115 Around 80% (107 out of 132) of the cases ended in a conviction.

physical hardships or psychological pressures, but it is clear that the religiosity of the population made it easier to enforce the strict legislation.[116]

Once criminal cases ended up in the court of appeal, the issue of culpability had usually already been resolved. The prosecuted persons had 'voluntarily admitted their grievous sin', they 'repented their crime', and now they 'tearfully' pleaded for 'mercy from the most esteemed authority'. In other words, the confession was directly followed by a passionate appeal for mercy. It is likely that an element of interaction played a decisive role for the conduct of the accused in court. In several cases, those who were guilty of committing crimes of incest had lived in secret with their sin for a long time. They had gone to church on Sundays and listened to the admonitions of the clergyman without being manifestly tormented by pangs of conscience or feelings of guilt, but when they ended up in court everything changed. The interrogation confirmed the immoral aspect of the relationship, the official condemnation of the act became obvious, and it is possible that a prosecuted person's own experience of the crime changed in consequence.

Ingemar Olsson had had a sexual relationship with his *stepdaughter* for several years. For a long time he had lived with the knowledge of his sin without its being made public and without his being tormented by any apparent feelings of remorse. At the final confession in the local court, Olsson, 'after repeated and serious exhortations, tearfully confessed and begged God to have mercy upon him and people to support him'.[117] He had thus refused to acknowledge his guilt to himself and to God until the matter became public knowledge and his crime could be reflected in the reactions of the people around him. A similar reaction can be seen in several of the people who were prosecuted for crimes of incest. At trial they broke down and the tears came.

It stands to reason that one also has to consider the impending secular punishment, which was surely the cause of great fear for anyone who ran the risk of being beheaded. Ingemar's pleas were directed both to God and to his fellow human beings, which indicates

116 On the one hand, the stay in prison was probably a very unpleasant experience even when not made more difficult by handcuffs that were screwed too tight or other special measures. On the other hand, not even a stay in a 'harsh' prison seems to have been an effective means of exerting pressure on a person. Liliequist 1992, p. 71.

117 GHA, BIIA:23, 1713, no. 135.

that he feared both the secular and the spiritual punishment. Nevertheless, the many confessions indicate that the prosecuted individuals accepted the official evaluation of the nature of the crime. If they had had sincere objections to the sinfulness of their acts – if they themselves did not believe that they had violated God's commandments and that they now risked the salvation of their souls – they would have been able to deny their actions to the very end and would probably have been acquitted. The common plea for mercy reveals that even if the prosecuted individuals admitted the criminality of their acts, they did not feel that these acts were unforgivable. To the very end they hoped for mercy and forgiveness, which was rare but not completely impossible if there were strongly mitigating circumstances.

Mitigating and aggravating circumstances

With respect to relationship categories in the more distant family degrees, *ignorance* was, as we have seen, used as an excuse for a criminal act both by the peasantry and by the authorities. Ignorance was thus a legitimate argument for completely acquitting someone of criminal liability or for reducing a sentence. This ignorance could manifest itself in various ways. On the one hand, the person in question could be unaware of the prohibition in itself. On the other hand, a person could unknowingly commit incest because they did not know of their partner's previous sexual contacts – for instance, when a man had sexual relations with two sisters on different occasions without being married to either of them and without their being aware of each other's activities. In connection with similar 'triangle cases', where all the parties were unmarried, it was always made clear whether there had been prior knowledge of the other relationship. If the answer was no, the ignorant party was completely acquitted of the accusation.[118] *Feeblemindedness*, in the sense of mental deficiency, could also, as an obvious consequence, be invoked as a mitigating circumstance by the accused or by their relatives.[119] Closely related to ignorance as an excuse, *youthful folly* could also be used as a defence for committing a sin. This line of reasoning was based on the idea that a young person had not always reached a complete understanding of right and wrong and of the message

118 See, e.g., GHA, BIIA:12, 1702, no. 14 or GHA, BIIA:14, 1704, no. 29.
119 E.g., GHA, BIIA:15, 1705, no. 104.

of Christianity, and for that reason the people around them could overlook their behaviour.[120]

Another common strategy was to emphasise the fact that the ill deed had been an *isolated mistake* or that it had happened while *under the influence of alcohol.* This defence becomes logical if we consider the ideas surrounding self-discipline and self-control, qualities that were regarded as being among the human virtues. Indeed, self-control was felt to constitute the decisive difference between humans and animals.[121] It was sinful to give in to physical appetites, to gorge on food, and to live out one's carnal desires.[122] Losing one's self-control was on the whole considered a failure, but it could be forgiven if it only happened on an isolated occasion or if a person had been strongly provoked.[123] If, in addition, a person had been intoxicated on this occasion, he or she was not thought to have been in full possession of his or her senses, which diminished the issue of responsibility even further. This was expressed in forthright terms in one case. The couple in question allegedly committed the crime of incest when 'in their cups', when they 'during the distillation of spirituous liquor [...] had surfeited themselves to such a degree, that they then did not know what they did'.[124]

Similarly, a single crime could in exceptional cases be forgiven with the justification that the person in question had been overpowered by desire that suddenly flared up. Both men's and women's sexuality were basically seen as positive. Sexuality was a gift from God so that men and women could experience joy in and lust for each other.[125] But the sexual drive was acknowledged and accepted only within marriage.[126] Passion and lust outside of the marriage bed was seen as

120 Lindberg 1992, pp. 391f.

121 Jansson 2002, pp. 54f; Thomas 1984, p. 37.

122 Lindberg 1992, p. 405.

123 This line of reasoning can be compared with that concerning violent crimes. A fistfight occasioned by a sudden conflict or by a powerful provocation did not have to be dishonourable, even if a person happened to seriously injure his or her opponent, while a fight between two sworn enemies had serious consequences because it was assumed that there had been evil *intent* in such a case. Jansson 2006, pp. 156f.

124 GHA, BIIA:14, 1704, no. 4.

125 Lennartsson 2009, p. 363; Jarzebowski 2014, pp. 171, 174.

126 Sexual relations within marriage were not just a right but also a duty, and there was no scope for either party to deny the other party sexual congress. Incapacity in bed could even be grounds for a divorce. Marklund 2004, p. 168.

a negative force which had to be controlled and repressed in order not to lead an individual into ruin and misery.[127] Repeating a crime of incest after having had the chance to stop and think was thus a severely aggravating circumstance. Both the local court and the court of appeal took into account whether the evil deed had only been committed once or on several occasions, which shows how important they felt this piece of information to be.[128] Both men and women could thus gain the sympathy of the court by emphasising that sexual congress had only happened a single time.

In legal proceedings, the *conduct and reputation* of the accused were considered as well. It was noted whether the prosecuted individual had illegitimate children, or whether he or she had been convicted of sexual relations outside marriage on previous occasions. In this context, it was also an advantage if the prosecuted person had *explicit support from the people around him or her*. It was fairly common for a married party to beg for his or her spouse's life, but other relatives or 'the rest of the peasantry' might also make statements about the behaviour and reputation of the accused.

If a woman claimed that the sexual act had happened *against her will*, her sentence could be reduced to a fine or corporal punishment. The man was usually older than the woman, and according to the ideas of the time he was the active party who seduced her.[129] When the woman claimed to have been 'lured', 'enticed', 'forced', or 'persuaded' by the man, this was thus in line with ideas surrounding male and female behaviour. To be sure, popular culture and theological discourse contained a parallel notion about the woman as a dangerous enchantress who could attract men to her;[130] but

127 Nilsson [Hammar] 2012, pp. 117, 123.

128 For instance, GHA, BIIA:8, 1698, no. 130; GHA, BIIA:14, 1704, no. 52; Bankekind Hundred, AIa:7, 1705, 8 April, p. 503; GHA, BIIA:136, 1705, no. 136.

129 Baldwin 1994, pp. 231, 234. A similarly gendered division between male activity and female passivity can also be found in mediaeval Swedish legislation, where the man alone was held responsible for sexual transgressions. Around the turn of the century, in 1700, the situation had begun to even out, and the woman was fined alongside the man in a more equal manner. Lennartsson 2009, p. 361.

130 In Catholicism sexuality was early on branded as something impure and indecent. At the same time sexuality and reproduction were associated with the woman, and she was characterised as wanton by nature and less resistant to the influence of Satan. The image of the woman as a dangerous seductress proved to be persistent during subsequent centuries. Baldwin 1994, p. 233; Brundage 1987; Ambjörnsson 1978, pp. 131–7.

in a court context the woman's role was presumed to have been passive, and the question of whether she had acted provocatively or inappropriately was not asked:[131] it was the image of the initiating male that prevailed. In cases where the woman was the older party, there are no arguments concerning seduction or enticement of the younger male.[132]

Both the debate and the actual legislation show that it did not matter whether a person was married or unmarried when the crime was committed. If someone violated the forbidden degrees this was seen as a crime against God's law, irrespective of whether there was an aggrieved wife/husband or not. But when actual criminal cases were tried, it was repeatedly indicated whether the crime was 'aggravated' by adultery or not. Sometimes individual judges recommended a reduction of the death penalty with reference to the crime having been committed after the spouse had died.[133] The marital state of the prosecuted individuals was thus used as a rhetorical manoeuvre by judges in order to influence the assessment in either direction in individual cases, but in practice this does not appear to have had any effect on the outcome.[134]

It was not entirely uncommon for a suspect who risked the death penalty to abscond before the trial began. It was mostly men who absconded, but in a few cases women did as well.[135] The court

131 Other researchers have also noted that representatives of the judicial apparatus were not as interested in the woman's actions as in the man's in connection with sexual crimes. Towards the end of the eighteenth century, the court's interest in the woman's actions increased as her role was subjectified in judicial contexts. Lennartsson 2009, p. 369; Jansson 2002, pp. 301, 305; Telste 1997, p. 120; Rublack 1999, p. 252.

132 GHA, BIIA:12, 1702, no. 109; GHA, BIIA:20, 1710, no. 107; GHA, BIIA:8, 1698, no. 204.

133 GHA, BIIA:23, 1711, no. 8; GHA, BIIA:25, 1716, no. 62; GHA, BIIA:6, 1696, no. 35; GHA, BIIA:7, 1697, no. 89.

134 In my material there are three cases where a man initiated a sexual relationship with his sister-in-law after his wife had died. In all these cases all the prosecuted individuals were sentenced to death. (One of the men had absconded and could for this reason not be prosecuted.) GHA, BIIA:9, 1699, no. 11; GHA, BIIA:16, 1706, no. 63; GHA, BIIA:23, 1713, no. 36. At the same time, there are examples of similar relationships where the prosecuted individuals had their death sentence reduced even when the spouse was alive. GHA, BIIA:3, 1694, no. 1; GHA, BIIA:3, 1694, no. 11; GHA, BIIA:9, 1699, no. 130.

135 In incest cases where the prosecuted individuals risked the death penalty (with the exception of *wife's niece*), twenty-two out of sixty men absconded

viewed absconding as a severely aggravating circumstance. It was felt that the criminal was not only confessing his or her crime by absconding, but also rebelling against justice and indirectly defying the authority of the court. However, it was difficult to stay away for a long period of time. Wherever the fugitive went, he or she risked people reacting and becoming suspicious. One solution could be to join the army, where it may be supposed that fewer questions were asked. But several fugitives returned sooner or later, and then the court was waiting for them.[136]

Although theoretical penal consequences had been established for different crimes, there was nonetheless scope for interpretation and negotiation in the practical administration of justice. In the interactions among suspects, the local community, and the authorities, the actors involved continually used informal norms in order to strengthen their arguments. In trial proceedings, several circumstances were invoked, and accepted, as mitigating circumstances. These norms were thus reproduced on a general level by both the authorities and the peasantry: from below by stating these circumstances as excuses for having committed the crime, and from above by explicitly mentioning them as reasons for a potential reduction of the punishment. *Ignorance*, *intoxication*, *an isolated mistake*, and *coercion* are a few examples of such excuses. However, none of these circumstances was guaranteed to result in a reprieve or a reduction of the punishment. The members of the court always made an assessment regarding credibility in each individual case; then, depending on their assessment, they could emphasise or ignore mitigating as well as aggravating factors.

It might be added that the relevant religious notions functioned as an obvious and unchallenged basis for the prohibitions. It was formally stated that the act was forbidden according to God's law in Leviticus, and the prosecuted individuals were called upon to 'confess the truth' so that their souls would escape eternal damnation.[137]

---

before the trial. The cases where it is made clear that the woman had absconded are few in number. GHA, BIIA:3, 1694, no. 11; GHA, BIIA:6, 1696, no. 35; GHA, BIIA:11, 1701, no. 11; GHA, BIIA:25, 1716, no. 241.

136 See, e.g., GHA, BIIA:10, 1700, no. 48; GHA, BIIA:13, 1703, no. 97.

137 The allusion to God's law was made in the vast majority of cases. See, e.g., GHA, BIIA:13, 1703, no. 60; GHA, BIIA:23, 1713, no. 135; GHA, BIIA:4, 1695, no. 103; GHA, BIIA:17, 1707, no. 1; GHA, BIIA:15, 1705, no. 136. A confession from the accused was also a central issue in all cases. See, e.g., GHA, BIIA:24, 1714, no. 272; GHA, BIIA:14, 1704, no. 29; GHA, BIIA:8, 1698, no. 180; GHA, BIIA:14, 1704, no. 133.

Other than this, however, religious arguments did not play a prominent role in the judicial process. For example, discovered crimes never led to pronounced apprehensions that God's collective punishment was at hand, or that the purpose of the punishment was to prevent such divine retribution. The religious motive was thus there as an incontrovertible point of departure for the prosecution, but in other respects religion was not used as an active argument during the proceedings.

Violence and exploitation

The question of whether the sexual act had been voluntary or not was never asked. The crime of incest was primarily connected with the *act*, not the *intent*. The act signified a violation of God's law and could in theory only be atoned for by the sinner being punished by death. By participating in the act, a person was guilty of the crime – regardless of whether the involvement in the sexual act had been voluntary or coerced. However, Lindstedt Cronberg, who has studied incest between parents and children in Sweden, shows that even if the court assumed that both parties were guilty of the crime of incest, there was scope for reducing the punishment when a young girl had been forced by her father or stepfather to commit the act.[138] How common were these abusive relationships in reality? And how was the issue of guilt assessed in these cases, compared to cases that did not contain elements of violence, threat, or obvious pressure?

My definition of violent or coercive relationships is comparatively broad in this context. I include all cases where the woman was considerably younger or where she, according to her own statement or other testimony, had been seduced or coerced by the man. Cases where the woman is said to have been feebleminded, or where there are indications that she had been paid for sexual services with money or goods, have also been categorised as coercive relationships. This is of course a very uncertain categorisation in respect of which all numbers should be taken with a large grain of salt. It is likely that many casual relationships occurred between men and, in particular, unmarried women where the women's freedom of choice might be questioned even when there were no pronounced elements of violence or coercion. In addition, as Jarzebowski has pointed out, it is likely that the very meaning of sexual violence has changed over time, as

138 Lindstedt Cronberg 2002, pp. 111–17.

has the definition of voluntary and involuntary relationships, which complicates the picture further.[139] But the interesting thing is not how we would have defined a relationship, but how the relationship was perceived at the time. If there are no traces of coercion in the court records, even though violence and coercion were seen as mitigating circumstances, we have to assume that neither the accused, nor the local community, nor the judging authorities perceived the relationship as a coercive one.

Earlier Swedish research shows that when the crime involved fornication (when both parties were unmarried and unrelated to each other), the relationships mostly appear to have been voluntary and reciprocal. In these cases, the woman was rarely in a formal position of dependency vis-à-vis the man; and to judge from comments in the judgement books, she had often been as interested in the relationship as he. If they were discovered, the women in particular risked the loss of their honour. The motive for nevertheless committing the act may, aside from sexual desire, be explained by a wish for marriage. Sexual congress can thus be seen as a conscious strategy for attaining the sought-after title of wife.[140] When, on the other hand, the crime involved adultery (i.e., when one or both parties were married), the woman repeatedly described how the man had 'long pursued her' until she had finally given in.[141] In the latter case, it thus seems as though the man was the active initiator of the sexual relationship. However, this does not necessarily mean that there was actual coercion or violence, and for a researcher it is difficult to determine whether the woman acted voluntarily, or whether she was forced to participate in the sexual act, exclusively on the basis of court records. The woman had nothing to gain from accusing the man of exploitation in this context. In her study of rape cases in Sweden between 1600 and 1800, Karin Hassan Jansson has drawn the conclusion that it was difficult for a woman to have a man convicted of rape during the early modern period. Ideally, she would have to prove her active resistance in the form of torn clothes and serious physical injury in order to have the slightest chance of having the man convicted.

---

139 Jarzebowski 2006, p. 29. See also the discussion on coercion in Rublack 1999, pp. 238f.

140 This tactic was used in particular by women who were not very well off; lacking a significant dowry, they were less sought-after in the marriage market. Lindstedt Cronberg 1997, pp. 101, 205. Telste 1993, p. 130.

141 Lindstedt Cronberg 1997, p. 101.

And even when these requirements were fulfilled, it was practically always 'unknown assailants' who were convicted, not the women's employers.[142] In those cases where the woman did not succeed in convincing the court that she had been forced to participate in the act, her testimony was taken as a confession of fornication or adultery, for which crime both parties were punished but in respect of which social stigmatisation had a more unfavourable impact on the woman. For this reason one may imagine that many women who were the victims of sexual violence chose not to talk about the incident unless they became pregnant.[143] In line with this reasoning I believe, as do several other researchers, that there is probably a large number of unreported cases of violence and exploitation in connection with sexual criminal cases in the reporting in the judgement books.[144]

When the crimes concerned sexual relationships between closely related people, the situation is different, though. If a regular rape was considered proven, the legislation prescribed the death penalty for the man. By instead defining the crime as a case of fornication or adultery, both the man and the woman were sentenced to a fine or, alternatively, to corporal punishment. In so doing, the court could avoid handing out a death sentence by dismissing the credibility of the woman's testimony. But if a man violated a close relative, the question of whether the act had been committed by force or not was immaterial: the punishment was death in either case. For the woman, though, the definition of the crime was crucial. If she had been forced to participate in the act, this could justify a reprieve for her.

The manner of defining the crime thus determined the final judgement that could be handed out. If there was no family relationship between the man and the woman, a death sentence (for the man) was avoided by dismissing the woman's claim of violence and coercion. But if, on the other hand, there was a family relationship between the parties, a death sentence (for the woman) could only be avoided if her story was accepted as true. Here the assessment of the members of the court may have been influenced by a desire to apply lenient case law. Previous research supports the assumption

142 Jansson 2002, p. 289. See also Lindstedt Cronberg 1997, pp. 125f.

143 Jansson 2002, p. 163.

144 Similar arguments for a significant number of unreported cases have been presented in Bergenlöv 2002, p. 179, and the literature referred to therein.

that this was a prioritised norm according to which the court of appeal acted in its everyday activities.[145]

This does not mean that the members of the court of appeal chose to ignore persuasive evidence, or that they avoided pronouncing death sentences at any cost. Instead, I see their actions as a subconscious *interpretation* of the chain of events that might affect the outcome in *uncertain* cases. Their interpretation was probably affected by several parallel and partly overlapping ideas surrounding, for instance, legal justice and general judicial ethics, but also by their own religious and gendered preconceptions. When a rape case where there was no family relationship between the perpetrator and the victim was defined as adultery or fornication, male patriarchy, women's subordination, and the basic hierarchical construction of society were indirectly defended while the lenient case law could still be maintained. In cases where the man and the woman were related, three of the first-mentioned norms came into conflict with the last-mentioned one. It was impossible to defend the superiority of the man in the social hierarchy and practise lenient case law at the same time. I believe that the *family relationship* thus acquired an active significance for the assessment of incest cases where the woman claimed to have been exploited by the man.

In cases where the court found it credible that the woman had been coerced or enticed into participating in the sexual act, she was reprieved from the death penalty but was forced to suffer corporal punishment in the form of birching. She was rarely completely acquitted, because she had in fact participated in an act that was forbidden by God.[146] In spite of this, violence and coercion were among her strongest arguments for obtaining any kind of reprieve from the death penalty. Hence there was a strong incentive for a woman to relate any abuse in cases where such circumstances actually existed. In the majority of incest cases from the period around the turn of the century in 1700, the woman's punishment was reduced not only in obvious rape cases but also when she claimed after the fact that she had been 'enticed', 'lured', or 'deceived' into committing the act.

145 Thunander 1993, pp. 107, 173.

146 See, e.g., GHA, BIIA:3, 1694, no. 88; GHA, BIIA:4, 1695, no. 103; GHA, BIIA:9, 1699, no. 130; GHA, BIIA:14, 1704, no. 123; GHA, BIIA:15, 1705, no. 136. In two out of twenty-two cases the woman was completely acquitted of any responsibility. GHA, BIIA:25, 1716, no. 162; GHA, BIIA:11, 1701, no. 35.

In 1701, Sven Ersson (forty years old) and his niece Anna Olofsdotter (fifteen) were accused of incest. Both 'freely' confessed their crimes and should, according to the law, have been sentenced to death. But Anna's father, Sven's brother Olof, 'tearfully' begged for his daughter's life before the hundred court, with the justification that she was very young and that Sven had 'lured and enticed' her to commit this 'grievous sin'. According to the father, the guilt was entirely Sven's. First, he was 'an old farmhand'; second, he had previously been convicted of fornication; and third, he had lived and worked as a farmhand on Olof's farm for ten years. Being forty, Sven could not blame his acts on youthful folly. His conduct and honour were not only sullied by his previous misdeeds, but also by his actions towards his brother and master. By seducing Olof's daughter, he had violated his master's trust. This crime appears to have been revealed only when the daughter became pregnant. There are no indications that Sven used physical violence or threats in order to persuade Anna to be together with him sexually. The court records only describe that he had lured and enticed her to come to him. He had quite simply seduced her in a way that, judging from the studies of Jansson and other researchers, would never have led to a conviction for rape if Sven and Anna had not been related. By emphasising Anna's youth and foolishness in parallel with Sven's shortcomings, all guilt was foisted onto him. Anna escaped with a birching, while he had to pay with his life.[147]

A seventeen-year-old girl, whose name was also Anna Olofsdotter, ended up in court in 1704 when it was revealed that she was pregnant. At first, she claimed that a farmhand was the father; but after lengthy interrogations she finally confessed that it was her brother-in-law who had 'enticed' her into having sexual relations with him on two occasions during the previous summer. Her sister and her parents begged for her life, and her sentence was reduced to being birched outside the door of the local courthouse on two occasions with fourteen days between them.[148]

Similarly, a thirty-two-year-old woman ended up in court in Lister Hundred in 1704 when it became obvious that she was expecting a child. This woman also initially identified a farmhand as the

147 GHA, BIIA:11, 1701, no. 10.

148 GHA, BIIA:14, 1704, no. 53. Her brother-in-law in this case absconded to Norway with his wife, but he returned to Sweden six years later whereupon he was apprehended, convicted, and sentenced to death for the crime of incest. GHA, BIIA:20, 1710, no. 31.

father, but later 'tearfully' confessed that it was her sister's husband who was the father of the child. The sexual relations were to have taken place 'once only, when they were both in their cups'. Her brother-in-law escaped before the trial. The woman's sentence was reduced to a birching with the justification that the crime had occurred a) once only, b) in the absence of the wife, and c) while intoxicated, and because the man who was just as guilty, or even more so, had absconded and thus escaped punishment.[149] Twenty-year-old Britta Andersdotter was also sentenced to a birching after claiming that her brother-in-law had lured her into drinking so much that she was severely intoxicated on one occasion, after which he abused her sexually and made her pregnant.[150]

None of the above-mentioned cases contain any description of physical violence, threats, or obvious situations of dependency. Not even Anna, who was very young, can be said to have been in her uncle's power, since he was a mere farmhand in the household where her father was the master. All the crimes were discovered several months after the sexual act in connection with the discovery that the woman was pregnant, and it was thus only after the fact that the women defended their actions with having been lured or enticed into committing the acts.

In cases where a woman was considered to have been forced or lured into participating in the sexual act, she often had the support of both the court and her family. The violence or abuse ended up as the focal point while the family relationship was toned down. At the same time, I believe it was *precisely the family relationship* that made it possible to focus on the abuse in these cases. By accepting the woman's description of the relations as having been forced, the judges could justify her reprieve. In opposition to what was the case when there was no family relationship between the parties, the judges were thus able to avoid a death sentence by believing the woman's words. Jansson, too, notes that in rape cases that were also incest cases, women often managed to persuade the court that their version of events was the true one.[151]

In another study, historian Eva Bergenlöv compares Swedish rape cases from the turn of the century in 1700. In one case she finds it 'noteworthy' that a man was convicted of rape although the victimised woman had not reported the crime immediately. According to the

149 GHA, BIIA:14, 1704, no. 4; GHA, AII:5, 1704, 10 February, p. 535f.
150 GHA, BIIA:9, 1699, no. 130.
151 Jansson 2002, pp. 94f.

court records, the man had confessed his crime orally on a previous occasion before two credible witnesses; Bergenlöv assumes that this was the decisive circumstance for the outcome of the case. The man in question is said to be the woman's stepfather, but because the family relationship was mentioned without being emphasised in the records, Bergenlöv dismisses its significance for the outcome of the case.[152] Conversely, I believe that the family relationship was probably the decisive circumstance in the assessment of this case.

It should, however, be emphasised that the court did not in any way lightly or routinely pardon women on such grounds. In some cases, the woman's position was improved by the man's absconding before court proceedings began, because this was considered indicative of his guilt. If one party was not present in court, the chances of escaping the severest punishment of the law increased for the party who did show up. The crime was then blamed on the party who was not present. Because (usually) the man had escaped secular punishment through absconding or death, it was considered wrong to let the woman alone answer for the crime.[153] When both parties were present, the woman's credibility might be questioned by the man's defence.

Anna Eriksdotter (twenty-four years old) worked as a servant for her uncle, Holsten Bengtsson (sixty-four). When Anna became pregnant, both confessed that they had had sexual relations on one occasion. But their accounts differed with respect to the circumstances of the crime. He claimed that she had taken the initiative by coming to him in bed, whereas Anna was prepared to 'swear on oath' that it was Holsten who had come to her and demanded sex when he was drunk.[154] Following both their confessions, the court of appeal found no reason to amend the death sentence handed out by the hundred court. The case was never referred to the Crown, and both

152 Bergenlöv 2002, pp. 196–8.

153 Seventeen women were pardoned, eleven after the man had absconded or failed to show up for some other reason. The corresponding number for men was a mere two. Another two men were, however, completely acquitted of accusations of incest, because the woman had first admitted the crime before witnesses and then died before prosecution could be brought. The most common situation was that the man had absconded (which increased his burden of guilt in the eyes of the court), and the court was then loath to allow the woman to answer for the crime on her own. See, for instance, GHA, BIIA:4, 1695, no. 103. In only six out of sixty-three cases were both the man and the woman pardoned when the act was considered proven.

154 Hammarkind Hundred, AIa:11, 1704, 30 April, p. 398.

Anna and Holsten were executed.[155] Anna was much younger than her uncle. She lived in his house and was dependent on him for her upkeep. In addition, she was prepared to swear that the crime had happened on his initiative; but this was not enough for her life to be spared.

This case shows that it was after all quite difficult to be reprieved from the sentence of capital punishment when the crime involved incest. It also underlines the fact that the court *always* assumed that both parties were equally guilty. Although most of those reprieves which were actually granted were given to women who claimed that they had been forced or lured into committing the act, this was never an active line of questioning that was initiated by the court. It was quite simply assumed that both had been willing participants in the act. Incest was thus not primarily associated with violence or situations of coercion. One reason for this may be that incestuous relationships based on coercion or exploitation were actually in a clear minority at this time.

On the basis of court records written around the turn of the century in 1700, it may be established that relationships between full biological relatives were the only relationship category where coercion and exploitation appear to have dominated. In five out of eight such cases, these circumstances were mentioned, but at the same time these relationship categories were clearly in a minority. As for the affinity categories, the percentage of criminal cases where aspects of violence or coercion were mentioned was at most around 30% in specific relationships, the average figure being just under 20%. See Table 7.

It is true that there may have been coercion or exploitation even in some other relationships that have been categorised as ‘unknown’, but the incentive of the woman to portray a relationship as coerced – whether this was the case or not – should have been great in relationship categories where there was a risk of capital punishment. She had everything to gain and nothing to lose by blaming the man. Thus, the likelihood increases that the category ‘enticed/forced’ contains relationships where the woman voluntarily participated in the sexual act only to blame the man after the fact.[156]

155 GHA, AII:5, 1704, 6 April, pp. 564f; GHA, AII:5, 1704, 27 May, pp. 582f; GHA, BIIA:14, 1704, no. 52. For other examples of the woman’s failing to obtain a pardon in spite of seeming to have been forced or grossly exploited, see, for instance, Lister Hundred, AIb:1, 1703, 14 April.

156 See, e.g., GHA, BIIA:17, 1707, no. 1 and GHA, BIIA:4, 1695, no. 103, which seem to be uncertain cases.

Table 7. Incest cases from GHA 1694–1716, the reciprocity of relationships

Relationship category	Relationship	Voluntary	Enticed/ forced	Unknown
Consanguinity				
First lineal degree	daughter		1	
First collateral degree	sister	2	2	
Diagonally	niece	2	3	1
	aunt		1	
Affinity				
First lineal degree	stepmother	2		
	stepdaughter	8	5	3
	stepgranddaughter	1		
	daughter-in-law	1		
First collateral degree	wife's sister	12	5	1
	brother's widow/wife	2		1
	two sisters, two brothers with the same woman	5*		
Diagonally	uncle's concubine/ widow	6		
	mother-in-law's half-sister	1		
	wife's niece	13	3	6

Source: GHA, series BIIA. A selection of categories where the defendants risked capital punishment. These numbers also include half-relatives.
* There are in fact seven cases in this category. In two cases the woman claimed that she was not aware of the man's previous relationship to her sister. The woman thus seemingly voluntarily participated in the sexual act, but could not, by reason of ignorance, take a position with respect to the kinship crime. For this reason, these cases have been removed from the statistics.

Swedish circumstances were thus similar to the situation in the Netherlands, because Dutch lawyers also tended to pardon women who claimed that they had been forced to participate in the sexual act.[157] In German-speaking areas, however, it was more difficult for women to gain a hearing for stories involving threats and violence.

157 Egmond 2001, pp. 24f.

Ulinka Rublack describes a culture where women were forced to endure sexual demands from their relatives and where no harm was felt to have been done as long as they did not become pregnant. According to Rublack's material, the woman was often economically dependent on the man, which resulted in her having problems defending herself from sexual pressures. Ideas regarding rape at this time assumed that the crime was committed in the forest or out in the fields by an unknown assailant, which made lawyers less than responsive to other scenarios or versions of events. To a large extent, women were therefore judged in the same way as men.[158] This difference might be explained by the fact that fewer relationships risked the death penalty in the German-speaking areas; consequently, the incentive to believe the woman diminished in accordance with the above line of reasoning.

In conclusion, a clear majority of all Swedish crimes of incest from the turn of the century around 1700 onwards appear to have been voluntary relationships between two adult individuals who were related through marriage (affinity relationships). In legal contexts it was assumed that both parties had participated voluntarily in the act, and only when the woman or her relatives claimed that she had been forced or lured into committing the sexual act was an assessment made as to whether this might be the case. If the woman managed to convince the court that she had been deceived or lured by the man into committing the act, her punishment was often reduced to birching. She was rarely completely acquitted, though, because she had – albeit involuntarily – participated in an act forbidden by God.

Love and passion

As the preceding section showed, the large majority of incestuous relationships reported to the Göta Court of Appeal around the turn of the century in 1700 were affinity relationships, or relationships between non-biological relatives. Most of these relationships appear to have been based on mutual voluntary participation. In spite of this, very few cases include references to the personal feelings of the couples involved. Descriptions of love and infatuation are thus conspicuous by their absence in the court records, which shows that love, lust, and longing were not considered legitimate excuses for violating incest prohibitions. But this does not mean that ideas

158 Rublack 1999, pp. 236–42.

8 A peasant couple from the eighteenth century.

surrounding love and sexuality were not important in these contexts. On the contrary, I believe that such ideas had a decisive significance for how individual incest cases were decided. In order to illustrate the ways in which this happened, I will analyse two incest cases where a man had a sexual relationship with his *wife's sister*. Both cases ended in the conviction of the accused with the death penalty as a consequence, but in the end a royal pardon was obtained for one of the couples. The interesting question here is why one of the couples were pardoned but not the other, although the family relationships were the same.

The first case concerns twenty-year-old Lars in Spånbacken. According to the court records, he had ended up on the floor in the straw together with his wife's unmarried sister, Britta Andersdotter (twenty-six years old), late in the evening after the festivities of the Christmas holiday. Lars was drunk on this occasion and the two of them had sexual intercourse, whereupon Britta became pregnant. Later, before the hundred court, they confessed their crime and humbly pleaded for mercy. During the interrogations they admitted that they knew that the family relationship aggravated the criminal act, and that they had hence committed a very grave sin. Lars's wife (who was thus Britta's sister) begged for mercy on behalf of her husband and said that she would gladly have him back if he could be reprieved from the death sentence.[159]

The second case concerns a forty-year-old gardener by the name of Abraham Andersson. After a sudden illness, Abraham's wife had died and left him alone with four small children. Shortly thereafter the unmarried sister of the dead wife, Catharina Olofsdotter, who was around thirty years old, began helping Abraham with the household chores and the care of the children. The following year Catharina gave birth to an illegitimate child, whereupon she was summoned to the local court for questioning. When asked about the father of her child, she said that it was a boatswain whose ship had left harbour several months earlier. But the members of the hundred court did not believe her, as the time when the ship sailed did not quite correspond to the duration of a normal pregnancy. The interrogation continued for another few hours, and eventually Catharina started crying. She went up to the hundred-court judge, who was in charge of the proceedings, and whispered a confession in his ear that it was actually her brother-in-law, Abraham, who was the father of the child. After Catharina had confessed, she displayed 'particular remorse for the sin and begged that her life might be spared by the esteemed authority', and she expressed pity for her little child, who now risked becoming an orphan. Abraham was brought in for questioning, and after a certain hesitation he too confessed to their crime. It was also revealed that it was Abraham who had encouraged Catharina to ascribe the paternity to the boatswain.

159 Vista Hundred, AIa:5, 1693, 18 October, no. 5.

Abraham and Catharina had a certain amount of support from the local community. The people assembled for the trial attested that neither Catharina nor Abraham was known for dissolute living; and the county sheriff Lars Bjälke, who was Abraham's neighbour, confirmed that Catharina had not been seen around Abraham's cottage before his wife died and that after the wife's death she had only been there to look after his little children.[160]

When Catharina gave birth to her child, she had been assisted by three women who also appear to have tried to protect the couple as far as possible. During the early modern period, it was the explicit duty of such birth assistants or midwives to ask unmarried women in labour who the father of their child was – preferably while the woman was racked by the most severe pain. Pronouncements made during labour had high credibility and could be equated with a deathbed confession.[161]

For this reason, the three birth assistants were questioned during Catharina's trial. At an early stage of the trial, before Catharina had confessed her guilt, the birth assistants unanimously claimed that it was true that Abraham had shown great concern for Catharina in connection with the delivery, but that the only father of the child who had been mentioned was the boatswain. Later, when both Catharina and Abraham had confessed to the crime, the same birth assistants were summoned again. Once more, the hundred court asked them if they really had not suspected that Abraham might be the father of Catharina's baby. The women then admitted that they had had their suspicions about Abraham's involvement, because he had been so very anxious while Catharina was giving birth. Catharina's delivery had been unusually difficult and protracted. On one occasion during the two-day-long delivery process, Abraham had a forcibly opened a bolted door and made his way in to Catharina, though the birth assistants had attempted to expel him from the cottage. He could not be prevailed upon to leave her but had sat at her side, holding her hand and apologising for having been 'too close' to her.[162]

160 Östkind Hundred, A1:4, 1713, 16 February.

161 Lindstedt Cronberg 1997, pp. 92–5. Only after 1778, when a new ordinance (the infanticide ordinance) was adopted, did it become possible for women to bear their children without having to answer troubling questions regarding paternity. Lindstedt Cronberg 1997, pp. 143f.

162 Östkind Hundred, A1:4, 1713, 16 February.

Once the crime had been confessed, the members of the court turned directly to Catharina and asked how in the world she had allowed herself to become involved in such a grievous sin. She answered that she had tried to resist Abraham when he pursued her, but that she had finally given in when she, 'so help me God, began to love him'. Abraham confessed that he had initiated the relationship, but firmly claimed that 'sinful as it was, it happened from a blinding love for Catharina'.[163]

These two criminal cases have several things in common. Both concerned a relationship between a man and his wife's sister. They were relatively close in time and space (1692 in Västergötland and 1712 in Östergötland, respectively). In both cases small children were involved, and the accused showed great remorse and humility before the court. In neither case is there any indication that the relationship was based on any form of violence or coercion, and in both cases a person from the local community had spoken up in favour of the accused. Both couples were considered guilty of the sexual act and were sentenced to death, but on recommendation from the Court of Appeal one of the couples was later pardoned by the king. What was it in the chains of events that differed in such a crucial manner that one couple was allowed to live but not the other? From a modern perspective, the answer to the question is not obvious; but on the basis of the cultural values of the time, the dissimilar outcomes may be explained.

Abraham and Catharina were both unmarried, whereas the crime of Lars and Britta was aggravated by the fact that Lars's wife was alive when the crime was committed. It followed from this that the couple were guilty of *both* adultery *and* incest. According to the law, the civil status of the offenders was not supposed to affect the assessment of the crime of incest; but the members of the court often cited as a mitigating circumstance that a criminal was unmarried, which suggests that this factor did affect the court's reasoning after all. Even so, it was Lars and Britta who were pardoned by the Crown after a petition for mercy from the Court of Appeal. The petition summarised the criminal charge and adduced the mitigating circumstances as perceived by the members of the Court. It was pointed out that Lars was very young, that the crime had occurred when he was drunk, that his wife begged for clemency on behalf of her husband, that the accused had been in 'harsh' prison

163 Östkind Hundred, A1:4, 1713, 16 February.

for a long time, and that the crime had only happened on *a single occasion*. In my view, this final fact constitutes the decisive difference between the two cases.[164] Abraham and Catharina were both uncommitted, they had a good reputation in the local community, and there were neighbours who spoke up for them; but they had been involved in a longer relationship. In spite of their knowledge of the prohibition, they had committed the crime again and again. That they appear to have been in love was not perceived as a mitigating circumstance.

During the early modern period both women and men were thought to have an active sexuality; and although marriages were often based on practical agreements, love and tenderness between spouses were regarded as praiseworthy and desirable. Indeed, they were considered to be among the marital duties. Previous research shows that this favourable discourse about love had the support of both the authorities and the peasantry during the seventeenth century. In contradistinction, the *purpose* of the love relationship was not primarily the happiness of individuals, but the promotion of marriage in itself.[165] Because marriage as an institution was considered to be one of the cornerstones of a stable society, conjugal love almost became a civic duty. First and foremost, it was supposed to promote marriage and consequently the good of society.[166] In other words, not only sexuality was channelled into marriage, but also all the tender feelings that men and women could have for one another.

In sharp contrast to conjugal love there was extramarital passion, which was perceived as a potentially dangerous instinct or disease that had to be controlled at any cost. Passionate love was considered unreliable and fickle. However favourable the effects of love within marriage might be, love's possible consequences outside the matrimonial union were dangerous in equal measure. In this context theologians emphasised original sin, which all people carried within them and which made them vulnerable to temptations of various kinds. Emotions and passions were perceived as weak points in the human defence against worldly temptations.[167] Historians have described the early modern period as a battlefield between good

164 For examples of other cases where the number of sexual acts engaged in is emphasised, see footnote 128.

165 Lennartsson 1999, pp. 121, 157, 181, 337, 351.

166 Luhmann 2003, p. 118; Jarzebowski 2014, pp. 170–2; Stadin 2005, pp. 400f.

167 Ambjörnsson 1978, p. 149; Nilsson [Hammar] 2012, pp. 103, 117, 123.

and evil, between God and the Devil. People were tempted by social prestige, physical pleasure, or spiritual satisfaction. But according to the prevailing, religiously influenced normative interpretation, these were illusions created by the Devil in order to lead people astray, away from God. Yielding to temptation would, according to early-modern rhetoric, only lead to a brief and false happiness. For this reason, it was thought to be of the utmost importance that people learned to govern their passions and firmly resist temptations.[168] To a certain degree, youthful indiscretions could be overlooked; but as people grew older and amassed greater life experience, they were expected to be able to control and assume responsibility for their actions.

On the basis of these ideas, prevalent at the time, the differing judgements become easier to understand. True, Lars and Britta had failed to control their desires. They had been carried away by their feelings, a failure partly explained by their youthful folly, partly by Lars's intoxication. The arguments presented in court were based on the idea that they could not be held completely responsible for their actions under the circumstances. At the same time, the support of Lars's wife implied that they were, at bottom, proper and devout individuals. The couple was sentenced to harsh corporal punishments: Lars had to run nine gauntlets, and Britta was severely birched at the door of the local courthouse; but at least they were allowed to live.[169]

For Abraham and Catharina there were no mitigating circumstances. Over a period of several months, they had repeated their crime again and again. They had had an opportunity to come to their senses, but had again fallen for the temptation of having 'carnal knowledge' of each other. In addition, they were forty and thirty years old, respectively, and were consequently held fully accountable for their actions. It did not matter that they behaved humbly and devoutly in all other respects – their relationship was a violation of God's laws and could not be excused or pardoned by a secular court.

---

168 Thomas 1984, pp. 36–41; Jarzebowski 2014, p. 175; Sanders 2001, p. 7; Luhmann 2003, p. 64. On the fickleness of happiness, see Savin 2011, pp. 85–7, 219.

169 GHA, BIIA:3, 1694, no. 1. In contrast to a regular birching, severe birching was performed by an executioner, which brought with it additional shame. Thunander 1993, p. 80.

Even though Abraham and Catharina pleaded with the authorities for mercy, they at the same time admitted their guilt and the justness of punishment for their actions. Both claimed to 'cheerfully wish to suffer their well-earned punishment', and they did not invoke any mitigating circumstances. The warm feelings they had for each other were only made clear as an answer to an explicit question by the hundred court. Catharina said that she had allowed herself to be tempted into committing the act when she, against her will, had begun to love Abraham; and as was stated above, Abraham explained his behaviour by referring to a 'blinding love' for Catharina. In both cases these were explanations of their behaviour, not excuses that they thought might lead to a reduction of their punishment.

The account of Catharina's final confession that is recorded in the judgement book is very interesting. Before the confession was made public, only Catharina, Abraham, and God (as far as we know) had any knowledge of the sin. As long as the crime was kept secret from the people around them, their feelings of guilt or shame were not so great that they were unable to keep them in check. Once the pregnancy was a fact, they attempted to use a lie to avoid suffering the consequences of their actions. But Catharina's claim that the boatswain was the father of her child was not believed by the members of the court, who continued to apply pressure on her. The hundred-court judge asked her to swear on the Bible, while he at the same time reminded her of the 'torments of her soul', the 'agony', and the secular and Christian punishments she might endure if she chose not to speak the truth. If she confessed the crime instead and showed due remorse, she could still save her soul. For 'over two hours' the hundred-court judge 'belaboured' Catharina in this way, whereupon she finally burst into tears and *whispered her confession.* She did not wish to speak it aloud and tried to keep it secret from the people around her for as long as possible. Catharina's reaction indicates that she expected condemnation. Regardless of whether she responded to the actual reaction of the people around her or to the reaction she expected would come, her behaviour reveals that she acknowledged the act as immoral and sinful.

It is striking how absent allusions to the emotions are in court records of this period, even though most incest cases appear to have been voluntary relationships. Not even in the few cases where the accused had lived together for years and had several children together were tender feelings mentioned. Personal feelings were quite simply not offered as an explanation or excuse on the part of the accused.[170]

Similar patterns are presented by other researchers with respect to crimes of adultery and fornication, where the argumentation was rarely made in terms of infatuation or attraction. Rather, infidelity was regarded as folly.[171] This confirms that the censorious attitude as regards extramarital infatuation was a powerful social norm that both the authorities and the peasantry supported, at least on the surface. The same norm was reproduced in the court proceedings by all the parties involved, by the members of the court as well as by the accused and by the witnesses.

A sexual relationship that had been repeated more than once could not be defended. On the contrary, it was as seen as an aggravating circumstance that the parties, in spite of having had the opportunity to come to their senses and reflect on their behaviour, had nevertheless repeated their crime. The then-current view of extramarital sexuality was of indirect importance to the assessment of these cases. Since extramarital love was perceived in such unfavourable terms, infatuation and love did not serve as a legitimate excuse for extramarital sexuality. The associations between unrestrained passionate behaviour and the Devil's influence over weak and sinful people may thus have contributed to the convictions. By repeating their crime, Abraham and Catharina had given in to the temptations of the Devil. The eternal life of the soul was in peril and could only be a saved by confessing and atoning for the crime – in other words, by the implementation of the death sentence. On 3 March 1713, Abraham's and Catharina's death sentences were upheld by the Göta Court of Appeal without referral to the king. As the sentence was carried out, five children were orphaned.[172]

---

170 See, e.g., GHA, BIIA:6, 1696, no. 35; GHA, BIIA:3, 1694, no. 118; GHA, BIIA:13, 1703, no. 51. There are, however, isolated exceptions; see, e.g., the prosecution against Anna Maria Larmen, who ran away with her sister's husband Lars Hindriksson. Lars claimed to have been married off to the sister in spite of loving Anna Maria more. Rudolf Thunander discusses this incest case in detail in Thunander 1992, pp. 41–8.

171 Lindstedt Cronberg 1997, pp. 107–9.

172 GHA, BIIA:23, 1713, no. 36. What happened to the children in this and other cases is not specifically mentioned. Court records often stated that funds would be taken from the property of the parents to pay for the upbringing of the children until they were able to support themselves, but nothing was mentioned about where they would be placed. From previous research, however, it is known that mortality among children born outside

Kinship

Historians such as Claudia Jarzebowski and Michel Mitterauer have shown that *family* and *kinship* are not static concepts but that they have changed radically over time, a circumstance that has also been crucial for the ways in which incest prohibitions have been formulated and practised.[173] Kinship and the formation of families are seen here as socially constructed, changeable, and negotiable. In accordance with this line of argument, it becomes reasonable to ask what importance various kinship categories had for negotiations surrounding the formulation and limitation of incest prohibitions in early modern Sweden.

Consanguinity and affinity

Comparisons of incest cases bring out certain patterns in the assessments of the court of appeal that can be linked to the family relationships of the prosecuted individuals. Above all, it becomes obvious that consanguinity relationships, especially in the first degree, were perceived as more offensive than affinity relationships although the law equated them. In practice, a distinction was thus made between biological and non-biological relationships.

The judgement-book material contains one single case where a man had assaulted his biological daughter. This was obviously perceived as a grosser crime than when a stepfather had taken advantage of his stepdaughter. In the latter cases, the crime was usually described as 'incest' (*blodskam*), 'aggravated incest' (*svår blodskam*), or 'outrage' (*missgärning*) in the court records. When the family relationship was biological, however, completely different turns of phrase were used. Here we find strong language such as 'the wicked deed' (*den ogudaktiga gärningen*), 'the sodomitic sin' (*den sodomitiska synden*), and 'the shameful, highly indecent and abominable act' (*den skamliga och mycket oanständiga samt vederstyggliga handlingen*).[174] Because of the biological family relationship, the relationship was perceived as not only illegal but as downright *unnatural*. The attitude to crimes of incest in the closest

wedlock was considerably higher when compared to that of children born to married parents. Lövkrona 1999, p. 209.

173 Jarzebowski 2006, pp. 15–19; Jarzebowski 2014, pp. 176–8; Mitterauer 1994, pp. 246f. For similar lines of reasoning, see also Gaunt 1996, pp. 188–91, 217.

174 GHA, BIIA:25, 1716, no. 162.

consanguinity degrees can be likened to the attitude to bestiality crimes, which were described in similarly condemnatory terms.[175]

German historian Ulinka Rublack has also noted that the crime of incest was equated with bestiality, and that both crimes were perceived as unnatural and brutish.[176] While Rublack does not distinguish between different relationship categories, only the closest consanguinity relationships were regarded in this manner in the Swedish material. Other crimes of incest might certainly be defined as morally or religiously reprehensible, but they were nevertheless accepted as human acts. In the case involving a father and his daughter, the members of the court of appeal showed great compassion for the victimised girl. She was completely acquitted of the incest accusation with the justification that she had been coerced. Maria – that was the girl's name – was sent to the local clergyman for comfort and support. It was also recommended that she should move to relatives who lived elsewhere in order to escape the 'offence' that the act had caused in her home village, so that she might 'by virtue of an honourable reputation enjoy a measure of happiness and prosperity in the future'.[177] True, stepdaughters who had been subjected to similar abuse by their stepfathers were in most cases reprieved from the death penalty; but they were nevertheless birched at the doors of the local courthouse as 'well-deserved chastisement', and nobody seems to have reflected on whether these girls might be in need of comfort or protection from gossip.[178] The crime to which the biological daughter had been exposed was perceived as being so heinous that her role as an innocent and helpless victim was not questioned, whereas the stepdaughters were to a certain extent considered to be accessories to the crime. In this extreme case, the biological family relationship thus led to a complete acquittal.

Conversely, the outcome tended to be stricter punishments for all parties involved if the case had to do with biological relationships rather than non-biological ones. Two pairs of *siblings* were convicted of incest. In the first case, both were sentenced to death although the sister was described as feebleminded – a mitigating circumstance that usually led to a reprieve. But the records stated that the woman

175 Liliequist 1992, pp. 1, 89f.

176 Rublack 1999, pp. 234f.

177 GHA, BIIA:25, 1716, no. 162. This case is also described in Lindstedt Cronberg 2002, pp. 116f.

178 See, e.g., GHA, BIIA:3, 1694, no. 88; GHA, BIIA:14, 1704, no. 123.

was able to do her work and say her prayers, and for this reason she was considered accountable for her crime.[179] In the second case, the female party was eighteen years old and in her brother's employ and household. He had taken the initiative, luring and coercing her, and when the crime was discovered he had absconded. Despite her youth and her brother's ill conduct, she was sentenced to death without compassion.[180]

Anna Eriksdotter (previously mentioned on pp. 95–6) was accused of incest with her biological uncle. She was considerably younger than her uncle, and according to her testimony he was responsible for the crime. Their sexual congress was said to have occurred on one occasion only and on his initiative when he was drunk. These were circumstances that usually entailed a reprieve for the woman, but Anna's death sentence was upheld without the case going to the highest instance. It is possible that the decision was affected by the fact that she was his biological niece.[181]

'Half-relative' status was occasionally invoked as a mitigating circumstance, but in practice this circumstance did not have any great effect on the court decisions.[182] A pair of *half-siblings* had grown up completely separately and only met when she was twenty-six and he was eighteen. The relationship appears to have been voluntary, and both were sentenced to death.[183] A man (forty-six years old) and his *half-niece* (forty-two years old) confessed that they had had sexual intercourse but claimed that they had not understood the severity of the crime. Both were sentenced to death.[184] Per Persson and his *half-niece* met the same fate after 'tearfully and freely confessing the sin and most humbly begging for a possible reprieve'.[185]

179 GHA, BIIA:13, 1703, no. 60.

180 GHA, BIIA:8, 1698, no. 130.

181 GHA, BIIA:14, 1704, no. 52.

182 Nevertheless, one case with this argument led to a reprieve: GHA, BIIA:4, 1695, no. 103. Here Karin Jönsdotter 'tearfully' confessed that she had had sexual intercourse with her *half-uncle*. The court reduced her sentence to being birched twice, with fourteen days in between, outside the door of the local courthouse, its argument being that 'both divine and secular law have wished to distinguish between full siblings and half siblings', and also because the guilt was mainly that of the man, who had absconded, and for this reason it would be cruel to let Karin alone answer for the crime.

183 GHA, BIIA:15, 1705, no. 46.

184 GHA, BIIA:22, 1712, no. 155.

185 GHA, BIIA:8, 1698, no. 71.

The material thus shows that the court of appeal, without using the family relationship as an active argument in their judicial decisions, tended to treat consanguinity cases more harshly and with less tolerance than affinity cases. Mitigating circumstances were less apt to entail a reprieve than was the case when the family relationship was not biological. Even though biological and non-biological relationships were completely equal according to the letter of the law, my survey thus shows that the members of the court of appeal considered consanguinity relationships to be more serious crimes than affinity relationships.

Lineal and horizontal affinity relationships

In affinity cases, a distinction was made depending on whether the family relationships were collateral or lineal. Relationships in the direct lineal degree, up or down (*stepmother*, *stepdaughter*, *mother-in-law*, *daughter-in-law*), made it most difficult to obtain clemency from the court. With respect to *stepfather/stepdaughter* relationships, the woman might have her sentence reduced to corporal punishment if she had been 'enticed' or 'coerced',[186] but no man was given a reprieve, and the court of appeal did not refer any case to the Crown where the relationship appeared to have been voluntary.[187]

A modern reader may spontaneously associate a relationship between a *stepfather* and his *stepdaughter* with abuse and exploitation, but in the interpretation of material from earlier periods one must be careful not to draw such quick conclusions. Since marriages came about because of economic or practical considerations to a greater extent than today, it was relatively common for a certain age difference to exist between husband and wife – especially in the second marriage – and the man was not always the older spouse.

186 For instance, GHA, BIIA:15, 1705, no. 136. This notwithstanding, 'coercion' and 'deception' were far from a guarantee that a woman would be reprieved in these kinship degrees. For instance, at the age of thirteen or fourteen, Elna Mattisdotter was said to have been lured and deceived into committing incest with her stepfather, who was twenty years her senior. The relationship continued until Elna became pregnant six years later. Both were sentenced to death. Lister Hundred, AIb:1, 1703, 15 April.

187 For examples of what I have assessed to be voluntary relationships, see GHA, BIIA:3, 1694, no. 118; GHA, BIIA:17, 1707, no. 142; GHA, BIIA:18, 1708, no. 125; GHA, BIIA:23, 1713, no. 8.

An older widow often remarried a younger man, which could result in his being closer in age to the widow's children.[188]

Around the turn of the century in 1700, the ages of the accused were not systematically stated in the Swedish material, which makes it harder to assess the nature of the relationships. Giöthar Olsson and his *stepdaughter* Sara Hindrichsdotter exemplify a relationship that I have considered to be mutual. It transpires that Giöthar wanted to marry Sara, who was the daughter of the house, seven years earlier. For various reasons that are not mentioned in the judgement book, but were attested to by several of the people present, he had nevertheless been forced to marry Sara's mother 'against his will'. The mother testified that the marriage had not worked out the way it should have done. The information that Giöthar had really wanted to marry Sara is important, because it indicates that Sara was of marriageable age when Giöthar married her mother. In other words, he did not function as an actual father figure to her during her childhood and adolescence. Giöthar absconded before the beginning of the trial, but Sara was sentenced to death. In accordance with common practice, however, the enforcement of the punishment was delayed until after she had given birth to the child she was expecting.[189]

Two other seemingly voluntary lineal affinity relationships concerned a *stepmother/stepson*. In both cases, the accused were sentenced to death without the case being referred to the Crown.[190] The same sentence was pronounced regarding Knut Larsson and his *daughter-in-law* Kirstin Andersdotter.[191] In the above cases, which concerned seemingly voluntary relationships between lineally related couples, there were thus no attempts to obtain a reprieve for the accused.

Collateral affinity relationships (*wife's sister*, *brother's widow*, *two sisters*), on the other hand, were somewhat differently assessed. Here, too, the court of appeal considered whether there had been any potential coercion or enticement of a young woman. But the court also called for a reduced punishment in some cases when the relationship was described as voluntary. The associate judges in

188 For instance, Sandén 2005, p. 178.
189 GHA, BIIA:9, 1699, no. 119.
190 GHA, BIIA:12, 1702, no. 109; GHA, BIIA:20, 1710, no. 107. See also Kåkind Hundred, AIa:38, 1710, 23 June.
191 GHA, BIIA:12, 1702, no. 45.

these cases emphasised the mitigating circumstances and referred the cases to the Crown. Seven out of eleven cases referred for potential reprieves dealt with seemingly mutual relationships between a man and his *wife's sister*.[192] The same pattern occurred with respect to other collateral relationships (*brother's widow*, *two sisters*).[193] In the highest instance only a minority were reprieved, but the assessment of the associate judges definitely diverged from the official norm.

Taken altogether, there were six cases where both parties were given a reprieve even though they were considered guilty. None of these relationships included a blood relationship, and most of them were collateral relationships. In two of these cases, uncertainty arose as to whether incest had actually been committed, because the accused men denied that the initial relationship had occurred.[194] The court appears to have been of two minds and chose to mitigate the sentences. In one case the accused couple claimed that they had been ignorant of the prohibition, a statement whose credibility was supported by the crime having been discovered when the man went to the local clergyman to ask to have the banns published.[195] There were only three cases where both the man and the woman were acquitted despite engaging in fully proven incestuous relations, all pertaining to brother-in-law/sister-in-law relationships.[196]

It is thus clear that lineal relationship categories were treated more harshly than horizontal ones. With few exceptions, only voluntary

---

192 GHA, BIIA:3, 1694, no. 1; GHA, BIIA:3, 1694, no. 11; GHA, BIIA:8, 1698, no. 42; GHA, BIIA:9, 1699, no. 11; GHA, BIIA:11, 1701, no. 93; GHA, BIIA:14, 1704, no. 4; GHA, BIIA:16, 1706, no. 63.

193 GHA, BIIA:12, 1702 no. 96 (*wife's half-sister*); GHA, BIIA:7, 1697, no. 89 (*brother's widow*); GHA, BIIA:10, 1700, no. 42 (*half-brother's wife*); GHA, BIIA:13, 1703, no. 51 (*two sisters*); GHA BIIA:14, 1704, no. 29 (*two sisters*).

194 However, in both these cases the circumstances suggest that they really had been guilty of incest as defined at the time. In one case the man had been engaged to the sister of his present girlfriend, but afterwards denied having had sexual relations with her. GHA BIIA:13, 1703, no. 51, (*two sisters*). In the second case, the man had been sentenced and had atoned for the paternity of another woman's child. He was later accused of incest with his *daughter-in-law*, but then claimed that he was not at all the father of the boy who had been raised as his son. GHA BIIA:25, 1716, no. 60, (*father and son*).

195 GHA BIIA:12, 1703, no. 79; GHA BIIA:13, 1703, no. 97 (*step-granddaughter*).

196 GHA BIIA:3, 1694, no. 1 (*wife's sister*); GHA BIIA:14, 1704, no. 30 (*wife's sister*); GHA BIIA:7, 1697, no. 98 (*brother's widow*).

collateral affinity relationships could occasion an application for mercy. Other than that, it was primarily relationships that included elements of violence or a suspected exploitation of the woman that led to a case being referred to the highest instance. This does not in any way mean that it was easy for a brother- or sister-in-law to have the punishment prescribed by law mitigated in the court of appeal. For this to happen, it was necessary for multiple mitigating circumstances to be present, such as the transgression only having taken place on a single occasion, preferably under the influence of alcohol; in addition, it was very helpful if people from the community of the accused put in a good word for them. But if conditions such as these were fulfilled, it was thus possible for both the accused to be reprieved.

Family position prioritised over age relationship

The fact that age was not stated systematically is interesting in and of itself. Occasionally, information concerning age is mentioned in passing, but in a majority of cases it is never made clear how old the prosecuted individuals were.[197] The absence of information about age in judgement books and cathedral-chapter records has also been remarked on by other researchers.[198] When information about age was provided, the individual in question was usually very young or very old. In these cases, information about age was primarily used in weighing the issue of guilt. In the case between Anna Olofsdotter and her uncle, her youth (fifteen years) was emphasised in comparison to his older maturity (forty years).[199] She was described as young and foolish whereas he, as a fully grown man, was held accountable for his actions. Similarly, the age of Lars in Spånbacka (twenty years) was emphasised as a mitigating circumstance when the court of appeal wanted to justify a reprieve. Conversely, Anna Eriksdotter, who had had sexual relations with her forty-years-older uncle on one occasion, could not be excused on the basis of youthful indiscretion. She was twenty-four years old while he was sixty-four.[200] Judging from this and other similar cases, a person was defined as

197 Out of a little over 220 prosecuted individuals, the ages for a few more than fifty of them were provided.
198 Lennartsson 2012, p. 97; Lennartsson 1999, p. 163.
199 GHA, BIIA:11, 1701, no. 10.
200 GHA, BIIA:14, 1704, no. 52.

young up until they were twenty years old.[201] Though teenage marriages existed, it was more common for men and women to marry when they were around twenty-five years old, at least among the general population. That fact is likely to have contributed to a twenty-year-old being considered young and foolish.[202]

While the family position was always stated very carefully, information about age was thus omitted unless youthful foolishness was specifically invoked as a mitigating circumstance. I interpret this as meaning that age was not considered relevant information for the assessment of the crime, as long as both parties were deemed to be old enough to be held accountable for their actions. Consequently, the family position acquires greater importance for the judicial decisions than the respective ages of the parties.

The importance of family position

The pattern of treating horizontal relationships more leniently than vertical ones can be recognised from the dispensational material. A relationship between a man and his *aunt's husband's widow* or his *stepmother's aunt* were not included in the prohibited degrees, but people in these relationships who applied for permission to marry were firmly advised against carrying out their plans by the members of the cathedral chapter. These relationships were thus not forbidden, but were still perceived as unsuitable by the members of the cathedral chapter.

In these cases, both the decisions of the court of appeal and those of the cathedral chapter may be connected to contemporary ideas about *family position*. People's relationships in society were ordered according to a strict hierarchy which was considered necessary for stability and balance to prevail. According to this social order, each

201 Examples of other cases where youth was emphasised as a mitigating circumstance: GHA, BIIA:20, 1710, no. 3; GHA, BIIA:3, 1694, no. 118; GHA, BIIA:13, 1703, no. 62; GHA, BIIA:14, 1704, no. 123; GHA, BIIA:14, 1704, no. 30; GHA, BIIA:14, 1707, no. 53.

202 Sweden followed the Western European marriage pattern: late marriage around the age of twenty-five; men and women were of the same age at their first marriages; and many women did not marry at all. For a more detailed description of the Western European marriage pattern with reference to research on the subject, see Lennartsson 2012, pp. 86–92; Coontz 2005, pp. 124–31; Carlsson 1977, p. 109; Gaunt 1996, pp. 14–19. Regarding the existence of younger brides, see Lennartsson 2012, pp. 103, 105, 114f, 118.

individual had a duty to act in accordance with his or her position in society. The hierarchy was considered to be God-given. It was God's wish that the king should rule over his people like a stern but just father in the same way as the master of the house should rule his wife, his children, and his servants. A child should show respect for his or her parents, in the same way that the peasantry should show respect for those who wielded authority. The duties of individuals thus followed from their social and family positions, but also from their civil status, their sex, and their age.[203]

Anna Hansen has studied the factors that predominated with regard to the position of an individual in different Swedish seventeenth-century contexts. For example, she shows that social position was more important than age and sex in the relationship between a young mistress and an older male farmhand. In the absence of the master, the mistress was, regardless of her age, responsible for any decisions that were made on the farm. In this situation, the woman's position as a mistress thus overshadowed her subordination as a woman.[204]

Sometimes there were tensions between different status positions, however, for instance in connection with generational takeovers. When a younger couple took over the parents'/parents-in-law's farm, but the parents(-in-law) continued to live there in a more modest dwelling on the property, set apart for that purpose (a so-called *undantag*), uncertainty could arise around the power order within the household. The question was whether the position of master was superordinate to the position of parent. As a child, a man had to show his parents(-in-law) respect and obedience; but in his role as the master of the farm, he was entitled to demand respect and obedience from the entire household, including his own parents(-in-law).[205] In her analysis, Hansen concludes that 'the respect for parents and older people took precedence before the authority that

203 The ideology underlying the hierarchical society was based on the Table of Duties and the Lutheran idea of the three estates, but also on the general division into estates, which in Sweden consisted of four parts (nobility, clergy, burghers, peasants). While the three estates were primarily a relational ideology, which defined people's duties vis-à-vis one another, the four-estate division regulated people's duties as citizens. Stadin 2004, pp. 17–30.

204 Hansen 2006, p. 288.

205 *Undantag* (lit. 'exception') was a kind of pension system that meant that the older generation handed over the farm to the younger generation in return for food and board for the rest of their lives.

a person might have because of his or her sex or position within the household', and that 'age was a factor that had far greater influence than previous scholarship has observed'.[206]

However, I would like to make a clearer distinction between age and family position. It is obvious that older people should be respected by younger people and that children should show deference to their parents. But what happened when the step-parent was younger than the child? What status position prevailed then?

Since there is no information about age in either the dispensation material or the judgement-book material, my opinion is that family position was more decisive for an individual's place within the family than his or her age. Sexual relations between people whose family positions crossed different generations were perceived as inappropriate because the individual's duties could become contradictory. For example, a man could not marry his stepmother because he then acquired different duties vis-à-vis the same person. A stepmother should be shown deferential respect and reverence by her stepson, whereas a wife should be dominated by her husband. The man's duties thus became incompatible and the relationship inconceivable. *Family position* was patently the decisive factor in this situation. Nobody asked what the age of the man or the woman was, either in the case of an application for dispensation or in connection with a crime of incest. Even though age was hardly a completely irrelevant factor in matrimonial issues in general, it appears secondary relative to family position in this context.

These ideas surrounding hierarchy and respect within the family probably affected both the associate judges of the court of appeal and the members of the cathedral chapter, because they tended to treat vertical family relationships with greater severity than horizontal ones. In addition, assessments of the cases may have been affected by whether it was the woman or the man who came from the older generation. A woman could dominate a man through her social position or her family position. After all, within a household a stepmother's authority over a stepson was recognised, and so was a mistress's authority over a farmhand.[207] But according to the prevailing gender ideas of the time, it was always the man who dominated the woman in a sexual relationship.[208] In other words,

206 Hansen 2006, p. 125.

207 Hansen 2006, p. 288.

208 For a discussion on the subordination of women, see Lennartsson 1999, pp. 23, 28f and the literature referred to there.

9 The authorities were apprised of several crimes via gossip and curious neighbours, but people from the local community could also make an investigation more difficult by withholding information or providing refuge for a fugitive. The image shows Swedish folk costumes from different parts of the country. The use of folk costumes decreased in the nineteenth century when factory-made clothes became more common.

a sexual relationship between a man and, for instance, his *wife's niece* may have violated social hierarchies; but if a woman's family position was superior to a man's (*uncle's widow*, *aunt's husband's widow*), it contradicted *both* social and gender-related ideas. The social structure, order, and hierarchy were turned upside down. On the basis of these notions, it was logical for the members of the cathedral chapter to oppose applications for marriage between a man and his *aunt's husband's widow* and his *stepmother's aunt*, even though these particular relationships were not included among the prohibitions.[209] In both of these family relationships the woman's family position was superior to the man's, and even if this line of reasoning was not voiced openly, it is probable that these ideas were what affected the assessments of the members.

209 According to K.R. 1703, 2 December, direct lineal relationships, such as stepmother's stepmother/stepfather's widow, were forbidden; by contrast, diagonal relationships were not prohibited in cases where two marriages separated the parties.

Consequently, it was *family position* that determined how a relationship was regarded when courts assessed family relationships, not the age relationship of the accused parties. The one time when age could be of interest in an assessment of the crime of incest was when either party was so young that youthful folly might justify a reprieve. From this, one may once more draw the conclusion that the application of the legislation was somewhat fluid, and that it was influenced by contemporary ideas surrounding age and family position.

The local community

Scholars have emphasised that sexuality was monitored not only by the official representatives of the state but also, and perhaps even more so, by the curious local community.[210] Even so, popular support for the norms of morality was far from absolute. For example, we know that premarital relationships were largely accepted by the peasantry and by the authorities alike, as long as the couple in question legalised their relationship with an official marriage before any children were born. Research has also shown that the local community to some extent turned a blind eye to a youth culture characterised by sexuality.[211] In addition, the importance of social position for the assessment of sexual crimes has been emphasised in both Swedish and Norwegian research. Masters, who had a high social position in the local community, were less often convicted of the crimes of rape or adultery than socially lower-ranking individuals such as soldiers or farmhands.[212] Besides, research has shown that the actions of the general public were affected by whether the expected punishment was thought to fit the crime or not.[213]

Many researchers argue that economic conditions form the main reason for the support for strict morality control which may after all be demonstrated among the general public. Extramarital contacts led to illegitimate children, who in their turn caused problems surrounding paternity issues, material support, inheritance, and ownership.[214] Illegitimate children were not only a problem for

210 For instance, Lindstedt Cronberg 1997, pp. 16f, 83f, 131f.
211 Jansson 2002, pp. 139, 145.
212 Jansson 2002, pp. 297f; Telste 1993, pp. 175f.
213 Rublack 1999, p. 35; Liliequist 1992, pp. 90–2.
214 Thunander 1992, pp. 12f; Telste 1993, pp. 16, 110f; Sundin 1992, p. 315; Sjöberg 1996, pp. 72f.

individuals and their families; they were also apt to entail increased pressure on public poor relief. In this way, illegitimate children became a common economic problem which afflicted society as a whole. That the economic perspective was important may be illustrated by the following incest case. A man who was accused of incest with his wife's subsequently deceased sister was given an opportunity to clear himself by way of an oath. He was requested to swear that he had not had illicit relations with the woman '40 weeks prior' to her giving birth to a child.[215] Hence, he did not have to deny ever having had a sexual relationship with the woman – he only had to clear himself of being the father. In this case the court prioritised ascertaining who the father was rather than investigating whether an incestuous act had in fact been committed. The following section presents a detailed account of the local community's reaction to those incest crimes that were revealed in their midst.

Keeping quiet and turning a blind eye

In August 1711, a suspected case of incest between the married man Torsten Nilsson and the spinster Tova Jönsdotter came up for trial. A few years previously, Torsten had been convicted of single adultery with Tova's sister, Olu, and now he had also made Tova pregnant. Torsten and Tova's relationship was thus defined as incest in the first collateral affinity degree, which in the event of a conviction would be punished by death; but before the interrogations began, Torsten absconded. Because his first crime of adultery with Tova's sister had been made public at the local court, everyone in the local community should have known exactly how serious the crime was. But when, in his search for the criminal, the county sheriff asked Torsten's friends and relatives where he was, they claimed to be 'entirely unfamiliar with and ignorant of his whereabouts'. At the same time, rumour had it that Torsten had been in the parish on a number of occasions. He allegedly stayed with two of his brothers and also visited his wife. According to the most recent rumour, however, he had crossed the county boundary into Blekinge. An epidemic was raging there, and that put a stop to further investigation.[216]

215 GHA, BIIA:3, 1694, no. 43 and no. 109.
216 Östra Göinge Hundred, AIa:32, 1711, 2 July.

In this case it is worth noting the timing of the events. The year was 1711. Sweden had been at war for a little over ten years, and it would be another ten years before there was peace in the country (the Great Northern War, 1700–21). The epidemic in Blekinge was the final great outbreak of the plague in Sweden (1710–13), and to make matters worse this part of the country had suffered crop failure a year or so earlier.[217]

During the entire seventeenth century, ideas about a God who actively interfered in everyday life prevailed. He handed out rewards and punishments on the basis of how well people adhered to his commandments. Everybody had a duty to maintain God's order on earth. Anyone who did not punish or report a known crime risked being struck by God's punishment themselves. 'A concealed sin was a shared sin', as Liliequist writes, which in his material provided a strong incentive for witnesses to come forward and report the commission of any bestiality crimes.[218] In addition to personal punishment, God's displeasure could also affect people collectively. His wrath would then take the form of major catastrophes, such as war, crop failure, and disease. These national scourges were, according to the rhetoric of the authorities, above all a consequence of the ways of sinful people.[219] And still Torsten, that obvious sinner, appears to have had marked support from the people around him, both family and friends. People were aware of his movements through rumours; but when the county sheriff came to look for him, nobody knew where he was. Torsten does not appear in later judgement-book material, and his final destiny is unknown; but Tova's death sentence was upheld by the Göta Court of Appeal on 20 October of the same year.[220]

The threat of divine retribution was thus not decisive with respect to how people chose to act. Neither the threat of personal nor of collective punishment prevented Torsten's friends from giving him their indirect support and protection. How can this curious fact be accounted for?

One possible explanation may be that the interpretation of Scripture made by the authorities did not always receive support from the peasantry when sinful ways were cited as the primary reason

217 Persson 2001, pp. 34, 163.
218 Liliequist 1992, p. 97.
219 Malmstedt 1994, pp. 173f, 177.
220 GHA, BIIA:21, 1711, no. 142.

for God's wrath. The peasantry emphasised other reasons for God's displeasure, for instance that Sundays were not kept holy in the same way as before, or that ancient holidays and ceremonies had been abolished.[221] The reason for the actions of the peasantry may also be that different models of interpretation could be activated in different contexts in the early modern world of ideas. While misfortune and adversity were explained as divine punishment or divine warning on a general level, the misfortune of single individuals was instead defined as a divine trial.[222] Also, in concrete contexts (for instance in legal documents) secular explanatory models dominated. One and the same event could thus be interpreted in very different ways (punishment, warning, or test) on different occasions.[223]

Both these explanatory models provide examples of people's capacity for stretching the boundaries of the prevailing religious order. When Torsten's acquaintances gave him their support in spite of their knowledge of his sinful behaviour, this does not mean that they acted in wilful opposition to this order. On the contrary, religion permeated Swedish society during this period – an opinion I share with other researchers. In spite of this, I wish to emphasise that people felt able to make independent interpretations and assessments within the religious framework and act accordingly.

In the case referred to above, Torsten was given passive support from the local community. Similar passive support can be discerned in other cases as well, especially when the issue was relationships that appear to have lasted for a fairly long period of time. The widow Estrid Jöransdotter and her deceased husband's stepson Lars Sörensson had been engaged for five years before she became pregnant and they attempted to make the union official, whereupon their relationship was exposed. Estrid was titled 'innkeeper', so she ought not to have been completely invisible in the local community. Nor is there anything to suggest that the engagement had been kept secret. Still, the couple was not reported to the authorities before the pregnancy exposed their relationship.[224] In another example, the boatswain Sven Stinner first had a relationship with Sissa Håkansdotter, which was made public at the local court. A few years after Sissa's death, Sven began a sexual relationship with her younger sister, Elin Håkansdotter. Sven and Elin had two children

221 Malmstedt 1994, pp. 207–11.
222 Savin 2011, pp. 209, 240f, 265.
223 Savin 2011, pp. 378f.
224 GHA, BIIA:20, 1710, no. 30.

together before they ended up in court accused of incest.[225] Everybody in the local community must have been aware of Sven's previous relationship with Elin's sister, as well as of the nature of Sven's and Elin's relationship. Even so, it took several years before the court was made aware of this matter.

There are hence several examples of people in the local community choosing to turn a blind eye to a suspected prohibited relationship, unless the relationship was exposed by a pregnancy. But not even an unwanted pregnancy was certain to lead to a relationship's being reported to the authorities.

False fathers

In 1707, Erik Johansson and his stepdaughter Brita Persdotter were tried on suspicion of having had sexual intercourse. Before the court they both persistently denied the accusation, and Brita instead identified Jöns Gustavsson as the father of the child she was expecting. Jöns admitted paternity and offered to marry her, whereupon Erik and Brita were acquitted of the accusation of incest and the case was dismissed.[226]

One year later the same couple were taken to court again, accused of the same crime. According to the court records, they had 'allowed some persons to observe' that Erik was 'not free of his stepdaughter', and after careful interrogations they finally admitted that they had had 'carnal knowledge' of each other on three occasions. During the new interrogations it was also revealed that it was Erik who had persuaded Jöns to accept paternity when Brita had become pregnant, which he had agreed to do 'with his parents' knowledge and consent'. Father and stepdaughter were sentenced to death. Jöns, who had married Brita despite knowing about her illicit relations with her stepfather, was sentenced to prison for fourteen days on bread and water. His parents had to sit in the stocks for one and two Sundays respectively, and an additional three people were fined three silver coins each for their 'disobedience and contumacy'.[227]

It is obvious that several people were aware of the relationship of Erik and Brita, but initially no one reported them. Nor do Erik and Brita seem to have felt particularly threatened, since they had

225 GHA, BIIA:13, 1703, no. 51.
226 GHA, BIIA:17, 1707, no. 142.
227 GHA, BIIA:18, 1708, no. 125; Norra Vedbo Hundred, AI:14, 1708, 21 November.

– according to the notes in the records – spoken of their crime in the presence of other people. The wording in the court records testifies to the indignation felt by the court at the insolent and disrespectful disobedience of people who had deliberately misled the court and withheld the truth. In consequence, the court demonstrated to whom power belonged by imposing public-shaming punishments and fines.

In another case, yet another prohibited relationship between a stepfather and his stepdaughter is described. When the daughter became pregnant the father is said to have persuaded another man to confess to being the father and marry the daughter. However, the relationship between stepfather and stepdaughter continued even after the daughter's marriage, which led to the crime being exposed a few years later.[228]

Voluntarily taking on paternity in the way that was done in these cases must be regarded as a patent challenge to the prevailing norms of morality. In both cases a 'nasty rumour' was in circulation concerning the relationship of the respective couple, which did not prevent the false fathers from accepting paternity. The phenomenon of false fathers has also been discovered in connection with crimes of adultery.[229]

My material contains several cases in which there are doubts as to who was a child's real father. Knut Larsson, Sven Stinner, and Pär Arvidsson all tried to acquit themselves from accusations of incest by claiming that they were not at all the fathers of children for whom they had previously accepted paternity. These arguments were partially successful: one of the men was acquitted, one had his sentence reduced to a fine, and only one was sentenced to death, although his crime was both incest and double adultery.[230] The assessments of the courts in these cases show that they accepted the possibility that the wrong father had been identified before. In two other cases the women had, on realising that they were pregnant, identified a relative as the father of their expected children before

228 GHA, BIIA:23, 1713, no. 126; Albo Hundred, A1a:10, 1713, 22 May. See also GHA, AII:10, 1715, 15 February, pp. 531f, where a couple were sentenced to imprisonment for allowing their daughter to marry a man they knew had had a sexual relationship with his stepdaughter.

229 Lindstedt Cronberg 1997, pp. 122–4; Jansson 2002, p. 109; Lövkrona 1999, p. 99; Telste 1993, pp. 166–8; Hansen 1993, p. 159.

230 GHA, BIIA:13, 1703, no. 51; GHA, BIIA:12, 1702, no. 45; GHA, BIIA:10, 1700, no. 42.

witnesses. When the hundred court summoned them to official interrogations, however, they recanted their confessions and instead named other men as being responsible for the pregnancies, whereupon they were acquitted.[231]

It is of course impossible to say what is true in these cases; but all in all, they show that paternity was not always obvious – not even after the local court had publicly identified a person as the father. Because it was recognised that false fathers were a possibility, the argument could also be used in the defence of a single individual.

Pregnancies

By comparing how many pregnancies were mentioned in the records of the courts of appeal in relation to the different relationship categories, it is possible to obtain additional information about the general attitude of the peasantry to different incestuous relationships. See Table 8.

The figures in Table 8 show how many pregnancies were mentioned in the records of the courts of appeal in relation to the respective relationship category. Even though the figures can only be considered approximate (pregnancies may have occurred without being specifically mentioned), it is possible to attempt a cautious interpretation.

Table 8. Incest cases from GHA 1694–1716, number of pregnancies.

Family relationship	Closeness	Absolute numbers	Per cent
Average of all incest cases		83/105	79
Consanguinity	First lineal degree	0/1	0
	First collateral degree	3/4	75
	Diagonally	5/7	71
Affinity	First + second lineal degree	20/21	95
	First collateral degree	25/28	89
	Diagonally	15/21	71

Source: GHA, series BIIA.
Note: Selected categories, including half-relatives.

231 GHA, BIIA:19, 1709, no. 199; GHA, BIIA:9, 1699, no. 159.

On average, children and pregnancy are mentioned in 79% of all incest cases. In other words, the court was made aware of, on average, four out of five crimes of incest because they had been revealed by a pregnancy. Consequently, figures greater than the average suggest a *lower* tendency to report these crimes, whereas lower figures indicate a *higher* tendency to report. The two categories where the figures clearly exceed the average (89% and 95%, respectively) are both affinity relationships where the accused risked being sentenced to death (*stepdaughter*, *wife's sister*, *two sisters*). With respect to these relationship categories, the court appears to have been made aware of very few cases without a revealing pregnancy necessitating an investigation. There was thus a lower tendency to report these crimes, and the harsh punishment is likely to have acted as a deterrent. In Norway, infringements against the prohibited degrees almost completely disappear from the legal sources towards the end of the seventeenth century. Kari Telste explains this decrease as a probable discrepancy between penal practice and the norms of the common people. Crimes of incest were quite simply not reported to the sheriff because people thought the punishment too harsh in relation to the offence.[232]

With respect to diagonal affinity relationships (*wife's niece*), where one might expect the sentence to be routinely reduced to a fine, the number of pregnancies is lower than average and the readiness to report the crime consequently higher. In my view, this supports the conclusion that the number of submitted reports was related to the harshness of the punishment. It was felt to be reasonable that a man and his *wife's niece* were sentenced to a fine when violating the norms of morality; but for a man and his *wife's sister* or a man and his *stepdaughter* to be sentenced to death for the identical crime did not have the same support in the local community.

The readiness to report consanguinity relationships is higher than average, even though these crimes were punishable by death. This means that consanguinity relationships in the closest degrees (*mother*, *daughter*, *niece*) were probably regarded as more serious crimes than affinity relationships. Here, then, the actions of the peasantry are in line with the tendency that the authorities evinced through their judicial decisions. In other words, both groups perceived a biological relationship to be more offensive than a non-biological one even though these relationships were equated in the Bible, which formed the basis of the legislation.

---

232 Telste 1993, p. 226.

Defending a criminal

Another way of determining the attitude of the general public to relationships within the prohibited degrees is to look at which criminals were supported by the people closest to them. In connection with proceedings at the local court, family and friends could support a criminal by testifying to his or her good reputation or by pleading for a merciful assessment and a reduction of the punishment.

For a family member to actively support a prosecuted criminal in this way was mentioned as a mitigating circumstance in some cases, but ignored in others. Sven Frendesson and his *wife's sister* could, for instance, not be spared simply 'because the wife pleads for her husband'.[233] In another case, Anna Ambjörnsdotter was accused of incest with her *sister's husband* (who had absconded). The hundred court summed up the case with three aggravating circumstances and three mitigating ones, of which one described how Anna's sister 'voiced an eloquent plea for her sister's life to be spared'.[234] The court of appeal did not comment on the mitigating circumstances at all, but repeated the aggravating ones and sentenced Anna to death.[235]

As the numbers are uncertain, a quantitative comparison of the support given to the accused will not be completely reliable; but it is clear that support was particularly frequent when a man had had sexual relations with his wife's sister.[236] Usually this support came from the wife of the accused man. She would emphasise that the marriage had functioned well previously, and that the man had fulfilled his duties as a husband and father of a family. Now and then the wife would stress the family's dependence on the man as the provider.[237] Previous research has shown that this was a common argument with respect to crimes of adultery as well, and it has been pointed out that the economic consequences may have played a

233 GHA BIIA:6, 1696, 21 March, no. 35.
234 The court records of Vista Hundred, AlA:12, 1694, 18 May.
235 GHA, BIIA:3, 1694, no. 49.
236 In ten out of eighteen cases (55%), one or both of the prosecuted individuals were given explicit support according to the documents of the court of appeal. Support was given in at least two more cases according to the records of the hundred court. This figure may be compared with other categories, where the support amounted to 25–37%.
237 See, e.g., GHA, BIIA:22, 1712, 9 October, no. 155.

decisive part when it came to securing a wife's support.[238] Even though it was usually the wife who interceded for her husband or her sister, it sometimes happened that other relatives pleaded for their loved ones, or that 'other members of the peasantry present at the local court' expressed their views regarding the good conduct of the accused persons.

There are examples of support given by relatives or neighbours in all relationship categories, even when the relationship concerned full blood ties. Marit Bengtsdotter, who was thirty years old and lived in her sister's household, was frequently interrogated after having given birth to an illegitimate child. Finally she 'tearfully' admitted that her sister's son Måns, who was now abroad, was the child's father. Both her sister and Måns's wife rallied to her support in spite of the close blood relationship. They expressed sympathy for Marit's misfortune and emphasised her imperfect knowledge of Scripture. The proceedings dragged on, but eventually Marit was reprieved to a birching after two and a half years in prison.[239]

Several seemingly voluntary relationships were given the support of the people around the culprits, regardless of their family relationships. This also pertained to relationship categories that crossed generational boundaries (e.g., *stepfather/stepdaughter*), although these may be said to have challenged the social order to a particularly high degree.[240] Married men were frequently supported by the people around them, even if they were guilty of both adultery and crimes of incest; conversely, unmarried men and women had fewer people around them who pleaded for them. Furthermore, there was a tendency for young people to receive more support from the people around them than did older people. Regardless of the family-relationship category, women who had been subjected to violence or coercion of some kind were often supported by the people around them, the blame in these cases being placed on the men.[241] In cases

238 Telste 1993, pp. 169–72; Lindstedt Cronberg 1997, p. 113. Both authors also speak about the loss of honour that befell a household when the man was convicted of adultery. In my material, there were only two cases where the wife expressly refused to plead for her husband. GHA, BIIA:4, 1695, no. 41; GHA, BIIA:16, 1706, no. 63.

239 GHA, BIIA:17, 1707, no. 1.

240 See, e.g., GHA, BIIA:9, 1699, no. 119; Lister Hundred, AIb:1, 1703, 15 April; GHA, BIIA:123, 1704, no. 123; GHA, BIIA:21, 1711, no. 202.

241 See, e.g., GHA, BIIA:11, 1701, no. 10; GHA, BIIA:15, 1705, no. 136.

where there are no notes regarding violence and exploitation, the support was distributed relatively equally between men and women.

All in all, support seems to have been less affected by family position than by who had committed the crime, what social network the person in question belonged to, and whether or not participation in the relationship had been voluntary.

Actively challenging the legal standards

In a few cases, the official legal standards were actively questioned in connection with the proceedings at the local court. When Arvid Månsson (forty-six years old) and his *half-sister's daughter* Elin Andersdotter (forty-two years old) were convicted of incest in October 1712, they protested vociferously. They did admit to having had sexual relations, but they claimed not to have understood that their sin was so great that they risked being sentenced to death. They argued that the crime was no greater than when 'unrelated folk' committed it. In other words, they protested against the idea that their family relationship aggravated the crime. The couple felt that the punishment should adhere to the penalty scale for adultery, which in practice meant a fine. Arvid's wife (sixty years old) supported her husband. She begged for his life and claimed that she and their four children would not be able to support themselves if they lost him.[242]

In another case Kirstin Olufsdotter, who had been guilty of incest with her *sister's husband* eight years before, claimed that at the time of the crime she had not realised that it was such a grave offence.[243] A similar argument was presented by Jon Larsson and his *wife's half-sister* Karin Jönsdotter when they were prosecuted for incest. They had not expected that their act could lead to a death sentence, because Karin was only the *half*-sister of Jon's wife. The couple was supported by their family and by the local farmers.[244]

In all those cases, it was the penalty scale that these people opposed. They recognised that the sexual act was an offence, but they equated it with adultery rather than with a capital crime. On the basis of the judicial decisions in all incest cases from this period, their opinions appear to have been shared by at least some lawyers,

242 GHA, BIIA:22, 1712, 9 October, no. 155.
243 Bråbo Hundred, AIa:4, 1701, 1 August.
244 The same case is mentioned in the preface to this book. Kåkind Hundred, AIa:38, 1702, 23 June.

because similar relationship categories (*half-niece*, *wife's sister*) led to a reprieve in exceptional cases.[245] But openly opposing the right of the authorities to judge was rarely productive. All the individuals in the above-mentioned cases were sentenced to death.[246]

The court of appeal thus defended the right of its members to interpret the crimes according to their own views. In connection with internal discussions about legislation or when assessing individual crimes of incest, the lawyers might disagree; but publicly they put up a united front. This becomes especially clear in a case regarding a man and his *wife's sister*. Even though the crime of incest in this case had been confessed to and proven in full, the hundred court in their official letter to the court of appeal suggested that the prosecuted individuals should be reprieved from capital punishment and instead be sentenced to a fine or corporal punishment. As mitigating circumstances, the court stated that the couple, together with the man's wife/the woman's sister, humbly begged for mercy. Here the court of appeal reacted forcefully. Having pointed out that the case was aggravated by the fact that the couple had previously run away together, the court unhesitatingly condemned them to death. In addition, the court of appeal dispatched a stern reprimand to the hundred-court judge who had, in the higher court's opinion, seriously overstepped his authority. He had consciously opposed 'God's and secular law', 'royal ordinances and official decrees', as well as 'ancient practice' and 'precedents'. The right to mitigate lay only with the Crown and the court of appeal, and the latter exhorted the high-court judge to refrain from 'such presumptuous arbitrations' in future.[247]

In summary, the official legal standards encountered both direct and indirect challenges in connection with the exposure of crimes of incest. In the trial processes that followed and in the judgements of the accused, the authorities attempted to re-establish the official legal standards. For this reason, the trials may be described as negotiations concerning the prevailing legal standards between the

245 Examples of pardons: GHA, BIIA:4, 1695, 19 December, no. 103; GHA, BIIA:3, 1694, 3 February, no. 1; GHA, BIIA:3, 1694, 16 May, no. 11; GHA, BIIA:9, 1699, 27 November, no. 130; GHA, BIIA:14, 1704, 10 February, no. 4.

246 GHA, BIIA:22, 1712, 9 October, no. 155; GHA, BIIA:11, 1701, 7 October, no. 93; GHA, BIIA:12, 1702, 15 October, 29/11, no. 96.

247 GHA BIIA:6, 1696, 21 March, no. 35. The hundred-court judge defended himself in a letter by claiming that the text in the Bible was vague and by pointing to similar cases where criminals had been reprieved.

authorities and the local community. There is no doubt that local control contributed to several crimes being brought to public knowledge, often in connection with the woman becoming pregnant. But although the norms of morality received a certain degree of support from the peasantry, and despite the prevalence of the idea of God's collective punishments, the analysis shows that there was scope for people to interpret relationships in dissimilar ways. Depending on the interpretations made, people from the local community could reinforce the official norms, for instance by reporting crimes; but they could also challenge the judicial system through various forms of resistance.

In preparation for the Civil Code of 1734

At the beginning of the eighteenth century, a comprehensive revision of Swedish legislation was undertaken, resulting in a new statute book in 1734. New laws are often made as a subsequent codification of the norms and values produced in society, and there is much to suggest that this was the case when the rules regarding the prohibited degrees were established in connection with the introduction of the new code.[248]

On the basis of the dispensation material, relationships in the second affinity degree (*wife's cousin*, *wife's brother's widow*, *wife's stepmother*) seem to have balanced on the boundary between what was permitted and what was forbidden. These relationships were a cause for concern for the members of the cathedral chapter, which is indicated by the fact that the assessments of the applications were not quite consistent. In 1727, the prohibition against marriages in relationships in the second collateral affinity degree (*wife's cousin*) was abolished, which confirms that the status of these relationships had been renegotiated.[249] However, the prohibition against lineal affinity relationships in the second degree (*wife's stepmother*) remained.[250]

---

248 The new code was passed by the Swedish Parliament in 1734 but did not come into force until 1736.

249 K.B., 1727, 3 March.

250 The prohibition against lineal degrees was established in a resolution in 1703: K.R. 1703, 2 December. For examples of compliance with this law, see, e.g., K.B. 1738, 15 February, where a man is denied permission to marry his *wife's stepdaughter*. See also the survey and explanation of the Marriage Code by Professor David Nehrman in Nehrman 1729, pp. 173–87.

The judgement-book material has shown that around the turn of the century in 1700, it was general practice to reduce the death penalty for diagonal affinity relationships (*wife's niece*). In addition, there was a tendency to reduce the punishment for horizontal affinity relationships (*wife's sister*, *brother's widow*) in exceptional cases, in particular when there were mitigating circumstances. Just before the drafting of the Civil Code of 1734, the penalty scale for precisely these relationships was the subject of animated debate. Draft bills of 1713 and 1723 had recommended the death penalty for all parties involved.[251] The minutes of the Law Commission of 1728 noted that all of the members agreed that the punishment for incest between a brother-in-law and a sister-in-law was too harsh, and that judges had sentenced such criminals to death 'with trepidation'.[252] In 1729 and 1731, it was proposed that sexual intercourse with a *wife's sister* and a *wife's niece* should only lead to a fine, imprisonment, or corporal punishment. This was subsequently established in the Civil Code of 1734.[253] Before the Code was printed, there had been a heated discussion between the clerical estate, who forcefully recommended that the death penalty should be retained, and the other estates. The issue had eventually been settled by way of a vote.[254]

Here all indications suggest that the new law was an adaptation to legal opinions among the general public. The death penalty was felt to be too severe in relation to the crime by both the peasantry and the lawyers, and an adjustment was thought to be necessary. After the Civil Code of 1734, crimes of incest between a man and his *wife's sister* were punished with forty pairs of rods for the man and thirty pairs of birch rods for the woman, or by one month in prison for each of them. Diagonal relationships were primarily punished by way of a fine. If the accused had no financial assets, the punishment could be replaced by one month's imprisonment on bread and water. The prison sentence should also be seen as a corporal punishment. One month on the meagre prison diet was quite simply what a healthy person was assumed to be capable of

251 *Förarbeten till Sveriges Rikes Lag 1686–1736*, v, p. 371. *Förarbeten till Sveriges Rikes Lag 1686–1736*, iv, p. 365.

252 *Förarbeten till Sveriges Rikes Lag 1686–1736*, iii, p. 309.

253 *Förarbetena till Sveriges Rikes Lag 1686–1736*, iv, pp. 402, 440; the Civil Code of 1734, the Misdeeds Code, Chapter 59, Sections 1–8.

254 *Lag-Commissionens förslag till Sweriges Rikes Lag af år 1734*, p. 161.

enduring without dying.[255] If neither party was married, the punishments were somewhat reduced.[256]

The international debate regarding incest prohibitions was going on all the time. In the 1710s, there was a rancorous debate between Danish lawyer and historian Andreas Hojer and Norwegian dramatist and historian Ludvig Holberg about the regulation of the prohibited degrees. In a text from 1718, Hojer claimed that the incest prohibitions did *not* have the support of either the Bible or natural law. Instead, he regarded them as human inventions derived from the Jewish tradition. True, he shared the idea that the prohibitions prevented undesirable and licentious living, which benefited both society and single individuals and families; however, he maintained that the law was not based on divine justice – it was merely a part of civil legislation. To Hojer, the revulsion and shame that most people felt with respect to the prohibited relationships were a consequence of upbringing and habit.[257] Hojer's views were radical for his time and encountered fierce resistance.

In a written rejoinder published in 1719, Holberg argued that the incest prohibitions had both natural and religious foundations. Among other things, he claimed that relationships between closely related individuals were contrary to both natural law and common sense.[258] It was not only Holberg who reacted to Hojer's claim regarding the origin of incest provisions. The text caused a commotion among theologians both within and outside the borders of Denmark–Norway. Hojer himself dropped this contentious issue, but his contribution appears to have functioned as a germ for further discussions in Denmark.[259] These discussions, which became particularly lively in the 1730s, aimed at clarifying whether the incest prohibitions were actually based on so-called *natural law*, which maintained God's order, or if they were solely to be regarded as secular rules rooted in an older Jewish society. The answer to this question determined whether or not a secular king or court had the right to change the legislative framework. However, there was no question of changing the practical treatment of crimes of incest; and during

255 Inger 2011, p. 148.

256 For the man thirty-two pairs of rods, for the woman twenty-four pairs of birch rods, or twenty-four days in prison. The Civil Code of 1734, the Misdeeds Code, Chapter 59, Sections 6–8.

257 Holberg 1974, pp. 72f. Spang-Hanssen 1963, pp. 21f.

258 Holberg 1974, pp. 81f.

259 Krogh 2000, p. 189.

the decades surrounding the turn of the century in 1700, it was considerably more customary for debaters to discuss *where* the limits should be drawn between what was permitted and what was forbidden than to question the very existence, or the origin, of the prohibitions.[260]

Partial summary and overview, 1680–1750

Around the turn of the century in 1700, Swedish society was permeated by religious ideas. The incest prohibitions were described in Leviticus in the Bible which had, by way of its addition to the national law code in 1608, been made the norm for Swedish legislation. The crime of incest was primarily perceived as an offence against God's law, a crime which could not be atoned for in any other way than by death. Previous research has shown that the penal legislation was made more stringent in all Protestant countries in connection with the Reformation, but the Nordic countries stood out as especially severe when it came to punishing those who had committed crimes of incest. During the final decades of the seventeenth century, penal practice was mitigated somewhat in Denmark–Norway and in Iceland; but in Sweden judges continued to rule according to the letter of the Bible for some additional decades.

Although the regulatory frameworks were very strict, there was a certain scope for independent interpretation in individual cases, which points to the capacity of an agent to act within the framework of the structure. Both crimes of incest that were discovered and applications for dispensation challenged the official legal standards; and in the practical handling of these cases, a pattern of cultural values appears which came to influence people's attitudes regarding these matters.

In the Swedish material, it is above all ideas surrounding kinship and family relationships that have affected the assessments made in individual cases. The hierarchy within the family, and in particular the parent–child respect, was indirectly defended by horizontal relationships being treated more leniently than vertical ones. In the applications for dispensation as well as in the criminal-case material, the relationships were always defined on the basis of the *family position* held by the individuals in question – not on the basis of their *ages*. The age relationship between a man and a woman was very rarely stated, which suggests that this information was not

260 Krogh 2000, p. 168.

thought to be an important factor when decisions were made in individual cases.

Views on love and passion also had consequences for how different incest cases were handled in practice. Although the majority of incest relationships appear to have been reciprocal in nature, they were rarely described in terms of love. This goes for both applications for dispensation and criminal cases. Love and tenderness were not thought to be legitimate arguments either when individuals wanted to circumvent the prohibitions and enter into marriage or when people wished to excuse a crime that had been committed. Love was perceived as a strong but potentially dangerous force which risked leading people astray unless subjected to control. The fact that extramarital love was encumbered with such unfavourable connotations lessened the chance of obtaining a reprieve and contributed indirectly to stricter assessments. The values mentioned above were not always actively articulated in the proceedings, but their effect stands out in the material.

The uncertainty that prevailed among Swedish theologians and lawyers with respect to drawing boundaries and creating reasonable penal consequences for crimes of incest had their equivalents on the European continent. The formulation of the Biblical prohibitions in relation to religious circumstances, ideas about natural law, and local customs were debated everywhere.[261]

In Holland, crimes of incest were handled at the regional level because of the lack of uniform national legislation. In general, incest was considered a serious crime with harsh punishments; but as was the case in Sweden, Dutch courts tended to reduce the punishment for women who had been forced to participate in sexual acts.[262] Prussian laws were similar to the Nordic legislation, but differed in that prohibitions against relationships in the second collateral affinity degree (*wife's sister*, *brother's widow*) and diagonal affinity relationships (*wife's aunt*, *wife's niece*) were considered to be secular matters. People who violated these prohibitions were thus punished less harshly; they might even, after an application for dispensation, be allowed to marry. After 1740, the prohibition against marriages between a brother-in-law and a sister-in-law was abolished by

261 Jarzebowski 2006, pp. 68f; Rublack 1999, p. 258; Denbo 2001, Chapter 3; Chammas 2011, p. 39; Egmond 2001, p. 24; Hehenberger 2003, pp. 197–201.

262 Egmond 2001, p. 24.

10 For centuries, regular church attendance was an important feature in the lives of Swedes.

Frederick II.[263] In Austria, only lineal consanguinity relationships were punished by death.[264] In France, incest in the closest degrees was also punished by death; but the application of the law varied significantly, depending on who had committed the crime. The higher the social rank, the lower the risk of being prosecuted – a circumstance that came in for criticism, for example in contemporaneous literature. Eventually, capital punishment was replaced by banishment.[265] The situation in England differed from that in other Protestant countries in that the handling of crimes of incest was the responsibility of ecclesiastical courts even after the Reformation. Consequently, the penalty scale was dominated by fines in the same way as it had been during the Roman Catholic era.[266]

All this research shows that consanguinity relationships were regarded as more heinous than affinity relationships, even though they were placed on an equal footing in the religious texts that formed the basis for all contemporary legislation. It is also obvious that vertical relationships were more severely punished than horizontal ones.

263 Jarzebowski 2012, p. 11.
264 Hehenberger 2003, p. 192.
265 Chammas 2011, p. 25.
266 Denbo 2001, p. 50.

3
Incest: a moral crime, 1750–1840

In the Age of Enlightenment

In comparison to many other European countries, eighteenth-century Sweden had a society that was highly homogeneous from economic, social, and religious points of view. This older authoritarian and patriarchal social order was to a great extent founded on various collectively held ideas about responsibilities and obligations. Towards the end of the century, however, the old order was challenged by new ideological impulses. Protestant orthodoxy encountered competition from religious movements such as pietistic and Moravian revivalist movements, where the individual was given greater responsibility for his or her religiosity and moral positions. At the same time, the image of God conveyed by the clergy and the authorities changed. In earlier times, God had usually been portrayed in an intimidating manner. His commandments had to be obeyed so that people were not struck by his wrath and vengeance. Now God's loving and forgiving traits were increasingly emphasised. Various forms of liberalism were also challenging forces in society. From an economic perspective, free-market competition was promoted above the prevailing system which consisted of guilds, privileges, and decisions made by authorities – decisions which limited an individual's freedom of choice. Simultaneously, demands for greater personal freedom and equal rights were voiced at all levels in society.[1]

The tendencies towards increased individualisation were supported by, among other things, the philosophical ideas of the Enlightenment being disseminated on the Continent. As in earlier times, social

1 For the general transformation of society, and for religious and liberal challenges, see, e.g., Jarlert 2001, pp. 126–8; Sundin 1982, pp. 50–2. For the altered image of God, see Malmstedt 1994, pp. 178–81, 187, 191, 204f.

order and balance were perceived as necessary factors for the welfare of the country; but the threat to this order had shifted. The dichotomy of God vs. Satan had been toned down to the advantage of the oppositional binary enlightenment–superstition. In other words, threats to society mainly consisted of things that were perceived as superstition, ignorance, or falsehood. Especially among educated social groups, reason and enlightenment were valorised while magic and superstition were described as remnants of a Catholic world-view, whose false and dishonest ideology lived on among common folk.[2]

The development of jurisprudence

European jurisprudence was also influenced by philosophical currents bearing Enlightenment ideas. The justice system was criticised for being arbitrary and for abusing individuals, for instance by using corporal punishment, which was considered both brutal and degrading. Demands were made for increased justice and more humane and predictable punishments. In addition, the punishments were to rest on secular rather than religious foundations. Critics demanded completely new ranges of punishment that were reasonably proportionate to the offences, and they insisted that all criminals should be sentenced in the same way for the same crimes. At the same time, fewer voices were raised in defence of the *principle of retaliation* (punishment with the aim of exerting revenge against the offender). As before, it was believed that the most important purpose of punishment was to *deter* people from committing crimes; but it was now claimed that this purpose could be equally successfully achieved by means of long prison sentences as by brief corporal punishments.[3]

Several of the liberalising and humanising tendencies can be derived from a novel interpretation of natural law and from changing attitudes to religion. In the past, the construction of society had been regarded as an expression of the divine order. In consequence, several crimes were defined as crimes against God himself; therefore, they had to be atoned for in accordance with the principle of retaliation. The new theories of natural law were based on a more rational conception of the construction of the state, which inspired a new view on punishment. It was no longer believed to be God's retribution

2 Oja 1999, pp. 42, 82, 110f, 168, 250.
3 Häthén 1990, pp. 39–41.

enforced by the authorities, but rather the authorities' means for preserving the social order. The purpose of punishment was hence conceived of in terms of its social usefulness. A person's duties to society and to his or her fellow human beings – duties exalted by, among others, the philosopher Samuel Pufendorf a hundred years earlier – increasingly developed into demands for human rights and individual freedoms. In theory, the new ideas had been discussed since the end of the seventeenth century; but the practical consequences in the administration of justice were not implemented until the second half of the eighteenth century and may be seen as a consequence of the impact of the Enlightenment.[4]

In Sweden, Enlightenment ideas were not particularly influential at first, even though the Swedish King Gustav III, who had come into contact with the philosophical ideas of the French Enlightenment in his youth, made a few attempts at reform in the 1770s. Among other things, he forbade torture in connection with interrogations and attempted to abolish the death penalty for incest crimes. However, this proposal met with fierce resistance from the estates of the realm with the justification that the crime was in opposition to God's law.[5] Thus, the death penalty remained in force until 1864 for the closest relationships in both consanguinity and affinity degrees. In practice, though, most people were reprieved from the death penalty.[6] Exactly when this milder practice was introduced is uncertain; but it is likely that Swedish case law followed – with a delay of a few decades – developments in Denmark and Norway, which would mean that the number of death sentences was reduced from the middle of the century onwards.[7] Although the legislation remained unchanged, the number of death sentences carried out hence declined towards the end of the century, which suggests that Swedish lawyers had been influenced by the European legal debate.

---

4 Häthén 1990, pp. 39–41; Lindberg 1976, p. 176.

5 Inger 2011, p. 199; Häthén 1990, pp. 148f.

6 According to the calculations of Swedish jurist Knut Olivecrona (1817–1902), no more than fifty-eight people were executed for incest in Sweden as a whole during the second half of the eighteenth century; Olivecrona 1866, pp. 51–90. The cases relating to incest have been compiled in Appendix Table 5.

7 Jónsson 1998, pp. 8f. No systematic examinations have been made of the period 1716–83. Nevertheless, a few random samples show that reductions to a month's imprisonment were made as early as the 1760s. GHA, BIIA:66, 1760, no. 61; GHA, BIIA:66, 1760, no. 88.

Except for the fact that incest criminals who had been sentenced to death were often reprieved towards the end of the eighteenth century, Swedish jurisprudence had hardly changed at all since the Civil Code of 1734. In contrast, more happened after the turn of the century in 1800. New ideas, primarily from German jurisprudence, gained a foothold in the Swedish debate as well. Conservative positions, which promoted the idea of retaliation, were confronted by fresh notions about punishment functioning as a *means* for achieving something else. There were discussions over whether the primary purpose of the punishment was to *deter from* or *prevent* crime. At the same time, new goals to do with trying to improve criminals and reintegrate them into society instead of punishing them were articulated; but these theories did not prevail in the Swedish debate until the later part of the nineteenth century.[8]

The decades around the turn of the century in 1800 were thus characterised by gradually changing attitudes to crime and punishment and by step-by-step reforms within the Swedish judicial system. This was also a period when legislation concerning the prohibited degrees began to be questioned to an ever greater extent, in everyday practice as well as in official debates. That is the topic of this chapter.

Applications for dispensation

An increase in the number of applications for marriage

During the whole of the eighteenth century, there were applications for dispensation from individuals who wished to marry in spite of being related to one another within the prohibited degrees; but towards the end of the century there was a dramatic increase in the number of applications received by the Judiciary Inspection. From a handful of cases per year at the beginning of the eighteenth century, the number rose to 200–300 applications per year around 1800.[9] See Graph 1.

Judging by the names and titles of the applicants, there were representatives from all social strata among them. Even so, the higher or middling social groups were overrepresented, considering that they only made up a small fraction (less than 5%) of the total

8 Häthén 1990, pp. 19, 148–56.

9 For more detailed information about which relationship categories the applications concerned, see Appendix Table 1.

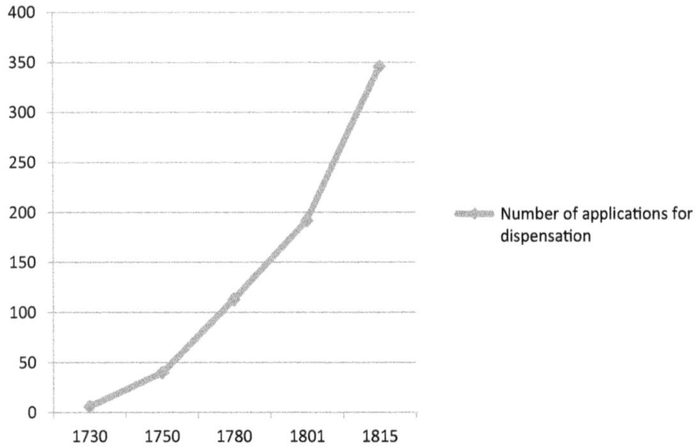

Graph 1. Applications for dispensation directed to the Judiciary Inspection, 1730–1815. Source: The diaries of the Judiciary Inspection for the years in question.

population.[10] Some of the titles mentioned are *captain*, *preacher*, *lieutenant*, *major*, *knight*, *county sheriff*, *sergeant*, *parish constable*, *shipmaster*, *count*, *merchant*, and *public prosecutor*. The female parties were in these cases given titles such as *miss*, *maid*, or *baroness*. Male applicants from the lower social strata were called *servant* or *farmhand*. In addition, there are titles such as *labourer*, *manservant*, *innkeeper*, *perpetual curate*, and *journeyman shoemaker* in the material. In such cases the female parties were usually entitled *maidservant* or possibly, in relevant cases, *widow* or *wife* (meaning 'former wife, now widow'). Applications were thus received from all social groups, and consequently the material may to some extent be said to reflect society at large.

10 In 1750, cousin marriages accounted for 3.5% of the marriages of the Swedish aristocracy. Within the nobility alone, the proportion of cousin marriages was over 13%. These figures can be compared with the figures for the population as a whole, which were at 0.3% during the same period; Alström 1958, p. 336. In my material, which has been collected randomly, the more exalted titles make up around half of all the titles. However, approximately every fifth application does not include a title. For the proportion of nobles, clergymen, and high-ranking commoners (*ofrälse ståndspersoner*) in the total population, see Carlsson 1977, p. 18.

As was mentioned earlier, the number of applications for dispensation rose during the whole of the eighteenth century – at first on a modest scale and then at an increasing rate – and it continued to rise during the nineteenth century. In 1845, the prohibition against cousin marriages was abolished, and in 1872 several of the affinity relationships were liberalised. The number of applications then decreased again as a natural consequence of the legal changes. Information about these relationships thus disappears from judgement books and application documents; but other research shows that the existence of, among other things, cousin marriages continued to increase even after the prohibition had been abolished.[11] During the same period, the relationship categories involved in applications for marriage shifted from the second and more distant degrees (e.g., *wife's cousin*) to the first collateral degree (e.g., *wife's sister*). Applications where the parties stood in a directly vertical relationship to each other (e.g., *stepdaughter*) were rare, however.[12]

How is this striking change to be understood? What prompted people to seek out these marriage alliances to a greater extent than before? During the greater part of the century, the increase occurred without any change in the law being implemented or even discussed; this indicates that the pressure for a liberalisation of the rules came from below, from the people. The change can be interpreted in several ways. There are, for instance, demographic explanatory models that foreground the connection between the significant population increase during the second half of the nineteenth century and the increasing number of marriages between individuals who were related. Families became larger when child mortality decreased, whereupon the number of presumptive marriage partners within the family increased. When birth numbers declined in the early twentieth century, the market for these marriages also slumped.[13] But the increase in the number of applications for dispensation began even before the commencement of the significant population increase, and there are no proportional connections between this and the number of applications for dispensation, which suggests

11 Cousin marriages seem to have been slightly more common in northern Sweden, where the population density was lower. Egerbladh and Bittles 2011, p. 414.

12 See Appendix Table 1.

13 Egerbladh and Bittles 2011, p. 415.

that the development had other driving forces as well.[14] For instance, ideas surrounding kin and family and the difference between vertical and horizontal relationships appear to have had a decisive influence on developments. These ideas in their turn interacted with economic and cultural changes in society that occurred in Sweden and also in Europe.

Economic and cultural transformations in society

As was pointed out above, it is difficult to draw any reliable conclusions about the cause of the substantial increase in the number of applications for dispensation, and it is likely that the process was influenced by several factors. It must, however, be noted that the development in Sweden was not an isolated occurrence but a part of a general trend across the whole of Europe. There was an increase in the number of marriages between persons related by blood and by marriage in several places. The anthology *Kinship in Europe* demonstrates – with examples drawn from among other countries France, Germany, Switzerland, and Hungary – that the function of the extended family changed during the period in question. Before the eighteenth century, *vertical* family relationships were foundational, because it was possible to claim a right to land or an office by dint of one's origins and ancestry; but from the mid-eighteenth century onwards, there was growing emphasis on *horizontal* networks and contacts. The economic conditions changed, and it was not as easy as before to claim the right to an estate or an office on the basis of one's lineage. Landed property and the titles of one's parents mattered less at a time when the privileges of the nobility were challenged by a new bourgeoisie with significant spending power. As capital became more mobile in society, professional competence and social contacts became more important than formal descent in the competition for economic and political positions. This can be traced in many ways: the choice of godparents and baptismal names; the persons an individual did business with or allied him- or herself with in a political context; but perhaps above all the person whom

14 Between 1720 and 1750, the Swedish population increased by about 15% while the number of applications for dispensation between 1730 and 1750 increased by more than 500%. In 1750–1800, the population increased by over 32%. During the same period, the applications for dispensation increased by almost 500%. Compare the population statistics in Hofsten 2001, p. 15, to Appendix Table 1.

an individual would choose to marry. Historian David Warren Sabean, who has made his own detailed studies of the development of kinship patterns in a German province between 1700 and 1870, has also collected material from several other European studies. The result is persuasive. Regardless of whether one follows kinship patterns between biological relatives (*cousins*, *second cousins*, *third cousins*) or relatives through marriage (*wife's cousin*, *wife's sister*, *two siblings marrying two other siblings*, etc.), a common developmental trend becomes visible. From the middle of the eighteenth century onwards, the number of matrimonial unions within people's own kinship groups steadily increased in all social groups. Between the final decades of the nineteenth century and the First World War the trend reached its peak, and after 1920 the numbers decreased again.[15] From the mid-eighteenth century onwards, more and more people thus chose their marriage partners from among their own immediate peers (*endogamous marriage pattern*).[16]

The new marriage pattern coincides with a change in the concept of love. After all, it was during the late eighteenth century that love matches began to be idealised. From this period, emotions and personal taste were assigned greater importance for marriage, and love was increasingly often described as a *heartfelt friendship*. The emotional bonds and familial nearness emphasised within the biological family, and especially among siblings, were simultaneously extended to include, for instance, school friends, business partners, and relatives by marriage. It became common for two business partners or childhood friends to call each other *brother*, and for brothers-in-law and sisters-in-law to call each other *brother* and *sister*. The difference between siblings and spouses decreased.[17] This general upgrading of sibling love can also be observed in the literature of the time.[18] The change primarily took place in the propertied

15 The various studies represent Northern, Central, and Southern Europe and include both Protestant and Catholic areas. Sabean 1998, pp. 428–48.

16 Sabean, Teuscher, and Mathieu 2007b, pp. 187f. See also Johnson and Sabean 2011. Similar research results with respect to Britain can be studied in Davidoff and Hall 1987, pp. 215–25; Davidoff, Doolittle, Fink, and Holden 1999, pp. 60, 77; Kuper 2009, pp. 24–8, 243.

17 Sabean, Teuscher, and Mathieu 2007b, p. 188; Johnson 2011, pp. 192f; Sabean 2001b, pp. 233–5; Davidoff and Hall 1987, p. 200; Davidoff, Doolittle, Fink, and Holden 1999, pp. 60, 77.

18 Johnson 2011, pp. 189f and the literature referred to therein; Corbett 2008; Hunt 1992, pp. 21–36; von Braun 1989, p. 105.

groups in society and seems to have been analogous in both Catholic and Protestant regions all over Europe.[19] Passionate love, which had previously been perceived as a dangerous disease or the call of the Devil, was still encumbered with unfavourable connotations. The sudden flare of emotion could not be trusted in the long run. Instead, the image of a deep and mutual friendship between spouses was idealised.[20]

In research, it is emphasised that women played a central role in the new horizontal networks. It was often women who, through their correspondence, visits, parties, and discussion groups, established and maintained valuable contacts in a family's social network. Swiss historian Elisabeth Joris also describes how women's right of inheritance and capital could become a pawn in men's political and economic activities. Mothers, wives, sisters, aunts, and sisters-in-law were expected to support male relatives by investing their capital in the men's businesses, often without any official partial ownership or written documentation regarding the right to potential profits.[21]

Developments in Sweden appear to have adhered to the processes seen in Europe to a considerable degree. Conditions for the transfer of property changed during the eighteenth and nineteenth centuries. Birthright, which regulated the rights of relatives to purchase land before strangers were allowed an opportunity to do so, decreased in importance as the number of relatives who had the right of priority was reduced. Instead, the right of ownership and the right of inheritance were strengthened, and it became easier to buy and sell land. In 1809, the aristocracy's monopoly on land was abolished completely, and one upshot was that it became possible to sell land previously owned by the aristocracy to commoners. Taxes were fixed; but there was at the same time a certain degree of inflation, and that gave farmers a surplus from production which could be invested.[22] As the mobility of capital increased in this way, people's attitude to women's resources changed as well.

Historian Maria Sjöberg, who has studied circumstances regarding property in relation to regulations concerning marriage and

---

19 Sabean 2011b, p. 222; Mathieu 2007; Bittles 2012, pp. 17f.

20 Luhmann 2003, pp. 118–20; von Braun 1989, pp. 85–7.

21 Joris 2007, pp. 242–50. The role of women in horizontal networks has also been highlighted after studies of French and English material. Davidson 2012; Davidoff and Hall 1987, pp. 276–81.

22 Winberg 1985, pp. 2–4, 149f, 200. On the significance of birthright and its deregulation, see Ågren 1997, pp. 250–61.

inheritance in a Swedish context, emphasises how economic, cultural, and social conditions interacted, gender roles being a factor that periodically had a decisive significance for circumstances regarding property. A woman's property was *under the control* of her male relatives; it was thus her father, brother, or husband who had the mandate to manage her property. In the earlier agrarian society, the influence of biological relatives over a woman's property was comparatively great in comparison to that of her husband; but when the capital market became more flexible, the balance shifted in a way that benefited the husband. When women were given equal rights of inheritance in 1845, it was primarily their husbands who profited from the reform, because it was husbands who were in control of women's property. Through the reform, it became easier for men in the peasant and burgher estates to acquire lands previously belonging to the aristocracy via strategic marriages; and in research it has been suggested that the entire reform may in fact be seen as a result of men's competition among themselves over resources, rather than a morally inspired striving for social equality. The competition among men may partly have played out between the classes; but, as Sjöberg points out, kinship has been of great significance, too. The fathers, brothers, and husbands of the women in one and the same social group had different interests with respect to women's property, and the right of disposal of this property increasingly favoured the interests of husbands, as did the legislation.[23]

A father's power over his daughter decreased, while a husband's influence over his wife remained the same. To be sure, unmarried women became free to invest their capital wherever they wanted; but they were expected to support their male relatives, especially when living in their households. In other words, the capital-owning woman's opportunities were limited, and her capacity for supporting herself was mediated through her male relatives.[24] In this context, it was not uncommon for a man to be in control of the resources of both his wife and her unmarried sister. Nor was this development, according to Joris, restricted to the higher social groups or to economic circumstances. Unmarried women were also expected to support their families by doing household work, caring for elderly relatives, looking after children, or doing needlework in the household

23 Sjöberg 2001, pp. 157–9, 171–3, 177f. See also Taussi Sjöberg 1994.
24 Göransson 1990, p. 529.

where they had board and lodging. At all levels, women's unpaid labour made up a kind of social safety net for the rest of the family.[25]

In summary, we may speak of a cultural change where a woman's loyalty was shifted from her biological family to the family she married into; where the father's structural influence decreased while the husband's was maintained or strengthened; where knowledge, contacts, and social networks became more important for a man's career than lineage; and where sibling love and sibling loyalty flourished both as an idea and in terms of concrete action. It would also be possible to describe this change as a shift in emphasis from vertical family connections to horizontal ones. The increase in applications for marriage in the prohibited degrees that took place towards the end of the eighteenth century, primarily involving horizontal or diagonal kinship connections, may, according to this line of reasoning, be at least partially linked to a change in the economic conditions in society – conditions that either led to or were affected by new cultural patterns. In this context it is difficult to say which came first, the egg or the chicken. There is likely to have been an interaction of cultural and economic factors.

What attitudes did people in power in Sweden have to these issues, and how did they react to the pressures that were brought to bear? It had long been comparatively easy for cousins to have their application for dispensation approved; but around the turn of the century in 1800 increasing numbers of applications were submitted concerning other relationship categories as well, for instance from men who wanted to marry a *niece*, a *wife's sister*, a *brother's widow*, or an *uncle's widow*. How did decision-makers respond to these new tendencies which indirectly challenged the boundaries drawn up between permitted and prohibited marriage relationships?

The applicants' arguments

Pure and Christian love

At the beginning of the eighteenth century, applications for dispensation had been relatively brief and to the point. Around the turn of the century in 1800, they became longer and more detailed. An increasing number of arguments were invoked in order to have an application approved, practical as well as emotional ones. In all cases, it was in one way or another emphasised that the relationship

25 Joris 2007, pp. 239, 248–50.

in question was based on a *pure* or *Christian* love and that the applicants were of *good repute* and *virtuous conduct*. In order to draw attention to each other's praiseworthy characteristics, the man and the woman sometimes each wrote a portion of the application. In this way they were able to stress each other's positive qualities, such as industriousness or piety, estimable behaviour or loyalty, and tender feelings towards the children in the family. In addition, the couple's good conduct was usually certified in a separate testimonial from a vicar.

One farmer who applied for dispensation was described as 'honest and obliging' with a 'good conduct in life' and 'free from all other connections'.[26] Another was attested to 'have good knowledge of Scripture', lead 'a Christian life', and desire his cousin, who was to be his wife, 'without any carnal commixtion, in a Christian manner'.[27] The Honourable Emanuel Stråhle and his cousin, Miss Elisabeth Stråhle, insisted that they felt an 'innocent declared love and affection' for each other and that they wished to enter into 'a sacred married connection'. In addition, they were both said always to have led a 'Christian', 'decent', and 'virtuous' life, as befitted their 'exalted lineage'.[28] One cousin couple wrote in their application that they had for several years enjoyed each other's company with 'a decent intimacy', which had grown in strength over time until it had been transformed into a 'pure and sincere love'.[29] Hans Knutsson and Pernilla Bengtsdotter wanted to have their application approved because they felt a 'pure and decent love' for each other.[30] Johannes Larsson and his cousin, maidservant Greta Johansdotter, asserted that their prospective marriage was 'founded in chastity' and had 'the purest, the most honest, yea the most justifiable intentions'.[31]

---

26 JR, BoA, 1780, 25 February, Nils Larsson, Ingrid Rasmusdotter (*cousin*).
27 JR, BoA, 1780, 17 March, Per Svensson, Anna Carlsdotter (*cousin*).
28 JR, BoA, 1780, 16 May, Emanuel Stråhle, Elisabeth Stråhle (*cousin*).
29 JR, BoA, 1801, 1 July, Johan Adolf Hedberg, Helena Sophia Hamisch (*cousin*).
30 JR, BoA, 1801, 7 October, Hans Knutsson, Pernilla Bengtsdotter (*cousin*).
31 JR, BoA, 1801, 28 October, Johannes Larsson, Greta Johansdotter (*cousin*). For additional examples of this kind, see JR, BoA, 1801, 28 October, Joseph Rautiain, Ulrika (*cousin*); JR, BoA, 1801, 13–14 May, B. N. Hanberg, Christina Elmgren (*wife's sister*); JR, BoA, 1802, 11 May, Olof Olsson, Karin Hansdotter (*wife's sister*); JR, BoA, 1801, 14 May, Olof Ersson, Maria Andersdotter (*brother's widow*), JR, BoA, 1801, 1 July, Anders Hansson, Catharina Ersdotter (*wife's niece*).

Many more examples could be provided. Irrespective of whether the applicants themselves felt that these were important circumstances, or if the argumentation was merely tactically employed in order to have the application approved, the argument of a *pure and Christian love* was frequently used in attempts to have relationships legalised. This indicates that virtue – just as in earlier periods – was an important factor for the relationship to be perceived as acceptable. Even so, the connection between virtue and love was much stronger at this time than during the early eighteenth century. The emotional bond between the applicants was highlighted again and again; but at the same time, it was emphasised that theirs was a virtuous love, not a passionate, heedless infatuation.

Individual happiness and bliss

Applications for dispensation often pointed out that the prospective marriage would lead to the applicants' *individual happiness* and *bliss*. In his official letter, Johan Adolf Hedberg stressed that his and his prospective wife's application was not at all made 'with the intention of satisfying fickle desires, but with a firm intention to seek [...] mutual bliss'.[32] Peter Brunström, too, associated the potential approval of his application with 'mutual bliss' for himself and his prospective wife.[33] Nils Berg Andersson called his application 'a plea for [his] happiness'. He expected that his and his fiancée's 'much longed-for happiness' would be great following the gracious approval of His Majesty the King.[34] One couple felt that their 'earthly bliss' would be 'made perfect' if they were allowed to marry, while another couple described how they, if their application was rejected, would be forced to 'wear sad faces and have lamentation in our hearts'.[35]

32 JR, BoA, 1801, 1 July, Johan Adolf Hedberg, Helena Sophia Hamisch (*cousin*).

33 JR, BoA 1801, 28 January, Peter Brunström, Anna Elisabeth Holmström (*wife's sister*).

34 JR, BoA, 1801, 7 October Nils Berg Andersson, Anna Maria Schultz (*cousin*).

35 JR, BoA, 1815, 24 May, Petrus Persson, Sara Jönsdotter (*wife's sister*); JR, BoA, 1801, 28 October, Johannes Larsson, Greta Johansdotter (*cousin*). See also JR, BoA, 1801, 27 April, 13 May, Johannes Håkansson, Brita Christina Jakobsdotter (*uncle's widow*); JR, BoA, 1801, 27 April, 13 May, Anders Eriksson, Maria Svensdotter (*half-uncle's widow*); JR, BoA, 1801, 4 February, Jon Månsson, Karin Månsdotter (*wife's niece*).

Individual happiness and mutual love were thus emphasised in a completely different way than previously. Margaret Darrow, who has studied applications for dispensation in southwestern France, notes a similar increase in emotional arguments from the applicants after 1770. She especially draws attention to the fact that the increased emphasis on mutual emotions between the applicants occurred both among peasants and the elite, and in the countryside as well as in towns and cities.[36] In applications for dispensation in the border region between Austria, Switzerland, and Italy the importance of mutuality, nearness, and familiarity between the presumptive spouses was similarly stressed.[37] This is also in line with research that describes the late eighteenth century as a period when emotions and love were valued. After the turn of the century in 1800, earthly happiness was valorised in a way it had not been before. Love, tenderness, and compassion were increasingly often described as Christian virtues, and happiness was something a person could hope to enjoy already during his or her earthly existence.[38] This cultural shift is clearly reflected in the material in that applicant couples argued in terms of love and happiness when attempting to have their relationships legitimised.

Practical advantages for household or family

In several cases, the applications for dispensation drew attention to a more practical perspective as well. While the applicants described their mutual friendship, affection, and respect, they also emphasised that the relationship was a mutual agreement and that they had the consent of their families. If the parties were approximately the same age, or if the solution was practical in terms of their economic situation, their household, or the composition of their family, that fact was highlighted.

The previously mentioned Peter Brunström's application may be used as an example of this practical perspective. In his letter he described how his and his prospective wife's situation would change if their marriage was to take place. Then she would 'from poor and impecunious circumstances be placed in what anybody would regard

36 Darrow 1985, pp. 268f.
37 Margareth Lanzinger also suggests that this emphasis on social hegemony may have paved the way for racist ideologies later on. Lanzinger 2015, pp. 278f, 343–7.
38 Nilsson [Hammar] 2012, pp. 152, 194.

as a better and happier situation'. As for Peter himself, he would simultaneously acquire 'secure support' in his housekeeping and help with raising his two daughters. The vicar also certified in two separate testimonials that the marriage between Peter and his prospective wife, Anna Holmström, would be especially advantageous because it would solve practical problems for both him and her. Because of his work, Peter was obliged to be away at sea for a week at a time, and during his absences he lacked help in his home. Anna had, for her part, been plunged into deep economic debt after the demise of her late husband. The social and economic problems of both would thus be alleviated if they were allowed to marry, although Peter had previously been married to Anna's now deceased sister.[39]

Another man claimed that his prospective marriage to his deceased wife's niece would not only satisfy his own wishes but also those of his mother- and father-in-law. They preferred to be looked after and cared for in their old age by their own grandchild because they then expected 'more tender treatment [...] than from a person unrelated to them'.[40] County sheriff Hanberg, who was forced to be 'continually absent' from his home because of his work, wanted to marry his *wife's sister* after his wife's death because she would, according to his estimation, be the person best suited to taking care of his son's upbringing.[41] Similar arguments were proposed by Olof Ersson and Emanuel Schagerström, who also wanted to marry their deceased *wives' sisters*.[42] The practical and economic advantages of a future marriage were also stressed by Olof Andersson, who wanted to marry his *uncle's widow*, a woman three years his senior. In connection with Olof's uncle's marriage, he had been given a homestead by his family. His widow was now unable to run the homestead on her own; and if she married an outsider, the right of ownership of the homestead might be called into question.[43]

39 JR, BoA 1801, 28 January, Peter Brunström, Anna Elisabeth Holmström (*wife's sister*).

40 JR, BoA, 1801 19 January, Nils Nilsson, Maria Johansdotter (*wife's niece*).

41 JR, BoA, 1801, 13–14 May, B.N. Hanberg, Christina Elmgren (*wife's sister*).

42 JR, BoA, 1802, 11 May, Olof Olsson, Karin Hansdotter (*wife's sister*); JR, BoA, 1790, 16 September, Emanuel Schagerström, Greta Stina Collin (*wife's sister*)

43 JR, BoA, 1790, 16 September, Olof Andersson, Britta Eriksdotter (*uncle's widow*).

All these applications embodied an implicit challenge to the officially prevailing norm. True, the existence of the prohibitions was recognised by asking for the king's permission to marry; but at the same time that action constituted a challenge to the legislative framework and to the system of norms on which it rested. The applicants obviously did not define their relationships as deviant or immoral, and they therefore tried to circumvent the legislation in order to legitimise the relationship. To strengthen their own positions, some of them referred to previous decisions where a permission to marry had been granted in opposition to the legal provisions currently in force.[44] From the perspective of the applicants, it was also considered completely reasonable to marry for practical reasons alongside the emotional ones. American historian Denise Z. Davidson, who has studied French collections of letters from the same period, claims that economic perspectives were directly interwoven with emotional ones – that is to say, a happy marriage could not be achieved if the economy was not secured.[45] Judging from the application material, Swedish couples reasoned along similar lines. A successful marriage was built on mutual respect and love *as well as* on a solid financial situation.

The argumentation of the applicants thus raised notions concerning *the right of the individual to love and happiness* in a general sense while confirming and reinforcing the idea of *pure* and *virtuous* love as a moral basis for marriage. In addition, *practical* and *economic* circumstances were highlighted in attempts to impart legitimacy to what was, at bottom, a prohibited relationship. The following section analyses the reaction of the authorities to the challenges represented by the applications.

The authorities' response

Virtuous conduct

In connection with the examination of applications for dispensation, it was repeatedly noted whether the applicants were of 'good repute' and exhibited 'virtuous conduct'; but, as in earlier periods, a couple

44 See, e.g., JR, BoA, 1774, 8 August, Friedrich Schuberts, Margaretha Liedman (*step-grandfather's widow*); JR, BoA, 1792, 24 April, Johan Assarsson, Maria Jonasdotter (*uncle's widow*); JR, BoA, 1801, 7 October, Erik Andersson, Anna Christina Jönsdotter (*wife's niece*); JR, BoA, 1801, 21 October, Adam Quist, Anna Elisabet Stark (*wife's niece*).

45 Davidson 2012.

who had had sexual intercourse could nevertheless be given permission to marry. However, practically all the couples who applied for a dispensation to marry despite having violated the norm of moral behaviour were cousins. For example, Jon Jönsson and his cousin were given permission to marry in spite of their 'premature carnality', and this happened to several other cousin couples as well.[46] Immoral conduct hence did not prevent cousins from obtaining permission to marry.

Only one application mentions premarital sexuality between applicants who were not cousins, but here the immoral conduct became decisive for the outcome. The case involved Lars Jönsson, who wanted to marry his deceased *wife's niece*, Bengta Nilsdotter. In July 1801, the Judiciary Inspection received the couple's application for marriage, where their good conduct was certified by their vicar. But in a new formal letter dated in December of the same year, the vicar distanced himself from his previous testimonial because he had discovered that Bengta was pregnant and that Lars had admitted to being the father. The couple was denied permission to marry, and the royal decision stated that the later information from the vicar regarding the couple's improper conduct had been conclusive for the decision.[47] Apparently, the combination of a challenging family relationship and unsatisfactory conduct was unacceptable.

Even though immoral conduct did not affect the authorities' decision when cousins applied for permission to marry, the failure of Lars and Bengta's application could be seen as an indication that more importance was attached to the norms of morality in cases involving relationship categories which formed greater challenges to the boundaries that prevailed at the time.

Family position before age relationship

In addition to information about virtue and conduct, the argumentation in the applications for dispensation indicates that efforts to attain individual happiness were increasingly important. Applicants

46 JR, D, 1775, 28 July, Jon Jönsson; JR, R, 1775, 22 November, Wilhelm Larsson, Marja Johansdotter (*cousin*); JR, R, 1775, 22 November, Per Kettunen, Karin (*cousin*); JR, D, 1801, 21 December, Per Larsson, Greta Nilsdotter (*cousin*). In fact, no rejections whatsoever have been found when the application involved two cousins.

47 JR, BoA, K, 1802, 12 January, Lars Jönsson, Bengta Nilsdotter (*wife's niece*).

often invoked other practical circumstances as well, but none of these arguments seem to have had a significant effect on the outcome.

Instead, the crucial factor in the decision-making process of the authorities was the *family position* of the applicants *relative to each other*. If the applicants' respective family positions entailed the crossing of a generational boundary – that is to say, if the deference between parent and child could be jeopardised – the relationship was considered dangerous to the social order. For this reason, no dispensation was given for marriages between persons whose family positions originated in two different generations (*wife's niece*, *uncle's widow*, *wife's stepmother*, etc.).

Clearly, then, great importance continued to be attributed to *filial deference*, or the hierarchical relationship between parents and children. The same principle had been mentioned as early as the end of the seventeenth century by Johan Stiernhöök in connection with legislative work. The principle was clearly indicated in the Lutheran Table of Duties, and it had significant consequences for the practical handling and assessment of dispensational cases throughout the eighteenth century. Several documents testify to this. In a royal letter from 1768, an application from a man who wanted to marry his *son-in-law's daughter* was rejected. The letter justified the rejection by stating that the woman would then 'become her stepmother's stepmother and her father's stepmother-in-law', which meant that the 'reciprocal duties incumbent on each individual would be confused, and the deference between parents and children lost'.[48] Similar arguments were used when a man was denied marriage to his *wife's stepdaughter* (1738), his *wife's half-brother's daughter* (1738), his *stepson's stepdaughter* (1744), and his *step-grandfather's widow* (1752).[49]

The relationship between generations originated in the fourth commandment in the Bible: 'Honour thy father and thy mother: that thy days may be long upon the land which the Lord thy God giveth thee.' But the hierarchical order went further than that. In addition to a person's own parents and the secular authorities, any step-parents and parents-in-law should be honoured, along with the master and mistress of a household.[50] The entire social order

48 K.B. 1768, 22 June.

49 K.B. 1738, 15 February; K. B. 1738, 16 March; K.B. 1744, 12 December; K.B.; 1752, 23 December. See also the examples in Marklund 2004, pp. 225f.

50 Odén 1991, pp. 90f.

11 The ‘Haustafel’ was a section in Luther’s Small Catechism, where the duties of the individual towards his or her fellow human beings were clarified on the basis of the person’s position in society.

rested on ideas surrounding high and low, super- and subordination. An individual's position in society was based on a number of different circumstances, such as occupation, sex, age, and civil status. Depending on the combination of these power-creating factors, expectations were formed concerning particular behaviour, both with respect to the individual in question and to the people surrounding him or her. Respecting older people, or those who held the position of a parent, had long been a well-established norm in society.[51]

The principle of filial deference was directly reflected in the matrimonial legislation. In accordance with the Civil Code of 1734, a father and his son were allowed to marry a mother and her daughter, on condition that it was the father who married the mother and the son the daughter.[52] The father could also marry the daughter or the son the mother, *but not at the same time*. If the father married the daughter while his son married the mother, the interpersonal relationships became more complicated, because individuals acquired conflicting duties vis-à-vis members of their family. This was seen as the son becoming the stepfather of his own father. From this followed that he was expected to show respect and obedience to his biological father while at the same time being expected to discipline and govern his stepson, who were one and the same person. His duties quite simply became incompatible, which is why these marriage constellations were expressly forbidden.

The same section of the law established that marriage between two brothers from one family and two sisters from another was entirely acceptable. But nothing was said about whether a father and a son from one family could marry two sisters from another. At the end of the eighteenth century, a few marriage applications of this kind were submitted to the Skara Cathedral Chapter; and although there was no formal prohibition against such relationships, the members of the cathedral chapter attempted to prevent these marriages. In answer to an application for permission to marry from a man and his *stepmother's sister*, the cathedral chapter wrote that the applicants should 'in all earnestness be dissuaded' from such a decision. When the couple stood firm, the consistory wanted to know which of the sisters was the eldest. It was considered interesting to know whether it was the younger or the elder sister who was marrying the stepson. If it had been the elder sister, the relationship would have been perceived as more problematic; but

51 Gaunt 1996, pp. 156–8; Hansen 2006, p. 23.

52 Civil Code of 1734, Marriage Code, Chapter 2, Section 8.

it so happened that it was the younger sister, and the couple were given permission to marry. But in reality the cathedral chapter did not have the authority to prevent this marriage regardless of which sister was the intended bride, a fact which the members recognised.[53] Even though there was no formal bar to these relationships, it is clear that they were perceived as improper and unsuitable by the members of the cathedral chapter, precisely because they challenged the principle of filial deference.

Johannes Håkansson (thirty-one years old) and his *uncle's widow*, Brita Christina Jakobsdotter (thirty-eight years old), were also eager to marry. They wrote in their application that they were convinced that the 'pure regard' that they felt for each other would lead to a 'happy marriage', that they felt a 'continuously increasing [...] love' for each other, and that their will to live would vanish completely if their application was rejected. In an appended letter, the local clergyman testified to their good conduct. According to his statement, the couple 'tearfully' protested their 'inextinguishable inclination towards each other'. The clergyman added that the 'small difference in age' between the applicants was far outweighed by the man's maturity.[54] In 1790, another man by the name of Olof Andersson (twenty-four years old) similarly applied for permission to marry his *uncle's widow* Britta Eriksdotter (twenty-seven years old).[55]

In one of these cases there were seven years between the man and the woman, in the other only three; but what determined these cases were the applicants' respective positions within their families. They came from different generations, a circumstance which was further complicated by the fact that it was the woman who came from the older generation. Although the age difference was quite small, and though the good conduct and scriptural knowledge of all parties were certified by their respective vicars, both applications were rejected.[56] It was quite simply felt that each man was in the

53 SD, AI:55, 1776, 25 September, no. 4, p. 259; SD, AI:55, 1776, 2 October, no. 3, p. 261, quote on p. 259. See also SD, AI:55, 1779, 5 August, no. 10, p. 1117; SD, AI:56, 1780, 7 June, no. 6, p. 171; SD, AI:60, 1796, 18 May, no. 4, p. 543, SD, AI:60, 1796, 27 June, no. 2, p. 619.

54 JR, BoA, 1801, 13 May, Johannes Håkansson, Brita Christina Jakobsdotter (*uncle's widow*).

55 JR, BoA, 1790, 16 September, Olof Andersson, Britta Eriksdotter (*uncle's widow*).

56 JR, R, K, 1801, 13 May, Johannes Håkansson and Brita Christina Jakobsdotter (*uncle's widow*); JR, K, 1790, 16 September, Olof Andersson and Britta Eriksdotter (*uncle's widow*).

position of a child with respect to his intended bride, which was not considered compatible with his role as a husband.

It is thus clear that respect between generations was a powerful norm which the authorities were anxious to uphold. Before 1790, virtually no information was provided about the applicants' ages, and any notes on the emotional, economic, or practical advantages that a potential marriage might bring were not commented on by the authorities. This indicates that information of that kind was not thought to be relevant. Here the hierarchical relationship between parent and child, and the deference that followed from it, appears to be an unshakeable principle which was considered important to uphold, regardless of whether the actual circumstances constituted a threat to it or not. One might say that the governing elite defended the *idea* of parental authority rather than taking a position with respect to social realities. In other words, the *kinship in itself* was less crucial to the assessment of the relationship than the *family position*.

Filial deference, *parental authority*, or *respect between the generations* is thus the principle and social norm that can account for the fact that biological cousins found it relatively easy to acquire dispensation for marriage during the whole of the eighteenth century while a man was not allowed to marry, for instance, his *uncle's widow* – a relationship completely without biological ties. Of course the assessment was also influenced by the fact that the Bible explicitly forbade marriages between a man and his uncle's widow, while the prohibition against cousin marriages was thought to be based on secular rules.[57] However, I would argue that parental authority had a stronger practical influence on the decisions, because this was the principle to which the Swedish decision-makers actively referred. In addition, incest in certain diagonal degrees (*niece*, *wife's niece*), like incest in the second affinity degree (*stepfather's widow*, *wife's stepdaughter*), was also secularly based; but these applications were nevertheless consistently rejected during the greater part of the eighteenth century, with the specific justification that the relationship was in opposition to filial deference. If the explicit prohibition in the Bible had played a decisive role in the making

57 According to the Protestant way of thinking, only prohibitions explicitly mentioned in the Bible were God's prohibitions, while any extensions to the prohibitions were seen as secular. See, e.g., the statement by Johan Stiernhöök in *Förarbeten till Sveriges Rikes Lag 1666–1686*, pp. 109f.

of the relevant decisions, these relationships should have been approved, in the same routine manner as the applications from two cousins.

Challenges to the generational order

During the greater part of the eighteenth century, the decisions of the authorities followed the pattern described above, the family position of applicants determining the outcome of applications for dispensation; but towards the end of the century, the assessments of several relationship categories changed even though no changes to the law had been implemented or even discussed.

Approval in spite of a challenging kinship position

In 1774, a journeyman chamois-maker and his *step-grandfather's widow* applied for permission to marry, first to the cathedral chapter and then to the Crown. The application pointed out that exceptions to the rules had been made on other occasions, and therefore the applicants hoped that their application could be approved as well. The couple presented both practical and emotional reasons for having their application approved. It seems that the man had for several years worked in the workshop which the woman had taken over when her husband died. Now she wanted to reward him by presenting him with '[her]self, [her] love, and [her] workshop'. However, both the cathedral chapter and the Crown felt that this relationship challenged the respect between parent and child and rejected the application.[58]

Six years later, another journeyman chamois-maker by the name of Magnus Norling (twenty-six years old) and his *stepfather's widow* Catharina Söderström (twenty-eight years old) applied for permission to marry.[59] Magnus was the son of a chamois-maker who had died when Magnus was nine years old. Magnus's mother had remarried a man named Hans Ekman, but she herself died shortly thereafter. When Magnus was nineteen years old, Hans Ekman, who was thus

58 JR, BoA, K, 1774, 8 August, Fredric Schubert, Margareta Lidman.

59 Lineal relationships were considered equally close regardless of the number of generations. *Stepfather's widow* was, in other words, comparable to *step-grandfather's widow* with respect to the closeness of the family relationship.

Magnus's stepfather, in his turn married Catharina, whereupon he, too, died after a few years. Left in the household were Magnus and Catharina, who after a few years applied for permission to marry. In their application they pointed out that they had already lived together for some time, and that Magnus was the one who managed the workshop. They expressed their concern that their mutual household might be disrupted, and the chamois-making business severely damaged, if they were not allowed to marry. They also pointed out that several people related by blood had been allowed to marry, whereas they themselves were 'only' related in the second affinity degree.[60]

In both of these cases the man had taken over the workshop when his step(grand)father had died. Both couples referred to previous exceptions in the dispensation procedure when attempting to have their applications approved. In the first case the ages of the applicants were not mentioned, but Magnus and Catharina were much the same age, she twenty-eight and he twenty-six years old. This closeness in age was specifically emphasised by the couple as an argument for filial deference not being challenged because of their marriage. That may have been decisive for the outcome. The Crown 'graciously' approved Magnus's and Catharina's application for marriage because of the 'existing special circumstances'.[61]

At approximately the same time, a similar change occurred in the decisions regarding relationships in diagonal affinity degrees. An application for marriage from a man and his *wife's half-niece* was rejected in August 1770.[62] Five years later, when a similar application was to be decided, the state councillors were in disagreement. The application was sent on to the Crown to be settled and was approved.[63] These are the first applications that I have found in the archives where marriage was permitted between people whose family positions were in different generations. In 1780, another two couples in the same relationship degrees (*wife's half-niece*) were

60 JR, BoA 1780, 25 February, Magnus Norling, Catharina Söderström (*stepfather's widow*).

61 JR, BoA, R, K, 1780, 25 February, Magnus Norling, Catharina Söderström (*stepfather's widow*).

62 JR, BoA, K, 1770, 23 August, Johan Hammarström, Stina Roos (*wife's half-niece*).

63 JR, BoA, R, 1775, 4 May, Per Ersson, Lisa Maris Persdotter (*wife's half-niece*). See also a letter patent in which marriage was allowed between a man and his *daughter's stepdaughter*, 1768. K.B., 1768, 19/6.

given permission to marry.[64] Ten years later, couples where the family relationship was full (*wife's niece*) were also given permission to marry.[65] At the beginning of the nineteenth century, at least three applications for marriage were approved from couples who were related in the second lineal affinity degree (*stepfather's widow*, *wife's stepdaughter*, *stepson's stepdaughter*).[66]

From the 1780s onwards, applicants in certain affinity relationships were thus given permission to marry despite the fact that their family positions transcended generational boundaries. In the second affinity degree, that is to say when two marriages separated the applicants, permission to marry was granted in the direct lineal degree (*wife's stepdaughter*, *stepfather's widow*). When only one marriage separated the applicants, permission was given for people in diagonal affinity degrees (*wife's niece*). However, when the relationship was in the diagonal degree it was crucial for the man's family position to originate in the older generation. While marriages between a man and his *wife's niece* were approved, applications from a man and his *uncle's widow* were rejected, though the kinship was equally close.[67] This shows that gender-based ideas had an effect on decisions. The authority of the husband was equated with that of the father; the social order was hence not challenged to the same degree when the woman's family position was in the younger generation as when it was in the older one. In these cases, morality also affected the outcome. Although a new liberal practice had been established at the end of the eighteenth century regarding, for example, a *wife's niece*, the previously mentioned Lars and Bengta had their application rejected when it transpired that he had made her pregnant.

In 1785, too, the first application for dispensation between a man and his deceased *wife's sister* was approved. The man in question

---

64 JR, BoA, K, 1780, 10 March, Lars Boman, Christina Lindman (*wife's half-niece*); JR, BoA, 1780, 28 January, Anders Svensson, Karna Åkesdotter (*wife's half-niece*).

65 JR, K, 1790, 22 March, Per Jönsson, Kristina Bengtsdotter (*wife's niece*); JR, D, 1780, 22 March, Elias Ribbing, Lena (*wife's niece*).

66 JR, K, 1807, 12 February, Gunnar Pehrsson, Brita Pehrsdotter, (*wife's stepdaughter*); JR, BoA, K, 1815, 26 July, Johan Emanuel Lundberg, Beata Ulrica Lindberg (*stepfather's widow*); JR, BoA, K, 1815, 24 May, Jakob Andersson, Anna Jönsdotter (*stepson's stepdaughter*).

67 See, e.g., JR, BoA, 1792, 24 April, Johan Assarsson, 25, Maria Jonasdotter, 29 (*uncle's widow*); JR, BoA, K, 1801, 4 June, Per Wretman, Elisabeth Nyman (*uncle's widow*); JR, D, 1802, 4 May, Johan Petersson (*father's uncle's widow*); JR, D, 1802, 4 June, Johan Andersson, Anna Johansdotter (*uncle's widow*).

was Lieutenant-Colonel Jan Gustaf Hägerflykt, who wanted to marry his deceased wife's sister, and the application was approved by the Crown without any detailed justification.[68] The decision was officially proclaimed on the same day, and it became precedential for future applications.[69]

The principles that had applied for the handling of dispensational cases during the entire eighteenth century thus gave way at roughly the same time as the number of applications for dispensation began to rise in earnest. The pressure of applications forced decision-makers to reflect on the boundaries that were valid at the time, and that resulted in a changed practice. In the renegotiation of boundaries that took place, it is clear that the principle of filial deference and notions regarding the relationship between two generations were central factors around which the renegotiations revolved. The fact that all relationships were no longer treated completely gender-neutrally also indicates that gender-related ideas were activated in the process of negotiation.

Age

There is much to indicate that this change may also be connected to a new interest in the ages of the applicants. Before 1790, ages were rarely stated at all; but after this date notes in pencil begin to appear on the applications, asking for or specifying the ages of the applicants.[70] After 1800, it became increasingly common for the ages of the applicants to be specified already in the application.[71]

Information on the ages of the applicants thus became more common in the dispensational material from 1790 onwards, and

---

68 Lower Judiciary Inspection (*Nedre Justitierevisionen*), FII:3, precedent 1780–99, p. 17.

69 K.B. 1785, 11 February. See, e.g. JR, BoA, K, 1790, 16 September, Emanuel Schagerström, Greta Stina Collin (*wife's sister*); JR, BoA, 1790, 16 September, Erik Larsson, Catharina Larsdotter (*wife's sister*); JR, BoA, K, 1801, 28 January, Peter Brunström, Anna Elisabeth Holmström (*wife's sister*); JR, BoA, R, K, 1801, 13 May, Jonas Fredrik Brink, Botella Kullenberg (*wife's sister*).

70 For instance, JR, BoA, 1790, 16 September, Olof Andersson and Britta Eriksdotter (*uncle's widow*); JR, BoA, 1790, 16 September, Anders Johansson, twenty-nine, Anna Maria Andersdotter, thirty-six (*uncle's widow*).

71 See, e.g. JR, BoA, 1801, 3 June, Anders Nilsson, Brita Eriksdotter (*half-niece*); JR, BoA, 1801, 28 October, Johannes Larsson, Greta Johansdotter (*cousin*); JR, BoA, 1802, 11 May, Olof Olsson, Karin Hansdotter (*wife's sister*).

in some cases the age-related information seems to have had an effect on the decisions. There were only two years between Magnus and his stepfather's widow Catharina, who were among the very first couples to be given permission to marry despite the lineal kinship tie. In their argumentation, the couple expressly referred to their ages when pointing out that filial deference would not be challenged by their potential union. Even though social circumstances may also have affected the outcome in this case, it is likely that the closeness in age between the applicants made a positive outcome possible.

Furthermore, it may be noted that applications for marriage from a man and his *uncle's widow* were usually rejected; but I have found two exceptions that can also be connected to the ages of the applicants. In 1790, Johan Lang applied for permission to marry his *half-uncle's widow*, Magdalena Jönsdotter. On the front page of the application, there is a note that urges the county sheriff to find out what the ages of the applicants were. It turned out that Johan was forty-four years old and Magdalena thirty-three. There were hence eleven years between Johan and Magdalena; but she was the younger party, and the couple were given permission to marry.[72] Similarly, Håkan Jönsson (twenty-eight years old) and his *half-uncle's widow*, Maja Nilsdotter (twenty-seven years old) were allowed to marry.[73] In the same year, two other couples with a similar kinship tie were denied permission. In one of these cases the man was twenty-four years old and the woman twenty-seven; in the second case he was twenty-nine and she thirty-six.[74] In other words, it made no difference if the man and the woman were nearly the same age. As long as she was older than he, the application for permission to marry resulted in a rejection. The fact that the kinship tie was only half between Johan and Magdalena, as well as between Håkan and Maja, is unlikely to have been decisive for their cases being an exception to common practice, since

72 JR, K, 1790, 23 September, Johan Lang, Magdalena Jönsdotter (*half-uncle's widow*).

73 JR, BoA, K, 1815, 24 May, Håkan Jönsson (twenty-eight), Maja Nilsdotter (twenty-seven) (*half-uncle's widow*).

74 JR, BoA, K, 1790, 16 September, Olof Andersson, Britta Eriksdotter (*uncle's widow*); JR, BoA, K, 1790, 16 September, Anders Johansson, twenty-nine, Anna Maria Andersdotter, thirty-six (*uncle's widow*); see also JR, R, K, 1801, 13 May, Johannes Håkansson, Brita Christina Jakobsdotter (*uncle's widow*).

other couples with half kinship ties were denied permission to marry.[75]

Here, then, a clear reformulation of both the gender-based and the generational order becomes visible. Previously, the prevailing view on the relationships of relatives had been governed by social factors. In other words, it was the family position that determined how the relationship between the people in question was perceived. From the turn of the century in 1800 onwards, though, family position was weighed against the age and sex of the applicants in a way that had not happened before.

In the Danish incest debate at this time, the age relationship between the man and the woman was specifically discussed. The attitudes in this debate reflected Swedish practice and were justified by the argument that there was an increased risk that the woman would not respect her husband to the desired extent if he was younger than she, and for this reason the authorities were loath to grant dispensations in such cases.[76] Unlike the situation in Sweden, the boundaries of incest prohibitions were repeatedly discussed by Danish politicians, and in 1770–1800 several Danish regulations were adopted where the rules were changed back and forth. The practical handling and assessment of dispensational cases in Denmark was, however, very similar to the treatment of these matters in Sweden during the same period, and the fact that applications regarding a *wife's niece* and an *uncle's widow* were treated differently probably reflects similar gender-related ideas in both countries.[77]

In spite of the newly-awakened interest in information about age, and in spite of individual dispensational cases where the decisions appear to have been affected by information about the applicants' ages, Swedish authorities still primarily acted on the basis of the family position in question. When a person had been given dispensation for marriage within a specific relationship category, the outcome often became precedential for later applications, regardless of the circumstances or of the ages specified. Even so, some deviations from this principle occurred during the decades around 1800, when

75 JR, BoA, K, 1801, 13 May, Anders Eriksson, Maria Svensdotter (*half-uncle's widow*); JR, D, 1802, 4 May, Simon Johansson (*half-uncle's widow*).

76 Koefoed 1999, p. 45.

77 For instance, in Denmark a dispensation regarding a *wife's niece* was denied in 1775 but granted in 1780. A dispensation for a *brother's widow* was granted in 1775 and for an *uncle's widow* in 1795. In 1799, the ages of the applicants began to be examined. Koefoed 1999, p. 69.

the practical handling of the dispensation applications changed.[78] When the case involved a man and his *uncle's widow*, the social order was challenged to a particularly high degree by the fact that she came from the older generation. But although such applications for dispensation were rejected even when the man and the woman were very close in age, we have seen that the authorities deviated from this practice when the woman was in fact younger than the man. The most likely explanation for these deviations is that the decision-makers allowed themselves to be influenced by the ages of the applicants. By the middle of the nineteenth century this inconsistency had disappeared, and applications from a man and his *uncle's widow* were approved according to the liberal practice that had been established for other relationships in the diagonal affinity degree, without any particular regard for the ages of the applicants.[79] In other words, the handling of applications for dispensation had been made uniform once more.

There may be several reasons why the importance of family position for the assessment of dispensational cases decreased or was renegotiated around the turn of the century in 1800. Previous research shows that the late eighteenth century was a period when the relationship between adult children and their parents changed in Sweden. David Gaunt observes that respect for the older generation was at its strongest in 1500–1750, and that it diminished steadily thereafter. Towards the end of the eighteenth century, conflict between generations increased, and unconditional respect for older people began to be questioned.[80] Similar results can be found in the research of Birgitta Odén. The number of conflicts between generations that ended up before a court increased significantly from 1780 to 1830.[81] Both Gaunt and Odén connect the changing attitudes towards older people to economic changes in society. In the older society, children

78 For example, in 1768 an application for dispensation for a marriage between a man and his *daughter's stepdaughter* was approved. In the same year another man was denied permission to marry his *son-in-law's daughter*, despite the fact that this relationship should be considered equally close. K.B. 1768, 19 June; K.B. 1768, 22 June.

79 See, e.g., JR, BoA, K, 1850, 22 January, Sven Börjesson (twenty-five years old), Stina Cajsa Carlsdotter (thirty-five) (*uncle's widow*); JR, BoA, K, 1850, 8 May, Grudd Andersson (forty-five), Margret Henriksdotter (fifty) (*uncle's widow*); JR, BoA, K, 1850, 5 June, John Hesling (forty-seven), Brita Andersdotter (thirty-seven) (*uncle's widow*).

80 Gaunt 1996, pp. 156–8.

81 Odén 1991, pp. 98, 104.

were often given permission to take over a farm in return for allowing their parents to continue living there, albeit in a more modest dwelling (a so-called *undantag*). This meant that parents received room and board for the rest of their lives. When agriculture was commercialised and mobility in the labour market increased, this system became ever more burdensome for the younger generation, who began to question whether they were actually obliged to take care of their parents.[82] Resistance against absolute filial deference has also been noted from the late eighteenth century in, for instance, French and English research.[83] Concurrently with the principle of filial deference being challenged, the importance of family position for the assessment of applications for dispensation thus decreased while interest in the ages of applicants increased.

The growing importance of age for the assessment of dispensational cases can also be viewed in relation to the new love-match ideal that was established at the same time. So-called widow conservation (*änkekonservering*), a form of 'widow inheritance' where a recently appointed younger clergyman married his predecessor's widow in order to secure her support, was relatively common. There was a similar system within different groups of artisans, too. In these cases, marriages primarily functioned as economic and practical transactions to arrange for the support of widows, and little attention was paid to the ages of the people involved. However, research has shown that these marriages became less popular towards the end of the eighteenth century; and both Solveig Widén, who has studied widow conservation within the clerical estate, and Kirsi Vainio-Korhonon, who has studied widow conservation within different groups of artisans, link the change to the new view on marriage. Tolerance for marriages of convenience, where a younger man married an older widow, decreased but did not disappear completely. Conservation within artisanal groups remained in existence well into the nineteenth century.[84]

The increasing interest in the age relationship between couples applying for dispensation thus partly coincided with a dwindling respect in society towards the older generation, partly with a new view on marriage in which mutual love and cordial companionship between spouses were foregrounded as ideals. Consequently,

82 Gaunt 1996, pp. 159–73; Odén 1991, pp. 107–9.

83 Hunt 1992, p. xiv, Chapter 2; Denbo 2001, pp. 202f.

84 Widén 1988, pp. 116f, 295; Vainio-Korhonen 1997, pp. 170–3, 175. Edgren 1983, pp. 10, 12.

12 The county sheriff announces a royal proclamation.

acceptance of marriages of convenience diminished. Because the new practices – that is to say, the increased number of applications from the general public and the changed assessment by the authorities of dispensational cases – coincided with a change in general social norms, it becomes logical to assume that these phenomena affected and possibly reinforced one another. The next section will focus on incest crimes in order to see if a similar process of change can be identified in the handling of criminal cases.

Criminal cases

Fewer criminal cases and milder punishments

Compared to the situation at the beginning of the eighteenth century, the number of incest cases in Swedish courts had more than halved by the turn of the following century. See Table 9. However, consanguinity relationships remained at a constant level, so the decrease is accounted for by affinity relationships.

It is difficult to draw any firm conclusions regarding the reasons for the significant decrease in the number of affinity crimes. The prohibitions for a *wife's cousin* and a *wife's brother's widow* were abolished following a royal regulation in 1727; but even with these

Table 9. Incest cases at GHA, 1694–1716, 1783–1800, 1810

Family relationship and closeness	**Relationship, a man and (his) …**	**1694–1716 (22)**	**1783–1800, 1810 (19)**
Consanguinity, first lineal degree	mother	–	3
	daughter	2	3
Consanguinity, first collateral degree	sister	4 (1)	4
Consanguinity, diagonal degree	niece	6 (3)	4 (2)
	aunt	1	1
Consanguinity, ≥ second degree	cousin, other	5 (1)	–
Consanguinity per year		**0.8**	**0.8**
Affinity, first lineal degree	stepmother, mother-in-law, a mother and her daughter, father and son with the same woman	10	2
	stepdaughter	21	12
Affinity, first collateral degree	wife's sister, two sisters, brother's widow, two brothers with the same woman	42 (2)	13 (1)
Affinity, diagonal degree	wife's aunt	8 (5)	3 (1)
	uncle's widow		
	wife's niece	22 (5)	6
Affinity, second degree	wife's cousin, two cousins, other	10	–
Affinity per year		**5.1**	**1.9**
Number of cases, total		**18+113=131**	**15+36=51**

Source: GHA, series BIIA.
Note: Within parenthesis = of which half-relatives

relationships removed from the statistics, affinity relationships had more than halved in the other categories. With respect to collateral and diagonal affinity relationships, the new dispensational procedure may have contributed to a reduction in the number of criminal cases, since it was possible to obtain permission to marry for these relationship categories from the 1780s onwards. However, this still does not explain why there was also a reduction in the number of lineal affinity crimes from one turn of the century to the next. This development is likely to have been influenced by a weakening of the connection between incest crimes and religion, which would mean that the crime in question was no longer felt to be quite so serious. Instead, incest crimes came to be associated with – and adhere to the development of – other sexual crimes; I will return to this discussion.

Except for the above-mentioned liberalisations, no changes to penal law had been made. Consequently, incest crimes were still regulated in accordance with the legislation of 1734, with the death penalty for the closest relationship categories. See Table 10.

Even though the legislation was all but unchanged at the end of the eighteenth century, a new, milder case law had been introduced, which meant that most of the people sentenced to death for incest crimes subsequently had their sentences reduced to corporal punishment or imprisonment.[85] Usually, these reductions were justified 'by benevolence and mercy' without invoking any specific circumstances.[86] Even if individual circumstances might have affected the assessment of some cases, the changes in the legal procedure should primarily be seen in relation to the contemporary jurisprudential debate on the death penalty and its purpose.[87]

The new, more lenient case law had a somewhat paradoxical consequence for the handling of crimes. Regardless of whether the statute book prescribed the death penalty or a gaol sentence for an

85 During the years 1783–1800+1810, eighteen people were sentenced to death for incest in the Göta Court of Appeal. Of these, sixteen people had their sentences reduced to imprisonment on bread and water and/or corporal punishment. Two death sentences were upheld. These death sentences were pronounced in a case concerning a man and his stepdaughter, who were in addition to the accusation of incest considered guilty of abortion. GHA, BIIA:120, 1796, no. 80; GHA, EIAC:17, 1796, p. 166.

86 See, e.g., GHA, BIIA:97, 1784, no. 105; GHA, EIAC:15, 1784, p. 235; GHA, EIAC:15, 1787, p. 454.

87 Olivecrona 1866, pp. 22–8.

Table 10. Incest prohibitions and punishments in accordance with the Civil Code of 1734

Family relationship	Closeness	Relationship, a man and his …	Punishment
Consanguinity	First/second lineal degree	mother, grandmother, daughter, granddaughter	Death by beheading Possibly breaking on the wheel or burning after death
	First collateral degree	sister	Death by beheading If adulterous, his body was to be broken on the wheel and her body to be burnt after death
	Diagonally	aunt, niece, grandniece	Death by beheading
	Second degree	cousin	Fine 40 thalers
Affinity	First/second lineal degree	stepmother, mother-in-law, stepdaughter, grandfather's widow	Death by beheading If adulterous, his body was to be broken on the wheel and her body was to be burnt after death
	First collateral degree +adultery	wife's sister, brother's wife, two sisters	Man: flogging 40 pairs/gaol 1 month Woman: birching 30 pairs/gaol 1 month
	First collateral degree –adultery	wife's sister, brother's widow, two sisters	Man: flogging 32 pairs/gaol 24 days Woman: birching 24 pairs/gaol 24 days
	Diagonally	uncle's widow, wife's niece, nephew's widow, grandmother's brother's widow	Man: fine 80 thalers/flogging 23 pairs/gaol 20 days Woman: fine 80 thalers/birching 18 pairs/gaol 20 days
	Second degree	wife's stepmother, wife's stepdaughter, stepson's widow, stepfather's widow	Fine: affinity 80 thalers + fornication (married 80 thalers, unmarried 40 thalers)

incest crime, the practical punishment became the same, i.e., imprisonment for twenty-eight days on bread and water. While the statute book differentiated between more or less aggravated offences, in practice all crimes had the same penal consequences.[88]

Fewer convictions

Compared to the turn of the century in 1700, the number of criminal cases had thus been significantly reduced; but the number of convictions had also decreased significantly from around 80 to 40%.[89] Previously, most decisions had been based on a confession by the accused, but now it was required that the confession should be verified by testimony for a conviction to be announced. An effect of this requirement was that prosecuted individuals were acquitted 'for want of evidence', even when they themselves confessed to the crime.[90]

In his research, Jonas Liliequist has shown how false confessions could be made tactically by people who were depressed or tired of life for the purpose of being executed. Because suicide was defined as a sin, the death penalty for these people could be seen as an opportunity to end their lives prematurely without risking the salvation of their souls. The death penalty adhered to a fixed ritual of preparations where the convicted person was comforted and guided by a clergyman. The person concerned was given the opportunity

88 The punishment for incest in the first consanguinity degree, in a diagonal consanguinity degree, or in a lineal affinity degree was death. But people convicted of these crimes had their sentences reduced to a gaol sentence on the same terms as people with collateral affinity ties, where the official punishment was imprisonment. Compare, e.g., GHA, BIIA:100, 1786, no. 49 and GHA, BIIA:97, 1784, no. 105 to GHA, BIIA:85, 1778, no. 24 and GHA, BIIA:104, 1788, no. 62. A few decades into the nineteenth century, the various crimes were again differentiated by sentencing people to hard labour in addition to the gaol sentence for the most aggravated offences.

89 In 1694–1716, 107 out of 131 cases (81.7%) ended in a conviction (one case with an unknown outcome). In 1778–1800+1810, nineteen out of fifty-one cases (39.2%) ended in a conviction (four cases with an unknown outcome).

90 It was regularly noted that a confession was supported by testimony or circumstances; e.g., GHA, BIIA:96, 1784, no. 72; GHA, BIIA:119, 1795, no. 166; Gärd hundred, AIa:67, 1784, 18 June, no. 74. For examples of people who were acquitted despite confessing, see GHA, BIIA:103, 1787, no. 130; GHA, BIIA:111, 1791, no. 150; GHA, BIIA:118, 1795, no. 7.

of confessing and receiving absolution before the execution was carried out. The risk of false self-denunciations was, according to Liliequist, one of the reasons why the evidentiary requirements were strengthened during the eighteenth century.[91] While some people were acquitted against their own confessions, others chose to deny the accusation to the very last, even if there were comparatively compromising circumstances.

Fisherman Olof Nyström (thirty-nine years old) and his *step-daughter* Rebecka Nilsdotter (twenty-five years old) were accused of sexual congress on a number of occasions. The first accusation of unchaste behaviour was registered in the minutes of a parish meeting in March 1783. On this occasion Olof and Rebecka were not accused of 'actual commixtion'; but their behaviour had aroused 'a good deal of attention and offence in the parish', and they were ordered to live separately in future on pain of a fine of 3 2/3 *riksdaler* in silver if they did not obey the decision of the parish meeting.[92] Later, during the spring and summer, the case was taken up by the hundred court as well, because there had been no change in the living arrangements or conduct of Olof and Rebecka. Witnesses who were summoned said that they had seen the couple lie undressed together in a bed, that they had accompanied each other at work 'like married folk', that they had slept together 'not once or twice, but they always live like married folk', that they had 'offered food to each other', that Olof had sat and held Rebecka 'tenderly', and that they had displayed 'much love for each other'.[93]

Olof and Rebecka flatly denied all accusations. They claimed that they had to spend a lot of time together because of their work. Because Rebecka's mother was old and infirm, Rebecka was needed at home to care for her and for the household. For purely practical

91 Liliequist 1992, pp. 112–14. In addition to false confessions, people with a death wish could also be tempted into committing crimes for the purpose of being sentenced to death, so-called murder-suicides. Jansson 1994; Lövkrona 1999, p. 15.

92 There are no minutes preserved from the parish meetings of Åkerbo for this year, but the case is mentioned in Åkerbo hundred, AIa:23, 1783, 23 April, no. 2, p. 1584. Somewhat different information about the couple's ages is provided in different minutes. I have chosen to state the ages which they themselves specified and which also recurred most often. Hammarkind hundred, AIa:81, 1786, 30 May, no. 98; Hammarkind hundred, AIa:81, 1786, 14 November, no. 135. The *riksdaler* was a new coin, introduced in 1777 and corresponding to six thalers silver.

93 Åkerbo hundred, AIa:23, 1783, 4 June, no. 51.

reasons, they often shared a bed; but Olof claimed that he was incapable of conjugal congress because of a physical defect. As evidence he presented a written testimonial, signed by barber-surgeon Gottfried Göhle from the town of Linköping.[94] Even if sexual intercourse could not be proven, the hundred court found, after the hearing concluded, that Olof and Rebecka had acted in an unchaste manner by

> always lying together in a bed, and always accompanying each other when they are out at work and on visits and when travelling, seeking out each other's company and bedfellowship whether there has been occasion for it or not and they had been offered the opportunity to lie separately, which, as is well known in the entire parish, has continued during all of the past year [...] and when in company with each other using unchaste gestures with kissing, stroking, and suchlike, which has caused general offence and outrage in the parish.[95]

Although the couple had been warned and threatened with a fine if they did not move apart, they had 'persisted in as indecent a life as before'; and even though they could not be accused of consummated incest, their behaviour was 'imprudent and loose, very much in breach of the rules of virtuous conduct and causing great offence', especially as they were stepfather and stepdaughter. Olof and Rebecka were sentenced to pay the fine imposed for their unchaste behaviour. In addition they had to sit in the stocks on a Sunday outside the church, whereupon Rebecka would have to move 'out of the house and out of the parish', if she did not wish to be put in the spinning-house 'until she improves her way of life'.[96]

Three years later, Olof and Rebecka turn up in the sources again. In the autumn after the couple had served their punishment in the stocks, they had moved to the district where Olof grew up, which was two hundreds away from where they had lived before. Here they had settled and still lived as a family together with Olof's wife/Rebecka's mother, who was now even more advanced in years and in poor health. Olof had taken up what used to be his father's profession as a tailor and travelled around in the parish doing various kinds of sewing work. He brought his stepdaughter with him and they often shared a bed; but they had, according to their

---

94 The wording of the testimony can be found in Hammarkind hundred, AIa:81, 1786, 14 November, no. 135.

95 Åkerbo hundred, AIa:23, 1783, 4 June, no. 51.

96 Åkerbo hundred, AIa:23, 1783, 4 June, no. 51.

own testimony, never 'committed carnal commixtion', which Olof proved by once again producing the testimonial from the barber-surgeon in Linköping. However, Rebecka had borne a bastard child, and even though she claimed to have been raped by an 'unknown man' there was a rumour afoot in the district that her stepfather might be the father of the child, which was why new court proceedings were initiated.

Once more, testimony was presented to the effect that Olof and Rebecka sought each other's company and that they chose to sleep together when they were travelling, in spite of being offered separate sleeping accommodation. At this hearing the accusations against the couple were more serious, because Rebecka had borne a child of whom Olof was suspected of being the father. This was no longer a matter of 'unchaste behaviour' but of incest in the first affinity degree, with the death penalty as a consequence upon conviction. The investigation was delayed for two years from one court session to another while the prosecutor collected evidence. The prosecutor requested a copy of the earlier judgement-book records and made enquiries regarding the authenticity of the testimonial that Olof used to confirm his innocence, in parallel with summoning and questioning additional witnesses.[97]

Seven years after the first official accusation about unchaste behaviour and after numerous court hearings, Olof and Rebecka were finally acquitted of the crime of incest. They had been questioned countless times over the years and prevailed upon to make a 'truthful confession' by lawyers and clergy. Threatened with flogging and imprisonment, they had been fined and sentenced to sitting in the stocks. The circumstantial evidence against the couple was convincing, but in light of their 'stubborn denial' they could not be convicted of consummated incest.[98] Olof and Rebecka thus consistently denied

97 Hammarkind hundred, AIa:81, 1786, 30 May, no. 98; Hammarkind hundred, AIa:81, 1786, 14 November, no. 135; Hammarkind hundred, AIa:82, 1787, 3 March, no. 156; Hammarkind hundred, AIa:82, 1787, 11 May, no. 83; Hammarkind hundred, AIa:82, 1787, 13 November, no. 47; Hammarkind hundred, AIa:83, 1788, 13 March, no. 187. The authenticity of the testimonal could never be proven because barber-surgeon Göhle turned out to be dead.

98 Hammarkind hundred, AIa:85, 1790, 13 March, no. 87; GHA, BIIA:109, 1790, no. 46. The final judgement is included in the register of the court of appeal but is missing from the judgement book itself. However, the decision will not have deviated from the decision of the hundred court based on previous statements in GHA, BIIA:105, 1788, no. 59.

all accusations of sexual intercourse. It is of course possible that they were innocent of the crime of which they were accused, but considering the circumstantial evidence and all the testimony, that seems unlikely.

Similarly, a number of witnesses provided incriminating testimony at the court hearing of shoemaker Lars Sundberg and his *sister* Britta Sundberg. This couple was said to have shown each other friendship and affection and to have been found in bed together in compromising situations on repeated occasions. As they stubbornly denied the accusations, however, they were eventually acquitted of incest, but were ordered to move apart.[99] When another man, named Jonas Eliasson, was accused of incest with his mute *sister*, the crime was verified by 'conclusive circumstances'; but because Jonas 'stubbornly denied' the act he, too, was acquitted.[100]

As these examples show, there were cases – especially when conviction could led to execution – where the prosecuted individuals were acquitted because they refused to confess that they had committed any type of crime, although there was strong circumstantial evidence against them.[101] The courts continuously worked in close cooperation with the clergy. The opinions of clergymen were actively requested by the court, and the clergy described – often in written reports – the scriptural knowledge, conduct, and general spiritual state of the accused. In addition, the clergymen stated how they exhorted the prosecuted individuals to confess to their crimes, and indeed several confessions were made precisely after such exhortations from clergymen or from members of the court.[102] As in earlier periods, the prosecuted individuals were thus subjected to serious admonitions towards the end of the eighteenth century, but there is nothing to suggest the use of physical force. At the turn of the century in 1700, there were occasions when 'harsh' and 'hard' prison was used; but there are no such references in the criminal-court material after 1783.

If it was the case that more people denied their crimes in spite of being guilty, there are several possible reasons for this. A more

99 GHA, EVII AABA:2621, 1785, no. 145; GHA, BIIA:99, 1785, no. 64; GHA, EVAC:52, 1785, no. 25.

100 GHA, BIIA:109, 1790, no. 102.

101 For other examples where the prosecuted individuals denied the charge and were set free, see Ölands Norra hundred, AIa:80, 1786, 21 March; GHA, BIIA:100, 1786, no. 67; GHA, BIIA:110, 1791, no. 65.

102 See, e.g., GHA, EVAC:52, 1785, no. 25; Gärd hundred, AIa:67, 1784, 15 June, no. 73; GHA, BIIA:120, 1796, no. 80.

humane treatment of suspects may be one explanation. The more stringent evidentiary requirements may be another. In addition, the altered image of the deity may have contributed to new behaviour. Previously, God had above all been delineated as a stern avenger whose wrath struck those who did not obey his commandments. Around 1800, the image of this avenging God had been toned down in favour of a mild and forgiving paternal figure. This makes it likely that the fear of God had become less important in comparison to what was the case in earlier periods. Finally, I would submit that the view of the crime of incest in itself had changed, from being primarily conceived of as a religious crime to being perceived as a moral crime to the detriment of general societal morality. In this way the seriousness of the crime had been reduced from something of a mortal sin to an immoral and depraved act, which may have diminished the prosecuted individuals' feelings of fear and guilt. I will return to this line of reasoning below.

In conclusion, it may be noted that higher evidentiary requirements in combination with fewer confessions led to fewer criminal trials ending in convictions around the turn of the century in 1800 in comparison to what was the case at the previous turn of the century.

Love: a mitigating circumstance

Previous research has identified the decades around the year 1800 as a peak period for the emotions. Motifs of love and happiness flourished in chapbooks and fictional literature, and the ideal marriage should, in addition to its practical goals, preferably also lead to personal happiness and bliss for the prospective spouses.[103] The changed discourse of love in society was reflected in the dispensational material in that the mutual emotions of applicants were often foregrounded as a reason why an application for marriage should be approved. This section analyses the question of whether this cultural change in society influenced the handling of criminal cases as well.

Some criminal-court records convey a distinct impression of the prosecuted individuals having warm feelings for each other; the case referred to above involving Olof and Rebecka is an example. Several witnesses testified to the couple seeking out each other's

103 See the discussion above on pp. 46–8.

13 A romantic encounter.

company and treating each other tenderly and lovingly. Their behaviour was disapproved of because of all the 'kissing, stroking, and suchlike'. In connection with the first parish meeting when the couple was accused of indecent behaviour, Rebecka is said to have become 'somewhat agitated' and threatened to take her own life if she could not be together with Olof. On another occasion, she had said that the fine of 3 2/3 *riksdaler* in silver was not enough to prevent her from wanting to sleep together with Olof.[104] In other words, it is clear that the relationship was reciprocal and that they were very fond of each other, even though they never used such expressions as *love*.

At around the same time, twenty-three-year-old Mårten Persson was prosecuted for having committed incest with his *stepdaughter*, Ingjär Pehrsdotter, who was seventeen years old. This relationship also appears to have been affectionate and reciprocal. According to a witness, Mårten had initially wanted to marry Ingjär; but because they had no farm of their own and thus could not support themselves, he had instead married her mother.[105] A month or two after the wedding the mother fell ill, and by the time the trial began in the following year she was dead. Witnesses said that Mårten and Ingjär behaved uncommonly kindly towards each other, that they accompanied each other to and from different tasks, and that they frequently held hands. On repeated occasions they had shared a bed, and they used to hug and kiss in the presence of other people. Most of this testimony, however, ended in assurances that the witnesses had never seen any truly 'indecent' or 'illicit' intercourse between Mårten and Ingjär. But there was one exception.[106]

One servant maid testified that she, when peeking through a bush, had seen Mårten and Ingjär lie together on the ground early in the morning of Midsummer Day. On that occasion, Ingjär was said to have lain beneath Mårten with her skirts drawn up so that her thighs were exposed. Mårten's 'trouser flap' was also said to have been open. The servant maid had not been alone on this occasion, but had been accompanied by the housewife Botill Carlsdotter, who also testified that she had seen Mårten and Ingjär. But Botill was not certain that Ingjär's clothes had been pulled up, nor that Mårten's 'trouser flap' had been open. Botill, who was a close

104 Åkerbo hundred, AIa:23, 1783, 4 June, no. 51.
105 Medelstad hundred, AIa:77, 1784, 9 December, no. 1.
106 Medelstad hundred, AIa:77, 1784, 6 December, no. 9.

neighbour of Mårten and Ingjär, had on several occasions seen the couple hug and kiss and share sleeping places when out at work, but she had not seen them do anything 'indecent'. The circumstantial evidence was grave, however, and after additional interrogations and exhortations, both Mårten and Ingjär admitted that they had had illicit intercourse on two occasions.[107]

It is obvious that Mårten and Ingjär had acted affectionately towards each other in public contexts, which had started a general rumour in the neighbourhood. Their conduct challenged both official and unofficial norms, which caused people around them to react. But although there were many witnesses who testified to seeing kisses and hugs, only one, a servant maid, believed that she had seen something truly 'indecent'. Not even Botill Carlsdotter wanted to testify that something really indecent had taken place. In her testimony, Botill claimed that she had had a branch in front of her, which had impeded her vision; she also said that she was ashamed of Mårten's and Ingjär's relationship and for this reason had not wanted to look.[108] Her actions must be seen as passive, because she could easily have moved the branch aside or moved herself so that she could see more clearly. Half of the twenty-odd witnesses who were heard by the court claimed not to know anything at all of the matter, even though Mårten and Ingjär, judging from the other testimony, had acted very affectionately towards each other in public places for several months. The clergyman who interrogated the imprisoned couple noted in a formal letter that the crime could not, in his opinion, be accounted for by any 'hardness or evil in the hearts' of the accused. On the contrary, both Ingjär and Mårten had, once they had confessed, displayed great 'concern', 'regret', and 'sadness'. Mårten in particular had feared that all the blame would be imputed to him 'as a father'. The clergyman emphasised that their crime had not so much arisen from 'evil and obduracy in sin' as from the fact that Mårten's wife had been much older and, in addition, infirm. These circumstances had led to such a temptation for the two accused that they had not, in the 'heedlessness of youth', been able to resist it.[109] By emphasising mitigating circumstances, the clergyman signalled that he would like to see Mårten and Ingjär's crimes judged as leniently as possible. He did not question

107 Medelstad hundred, AIa:77, 1784, 6 December, no. 9; Medelstad hundred, AIa:77, 1784, 9 December, no. 1.
108 Medelstad hundred, AIa:77, 1784, 6 December, no. 9.
109 Medelstad hundred, AIa:77, 1784, 15 December, no. 14.

the seriousness of the crime but underscored that the couple's *intent* had been without malice.

Because Mårten's and Ingjär's confessions were supported by the servant maid's testimony all evidentiary requirements were fulfilled, and the couple was sentenced to death by beheading, according to the law. The sentence was upheld in the court of appeal; but in the highest instance the couple, according to the new practice of the time, had their sentences reduced to imprisonment on bread and water. Although the maximum gaol sentence was twenty-eight days, Mårten and Ingjär were sentenced to 'only' sixteen and twelve days, respectively.[110]

The local community and the clergy, as well as the authorities, showed leniency and tolerance towards Mårten and Ingjär. The youth of the couple was emphasised by the clergyman as an explanation for their inability to resist the temptation to be together. Youthful indiscretion had been used as a mitigating circumstance before in similar incest cases, but never when the criminal act had been repeated. By emphasising that the couple's intent had not been malicious, the clergyman also placed a new focus on the intent rather than on the criminal act itself, which had not been the case around the previous turn of the century. In addition, love seems to have gained new legitimacy as a mitigating circumstance. The fact that the information provided by the witnesses concerning the nature of the relationship was written down shows that the authorities paid more attention to such aspects than they had done in the past. Similar sentence reductions were also given to other couples where mutual feelings appear to have been the only mitigating factor. Olof Mattsson and his *niece* Brita Svensdotter claimed to have begun to feel 'extreme affection and friendship' for each other, an affection which had eventually blossomed into 'illicit love'. Ideally, they wished to marry; but that could not be countenanced because of their close family relationship. However, the county sheriff recommended that their crime should be judged in the 'most lenient way' possible. The Crown reprieved them from the death penalty and sentenced them to twenty days in prison.[111] In another case, Ingeborg Persdotter,

110 Medelstad hundred, AIa:77, 1784, 15 December, no. 14; GHA, BIIA:98, 1785, no. 3. The couple were also sentenced to a penalty of eight pairs of rods for him and six pairs of birch rods for her if they were ever to reside in the same location again.

111 GHA, BIIA:119, 1795, no. 166.

who had first committed single adultery with Erik Jonasson and then conceived a child under a promise of marriage with Erik's brother Jon Jonasson (since deceased), was sentenced to twenty-four days in prison instead of the official twenty-eight.[112]

In the above cases, the prosecuted individuals were punished more leniently than what both the law and practice actually prescribed, and I think it likely that the nature of the relationships contributed to the more lenient decisions. Because the justifications for the final judgements were expressed in vague turns of phrase, such as 'owing to special circumstances' and 'by benevolence and mercy', the authorities' justifications for these more lenient punishments cannot be determined with certainty. Nor was the tendency to treat affectionate relationships more leniently entirely uniform. Knut Ringsten (sixty years old) and his daughter-in-law, the widow Märta Nilsdotter (over thirty years old), described their crime as the result of there being an 'ardent friendship and love' between them. They were reprieved from the death penalty but were sentenced to the maximum gaol sentence of twenty-eight days each.[113] It is possible that the relatively severe gaol sentence could be connected to the increased interest in age that is manifested in the dispensational material. Unlike, for instance, Mårten and Ingjär, who were of the same age, this relationship violated the prevailing norms for sexual relations both because of the significant age difference between the man and the woman and because of the lineal family relationship.

In some cases, for example when the relationship was described as affectionate and reciprocal, the sentences of the accused were thus reduced to shorter prison terms than what was, strictly speaking, normally the case. This reduction of the punishment could be implemented regardless of whether the case involved lineal, diagonal, or horizontal relationships. The *nature* of a relationship hence emerges as a circumstance that affected the outcome of a case more than previously. But irrespective of whether the nature of the relationship actually affected the judicial decisions or not, it is in any case clear that emotions between the accused were described in a more detailed manner than before, which in itself suggests an increased interest in these circumstances.

112 GHA, BIIA:112, 1792, no. 3. See also GHA, BIIA:96, 1784 no. 72.

113 GHA, EVAC:86, 1791, no. 26. There are also cases where the punishment was reduced without it being clear whether the prosecuted individuals had any affectionate feelings for each other.

Violence and coercion

Pronounced violence or coercion was rare among the criminal cases from the late eighteenth century. In a total of four out of fifty-one cases, the woman claimed that she had been forced or enticed into committing the act. One of these cases concerned a father who had tried to force himself on his thirteen-year-old *daughter*, but because the act had not been consummated both were acquitted of the accusation of incest. However, the father was sentenced to corporal punishment and hard labour for attempting to rape his daughter.[114]

In the three cases (one *daughter*/two *stepdaughters*) where the crime was considered to have been proven, the man and the woman were sentenced to equivalent punishments. In other words, no allowance was made for her claim of having suffered an assault. In all these cases, the woman was an adult when the crime was discovered (between twenty and twenty-seven years of age); and even though she in one case claimed that the sexual relationship had been going on since she was a child, this could not be proven. The incestuous act had also been repeated several times in all three cases.[115]

The point of departure for the assessment of the court was thus the same as a hundred years earlier. It was the act that had to be proven, and it was assumed that both parties had participated voluntarily. However, unlike the situation at the previous turn of the century, no woman received a reduction of her sentence after claiming that she had been subjected to violence and coercion. Nevertheless, the number of cases from the later period is low, and they cannot form a basis for drawing general conclusions. Besides,

114 GHA, BIIA:105, 1788, no. 69. This case is described in its entirety in Lindstedt Cronberg 2002, pp. 118–22.

115 Gärd hundred, AIa:67, 1784, 28 April, no. 1; Gärd hundred, AIa:67, 1784, 15 June, no. 73; Gärd hundred, AIa:67, 1784, 18 June, no. 74; GHA, BIIA:97, 1784, no. 105 (*stepdaughter*; the relationship appears to have been coercive for several years); Ölands Södra hundred, AIa:90, 1795, 17 July; Ölands Södra hundred, AIa:91, 1796, 26 March; GHA, BIIA:120, 1796, no. 11; GHA, BIIA:120, 1796, no. 80; GHA, EIAC:17, 1796, p. 166 (*stepdaughter*; even though the woman claimed at one time that the man had 'beguiled' her into committing the act, the relationship appears to have been voluntary; the couple was sentenced to death because they were considered to be guilty of abortion as well); GHA, BIIA:114, no. 4 (the *daughter* described four occasions when her father had forced himself on her before she herself chose to report the crime; this crime is described in Lindstedt Cronberg 2002, pp. 122–4).

the accused woman was an adult in all three cases, and the act had been repeated on more than one occasion, which would have been considered aggravating during earlier periods as well. In addition, a potential incentive for the earlier sentence reductions had disappeared. At the turn of the century in 1700, a woman's life could be saved if the members of the court chose to accept her version of the course of events. The crime would then have been defined as rape, which justified a reduction of her sentence. But because all death sentences were routinely reduced to gaol sentences at the end of the eighteenth century, the definition of the crime was no longer a matter of life and death for anyone.

Previous research has shown that attitudes to men's and women's sexuality have varied over time. Up until the turn of the century in 1800, responsibility with respect to social morality was laid primarily on the man who, in his position as master, should discipline both his wife and the other members of his household into becoming virtuous and honourable individuals. The man was perceived to be active and in charge, while the woman was regarded as being more passive. Women were described as emotional and less reliable because they were more apt to allow themselves to be misled by the Devil into committing sinful acts. A man's role as a rational leader was therefore considered both natural and necessary. After the turn of the century in 1800, a man's sexual desires were increasingly often described as stronger than a woman's, which increased the risk of his being taken in by her seductive wiles. Because a woman's sexuality was now considered weaker than a man's, responsibility for married life and social morality was gradually transferred to her. By creating a harmonious and loving home where a man could find rest and peace, a woman was believed to indirectly create stability and balance throughout society.[116]

The altered view of male and female sexuality led to an increased interest in women's behaviour in connection with sexual offences. When a woman claimed that she had been subjected to violence or coercion, it became more important to investigate whether she had acted provocatively – and thus contributed to the course of events – than to establish how much violence the man had used.

116 Liliequist 2007, pp. 167, 172f; Marklund 2004, pp. 74–6. Davidoff, Doolittle, Fink, and Holden 1999, pp. 57f, 66, 141. The image of woman as a dangerous seductress exists in many religions and was also taken over by the Catholic Church and implemented by church fathers and theologians. Baldwin 1994, p. 233; Brundage 1987.

Consequently, the woman's credibility was reduced, and her position in legal contexts was weakened.[117] This circumstance may also contribute to explaining why the proportion of cases where violence and coercion are mentioned decreased. If people were aware of the fact that women rarely gained a hearing for their stories about coercion and threats, the reason for mentioning these things decreased. The punishment would be the same, no matter how the crime had occurred.

Women's position in German courts was also relatively weak. True, the courts investigated claims of violence and coercion in connection with German incest cases; but because a man had the right to physically punish both his family and his servants for the purpose of disciplining them, the courts focused on assessing the nature of the violence. The question was thus not whether the man had used violence, but whether he had used excessive force, thereby abusing his authority as a father or master. In this assessment, the number of offences became decisive. If the sexual act had been repeated more than once, the members of the court regarded that as proof that the parties had been in agreement. In consequence, both were thought to be equally guilty.[118]

Clearly, then, neither Swedish nor German courts took account of the inequality in power positions that existed between a child – even if that child had reached adulthood – and his or her (step) parent. Although the number of incest cases that included violence is low in the Swedish material, it may be noted that alleged violence was more or less ignored by the members of the court. Quite simply, the members of the court do not appear to have reflected at all on the vulnerability and position of dependency of the younger party when these crimes were assessed.

The idea that the crime of incest was a prohibited act committed by two offenders thus persisted in Swedish society. By contrast, the religious interpretation of the crime had decreased in importance. That decrease forms the subject of the following section.

Incest: a moral crime

Around the turn of the century in 1700, incest had been treated as a religious crime. Even though exceptions had been made in individual cases when several mitigating circumstances existed, the majority

117 Jansson 2002, pp. 305f.
118 Jarzebowski 2006, pp. 260–2.

of the judgements had adhered to the established laws, which were primarily based on religious ideas. Crimes that according to the Bible should be punishable by death led to a death sentence being carried out in 70 to 75% of the cases. At the turn of the following century, milder case law had been introduced, and the death penalty was only implemented in exceptional cases. Death sentences were now reduced to imprisonment on bread and water for up to a month's time. In other words, the religious message was not followed to the letter as it had been before.

The religious rhetoric had also been toned down, and incestuous acts were instead described as crimes against *morality* and *social morals*. In the case against Olof and Rebecka, it was noted that the conduct of the couple was 'to the highest degree incompatible with good manners', which aroused 'offence' in the entire community.[119] Another court record defined their 'cohabitation' as 'highly indecent and punishable' because it violated 'good manners'.[120] The couple did not behave in a way that befitted a 'child and father', but their behaviour was 'unchaste' rather than sinful.[121] In another case, Karin Larsdotter and her *stepfather* were accused of harbouring a 'lewd inclination' for each other, which led to 'highly indecent and shameless' conduct.[122] In addition, the use of the concept 'illicit sexual behaviour' (*otukt*) to refer to incestuous relationships became more common around the turn of the century in 1800.[123] As time went by, these descriptions of the crime of incest as indecent and immoral came to overshadow descriptions of a religious sin.[124]

---

119 Åkerbo hundred, AIa:23, 1783, 4 June, no. 51.

120 Hammarkind hundred, AIa:83, 1788, 13 March, no. 187.

121 Åkerbo hundred, AIa:23, 1783, 4 June, no. 51; Åkerbo hundred, AIa:23, 1783, 23 April, no. 2; Hammarkind hundred, AIa:82, 1787, 11 May, no. 83.

122 Ölands Södra hundred, AIa:90, 1795, 17 July; GHA, BIIA:120, 1796, no. 80.

123 See, e.g., Kulling hundred, AIa:32, 1778, 24 January, no. 49; Kulling hundred, 1786, AIa:40, 4 May, no. 30; Västbo hundred, AIa:65, 1791, 3 March, no. 71; Medelstad hundred, AIa:85, 1792, 31 October; GHA, BIIA:120, 1796, no. 80.

124 Around the turn of the century in 1700, the ratio between, on the one hand, the three concepts of 'illicit sexual behaviour' (*otukt*), 'unchaste' (*okyskt*) behaviour and 'indecent' (*oanständigt*) behaviour taken together, and on the other hand the concept of 'sin', was one to ten. At the turn of the century in 1800, the frequency of use between these concepts had been inverted to around two to one.

In most of the criminal cases where 'indecent conduct' could be established, references were made to the 'offence' that this aroused in the local community; and irrespective of whether the crime could be proven or not, several hearings ended with an exhortation to the accused to move apart. In order to ensure that this admonition was respected, it was made under threat of a conditional penalty (*vite*), that is to say a fine, a gaol term, or a sentence of corporal punishment, if the order was not obeyed. Bengt Säf and his *daughter* were acquitted of the suspicion of having committed a crime; but in order to avoid public 'offence', they were told not to 'reside together in the same hundred or location' in future on pain of six pairs of rods for him and five pairs of birch rods for her.[125] Widower Mattias Johansson and his *stepdaughter* Brita Bengtsdotter were informed that they would be sentenced to a penalty of seven pairs of rods for him and five pairs of birch rods for her if they were to reside in the same location in future.[126] The penalty for farmer Per Olofsson and his *half-niece*, widow Margareta Hansdotter, was similar: eight pairs of rods and four pairs of birch rods, respectively, if they in future resided in the same location.[127] In the same way, a penalty of flogging and birching was conditionally imposed on Giöthar Dahl and his *stepdaughter* Annika Svensdotter and on Olof Jönsson Häll and his *niece* Brita Maria Larsdotter.[128] Still other persons were warned in more general terms or threatened with different sums in fines, or with a gaol sentence, if they did not stay away from each other in future.[129]

In the above-mentioned cases, the prosecuted individuals had violated established social norms regarding how family members should behave towards each other. The fact that several couples seem to have been unwilling to change their behaviour can be seen as a challenge to the prevailing norms for sexual relationships, but it was always an indirect challenge. Olof and Rebecka had clearly challenged the prevailing norms for the behaviour of family members by displaying greater intimacy and friendship towards each other than what was considered appropriate for a stepfather and

125 GHA, EIAC:15, 1788, p. 507.
126 GHA, BIIA:96, 1784, no. 72.
127 GHA, BIIA:99, 1785, no. 25.
128 GHA, BIIA:102, 1787, no. 39; GHA, BIIA:100, 1786, no. 49. See also GHA, BIIA:103, 1787 no. 130.
129 Hanekind hundred, AIa:34, 1784, 10 February, no. 2; GHA, BIIA:109, 1790, no. 102; GHA, BIIA:113, 1792, no. 89.

stepdaughter. A potential sexual relationship between them would have violated the social norms in several ways: first, by being a relationship outside marriage; second, by being a relationship between different generations; and third, by being a relationship between two family members. Olof and Rebecka never actively questioned these norms. Instead they defended their behaviour by referring to ideas about the loyalty of family members towards each other. In this context they claimed that their relations were perfectly natural. They belonged to the same family, worked close to each other, and helped each other as relatives should. The challenges were thus subtle and indirect, and nobody questioned either the legislation or social morality. Nevertheless, the criminal cases amounted to a strain on the system of norms.

The main reason for the conditional penalties will have been a wish on the part of the authorities to prevent what was considered to be indecent conduct. By way of these penalties, general 'offence' in the local community could be avoided. Even couples who were acquitted of the accusation of incest might be threatened with a penalty, as in the case of Olof and Rebecka. A conditional penalty can thus be seen as an attempt on the part of the authorities to inculcate correct behaviour in the accused and reintegrate them into the current norms as to how family relationships were supposed to function. This creates the impression that the authorities were more interested in preventing future indecencies than in punishing old transgressions. From a perspective of social morality, it was hence more important to penalise behaviour that was considered indecent than to establish whether an incest prohibition had actually been violated.

The transition from religious ideals to a more morally based ethics of virtue around the turn of the century in 1800 has been observed by other researchers as well, and it is completely in line with other social transformations.[130] With respect to France, Germany, and Denmark, a similar decrease in religious arguments in the assessment of incest cases has been shown to occur towards the end of the eighteenth century. In France, all incest prohibitions were completely abolished in 1791 in connection with a desire to eliminate religious hypocrisy;[131] and in Germany, incest prohibitions were primarily linked to a policy for family health. Because stable family relationships

130 Marklund 2004, pp. 74f; Nilsson [Hammar] 2012, pp. 192f.
131 Giuliani 2014, pp. 27–31.

without jealousy or abuse were perceived to be foundational for the whole of society, the court hearings came to focus on questions of morality and excessive violence. When voluntary relationships (usually *brother-in-law/sister-in-law* or *stepmother/stepson*) were to be assessed, the decisive factor became whether the relationship had been initiated before or after the husband/wife had died. When a person claimed that violence had been used, it became the task of the courts to determine whether the violence should be defined as legitimate, i.e. as occurring within the framework of disciplinary physical chastisement, or illegitimate. Jarzebowski maintains that the bourgeois family ideal eventually replaced the religious arguments that had previously been used to justify incest prohibitions. The crime of incest was no longer punished because it was seen as a sinful act, but because it was regarded as a threat against family solidarity at a time when the value of the family was rising.[132]

According to Danish historian Nina Koefoed, a radical change also occurred in the climate of Danish debate during the last decades of the eighteenth century. Around 1770, God's law was still used as an immutable baseline value for incest crimes, and the absolute power of the king to judge or reprieve criminals was not questioned. Thirty years later, by contrast, questions of religion, morals, and decency were settled with recourse to rational arguments. The church was no longer accepted as a guardian of social morality on behalf of the state. Instead, citizens themselves were expected to take responsibility for their own morals, and the task of the state could be described as that of defending civil rights.[133] However, another Danish historian, Tyge Krogh, shows that the change was not quite that radical. Whether incest prohibitions should be held to constitute a divine and thus immutable law had been debated off and on ever since Andreas Hojer raised the issue shortly after the turn of the century in 1700.[134]

No matter how rapid the process of change had been, it is clear that the legitimacy of religious arguments for incest had decreased towards the end of the century and that new arguments were brought forth as replacements. In Swedish case law, social morality and decency were given the largest space in the renegotiation of the actual purpose of incest prohibitions. The focus was on re-establishing

132 Jarzebowski 2006, pp. 257–63. See also Kerchner 2003, pp. 251f.
133 Koefoed 1999, pp. 24, 52–7.
134 Krogh 2000, p. 189.

14 A discussion in the Council of the State.

correct behaviour in the prosecuted individuals rather than on punishing them for the crimes they had committed in the past. Both parties were assumed to have participated voluntarily, and incest cases were primarily treated as *moral crimes*.

Incest prohibitions in public hearings

Up until now, this study has shown that the number of applications for dispensation increased significantly in Sweden towards the end of the eighteenth century. It did not take long for this increase to bring about an altered and more liberal assessment of certain relationship categories. At the turn of the century in 1800, a man and his *wife's sister*, *wife's niece*, and *stepfather's widow* could acquire royal permission to marry without much difficulty, unless there were other impediments to the marriage aside from the family relationship. At the same time, case law had changed in that fewer suspects were convicted of incest crimes, and those who were often received more lenient punishments than the ones prescribed by law. Clearly, then, the enforcement of incest prohibitions had been weakened in the practical handling of incest cases. However, no major changes to the law, or even discussions regarding legislative changes, had taken place. This would change in the nineteenth century.

On 9 June 1809, a bill was brought before the Swedish Parliament (the *Riksdag*) which initiated decades of discussion about the regulation of the forbidden degrees. The initiator of the bill was Henning Adolf von Strokirch, an associate judge of the court of appeal with twenty-five years of experience of working in the courts and a member of the Riksdag for the estate of the nobility.[135] Von Strokirch claimed that the law fell short when it came to the regulation of marriage prohibitions. The Swedish application of incest prohibitions, he said, had been pushed far beyond the limits of reason and beyond the assessments made in other nations. The text of the law was too strictly regulated and left no scope for a judge to take account of special circumstances that arose in real life, which resulted in a conflict between the 'flinty application of the law' on the one hand and 'the moral assessment' on the other. Von Strokirch thus described a discrepancy between the legislation and the general sense of justice. In order to remedy these problems, he proposed the abolition of several incest prohibitions.[136]

The proposal occasioned a detailed examination of the prohibitions. The original purposes of the prohibitions were discussed, as was the effect they were assumed to have on society as well as what was believed to be public opinion about the issue. After heated debate, Strokirch's bill resulted in a royal regulation in 1810 which meant that people who were related in different affinity degrees (among others *wife's sister*, *brother's widow*, *wife's niece*, *stepfather's widow*) became free to apply for a dispensation for marriage.[137] Consequently, the law was adapted in accordance with the practice that had developed over the past thirty years.

But that was not the end of the matter. On several occasions during the ensuing decades, new debates were initiated in the Riksdag regarding further liberalisation of the incest prohibitions; and the 1815 proposal for a new marriage legislation suggested that a number of incest prohibitions should be abolished completely. Opinions were divided, though.[138] Between 1823 and 1871, the issue was raised in eleven different sessions of the Riksdag. The incest relationships regulated in Chapter 2, Sections 3, 5, and 6 of the Marriage Code

135 Henning Adolf von Strokirch (1757–1826), during his career a hundred-court judge in Vartofta county, a member of the Göta Court of Appeal and later of the Supreme Court, Justice of the Supreme Court and President of the Svea Court of Appeal.

136 *RoA 1809*, pp. 646–54. Quotation on p. 646.

137 K.F. 1810, 10 April.

138 The proposal concerned *cousin*, *nephew's widow*, *wife's aunt*, *wife's niece*. *Förslag till Giftermåls Balk*, pp. 2–4.

were subjected to particularly intense discussion. These sections regulated cousin relationships (Section 3); collateral and diagonal affinity relationships, for instance *wife's sister*, *brother's widow*, *wife's niece*, or *uncle's widow* (Section 5); and affinity relationships in the second degree, for instance *wife's stepmother*, *stepfather's widow*, and *son-in-law's widow* (Section 6). The purpose of incest prohibitions, and the issue of how boundaries should be drawn, was also discussed in a thesis from 1813 written by future lawyer Carl Johan Schlyter.[139] This thesis was commented on anonymously in the law journal *Juridiskt Arkif* twenty years later.[140]

There is thus a wealth of preserved source material where the incest prohibitions were debated by lawyers, theologians, and politicians, material which provides a clear picture of the opinions articulated by these men during the first half of the nineteenth century. Some wanted to abolish the prohibitions while others wished to retain them; but at bottom everybody agreed that the relationships mentioned in Chapter 2, Sections 3, 5, and 6 of the Marriage Code were not harmful from a moral or a religious perspective.[141] In spite of this shared fundamental persuasion, people nevertheless chose different standpoints on the issue. The ensuing section analyses the arguments in the debates in order to bring out the norms and ideas that formed the basis for the views of the politicians. While the burgher and peasant estates were, in general, in favour of further liberalisation, the proposals caused much debate among the nobility and the clergy, where opinions were more mixed and decisions more often settled by way of a vote.

For protection against immorality

It is clear that the previously unchallenged explanatory basis for the drafting of the incest prohibitions, that of religion, had lost some of its credibility. Those who promoted a liberalisation of the legislation questioned the actual purpose and origin of the prohibitions. Some claimed that the incest prohibitions had been drawn up by and for the Jewish people in the political and cultural climate

139 Schlyter 1813.

140 Anonymous 1831/32.

141 See, e.g., *RoA, 1809*, pp. 1236, 1239; *RoA, 1809*, volume 3, pp. 150–2; *RoA, 1809*, volume 4, p. 832; *Pr, 1809*, volume 3, pp. 393, 400; *Lagutskottets betänkande nr 11* ('Report no. 11 of the parliamentary committee on legislation'), *1828/29*.

at the time of Moses; but since society had changed since then, it was reasonable for these laws to be adapted in accordance with social developments.[142] Others felt that the prohibitions were remnants of the heresies of Catholic priests.[143] These arguments are strongly reminiscent of those used by Andreas Hojer a hundred years earlier in Denmark. But these arguments, which had created such a stir during the early eighteenth century, were now accepted without any major challenges in the Swedish parliamentary debates.

Even though individual debaters maintained that the prohibitions were of divine origin, it was more common for the religious arguments to be reformulated in accordance with the contemporary demand for arguments based on reason. For example, the anonymous author of the previously mentioned article in the law journal *Juridiskt Arkif* claimed that there was no contradiction between attitudes based on religion and on natural law as regards incest prohibitions, because they both arose from 'the special commandments of conscience' that existed within a human being. Both reason and religion proceeded from a 'common traditional source' or an 'inherited conviction'. This common origin guaranteed the legitimacy of the prohibitions; and according to the article's author, it justified the idea that the Swedish legislation should be respected in its current form.[144]

The basic idea, i.e., that the laws were not divine or immutable, was thus to a great extent accepted by both the promoters and the opponents of the liberalisation of the incest prohibitions. Instead of allowing themselves to be governed by religious principles, they attempted to find a *basis in natural law* building on lines of reasoning regarding human nature.[145] In line with this approach, people spoke about incestuous relationships being circumscribed by 'a natural revulsion' or that there was a 'natural rein' that should be supported in law so that it was not weakened.[146]

142 *RoA, 1809*, volume 3, p. 152; *Bd, 1823*, volume 2, p. 704; *Utlåtande, i anledning af Anmärkningar wid Förslaget till Allmän Criminallag, af Lagcommiteen*, p. 132.

143 *RoA, 1809*, volume 3, p. 152.

144 Anonymous 1831/32, 329f.

145 *Utlåtande, i anledning af Anmärkningar wid Förslaget till Allmän Criminallag, af Lagcommiteen*, p. 131. According to Bo Lindberg's interpretation, the rhetoric surrounding the idea of natural law mainly served to impart legitimacy to legal assessments without really entailing any major changes; Lindberg 1976, pp. 171–6.

146 *Lagutskottets betänkande nr 31, 1823*, p. 109. Schlyter 1813, p. 11.

But what was thought to be the true purpose of the incest prohibitions?

In his thesis from 1813, Schlyter wrote that the incest prohibitions in the closest degrees promoted social virtue and that they had a beneficial influence on individual citizens as well as on the nation as a whole. The lineal consanguinity prohibition was, according to him, the most important prohibition:

> [F]rom the beginning [, this prohibition] was occasioned by revulsion against these connections, a revulsion which, albeit not an immediate instinct, should nevertheless be considered natural. Certain legislators have realised the good effect of such ways of thinking on upbringing, on customs, and on the vigour of the nation. Through these prohibitions, along with the penal laws against incest, they hence sought to prevent the natural revulsion from being weakened.[147]

Here the idea of the *natural* origin of the prohibitions recurs. The purpose of the prohibitions was to strengthen a sense of morality in young people, who in the long run provided the basis for a strong and healthy nation. In connection with the parliamentary session of 1809, it was similarly claimed that the purpose of the prohibitions was to promote 'social order, [and] the advancement of general and individual welfare'.[148] Another speaker felt that the incest prohibitions entailed moral benefits for the community and that their primary purpose was to 'retain the purity of customs'.[149]

The collateral affinity relationships (*wife's sister*, *brother's widow*) and the cousin relationships were not deemed to be criminal or immoral in themselves, which explains why these particular relationship categories were the subject of the majority of the proposals for liberalisation.[150] People agreed that crimes against these commandments were often committed because of 'thoughtlessness, without the intention to cause any evil, and [without] proper insight into the evil consequences of the act'.[151] In spite of this, several debaters argued that the crimes had to be assessed with reference to their social consequences rather than the actual intentions of the agent.[152] The purpose of the law was to retain the 'purity of customs'

147 Schlyter 1813, p. 11.
148 *Bd, 1809–1810*, volume 4, p. 466.
149 *RoA, 1809*, volume 3, p. 154.
150 Among these, diagonal degrees were also occasionally included, e.g., *niece*, *uncle's widow*.
151 *RoA, 1809*, p. 1236.
152 *Pr, 1809*, volume 2, p. 636; *Pr, 1809*, volume 3, p. 404.

and the 'social virtues'.[153] It was believed to counteract general immorality while having a favourable effect on young people's sense of morality and on their upbringing. One bishop felt that the relationships in fact 'had to be considered permissible by God himself', but that the prohibitions were nevertheless reasonable on account of what was 'best for society'.[154] Without the protection of the prohibitions people would more easily fall victim to the allure of desire, with – it was feared – unfavourable consequences for both households and society.[155] The removal of the prohibitions would therefore give 'occasion for seduction, for crimes against modesty and fidelity, and various disorders'.[156] Quite simply, the prohibitions promoted 'the necessary care for the preservation of decency'.[157]

Furthermore, the more conservative speakers claimed that the prohibitions functioned as a wall, a boundary, or what we might call a buffer zone between what was allowed and what was forbidden. A representative of the clerical estate described the prohibition of cousin marriages as 'beneficial and based in nature, like a kind of entrenchment or outworks for the sanctity of the [sibling prohibition]'.[158] Another member of the same estate felt that it was 'highly dangerous to disturb the barrier which, through the conditional prohibition in the law for the marriages of siblings' children [i.e., cousins], had been constructed to secure the sanctity of closer consanguinity degrees'.[159] A third voice pointed out that the prohibition, in spite of the possibilities of obtaining a dispensation, was 'a reminder that the boundary of the sacred, the inviolable, was [...] close'.[160] Without the boundaries formed by the prohibitions, the 'thoughtless crowd' in particular risked having diminished respect for the sacred.[161] As one speaker expressed it, the 'most hallowed

153 *RoA, 1809*, volume 3, p. 154; *Bd, 1809–1810*, volume 4, p. 451; *Utlåtande, i anledning af Anmärkningar wid Förslaget till Allmän Criminallag, af Lagcommiteen*, p. 132; *RoA, 1809*, volume 4, p. 830.

154 *Pr, 1823*, volume 5, pp. 101f.

155 *RoA, 1809*, volume 3, pp. 154f; *Lagutskottets betänkande nr 11, 1828/29*, pp. 24f.

156 *Pr, 1809*, volume 2, p. 636.

157 *Lagutskottets betänkande nr 31, 1823*, p. 107.

158 *Pr, 1823*, volume 5, p. 100; *Lagutskottets betänkande nr 11, 1828/29*, p. 22.

159 *Pr, 1829*, volume 2, p. 373.

160 *Lagutskottets betänkande nr 11, 1828/29*, p. 22. See also *Lagutskottets betänkande nr 135, 1823*, p. 742.

161 *Pr, 1823*, volume 5, p. 98.

bond of nature' might be torn asunder and trodden underfoot 'until the closest lineal blood relatives, former and future, considered themselves exempted by human laws from the commandments of divine law, and eventually entitled to descend from humans and Christians to animals'.[162]

According to their supporters, the prohibitions were to function as a warning bell for the people, and they were believed to be necessary in order to safeguard public decency. Politicians of a conservative bent thus feared the consequences that would follow any liberalisation of the marriage prohibitions. Even if the relationships in themselves were not perceived to be immoral, the prohibitions drew a line between what was forbidden and what was permitted. Without this distinct boundary, it was feared that people – especially those with little education – would initiate sexual relations in closer kinship degrees as well. By contrast, those who argued for a change in the law effectively questioned the connection between the statutory incest prohibitions and general morality in society.[163]

In support of healthy family relationships

During the nineteenth century, the general structure of the family changed. Previously the household – including any servant maids, farmhands, and other servants – had made up a collective work unit that lived in relative openness vis-à-vis the local community. Later, the idea of a private nuclear family emerged, one whose closeness was based more on love and care than on mutual economic dependency. The new family ideal developed first within the emergent bourgeoisie, but soon spread to other social groups as well.[164] These cultural changes had not become generally accepted in Swedish society at the turn of the century in 1800, but ideas about the nuclear family as the mainstay of society are clearly manifested in the parliamentary material. A large proportion of the nineteenth-century incest debate revolved around issues regarding the nuclear family and the drawing of boundaries between the innermost family circle and the rest of society. The debate also raised questions as

162 *Pr, 1823*, volume 5, p. 100.

163 *RoA, 1809*, volume 3, pp. 151f; *Lagutskottets betänkande nr 135, 1823*, p. 736. *Lagutskottets betänkande nr 11, 1828/29*, pp. 16f; *RoA, 1844*, part 4, p. 353.

164 See, e.g., Coontz 2005, pp. 128, 140–5, 173; Davidoff, Doolittle, Fink, and Holden 1999, pp. 37–9.

to how various family members were expected to behave towards one another. One thing that all prohibitions had in common was that their purpose was linked to contemporary ideas about kinship and family constellations. Discussions about the prohibitions were hence essentially concerned with what family relationships looked like in society, and how the prohibitions were assumed to affect everyday family relationships.

Preventing premature sensuality in children

The sibling and cousin prohibitions were considered to have the same original purpose; that is, to prevent 'premature sensuality' in children growing up close to one another. Schlyter wrote that 'the legislator wanted to fulfil the parents' wishes to prevent, by removing all thoughts of any future legal connection, a premature sensuality in children, who as a rule are always brought up in the same house'.[165]

It was considered important to make sure that children who grew up in physical proximity did not develop any form of sexual relationship. This was true of siblings as well as of cousins, who were sometimes raised together 'like siblings'. But even cousins who did *not* grow up in the same household might have a sibling-like relationship because their parents were siblings and they were therefore presumed to have close and everyday dealings with each other.[166] There was quite simply a danger in frequent and intense social intercourse during childhood and adolescence. The natural sibling-love and intimacy among cousins, which in itself was an asset for the individual and for all of society, then risked being transmuted into a harmful sexual relationship. For this reason, the prohibitions served as a constant reminder that such relationships were unnatural and improper.[167]

---

165 Schlyter 1813, pp. 13f.

166 *Lagutskottets betänkande nr 31, 1823*, p. 108. According to this justification, the relationship between, e.g., *step-siblings* or *foster children* should, logically speaking, also be forbidden, which Schlyter also pointed out. Nevertheless, extending the prohibitions never seems to have been up for discussion. Schlyter 1813, pp. 30f, note v; *Pr, 1823*, volume 5, p. 99.

167 For statements maintaining that families and laws should be considered to be unchanged, see *Lagutskottets betänkande nr 11, 1828/29*, pp. 21, 26; *Bo, 1828/29*, volume 1, p. 696; *Lagutskottets betänkande nr 135, 1823*, p. 740.

Nevertheless, during the first half of the nineteenth century many members of the Riksdag agreed that the cousin prohibition was obsolete because families did not associate with each other in the same way as before. On several occasions, it was emphasised that 'in older times' the family had made up 'a whole' in which cousins associated with each other 'as much as did siblings', but this was no longer the case.[168] Similarly, in 1809 the parliamentary committee on legislation pointed out that the justification for the cousin prohibition had 'ceased to be valid since families had begun to be more dispersed'.[169] In the parliamentary session of 1823, one speaker claimed that 'cousins have a relationship with each other that is no different from that between people who are completely unrelated'.[170] Several members of the Riksdag thus felt that everyday relations between cousins had changed and that the prohibition had consequently lost its function. Similar arguments about a reduced family intimacy were also voiced with regard to relationships in the second affinity degree (*wife's stepmother*, *stepson's widow*).[171]

Preventing jealousy and discord within the family

As was pointed out above, relationships between a woman and her brother-in-law, and between a man and his sister-in-law, were not regarded as immoral in themselves if the spouse in question was no longer alive. It was even recognised that there were advantages to a relationship of this kind. For example, a member of the clerical estate argued that a man could hardly find 'a more tender stepmother for his children than the sister of their deceased mother'.[172] In spite of this, people with a more conservative outlook felt that it was important to keep the prohibitions 'so that, while the wife lives, the idea of a connection with her sister is removed'.[173]

Everyday relations between a woman and her brother-in-law and a man and his sister-in-law left room for 'more intimate social

168 *RoA, 1809*, p. 1238. For additional examples, see *Pr, 1809*, volume 2, p. 630; *RoA, 1844*, part 4, p. 354; Schlyter 1813, p. 15.

169 *RoA, 1809*, p. 1238.

170 *Lagutskottets betänkande nr 135, 1823*, p. 737. See also *RoA, 1844*, part 4, p. 354.

171 *RoA, 1810*, volume 6, p. 1568. See also *Lagutskottets betänkande nr 35, 1847/48*, p. 2.

172 *Pr, 1809*, volume 3, p. 405.

173 *RoA, 1859/60*, volume 3, p. 208.

intercourse' than other relationships, which might lead people astray under the wrong circumstances.[174] The relationship between brother-in-law and sister-in-law was considered to have its foundation in 'a natural affection' that arose from their spending more time with each other than with other people. However, these close relations entailed the possibility that 'the sacred rights of intimacy and friendship [...] might [...] be abused'.[175] It was necessary to thwart the possibility of sexual relations between these people. Any infidelity between a brother-in-law and a sister-in-law was, in addition, held to lead to especially serious consequences for the family because such a betrayal was perceived to be 'more dreadful' and 'corrosive' for family members than if the betrayal was perpetrated with a stranger.[176]

The prohibitions hence aimed to promote a well-functioning family relationship by preventing affectionate relations between brothers-in-law and sisters-in-law from assuming a sexual character. Without prohibitions, there was risk that the frequency of infidelity would increase, which threatened to destroy a domestic and affectionate coexistence.

Promoting filial deference

The prohibitions against lineal relationships in both consanguinity and affinity degrees had a completely different, if equally important, purpose: to support and strengthen children's respect for their parents. In a report from 18 August 1809, the parliamentary committee on legislation discussed why filial deference was so important. It was pointed out that even though everyone was born with a capacity for rational thinking, sensuality was extra powerful during the years of youth and therefore had to be 'bent under the reason of others and be habituated to obedience' until the individual had matured and was 'able to listen to his or her own reason'. In order to maintain and protect the natural deference and respect felt by the younger generation for the older, it was therefore important to avert all thoughts of intimate relations between them. Parents were thought to be the people who were by nature primarily responsible for their children's upbringing, but if the parents died before their children

174 *Lagutskottets betänkande nr 31, 1823*, p. 107; *Pr, 1823*, volume 5, p. 99. See also *RoA, 1809*, volume 3, p. 154.
175 *Pr, 1809*, volume 3, p. 401.
176 *Pr, 1809*, volume 2, p. 636.

reached their majority, their siblings or spouses were expected to take over this responsibility.[177] The idea was to ensure that 'by removing all thoughts of a lawful connection between these possible rearers and the reared, the authority of the former can be preserved and promoted'.[178] One speaker made it clear that the prohibitions were necessary because nothing could 'undermine and vitiate' deference as much as the 'mere thought' of a sensual union between 'a rearer and the reared'.[179]

Here the debaters directly or indirectly alluded to the Lutheran Table of Duties, which had previously formed the obvious foundation of society and which retained its normative function far into the nineteenth century. Family relationships were characterised by deference and respect between the generations, and the importance of upholding these hierarchies could not be emphasised strongly enough. The subservient position of the child, which was regarded as necessary and healthy, was hence imperilled if the mere thought of a sexual relationship between the rearer and the child took hold. The relationship between the generations was nevertheless seen as reciprocal, with rights and obligations in both directions. The younger party should show respect and obedience vis-à-vis his or her rearer but was also entitled to expect protection and help from the older generation.[180] Consequently, prohibitions had the dual purpose of maintaining the deference between the generations while preventing a rearer from abusing his or her position of authority by exploiting the person who was under his or her protection.

Promoting closeness among family members

Regardless of which type of family relationship was involved, it was assumed that there was a special friendship and closeness between the persons in question, and the incest prohibitions contributed to protecting that. August von Hartmansdorff of the noble estate pointed out that the law protected cousins so that they could live close to and support each other without any suspicion of immorality.[181] Another nobleman feared that many needy people would be deprived

177 *RoA, 1809*, pp. 1234f, quotation on p. 1234.
178 Schlyter 1813, p. 14; *Förslag till Allmän Civillag, 1838*, p. 7.
179 *Lagutskottets betänkande nr 35, 1847/48*, p. 3. See also *Pr, 1829*, volume 2, p. 372.
180 *Lagutskottets betänkande nr 29, 1844/45*, p. 15.
181 *RoA, 1823*, volume 3, p. 585.

of the support of their relatives if the prohibition against cousin marriages was abolished, because they could no longer 'without blame [...] seek refuge' with a cousin if they needed to do so.[182] Similarly, hundred-court judge Arvid Ribbing claimed that repealing the current legislation would damage family solidarity and put obstacles in the way of charitable support between relatives in need.[183] If the incest prohibitions were to be abolished, people would be forced to change their behaviour towards each other in order to avoid suspicion of indecency, said yet another representative of the nobility. Friendship and intimacy within the closest family would have to be sacrificed, and family members would become as 'strangers to each other'.[184]

Incest prohibitions were also believed to be a prerequisite for people being able to receive economic support from their nearest kin without feeling disgraced. Relatives had a duty to help one another, and for this reason it was not humiliating to accept help from them in the way it would have been if the helper had been a stranger.[185]

The arguments thus aimed to show that the incest prohibitions made close social intercourse among family members possible. Indeed, the prohibitions were viewed as a *prerequisite* for affectionate relations. A single man or woman could move in with his or her married sibling without risking rumours of indecency, and cousins could live in the same household without the people around them becoming suspicious about their leading an immoral life. Kinship entailed rights as well as obligations. It functioned as a social and economic safety net on which everyone depended, not least the impecunious social categories. The incest prohibitions hence contributed to family members being able to live close to, and receive assistance from, one another without arousing suspicions of impropriety among the people around them.

182 *RoA, 1823*, volume 7, p. 437.

183 *Lagutskottets betänkande nr 135, 1823*, p. 741. See also p. 734.

184 *RoA, 1828/29*, part 12, pp. 127f, quotation on p. 128. For additional examples of a similar argumentation, see *RoA, 1844*, part 4, p. 353; *Pr, 1809*, volume 2, p. 637; *RoA, 1823*, volume 3, pp. 585f; *Lagutskottets betänkande nr 31, 1823*, p. 108.

185 *RoA, 1828/29*, part 12, p. 128; *RoA, 1844*, part 4, pp. 351f. On duties and solidarity among relatives, see also Rundquist 1989, pp. 284–7. See also *Lagutskottets betänkande nr 16, 1859/60*, p. 20.

Economic concerns and demands for justice

The drawing of boundaries with regard to incest prohibitions was also discussed on the basis of the economic and practical consequences that a liberalisation might entail. One nobleman claimed that the prohibitions were politically useful because they prevented estates from accumulating 'in the hands of one man', which was not in the interest of the state.[186] Several debaters said they thought that economic motives were the main reason behind most cousin marriages, and they feared that rich families would increasingly marry within their own group if the prohibitions were abolished. Abolition would thus lead to estates accumulating within individual families, whereas it was in society's interest that they should be distributed among all citizens. The forming of alliances between different groups and families, a process which the prohibitions encouraged, was also believed to be good for the nation.[187]

By contrast, the more liberal speakers maintained that the dispensational procedure involved an unnecessary workload for the state's civil servants while the procedure was expensive and time-consuming for individual citizens.[188] In addition, the system was said to be unfair because not everyone had the same opportunity to pay the stamp charge which the application involved.[189] Among those who rejected this argument were a couple of representatives from the clerical estate who said that poor people rarely wished to enter into such marriages, and if they really wanted to do so it was

186 *RoA, 1809*, volume 3, p. 154.

187 *Pr, 1809*, volume 2, p. 637; *Pr, 1823*, volume 2, p. 549; *Lagutskottets betänkande nr 31, 1823*, p. 109.

188 *Bd, 1823*, volume 2, p. 704; *Bd, 1828/29*, volume 1, p. 301; *Lagutskottets betänkande nr 31, 1823*, p. 107.

189 An application for dispensation cost about eight to ten *riksdaler* in *riksgäld* coins, which was the approximate equivalent in value to a quarter of an ox. In the early nineteenth century, banknotes were printed in parallel by the Riksbank, the Swedish central bank, and a national administrative authority called Riksgälden (approx. 'the national debt office'). Because of inflation, the value of the notes varied; therefore, it was important to be aware of which particular currency a person was referring to. See Lagerqvist and Nathorst-Böös, p. 16. *RoA, 1828/29*, part 12, pp. 130, 133; *RoA, 1844*, part 4, p. 354; *Pr, 1859/60*, volume 1, p. 41. Additional examples of the same argument can be found in *Pr, 1823*, volume 2, p. 548; *Bd, 1828–29*, volume 1, p. 301; *RoA, 1828–29*, part 12, p. 135; *RoA, 1809*, volume 3, p. 152; *Bd, 1834*, volume 5, p. 5.

also because of economic advantages, and then they were perfectly able to pay the fee.[190]

In 1829, the attention to and understanding of the situation of the poor that was nevertheless demonstrated by many people resulted in a royal proclamation which made the application procedure for cousin marriages free of cost.[191] However, the fees for applications for marriage in other relationship categories seem to have been retained.[192]

The dispensational procedure was perceived to be unfair from another perspective as well. The fact that the sole purpose of some prohibitions was that of serving as a warning against other, more forbidden relationships, while the expressly forbidden relations were not in fact thought to be immoral in themselves, amounted to sacrificing the individual for the good of the collective. This view was criticised by the proponents of liberalisation, who argued that neither the king nor the state had the right to interfere in the private affairs of individual citizens. In other words, single individuals should not have to forego a desired marriage in order to promote the common social morality. In addition, retaining a law that was in conflict with the people's sense of justice risked undermining confidence in the law and the judicial system. Consequently, the entire dispensational procedure as such was warped. That the same act was forbidden and criminal in one case and permitted in another was simply not logical. The question that arose from this was whether the system was at all morally defensible.[193]

There was a certain amount of disagreement about how public opinion regarded the incest prohibitions. Some people claimed that all relationships which were the subject of the liberalisation debate were accepted and well-liked by the people, whereas others wished to retain the prohibitions out of respect for those who viewed the prohibited acts as immoral.[194] As a golden mean, it was suggested

---

190 *Pr, 1823*, volume 2, pp. 549f.

191 K.F. 1829, 8 September.

192 In 1840 a man and his *brother's widow* refrained from applying for a dispensation for marriage because they felt it was too expensive. GHA, EVAC:937, 1840, no. 27.

193 *Bd, 1809/10*, volume 4, p. 453; *RoA, 1809*, p. 1236; *RoA, 1823*, volume 7, p. 427; *RoA, 1828/29*, part 12, p. 133; *RoA, 1840*, part 3, p. 217; *Lagutskottets betänkande nr 167, 1840/41*, p. 15.

194 *Lagutskottets betänkande nr 167, 1840/41*, p. 18; *Bd, 1840*, volume 2, p. 473; *RoA, 1844*, part 4, pp. 351f.

that the dispensational procedure should be used in order to slowly accustom the people to the drawing of new boundaries.[195] When comparisons to the legislation of other countries were made, the Swedish legislation was found to be stricter than Norwegian, Danish, and Prussian law, a finding that was also used as an argument in favour of making the legislative framework more lenient.[196]

Finally, some members of the Riksdag expressed concern that close kinship connections might have an adverse effect on the health of offspring. One of the representatives of the estate of the nobility had heard rumours that such relationships might entail 'injury to the mental faculties of descendants'.[197] Another had heard that 'certain noble as well as princely families who marry much among themselves become ever more stupid and maladroit'.[198] During this period, the subject was never debated widely and in earnest; but interest in hereditary consequences would increase over time, as will be seen below.

In summary, there was agreement on certain foundational ideological principles, such as the importance to society of social morality and the family. The function and value of the family were highly regarded by everyone. No one opposed the idea that there was a higher degree of intimacy within the family, and that this should be safeguarded; that there was a hierarchical division between generations, where the parental generation was entitled to demand the respect and obedience of younger generations; or that a family and their closest kin functioned both as economic and as social support among themselves. Everyone also agreed that sexual relationships might jeopardise these principles.

Instead, a large proportion of the debate had to do with establishing where the boundary of the innermost family circle should be drawn. Those who promoted the liberalisation of the prohibitions claimed that relations within the family had changed and that the boundaries between family, kin, and society had to be adjusted. There was no longer any obvious difference between cousins and neighbours, or between remote relatives by marriage and other friends. Other debaters felt that the relationships of family and kin

195 *RoA, 1809*, volume 4, p. 831; *Lagutskottets betänkande nr 31, 1823*, p. 107; Schlyter 1813, p. 15.

196 *Lagfarenhets-Bibliothek*, p. 728; *Bd, 1847/48*, volume 2, p. 393; *Bo, 1859/60*, volume 2, p. 294.

197 *Lagutskottets betänkande nr 31, 1823*, p. 108.

198 *RoA, 1844*, part 4, p. 352.

were essentially unchanged, that relatives still lived in closer proximity to one another, and that the prohibitions were needed as a protection for their intimate relations. The definition of the family, and conceptions as to the nature of different familial relationships, thus played a prominent role in the debate concerning the liberalisation of the incest prohibitions.

Partial summary and overview, 1740–1840

Towards the end of the eighteenth century, European society was increasingly characterised by revolutionary political, social, and cultural changes which led to the questioning of the incest regulations in force at the time as well as the norms on which the older legislation was based. Firstly, the position of religion in society changed, whereupon the incest prohibitions could no longer be justified by way of theological arguments alone. Secondly, the judicial system and penal legislation were criticised by proponents of the philosophical ideas of the Enlightenment, prompting demands for increased equality before the law and more lenient case law. Thirdly, the acceptance of marriage alliances between related people increased as a consequence of economic and cultural changes.

In Sweden, the negotiation process surrounding the configuration of incest prohibitions was brought to the fore during the decades before the turn of the century in 1800, which eventually resulted in a change of practice with regard to applications for dispensation and crimes of incest. Increasing numbers of people applied for permission to marry, and their applications were increasingly often approved with regard to a greater number of relationship categories. At the same time, fewer and fewer people were convicted of crimes against the incest prohibitions, and those who were convicted were often given more lenient punishments than those prescribed by law. In this way, a discrepancy between theoretical and practical positions was created, giving rise to official discussions among lawyers, theologians, and politicians during the first half of the nineteenth century.

In the official debate, various theories on the origin, purpose, and usefulness of the prohibitions were presented, as well as different opinions as to where boundaries should be drawn and which legal rules were felt to be reasonable. These debates emphasised the connection between incest prohibitions and moral norms, but ideas about the family and about relationships between family members were also brought into play. Among other things, there was an adjustment of the importance of filial deference for the assessment of incestuous relationships. Previously, relationships had only been assessed on the basis of people's positions in the family relative to each other, and horizontal relationships were treated more leniently than vertical ones, regardless of the age or biological closeness of those involved. After the turn of the century in 1800, information about the protagonists' respective age was taken into account in a way that had not been done before. Previous research has shown that respect towards the older generation decreased in society at the same time, and the new practice may be seen as an expression of the relationship between generations being renegotiated in society as a whole.

The material also reflects a change of mentality with respect to the view on emotions. Earlier, reason had been idealised above feeling; but now emotions acquired more favourable connotations, and the love match was increasingly valorised. This change was observed by previous researchers and seems to have occurred in Europe as a whole at slightly different times. In the Swedish dispensational material from the relevant period, this change can be seen in the fact that couples applying for dispensation to marry often emphasised that they loved each other, and that their marriage could therefore be expected to be a happy one. Another difference in comparison to earlier periods is that sentences were increasingly often reduced for prosecuted couples whose relationships were described as reciprocal and affectionate.

If one assumes that interactions among people and groups in society indirectly affect norms and values, this development becomes logical. Seen from this perspective, it was thus political pressure and questionings from the population at large that led to changed practices; and these changes, in their turn, became the driving force behind an official renegotiation of the drawing of boundaries with regard to incest prohibitions. In this discursive process of negotiation, older notions pertaining to religion and family hierarchies were contrasted with new ideas on social morality, kinship, and the right of the individual to freedom and happiness. The outcome was a change of attitude regarding the purpose and origin of incest prohibitions, and an adjustment of the drawing of boundaries between legal and illegal relationships.

Challenges to the prevailing, religiously justified, norms happened in parallel in places all over Europe. The penalties imposed for several crimes were reduced towards the end of the eighteenth century, while the number of marriages between related persons increased.[199] Legal, theological, and political debates regarding the configuration of the prohibitions were continually taking place in, among other countries, Britain, Germany, Austria, and France. There were debates outside the borders of Sweden even before the turn of the century in 1800; but the arguments that were presented were often similar.[200] In Prussia, incest prohibitions were renegotiated into laws against secularised crimes whose judicial assessment rested on ideas about the family and 'the common good'. Unlike the situation in Sweden, incestuous desires were now described as natural in Prussia, but the acts were nevertheless prohibited because they were thought to harm the family and society.[201] In Denmark, one new regulation followed upon another in the period between 1770 and 1800.[202] Nowhere, however, was the change as radical as in France. Here all incest prohibitions were abolished in connection with the French Revolution as being religious prohibitions that had unjustly been imposed on the people. Henceforth, incest was discussed wholly on the basis of ideas about sound family relationships and social morality. Exploitation and violence against underage relatives could still be prosecuted under other crime headings, but incestuous acts were primarily regarded as a private family matter.[203]

Although punishments were generally speaking reduced in all of Europe towards the end of the eighteenth century, Sweden still stood out with harsher punishments and a lower degree of tolerance. In Britain, the worst that could happen to non-biological relatives who married in opposition to religious law was that their marriages might be declared invalid (if they were reported), whereas Swedish couples who violated the incest prohibitions risked being put in jail on bread and water for up to twenty-eight days.[204] In Prussia, relationships between brothers-in-law and sisters-in-law were liberalised as early as 1740.[205] In Sweden, by contrast, the first

199 E.g., Sabean and Teusher 2007; Saurer 1997, pp. 356–9; Darrow 1985; Johnson 2011.

200 Denbo 2001, pp. 161–98; Kuper 2002, 160–8; Kercher 2003; Saurer 1997, pp. 350–6; Giuliani 2009b, Giuliani 2014; Hunt 1992, pp. 5, 17, 41.

201 Jarzebowski 2003, pp. 163, 167–71; Jarzebowski 2006, pp. 257f; Kerchner 2003, pp. 252f.

202 Koefoed 1999, pp. 52–9.

203 Giuliani 2014, pp. 14, 32f; Giuliani 2009a, p. 923.

204 Morris 1992, pp. 143, 152f.

205 Jarzebowski 2003, p. 165.

dispensation was granted in 1785, and the prohibition remained in force until 1872. In Austria, relationships between in-laws were certainly forbidden; but they were fairly widely accepted in society. From the late eighteenth century onwards, people frequently applied for dispensation for marriage both in the horizontal (*wife's sister*) and vertical affinity degrees (*stepmother*, *stepdaughter*).[206] Applications from couples who were related in a vertical degree were extremely rare during the entire nineteenth century in the Swedish material, and none were given permission to marry.

One common factor of all the countries mentioned here was that the renegotiation of the drawing of boundaries with respect to incest prohibitions was interwoven with new definitions of the family, with ideas regarding morals and decency, and with cultural challenges to paternal authority.

---

206 Saurer 1997, pp. 358–60.

4
Incest: a crime of violence, 1840–1940

Not until the second half of the nineteenth century did Swedish agrarian society enter a new age of industrialisation and urbanisation. The population grew steadily, which led to increasing social problems in the country. In the countryside, an ever-increasing proportion of the population lived in poverty, and in the cities the authorities struggled against overcrowding and worsening hygienic conditions as well as against rising crime, alcoholism, and prostitution. The number of marriages decreased while the number of illegitimate children rose, which reinforced the impression of a society in moral decline.[1] In this context, the lower classes were frequently portrayed as a menace to bourgeois society. The poor were believed to threaten society economically through the cost of poor relief and the fight against crime, but also morally through their lazy and sinful ways of life.[2]

Liberal ideas, whose proponents advocated greater freedom and equality in society, slowly gained ground in relation to the conservative forces that protected the older social order. The old society of estates lost its legitimacy, and in 1866 the Riksdag of Estates was abolished in favour of a parliament with two chambers. The guild system was abolished and freedom to conduct business was introduced, entailing greater social mobility. During the same period there was a clear shift in power from the king to the Riksdag and the government.[3] Ideologically speaking, the unified Lutheran church

1 Levin 1994, p. 45. The population increase was at its greatest during the first half of the nineteenth century. The 'social question' had been debated even before industrialisation and urbanisation made the situation in the cities worse. For the poverty debate during the whole of the nineteenth century, see Petersson 1983.

2 Sjögren 1997, pp. 22, 158; Nilsson 2008, p. 141.

3 Inger 2011, pp. 208f.

was challenged partly by various nonconformist denominations and partly by an increased incidence of atheism, which led to a general secularisation of society. This did not mean that religion disappeared. Rather, it changed character in that the significance of religion in the public space dwindled while it continued to be an important part of the lives of individuals and groups. Religious worship became a matter of personal allegiance. This development has been described as a *privatisation* of religion.[4] Liberal and nonconformist groups questioned the prevailing religious compulsory system. As a result, the regulatory frameworks of several religious rites that had previously been obligatory, for instance communion and christenings, were loosened.[5] In 1908, civil marriage was introduced as an alternative to church weddings.[6]

The balance of power between the sexes changed as well. Various reforms boosted women's opportunities to support themselves, and at the same time men's guardianship over them was reduced.[7] The year 1919 saw the introduction of female suffrage in parliamentary elections. Even so, marriage as an institution continued to be regarded as one of the mainstays of society.[8]

Swedish society was thus transformed on a number of levels, economically and demographically as well as ideologically and culturally. The third and last part of this study examines how the general attitude to and assessment of incestuous relationships were affected by these revolutionary social developments. The investigation continues where the previous part ended, in the middle of the nineteenth century, with the then topical debate on potential liberalisations of the affinity prohibitions in collateral and diagonal degrees.

---

4 The changed role of religion in society has also been described as a *pluralisation* or a *feminisation*. On the changed role of religion in European society, see, e.g., Mcleod 2000a; Mcleod 2000b; Brown 2001. Swedish developments around the turn of the century in 1900 have been described in Bexell 2008.

5 Bexell 2008, p. 64; Inger 2011, pp. 240f.

6 Inger 2011, p. 219.

7 For instance, in 1845 equal rights to matrimonial property and rights of inheritance were introduced for men and women. Women gained their own majority gradually through reforms in 1858, 1863, 1874, and 1884. Inger 2011, pp. 218, 244.

8 Inger 2011, p. 248.

An intermediate period, 1840–72

The Penal Act of 1864

During the first half of the nineteenth century, a legislative committee worked on proposals for a new civil and penal act in Sweden. The first proposal was presented as early as 1832, but it was not until 1864 that a new penal act could be adopted by the Riksdag. In the preparatory legislative work, the legislators were first and foremost inspired by German jurisprudential debates.[9] From a socio-economic perspective, proponents of the new ideas argued that it would be better if punishments were focused on *improving* the criminal and *preventing* new crimes, rather than on avenging criminal acts that had been committed. The retention or abolition of capital punishment continued to be debated vigorously, while public-shaming punishments and corporal punishments were increasingly questioned. Punishments involving flogging were no longer considered compatible with 'the sense of justice and way of thinking of the Swedish people'. It was feared that corporal punishment would make the criminal unfavourably disposed towards society, which would lead to the commission of new crimes.[10] With milder punishments, which were nevertheless in reasonable proportion to the crime, it was hoped that general criminality could be reduced.[11] However, not all legislators embraced these new ideas, and the Act of 1864 became a compromise between older and newer criminological influences.[12]

Unlike the state of things in previous periods, the penalties imposed were now put in relation to the injury or damage that various crimes had caused to people or property. This new way of thinking entailed changes in the status of religious and moral crimes. They were still believed to have a detrimental influence on society from a moral perspective; but, for all that, they were less serious than crimes aimed directly at the state or the individual. The set penalties could

9 Inger 2011, p. 210.

10 *Juridiskt Arkif*, volume 9, 1838–39, pp. 14, 17. Quotation on p. 14. In 1841, the punishment of breaking on the wheel and aggravated capital punishments (chopping off one hand, displaying the dead body in public after execution, burning at the stake) were abolished, as was sitting in the stocks. In 1855, birching and public penance were also abolished. Inger 2011, p. 298.

11 *Kongl. Maj:ts och Rikets Svea Hof-rätts Underdåniga Utlåtande*, pp. 5, 9f; Häthén 1990, pp. 159, 198, 212f.

12 Inger 2011, pp. 299f.

therefore be reduced.[13] The Penal Act of 1864 abolished the death penalty for incest, replacing it with hard labour.

As was pointed out above, several incest prohibitions had been questioned in repeated parliamentary debates during the first decades of the nineteenth century. The relationship categories that had caused the most heated debates were the second collateral consanguinity degree (*cousin*), the first collateral affinity degree (*wife's sister*, *brother's widow*), the diagonal affinity degree (*wife's niece*), and the second affinity degree (*wife's stepmother*, *stepson's widow*). Following the royal regulation of 1845, the prohibition against cousin marriages had been abolished, but other prohibitions remained in force. As the Penal Act of 1864 became valid, the new reduced penalties were introduced, and incestuous relationships were assessed and punished as shown in Table 11.

As can be seen from the table, the maximum penalty imposed for incest crimes was reduced from the death penalty to hard labour for eight to ten years. In practice, though, the death penalty had all but ceased to be applied long before this legislative change.

The Act of 1864 introduced a differentiation between adults and children for the first time, the maximum penalty imposed for minors being set at roughly half of that for an adult. Children under the age of fifteen were completely exempted from punishment. For the first time, an adult party's guilt and responsibility for a crime was separated from that of a minor. In spite of this, legislators assumed that incest between parents and children was a question of abuse of parental authority through *seduction* rather than through *violent assault*. In cases where the younger party had not been subjected to physical violence, it was assumed that the child had not suffered any actual harm.[14] If an incestuous relationship had begun before the child was fifteen years old but was discovered only after she (or he) had reached the age of criminal responsibility, the younger party could also be convicted of the crime.[15]

In addition, the law involved an increased differentiation between consanguinity and affinity incest. The first differentiation in this direction had been introduced in connection with the Civil Code of 1734, when capital punishment for affinity incest in collateral degrees (*wife's sister*, *brother's widow*) had been replaced by a

13 See the summary of the 1832 legislative proposal in *SOU 1935:68*, p. 39; Häthén 1990, pp. 198f.

14 Bergenheim 1998, p. 136.

15 Lindstedt Cronberg 2002, pp. 130f; Bergenheim 1998, p. 132.

Table 11. Incest prohibitions and punishments in accordance with the Penal Act of 1864

Family relationship	Closeness	Relationship, a man and his …	Punishment
Consanguinity	First/second lineal degree	mother, grandmother, daughter, granddaughter	Adult: Hard labour 8–10 years Child: Hard labour 6 months–4 years
	First collateral degree	sister	Hard labour 2–6 years
	Diagonally	aunt, grandfather's sister	Hard labour max 2 years
		niece	
Affinity	First/second lineal degree	stepmother, mother-in-law, grandfather's widow, stepdaughter, daughter-in-law	Adult: Hard labour 6 months–4 years Child: Gaol, max 6 months, or hard labour max 2 years
	First collateral degree	wife's sister, brother's wife	Fine
	Diagonally	uncle's widow, wife's niece, nephew's widow, grandmother's brother's widow	Fine
	Second degree	wife's stepmother, wife's grandmother, stepson's widow, grandfather's widow	Fine

15 Negotiations in the Second Chamber of the Riksdag.

prison sentence, while consanguinity incest in collateral degrees (*sister*) continued to be punishable by death. The Act of 1864 brought differentiation with regard to the range of punishments in lineal degrees, in that biological relatives who violated the incest prohibition were sentenced to nearly twice as long a period of hard labour as people who were related through affinity relationships.

Even after the change in the law, new bills continued to be submitted to the Riksdag, with renewed demands for the liberalisation of additional relationship categories.[16] The initiators of the bills sat in the Second Chamber, which was dominated by farmers, but these proposals also had the support of members of the First Chamber, who were mainly higher officials, estate owners, and factory owners.[17] On a couple of occasions, the king put a stop to a legislative change; but in 1872 political pressure resulted in the abolition of the affinity prohibition in the first collateral degree, the diagonal degree, and the second degree.[18]

16 Bills were submitted in 1868, 1870, and 1871.

17 On the division of the Chambers, see Inger 2011, p. 209. On the attitudes of each Chamber, see *Lagutskottets Utlåtande nr 47, 1868*, pp. 8f; *F.K. 1868*, volume 4, pp. 569f; *A.K. 1868*, volume 4, p. 469.

18 K.F. 1872, 24 May. Example of a previous rejection of a bill by the king: *Kunglig Skrivelse nr 7, 1869*, pp. 1f.

Contributions to the debate that led up to the legislative change described the older law as obsolete. In a report of 5 May 1868, the parliamentary committee on legislation noted that there was no longer any 'valid reason' for keeping the prohibitions against horizontal and diagonal affinity relationships. Applications for permission to marry submitted by people in these relationship degrees were never rejected, and the prohibitions appeared a 'purposeless formality' that was 'an obstacle to everyone and expensive to those of small means'.[19] Ola Månsson, a representative of the Second Chamber and the initiator of a couple of bills, argued that it 'frequently' happened that 'on the death of either spouse, the survivor wish[ed] to enter into marriage with one of the siblings of the deceased'.[20] Count Erik Sparre of the First Chamber claimed that 'the general opinion in the country' was in favour of such marriages.[21] A similar opinion was expressed by Count Oscar Mörner when he claimed that there was a 'fairly general desire' for the legislation to be changed.[22] Even though individual members still expressed their doubts about a potential liberalisation, they were in a clear minority. When the Speaker of the Second Chamber, after the conclusion of a discussion in the parliamentary session of 1868, asked if the proposal for liberalisation should be supported, 'there were many cries of yea along with a very occasional nay'.[23]

A large majority of the Riksdag members from both chambers hence described what they perceived to be changed norms in society. Marriages between people related through matrimony were no longer thought to give offence; on the contrary, they appeared to be popular and even desirable.

Applications for dispensation

The Riksdag members' contention that collateral affinity relationships were generally accepted in society is confirmed by other source material. The number of applications for dispensation from people

---

19 *Lagutskottets Utlåtande nr 47, 1868*. See also *Lagutskottets Utlåtande nr 16, 1859/60*, p. 17.

20 *Motion, nr 302 (Bill no. 302), 1868*, pp. 3f.

21 *F.K. 1868*, volume 4, p. 269.

22 *F.K. 1871*, volume 2, pp. 31f. Here Mörner bowed to the 'general desire', in spite of his claim that he himself sympathised with those who wanted the prohibitions to be retained.

23 *F.K. 1868*, volume 4, p. 270.

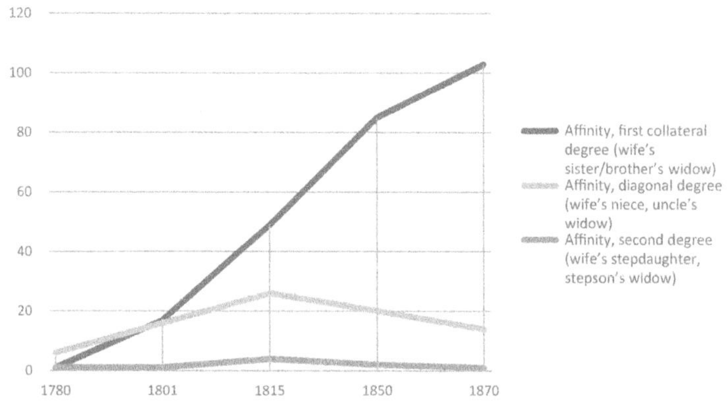

Graph 2. Applications for dispensation directed to the Judiciary Inspection, 1780–1870, selected categories. Source: The diaries of the Judiciary Inspection for the year in question.

related by marriage increased continuously during the whole of the nineteenth century. The applications were received by the Judiciary Inspection and routinely approved.[24]

Graph 2 shows the number of applications for dispensation for affinity relationships that reached the Judiciary Inspection during the century preceding the legislative change in 1872. Lineal affinity relationships were not the subject of a liberalisation debate during the nineteenth century and are hence not included in these statistics.

As the table shows, it was only the category of first collateral affinity degree (*wife's sister*, *brother's widow*) that stood out with a continuous and significant increase in the number of applications during the whole of the period. Nevertheless, the other affinity categories were lumped together with this one in the debate. The relationships were assessed in similar ways, and when one category was liberalised, the other categories followed suit.

As in the rest of Europe, marriages between related couples hence continued to increase in popularity in Sweden throughout the nineteenth century. Cousin marriages, liberalised as early as 1845,

24 On 21 November 1850, applications for marriage from five couples were approved simultaneously. JR, R, 1850, 21 November. On 11 February 1870, permission to marry was granted for five couples; and on 25 February of the same year, three more couples received approval. JR, K, 1870, 11 February; JR, K, 1870, 25 February.

are not included in these statistics either, but these marriage constellations also continued to increase in the same way.[25] The popularity of marriages between relatives culminated just before the First World War.[26] As was discussed above, this development may in part be linked to changed economic and cultural conditions in society. Marriages within the family were still particularly common in noble circles, but several studies describe a stronger tendency also to accept strategic marriage alliances within the family in the burgeoning bourgeoisie of the nineteenth century.[27] British social anthropologist Adam Kuper has described how some of the most successful middle-class families in Britain created large networks of family alliances during the nineteenth century with the help of systematic cousin marriages. These family-based networks provided advantages for the group in question in the general competition for capital and offices. Similar systems were used by burghers in several European countries during the early nineteenth century.[28]

With respect to Sweden, historian Anita Göransson has shown that similar strategies were used by Swedish merchants and factory owners during the same period. Within these groups, cousin marriages were strikingly common, as were other matrimonial family alliances, for instance two brothers from one family marrying two sisters from another or, alternatively, a man marrying his deceased wife's sister. Göransson notes that the likely purpose was to keep property together within the family in order to remain strong in the competition with the outside world.[29]

Even though the upper social groups are over-represented in the dispensational material in relation to the composition of the population, economic motivation for the formation of marriages affected lower social groups as well. A study of marriage patterns in north-eastern Sweden established that there was a preponderance of marriages between relatives in the peasant-proprietor class in comparison to unpropertied groups.[30] In addition, many applicants are entitled 'leaseholder' or 'artisan' in the dispensational material.

25 Egerbladh and Bittles 2011, pp. 413, 418.

26 Alström 1958, p. 300. Sabean 1998, p. 436.

27 In 1800, the proportion of cousin marriages within the nobility was 6 to 13%, in 1850 5 to 20%. The corresponding number for the entire population at the same time was 1–1.5%. Alström 1958, p. 336.

28 Kuper 2009, pp. 24–8, 243. Sabean 1998, pp. 428–48; Sabean, Teuscher, and Mathieu 2007b, pp. 187f; Johnson 2011.

29 Göransson 1990, pp. 525f, 540.

30 Egerbladh and Bittles 2011, pp. 413, 419.

16 In the nineteenth century, the hundred court was still led by the hundred-court judge and the co-opted lay judges.

Consequently, this phenomenon was not confined to specific social strata but more or less generally accepted.

Criminal cases

In the mid-1800s, approximately as many incest crimes were heard in Swedish courts as at the beginning of the century, and the distribution of the different relationship categories was similar.[31] In the material from the mid-nineteenth century, however, greater tolerance of relationships between relatives is discernible. At the turn of the century in 1800, the regulatory framework had been challenged by couples related through marriage behaving towards each other in what was felt to be a much too affectionate manner in public contexts, as was illustrated by the cases described in the previous chapter. But this had mostly amounted to an indirect questioning of the incest prohibitions, because the people in question often lived in

31 This statement is based on the material of the Göta Court of Appeal. For more detailed criminal statistics, see Appendix Table 3.

the same household in a relationship that was superficially legitimate. People who lived in the same family and household defended their conduct by claiming that showing affection and tenderness within the family was a desirable kind of behaviour without admitting that their physical relations transgressed a moral boundary. There are also examples where a man and a woman lived together under the pretext of her being his housekeeper.[32] There was thus no question of an open challenge to the norms at this time.

Fifty years later, in the middle of the nineteenth century, the official norms were challenged in a more obvious way. At this point in time, a man and a woman might live openly together as a loving couple, even after having been warned that their relationship was impermissible because they were related. When summoned to a judicial inquiry, such a couple might ignore the summons and quite simply fail to appear at the hearing. These patent challenges to the official legislation were particularly common when horizontal affinity relationships (*wife's sister*, *brother's widow*) were at issue. Anders Larsson Röding was, for instance, prosecuted for fornication with his deceased *wife's two sisters*, with one of whom he had formed a household and also wanted to marry.[33] Mårten Persson and his deceased *brother's widow* moved in together and had children without having been granted official permission to marry by the Crown.[34] Nils Erik Fagerström and his *wife's sister* Eva Sofia Olsdotter agreed to marry, moved in together, and lived as a married couple. When summoned to the local court, they failed to appear until the prosecutor had them picked up.[35] Widower Anders Olofsson wanted to marry his *niece* Anna Cajsa Johansdotter and went to the local clergyman to have the banns published. He was then told that their relationship was prohibited; but as neither Anders nor Anna was able to see 'the criminal nature' of their relationship, they nevertheless moved in together and lived as a married couple. Only when Anna became pregnant and bore an illegitimate child did the vicar report them to the county sheriff, who then prosecuted them.[36]

32 GHA, BIIA:98, 1785, no. 43; Hanekind hundred, AIa:34, 1784, 10 February, no. 2.

33 GHA, BIIA:318, 1851 no. 128; Stranda hundred, AIa:132, 1851, 24 September, no. 239.

34 GHA, BIIb:21, 1841, 5 November, no. 159.

35 GHA, BIIA:342, 1855, 26 September, no. 53; GHA, EVAC:1235, 1855 no. 53.

36 GHA, BIIA:293, 1845, 8 April, no. 37.

As in earlier periods, pregnancy in particular often brought matters to a head, but in some cases not even an illegitimate child led to any immediate reaction from the people around the couple in question. Börje Larsson and his *brother's widow* Anna Jönsdotter moved in together and had a child with the explicit intention of getting married. They were not prosecuted for incest by the county sheriff until the child was three years old.[37] Johannes Holm and his *brother's widow* Maja Lisa Petersdotter also formed a household, stating their intention to get married. When Maja Lisa became pregnant two years later, Johannes tried to have the banns published but was then told that they had to apply for a dispensation from the king in order to be allowed to marry. They thought this was too expensive and refrained from making the application, but continued to live together. When the couple finally ended up in court, their child was four years old.[38]

The decades around 1850 hence witnessed a more pronounced resistance towards certain types of incest prohibitions. Couples lived openly together in what the law defined as incestuous relationships for several years without anybody intervening, having children and planning a future together as husband and wife. In all these cases, the people involved displayed a striking lack of respect for and indifference to – or, alternatively, ignorance of – the applicable rules. By their actions, they rejected the official definition of their relationship as deviant or immoral. To be sure, they also challenged the norm that sexual relations should only occur within marriage; but in this respect they often attempted to achieve full legitimacy by expressing – in writing or orally – their desire to get married. These people thus seem to have had a certain amount of respect for the legitimacy of the marriage norm.

Two tendencies that may be discerned in the court material from the turn of the century in 1800 had been reinforced by mid-century. First, there was a tendency on the part of the authorities to reduce the punishment for couples who were found guilty of the crime of incest if their relationship appeared to be voluntary. In six out of nine cases where the prosecuted couple had violated the affinity prohibition in the first collateral degree, the punishment was reduced from twenty-eight to twenty-four days in prison. The common denominator of these cases was that the relationships were described as voluntary, or, alternatively, that the prosecuted

37 GHA, BIIA: 279, 1841, 11 October, no. 47.
38 GHA, EVAC:937, 1840, no. 27.

individuals said that they wished to be allowed to marry.[39] Even the *full siblings* Johannes Heberg and Anna Svensdotter had, to all appearances, a voluntary sexual relationship. They had been separated as children and had grown up apart. When they met as adults (she at the age of eighteen, he at the age of twenty-eight) they began a sexual relationship. They lived together for two years before they were prosecuted because of an illegitimate child. Before the court they confessed their crime, which was also confirmed by several witnesses. The witnesses described theirs as an 'unusually affectionate relationship'. They were to said to have 'sought solitude together' and had been seen lying together in the same bed on repeated occasions. According to one witness, they behaved 'as man and wife or as people betrothed'. Another witness based a suspicion of illicit relations on the mutual 'love' shown by the couple. The suspicions were confirmed later when the witness, peeping through a crack in the wall, watched them having 'carnal congress'.[40] Johannes and Anna were found guilty of incest and were sentenced to death, but had their sentences reduced to imprisonment according to the then current practice. But although the crime of incest in this case had been fully proven by the couple's own confessions and by the testimony of several others, and even though the relationship was between two biological siblings, the couple was not sentenced to the maximum prison sentence of twenty-eight days but only to twenty days in gaol.[41] The reprieve was merely justified with the phrase 'on account of particular circumstances'.[42] In my view, though, it is highly likely that this expression referred to the voluntary aspect of the couple's relationship, and that it was this circumstance that determined the more lenient sentence. The authorities were quite

39 GHA, BIIA:342, 1855, no. 53; GHA, BIIA:273, 1840, no. 27; GHA, BIIA:279, 1841, no. 47; GHA, BIIA:275, 1840, no. 29; GHA, BIIA:318, 1850, no. 98; HSoB, BIIb:21, 1841, no. 159.

40 GHA, BIIA:292, 1844, no. 93.

41 In the middle of the nineteenth century, hard labour was more or less routinely imposed in addition to gaol sentences for the most aggravated offences. Johannes and Anna were sentenced to five years of hard labour each after having served their gaol sentences. They were also threatened with flogging and birching if they resided in the same location in future. GHA, EIAC:22, 1845, p. 13. See also a case where a voluntary relationship between a man and his niece was punished by a mere sixteen days in prison and two years of hard labour. GHA, BIIA:293, 1845, no. 37; GHA, EIAC:22, 1845, p. 28.

42 GHA, EIAC:22, 1845, p. 13.

simply more tolerant of voluntary incestuous relationships than before.

As was observed above, reactions in local communities had been affected by how individual relationships functioned even during the most theocratic period in the past. If a relationship was perceived to be voluntary, there was a greater propensity to support and protect those who were prosecuted for incest, regardless of how close the family relationship between the prosecuted individuals was. In the middle of the nineteenth century, these circumstances also influenced the assessment of the authorities and thus also the final sentences. Mutuality had to all appearances gone from only influencing the closest relatives and friends of the accused into being recognised by the authorities as a mitigating circumstance which could justify reducing the punishment. This change may also be described as an informal norm becoming officially accepted in society.

The second tendency that becomes visible in the criminal cases of the middle of the nineteenth century is the accused parties' readiness to deny the charge even when there were extremely compromising circumstances. The case of Jakob Larsson (forty-four years old) and his *niece* Greta Andersdotter (twenty-nine years old) may be quoted as an example. They were accused of incest in 1841. Greta had kept house for Jakob for nine years, but in reality they had wanted to get married. About a year earlier, Jakob had urgently asked the local judge to write an application for marriage for them, a plea with which the judge had reluctantly complied. The couple's application was rejected, though, and when Greta later became pregnant they were prosecuted for incest by the county sheriff. Both Jakob and Greta stubbornly denied the accusation and were acquitted because of a lack of evidence.[43] Other couples who denied the charge were acquitted, too.[44] Of course, there is a theoretical possibility that the couples who denied the charges were not in fact guilty, but

43 GHA, EVAC:971, 1841, no. 47; GHA, BIIA:280, no. 43.

44 See, e.g., GHA, BIIA:293, 1845 no. 103; GHA, EVAC:1041, 1845, no. 103; HSoB, BIIb:31, 1851, no. 6. Another, more depressing, example is Kjerstin Mattisdotter, who claimed before her mother and sundry witnesses that her stepfather had raped her. However, at trial both of them denied the crime and were acquitted, 'yet her entire being betrayed great dejection'. Witnesses stated that the girl had been urged not to lay the blame on her stepfather in order to avoid making them both 'unhappy'. Medelstad hundred, AIa:133, 1840, 13 February, no. 429; 29 February, no. 445; 11 May, no. 249; 5 June, no. 462; HSoB, BIIb:20, 1840 no. 123.

it is not reasonable to assume that all of them were innocent. Rather, the denials form part of a new pattern of behaviour in the accused.

The fact that more people chose to deny committing the crime, in spite of all the circumstances that indicated their guilt, may – as was the case before – be explained by it being easier to escape conviction because the evidential requirements had become more stringent. But considering that the challenges to the regulatory framework were more overt, it is also likely that the official definition of the relationship as a criminal act was rejected by those who violated the rules. This was probably the case with several couples who were related in collateral affinity degrees, because these couples chose to live together openly in direct violation of the applicable rules. In criminal cases concerning other relationship categories, the obstinate denials may have been occasioned by the prosecuted individuals questioning the reasonableness of the penal consequences.

When Börje Bengtsson was prosecuted for committing incest with his *daughter* Inger, he chose to stubbornly deny the accusation before the court. Inger, who was Börje's illegitimate daughter, had grown up with her mother and moved to her father aged seventeen, whereupon father and daughter appear to have developed a liking for each other. According to testimony, Börje – in a state of 'intoxication' – admitted to being the father of both Inger and her illegitimate child. But in court he denied all culpability. Before a witness, he apparently said that he did not want to confess because he risked ending up in 'the hands of the executioner'. When the members of the hundred court urged him to confess his crime, he reportedly answered that he 'would not confess before those who wished to commit murder'.[45]

Börje was thus well aware of the legal consequences of his crime, but he did not acknowledge the right of the authorities to put him to death. He described the anticipated punishment as a murder – an unjust killing – and it was obviously the penalty to which Börje objected. By way of various statements, he indirectly admitted that he, too, understood the relationship as illicit. Before one witness, he stated that he had 'found himself sorely tempted', and before

45 At the beginning of the trial, Inger accused her father of having forced her to have sex. However, the 120-page records give a clear impression that the relationship was completely voluntary and that Inger's statement was an attempt to minimise her own guilt. She later retracted her confession, and the couple were acquitted from a lack of evidence. GHA, EVAC:1003, 1843, no. 14; GHA, BIIA:286, 1843, no. 14.

another acquaintance he said that he believed that a 'confession before God was enough to receive absolution'.[46] Börje thus did not protest against the definition of the relationship as sinful and prohibited, but against its penal consequences.

Taken together, the tendency for more couples to deny committing a crime and the tendency for the punishment to be reduced when the relationship appeared to be voluntary confirm that the crime of incest had acquired a changed status in society. The link between incest and morality norms appears even more patent than it did at the turn of the century in 1800.

Any change must of course also be put in relation to the changed attitudes in society to other moral crimes during the same period. With respect to how the accused acted before the court, Marie Lindstedt Cronberg describes a very similar development regarding 'ordinary' sexual crimes in Sweden from 1680 to 1880. Up until 1778, both men and women usually confessed their crimes with an almost 'naive sincerity'. In 1778, the so-called *infanticide proclamation* was announced, making it possible for women to bear illegitimate children without naming the father. After this turning-point, women increasingly often claimed to have been bedded by an 'unknown man'; but in cases where the woman named a man as the father of her child, he usually denied the accusation and escaped punishment. Lindstedt Cronberg connects the change in behaviour to general social developments. Attitudes to sexual crimes had become more lenient, which made it easier to deny committing them.[47] The change is illustrated by the fact that the number of illegitimate births increased continuously during the nineteenth century while the general frequency of marriage tended downwards. A changed attitude to sexual crimes also comes out in the legislation in that the regulatory framework for extramarital sexuality was made more lenient in the course of the nineteenth century. These legislative changes led to a gradual reduction of the number of sexual crimes

46 In total, around fifty witnesses were heard. Six claimed not to know anything. Approximately thirty witnesses described compromising circumstances in the form of suspicious statements or acts by the accused. Around twenty witnesses claimed that either Börje or Inger had confessed their relationship to them. Two men claimed to have been offered economic compensation for admitting to being the father of Inger's child and marrying her. GHA, EVAC:1003, 1843, no. 14.

47 Lindstedt Cronberg 1997, pp. 73f, 142–50, quotes on pp. 143, 145.

in Swedish courts, and around 1870 they had all but ceased to appear.[48]

Both the legislative changes and the behaviour of the accused in court indicate a cultural shift with respect to attitudes to sexual offences in general, and there are strong indications to the effect that attitudes to some incestuous relationships adhered to this trend.[49] This might account for the general reduction in the number of incest crimes that has been noted between the turn of the century in 1700 and the turn of the century in 1800. The crimes were simply increasingly rarely reported. In some incest cases, it is difficult to determine whether the family relationship played a role at all; the following case supplies an example.

In 1843, Nils Larsson accused his brother-in-law, former hussar Sven Wall, of having made Nils's daughter Anna pregnant. Nils demanded that Sven should pay for the child's upkeep. But Anna herself, who worked as a servant in Sven's household, absolved Sven from responsibly and claimed that it was a pedlar who was the father of her baby. A witness described that he had seen Sven and Anna lie together in bed at night, and that the relationship between them in general was friendly and intimate; but the same witness swore that he had not seen any direct 'illicit congress' at the time of conception. Anna's father for his part was entirely convinced of how things had happened, and he expressed his view of the case in a formal letter to the court:

> Because of the seductive actions of Sven Wall, my daughter has violated both secular and divine law and thus caused herself to be hated and reviled among the citizens in [our] community. And more than that, she has laid a heavy burden on us, her aged parents who are approaching our graves, hastening [our] descent into the grave with her [...] way of life and great disobedience. Not only did she,

---

48 Nilsson 2011, p. 76; Carlsson 1977, p. 14. In 1810, the secular punishment for fornication was abolished for women at the first and second violation. After 1864, public prosecution was no longer brought for sexual offences. However, fornication was not decriminalised until 1918 and adultery not until 1937. Inger 2011, pp. 300f, 373.

49 Examples of incest cases where a man, in a manner resembling that described by Lindstedt Cronberg, was identified as the father of a child by the woman but denied committing a crime can be found in GHA, EVAC:1066, 1846, no. 31; GHA, BIIA:298, 1846, no. 30; GHA, BIIA:322, 1851, no. 93; GHA, EVAC:1083, 1847, no. 105; GHA, BIIA:304, 1847, no. 105; GHA, BIIA:323, 1851, no. 135.

> in opposition to the admonitions given by us, commit adultery with Sven Wall, but she eventually [made] her father a liar both in writing and in speech [by] brazenly absolving Sven Wall before the lawful hundred court from having made her with the child whose upkeep is the subject of the present matter.[50]

In view of several compromising circumstances, the suspicion that the prosecuted individuals were guilty of the crime of which they were accused seems natural; but regardless of whether Sven was the father of Anna's child or not, Anna's father was sure of his brother-in-law's guilt. It is, however, uncertain whether it was the family relationship in itself which angered him most. Nowhere did he emphasise that it was the family relationship that was the main cause of his indignation. He referred to the crime as 'adultery' instead of adultery or fornication *in a prohibited degree*, which was a more common description of incest crimes. He was horrified that his daughter had lost her honour and the respect of the community through her actions, and that her child was not properly supported. He placed the guilt for his daughter's situation on Sven, who had lured the girl to her ruin with 'seductive actions'.[51]

Would Nils have reacted differently if there had been no family relationship between Anna and Sven? If the act had 'only' violated the norm that sexual activity should take place within marriage? There is no certain answer to this question, but my impression is that at this time, incest crimes in the more distant degrees – as was the case in this example (diagonal affinity degree) – were often handled without any particular emphasis being placed on the family relationship.[52] Consequently, it is hard to assess exactly which norm was under negotiation – extramarital sexuality, or extramarital sexuality *in the prohibited degrees*.

Both Riksdag records and applications for dispensation, as well as the criminal-case material, show that social attitudes to incest crimes continued to move in the direction of increasing tolerance. Affinity relationships in collateral and diagonal degrees were largely

50 GHA, EVAC:1013, 1843, no. 111.

51 GHA, EVAC:1013, 1843, no. 111.

52 In another example, the family relationship between the man and the woman was treated as only one offence among several petty crimes. Apart from the affinity crime, the man was also accused of 1) having moved into the poorhouse without permission, 2) stealing a hat, 3) breaking the Sabbath, and 4) three 'shovings'. Västbo hundred, AIa:202, 1849, no. 173, 19 June; 20 June, no. 197; GHA, BIIA:314, 1849, no. 100.

17 In connection with the Industrial Revolution the population in Swedish cities increased greatly, creating a need for altered urban environments. During the late nineteenth century, many old city blocks were torn down and replaced with large, modern stone buildings. This picture shows the Swedish capital, Stockholm, at the end of the nineteenth century.

treated as any other moral crime without the family relationship being foregrounded as an aggravating circumstance. The importance of the family relationship for the assessment of the crime thus seems to have vanished, or at least to have been significantly reduced. When the prohibitions against marriage in collateral and diagonal affinity degrees were abolished in 1872, it was thus an adaptation to this new norm. Once more, then, the legislative changes functioned as a codification of new ideas that had emerged in Swedish society during the first half of the nineteenth century.

The turn-of-the-century world of ideas, 1872–1940

Around the turn of the century in 1900, science had begun to replace religion as a normative basis for ethics and morals. As religion was increasingly privatised, the general social influence of the clergy lessened, doctors and scientists stepping up instead as obvious new spokesmen for the good of society. Family life and sexuality became an issue for medical experts.

Through Charles Darwin's theory of evolution the animal origins of the human race were made visible, which contributed to the increasing tendency of science to see sexual drives as natural instincts.[53] True, sexuality had also been perceived as natural according to Lutheran ideology, but sexual desire should be channelled into the marriage and the system of human reproduction established by God. During the second half of the nineteenth century, doctors began to argue that sexuality affected the well-being of the individual. Sexual satisfaction became a health-related issue.[54] This development has been described as a separation of romantic love and sexual desire, sexual desire being considered an innate, seething power in the human being. Passions were no longer seen as harmful animal lusts that had to be controlled and suppressed, but as a positive natural force for everybody to embrace. If the natural drives were suppressed, this might lead to sickness or depression. In addition, men's sexual needs came to be regarded as stronger than those of women; consequently, it was considered particularly important that their needs be satisfied. It was feared that a repressed male sexuality could lead to 'unnatural' sexual acts, such as masturbation, rape, or incest. A man who did not have an outlet for his natural lusts was therefore seen as a potential threat to the chastity of virtuous women. At the same time, most men had to wait until their thirties before they could get married, because it was not until then that they had a steady income and could support a family. According to this line of reasoning, the average man hence constituted a potential danger to himself and to the women around him for ten to fifteen years before marriage provided him with a natural outlet for his desires. The solution to this dilemma was an established double standard, where extramarital sexuality was forbidden while state-regulated prostitution was introduced. Apart from certain delays and minor national variations, developments were similar in several European cities.[55] The double standard was, however, criticised from

53 *On the Origin of Species*, where Darwin presented his theory, was published in 1859. On the link between race biology and Darwin's ideas, see Broberg and Tydén 1991, p. 11.

54 Lundquist 1982, p. 409; Ekenstam 1993, pp. 261, 263; Bergenheim 1998, p. 122.

55 With respect to Sweden, see Lennartsson 2001, pp. 95–101. Quotation on p. 95. Lennerhed 1994, Chapter 1. Tommy Lundquist provides a detailed

several directions, which resulted in heated social debates in the decades before the turn of the century. This criticism led to a deregulation of prostitution in Great Britain and the Scandinavian countries, whereas control of prostitutes continued in France, Germany, and Italy.[56]

The Swedish debate on morality and prostitution that arose in the 1880s may be described as a fiercely ideological battle. In this morality debate, which later became very well known, the focus was on family life and marriage as an institution. Some people promoted new – and challenging, for their time – ideas about free love and the use of contraceptives. Others defended the importance of marriage and monogamy for the happiness of the individual while simultaneously arguing for women's equality with men.[57] Although it was possible to live together without being married at this time, marriage was still considered the only legitimate way of cohabiting.[58]

The publication of the Darwinian theories of evolution not only contributed to shifts in views on sexuality, it also led to greater interest in the biological development of the human race. Once the first shocking insight that human beings might be descended from apes had settled, theories were formulated about the human civilising process. This development was described as a process of advancement, where people went from an originally primitive condition towards an increasing degree of civilisation and refinement. Animals were of course ranked as lower-standing creatures in relation to human beings, but human races were also divided according to how far they were considered to have progressed in the development of their civilisation. Unsurprisingly, white Westerners were put at the top of the evolutionary ladder, while groups that were defined as primitive tribes or aboriginal people from other parts of the world were placed further down the scale. The notion of the civilised white male

---

picture of the history of the regulation of prostitution in Sweden, from its introduction in the mid-nineteenth century to its abolition in 1918, in Lundquist 1982. For developments in Britain and Germany, see Walkowitz 1982 and Meyer-Renschhausen 1997. For a general overview of developments in Europe, see Blom 2012, pp. 25–32. For an overview of the debate in French and German forensic medicine, see Bergenheim 1998, pp. 122–31.

56 Blom 2012, p. 32.

57 Levin 1994, pp. 144–62.

58 The number of extramarital births had increased steadily in Sweden during the nineteenth century, and at the turn of the century in 1900 they made up approximately 15%. Nilsson 2011, p. 76.

helping other peoples to attain a similar degree of civilisation was, among other things, used to justify colonisation and imperialism.[59]

Ideas of race biology also spread to the social sciences, and soon eugenic terminology was being used to explain social differences in society.[60] The argument for these social-Darwinist ideas may be summarised as follows: those who managed successfully in society did so because they had received strong and vigorous genes, whereas poor people and social outcasts had probably been equipped with more deficient genes in the game of hereditary biology.[61] It was consequently believed that the development of the individual contained an element of biological determinism. On the heels of the ideas concerning the increasing degree of civilisation and refinement of the human race followed, as a logical consequence, the insight that this development could be reversed. The race might degenerate, or regress to an earlier stage of development. For the eugenic movement, it thus became an important goal to improve the human race by controlling procreation in the country. Similar ideas existed in several European countries, as well as in Russia, the United States, and China; but after Germany, Sweden may be said to be one of the countries where ideas on racial hygiene and positive and negative eugenics gained the strongest foothold, both scientifically and politically.[62]

The marriage act of 1915

In this eventful period of cultural and political turbulence, a review of the incest legislation took place. This time the Swedish law-drafting committee worked in close cooperation with the other Nordic countries, which resulted in a new Swedish marriage act in 1915 – the Act on the Celebration and Dissolution of Marriage. In the discussions that preceded the legislation, race-biological views were clearly expressed. New medical impediments to marriage were introduced, and the justification of the new law stated that its purpose was to protect 'future generations, in the interest of maintaining and improving the human race'. The desire was to 'both promote

---

59 Eriksson 1983, p. 125.

60 Tydén 2002, pp. 21–41. The Swedish debate contained parallel interpretations which emphasised the importance of social and cultural differences above that of racial differences. Tydén 2002, p. 22.

61 Eriksson 1983, p. 125.

62 Broberg and Tydén 1991, pp. 16–32.

the marriage frequency in the best of our members and prevent the procreation of the inferior' in order to 'gain the most able offspring from marriages'.[63]

Around the turn of the century in 1900, health-related consequences for the human race were thus at the centre of the Swedish incest debate. Within medicine, it was assumed that the risk of a disease being transferred to the next generation increased if both parents carried the same predisposition for that disease. But there was no evidence of an increased risk of disease for children with closely related parents, unless there was a predisposition for disease in the family. This explains why the authorities came to display a great deal of interest in the health status of couples applying for dispensation and their families.[64]

In comparison to Danish and Norwegian legislation, the Swedish incest prohibitions were more restrictive in the sense that marriages between people in the diagonal consanguinity degree (*aunt*, *niece*) were completely forbidden. In Denmark and Norway, a dispensation was required for marriages between a man and his aunt; but there were no restrictions for marriages between a man and his niece.[65] The dissimilar rules were seen to be problematic, though, in that people could travel across the border in order to get married, causing doubts about the validity of their marriage. The perception as to whether the marriage was valid or not determined whether any children had a right of inheritance after their parents.[66] In order to reduce the risk of later disputes, some couples applied for foreign citizenship before travelling across the border to get married, whereupon they returned to Sweden as foreign citizens.[67]

In order to adapt the Swedish legislation to the regulatory framework of the other Nordic countries, Sweden introduced an opportunity to apply for dispensation for marriage in the diagonal consanguinity degree in connection with the new marriage act. But the explanatory remarks to this act emphasised that such applications

63 *Lagberedningens förslag till revision av giftermålsbalken...I*, p. 131. The same justification was emphasised in brief summaries of the legislation. *Lag om äktenskapets ingående och upplösning*, p. 32.

64 *Lagberedningens förslag till revision av giftermålsbalken...I*, p. 198.

65 In Germany similar marriages were also permitted. *Nya äktenskapslagen med förklaringar*, pp. 52f.

66 See, e.g., *Nytt juridiskt arkiv, afd. I.*, 1907 (dispute about inheritance), p. 82, or *Nytt juridiskt arkiv, afd. I.*, 1883, p. 13 (attempt at ex-post legalisation of a marriage that took place abroad).

67 *Lagberedningens förslag till revision av giftermålsbalken...I*, pp. 199f.

would only be approved if the good health of the applicants and their families could be verified, or, alternatively, if the marriage was expected to be childless. With the Act of 1915, the regulations regarding kinship in affinity degrees also changed. Previously it had been the *sexual act* itself that bound two people together in a family relationship in affinity degrees; but from 1915 and onwards, it was instead the *marriage* that became the defining element for this family relationship.[68] Among the affinity prohibitions only one remained, the lineal one (*stepmother*, *stepdaughter*, *mother-in-law*, *daughter-in-law*). This was also the only impediment to marriage to be justified with moral instead of eugenic arguments.[69]

In line with the new eugenic ideas, all applications for dispensation for marriage were sent to the National Swedish Board of Health (*Medicinalstyrelsen*) for medical vetting before a decision on whether to approve or reject them was made. The Crown had the ultimate power to decide the outcome of these cases, but the recommendation of the National Swedish Board of Health was followed to almost 100%.[70] Consequently, the assessment of the dispensational cases had been moved to the medical profession, whose members were considered to represent objectivity and scientific knowledge, in line with the ideals of the time.

Applications for dispensation

The new marriage act led to a significant increase in applications for dispensation for marriages in diagonal consanguinity degrees (*aunt*, *niece*). During the five-year period preceding the introduction of the Act, there was no such application for dispensation. Between 1915 and 1920, sixty-four applications for dispensation were submitted to the Ministry of Justice, of which sixty-three came from couples who were related in precisely this way.[71] Most of the applications

68 *Lag om äktenskapets ingående och upplösning*, p. 46.

69 *Nya äktenskapslagen med förklaringar*, p. 53.

70 In four out of sixty-four cases (approximately 6%), the king chose to reject an application for dispensation in spite of the National Swedish Board of Health having established that no medical reasons created an impediment to the marriage. No documented argumentation clarifies why this happened in these four particular cases. See, e.g., JD, Cabinet-meeting document (*konseljakt*), R, 1917, 20 July, no. 23, Knut Westin, Gerda Lundgren; JD, K, 1917, 20 July, Knut Westin, Gerda Lundgren.

71 The Ministry of Justice received thirty-eight applications for dispensation for marriage between the years 1910 and 1914, but only one concerned

were submitted in the same year as an amendment of the law came into force (1916) or the year thereafter, as can be seen in Table 12.

Several applications involved relationships where a man and a woman already lived and had children together. When the amendment of the law opened up new opportunities, they wanted to legalise their relationships; but because the relationships were, properly speaking, prohibited and punishable, their character is rarely made immediately apparent in the material.

Two couples applied for dispensation for marriage as early as 1915; that is, before the new marriage act had come into force. The applications of both couples were rejected, causing re-submission at a later date. In both cases, it is only the later application that makes it clear that the couple lived together and had had children.[72] A third couple applied for permission to marry via a lawyer's office in 1916. The first official letter was brief and relatively impersonal; but because the National Swedish Board of Health asked for complementary information, the lawyer revealed that this couple, too, lived together and had had four children. He had deliberately omitted this information before, as 'their relationship was actually punishable before the amendment of the law'.[73]

The amendment of the law was thus immediately used when it became known, but it had not been preceded by any active pressures in the form of an increase in the number of applications for dispensation before it was adopted, as had happened in connection with previous legal amendments. After peaking during the initial years after the Act came into force, the number of applications for dispensation stabilised at less than ten per year for the entire country. It is hence not appropriate to speak of massive pressure or widespread popularity for these relationships either before or after the amendment of the law.

---

a too close family relationship. This case involved a family relationship in an affinity degree, not a consanguinity degree. SVAR's digital database for Cabinet-meeting documents in the Ministry of Justice (search term: 'äktenskap* hinder' ('marriage* impediment')).

72 JD, Cabinet-meeting document, 1915, 6 August, no. 29, Wilhelm Kaesen, Elisabeth Kaesen; JD, Cabinet-meeting document, 1917, 16 February, no. 39, Wilhelm Kaesen, Elisabeth Kaesen; JD, Cabinet-meeting document, 1915, 3 September, no. 37, Johan Skog, Emilia Skog; JD, Cabinet-meeting document, 1918, 31 July, no. 46, Johan Skog, Emilia Skog.

73 JD, Cabinet-meeting document, 1916, 17 November, no. 32, Anders Lindh, Anna Svensson.

Table 12. Applications for dispensation directed to the Ministry of Justice, 1915–20

Family relationship	Relationship	1915	1916	1917	1918	1919	1920	Total
Consanguinity, diagonally	niece	2	14	11	1	6	4	38
	aunt		2		1	1		4
	half-niece	1	5	4	5		1	16
	half-aunt		3				2	5
	Sum total, consanguinity	3	24	15	7	7	7	63
Affinity, first lineal degree	stepdaughter						1	1
	Sum total, affinity						1	1
Total		3	24	15	7	7	8	64

Source: SVAR's digital database for Cabinet meeting documents in the Ministry of Justice. Search terms: 'äktenskap* hinder' ('marriage* impediment').

A mild case of varicose veins and flatfoot

The importance of contemporary eugenic ideas is clearly reflected in the formulation of the applications for dispensation. In new, standardised forms, the applicants had to answer questions about their health and family relationships. They were obliged to undergo a medical examination and be declared free of 'congenital deformities and physical and psychological disorders' by a practising physician who had 'knowledge' of the applicants' family relationships. At least two credible witnesses who knew the families of the applicants well had to certify that the applicants were not tainted by hereditary disease, such as 'mental disorder, mental deficiency, falling sickness, chronic alcoholism' or 'suicide'. In addition, the family relationship of the applicants relative to each other, as well as the health status of the families of each of them, should be certified by the clergyman on duty on a third form.[74]

The application documents were thus increasingly dominated by detailed descriptions of the applicants' physical health status. One person was said to have a 'healthy appearance and a good physique'. This person lacked any signs of 'contagious disease' or other 'predisposition for disease'.[75] After conducting an examination of housekeeper Anna Westerberg, district physician Herman Melén certified that she was 'healthy and free [from] detectable predispositions for disease and had a normal physique without any deformities'.[76] Olga Hagström was described by her doctor as 'healthy and strong but pregnant', and Amanda Wretholm was said to be 'healthy and in particular free from nervousness and nervous disorders'.[77]

Whenever a physician found physical weaknesses in the applicant this was stated, regardless of whether or not these weaknesses were included in the abovementioned liabilities. For example, Carl Carlsson's physician described him as 'free of congenital deformity and physical and psychological signs of disorder', but 'with the exception

74 See heredity form I–III in, e.g., JD, Cabinet-meeting document, 1917, 16 April, no. 38, Knut Törnquist, Maria Törnquist. *Falling sickness* is an older term for epilepsy.

75 JD, Cabinet-meeting document, 1915, 6 August, no. 29, Wilhelm Kaesen, Elisabeth Kaesen.

76 JD, Cabinet-meeting document,1916, 14 July, no. 30, Johan Westerberg, Anna Westerberg.

77 JD, Cabinet-meeting document,1916, 24 March, no. 43, Johan Hultkvist, Olga Hagström; JD, Cabinet-meeting document, 1916, 24 March, no. 41, Anders Bengtsson, Amanda Wretholm.

of a mild case of varicose veins on both legs, a moderate case of flatfoot in both feet, and a visual acuity of 0.8 in the left eye'.[78] One woman was said to be blind in one eye, and in another case it was noted that a man had reduced hearing.[79]

The applicants' arguments

The application documents were no longer dominated by people from the highest echelons of society. Indeed, the titles provided suggest that the majority of the applicants were from the working class. Only isolated cases concerned higher officials, such as engineers or managers.[80]

To all appearances, the applicants accepted the basic medical requirements. Men and women went to see a doctor and allowed themselves to be examined without objections, and childhood friends or acquaintances informed the authorities in detail about the family's general medical history. The medical circumstances were hence confirmed and reproduced as legitimate reasons for marriage impediments both from above and from below in society. Apart from this crucial factor, the lines of argument employed by applicants varied from being rational and matter of fact to emphasising personal emotions and expressing hopes for a happy marriage.

A hundred years earlier, at the turn of the century in 1800, applications for dispensation had been characterised by the applicants invoking practical as well as economic and emotional circumstances. Later in the nineteenth century, applications for dispensation increased in number, but the phrasing became more succinct and impersonal, and the emotional character was toned down. As the applications were very routinely processed by the middle of the nineteenth

78 JD, Cabinet-meeting document, 1916, 7 April, no. 37, Carl Carlsson, Emma Carlsson.

79 JD, Cabinet-meeting document, 1917, 2 February, no. 27, Fritiof Hjelm, Sofia Petersdotter; JD, Cabinet-meeting document, 1916, 29 September, no. 36, Hjalmar Andersson, Anna Linder.

80 The material contains sixty-four applications from fifty-three different couples. The men's professional titles included forty-three labourers, freeholders, or the equivalent (this includes, e.g., foundry workers or mill hands, farm and forest labourers, house owners, farm labourers paid in kind, seamen, linemen, station hands, painters, corporals, shopkeepers, smiths); six with middle positions (e.g., railway-line inspectors, master builders, packing-masters, supervisors, and engineers); one factory owner; and one manager. Two cases do not contain a title.

century, there was no actual reason for arguing one's cause in great detail.

For the first time ever in Sweden, the amendment of the law in 1915 opened an opportunity for applying for dispensation in a new family category – diagonal consanguinity relationships (*aunt*, *niece*). But it was uncertain whether an application for such a marriage would be approved. This family relationship was perceived to be relatively close, and new medical arguments made the authorities disinclined to approve these marriages. Here, there was thus a new need for putting one's case in some detail. At the same time, the wording reveals an initial belief on the part of applicants that as long as the official requirements were fulfilled (health certificate, family-relationship certificate, and a testimonial from a clergyman), the application would be approved. Emanuel Carlsson wrote in his application that he and his *niece* had decided they wanted to marry. He invoked the new law, enclosing certificates on their state of health and their family relationships.[81] When the application was rejected, the couple submitted a new application in which the tone was considerably meeker. Emanuel now asked 'most humbly' that the king 'by [his] grace' might approve their marriage. He claimed that it would be 'peculiarly hard' for them to separate, and that his future would in such a case be 'ruined'.[82] Knut Törnquist and his *niece* Maria Törnquist had a similar experience. Initially, they noted that they had 'taken a fancy' to each other, which is why they applied for formal permission to marry.[83] When the application was rejected, they dispatched a new one containing a more detailed account of their 'mutual, heartfelt, and irresistible longing' to be married. They also wrote that a new rejection would cause them 'unsurmountable pain'.[84] When this application was also rejected, they sent in a third request. Here they revealed that they already had a child together and enclosed a petition for clemency from Maria's parents, who made a 'heartfelt' and 'fervent' appeal for their daughter so that 'her grief would not send her to an untimely

81 JD, Cabinet-meeting document, 1916, 27 October, no. 33, Emanuel Carlsson, Anna Olsson.

82 JD, Cabinet-meeting document, 1916, 22 December, no. 32, Emanuel Carlsson, Anna Olsson.

83 JD, Cabinet-meeting document, 1917, 27 April, no. 38, Knut Törnquist, Maria Törnquist.

84 JD, Cabinet-meeting document, 1917, 14 June, no. 48, Knut Törnquist, Maria Törnquist.

grave'. The parents claimed that there was no impediment to the marriage that was not outweighed by 'Christian love' and the need to support the small child.[85] Although this application was rejected too, the couple did not give up. In a fourth and final application, they once more emphasised that they felt a 'deep and lasting' love for each other and invoked two new circumstances in their favour. Their persistence paid off, and in December 1918 they were finally given official permission to marry.[86]

As these cases show, a number of applications initially employed a rather businesslike tone of voice; but when the applicants were put under pressure, the tone became more personal and the argumentation more emotional. In various ways, the applicants emphasised that they loved each other and that their future happiness depended on their being allowed to marry.[87]

Even though several couples had 'lived in sin', their wish to legalise their relationship with a formal marriage appears to have been important to them. In their final application, Knut and Maria Törnquist pointed out that a marriage between them could not be considered 'offensive' by the public, whereas their relationship in its current form might well cause 'offence and aversion'.[88] In other words, it was more important for them to maintain and reproduce the marital norm than the incest prohibition. Knut Westin and his *niece* argued in a similar way in their second application for permission to marry. As they were already a couple and had children together, it should 'for civic reasons be of value that the [...] existing relationship was legalised'.[89]

---

85 JD, Cabinet-meeting document, 1917, 14 December, no. 41, Knut Törnquist, Maria Törnquist.

86 JD, Cabinet-meeting document, 1918, 13 December, no. 108; JD K, 1918, 13 December, Knut Törnquist, Maria Törnquist. For more details regarding this case, see p. 249.

87 For additional examples where a couple's feelings for each other were emphasised as an argument for approval, see JD, Cabinet-meeting document, 1916, 12 May, no. 40, Anders Andersson, Augusta Gustavsson; JD, Cabinet-meeting document, 1917, 13 August, no. 28, Hjalmar Andersson, Anna Linder; JD, Cabinet-meeting document, 1917, 2 February, no. 27, Fritiof Hjelm, Blända Petersdotter; JD, Cabinet-meeting document, 1916, 24 March, no. 42, Martin Viberg, Hanna Blomberg.

88 JD, Cabinet-meeting document, 1918, 13 December, no. 108, Knut Törnquist, Maria Törnquist.

89 JD, Cabinet-meeting document, 1917, 18 January, no. 62, Knut Westin, Gerda Lundgren.

Similar values occur in the testimonials submitted by clergymen. In the testimonials from the middle of the nineteenth century, the clergy often provided neutral information about the repute and scriptural knowledge of the applicants. To be sure, one might say that the clergymen in question supported the applicants' desire to marry by writing testimonials in the first place; but this stance was not actively articulated.[90] In the applications from the 1910s, by contrast, a vicar often supported the cause of the applicants by conveying personal views and recommendations. One perpetual curate wished 'most heartily' to recommend a marriage between two applicants.[91] One vicar felt that a marriage would be 'desirable' for several reasons.[92] Another vicar felt that it would be better 'from the societal point of view' if a couple were allowed to marry, because they already lived together and because it was likely they would continue to do so even if the application was rejected.[93] In one application for dispensation, a vicar recommended that the desired marriage should be approved because the woman in question and her extramarital children would thereby be supported and 'not have to be a burden on the poor relief'.[94] In another case, a lawyer supported a couple who also applied for permission to marry.[95]

---

90 For instance, in material from 1850 the clergyman in question testified to conduct, repute, and scriptural knowledge in an impersonal way in twenty-nine out of thirty-five applications. In a mere two cases were statements made that may, with some generosity, be thought to amount to an active adoption of a position, i.e., JR, BoA 1850, 17 April, Lars Rasmusson, Kierstin Pehrsdotter; JR, BoA 1850, 9 July, Jan Jansson, Anna Andersdotter.

91 JD, Cabinet-meeting document, 1917, 2 February, no. 27, Fritjof Hjelm, Blända Petersdotter.

92 JD, Cabinet-meeting document, 1917, 23 March, no. 32, Valfrid Andreasson, Ellen Karlsson. The reasons stated were that the man was quite poor and had a wooden leg, which made it improbable that anybody else would want to marry him; that the man lived with his mother who was old and for this reason incapable of keeping house; and that the couple already lived together and were expecting an addition to the family.

93 JD, Cabinet-meeting document, 1917, 6 July, no. 34, Oskar Carlström, Helga Carlström.

94 JD, Cabinet-meeting document, 1919, 13 January, no. 38, Olof Dalberg, Sigrid Dalberg. For additional statements, see, e.g., JD, Cabinet-meeting document, 1916, 12 May, no. 40, Anders Andersson, Augusta Gustavsson; JD, Cabinet-meeting document, 1919, 18 January, no. 67, August Lundskog, Kristina Lundskog; JD, Cabinet-meeting document, 1919, 28 May, no. 41, Salomon Karlsson, Olivia Mårtensdotter; JD, Cabinet-meeting document, 1916, 14 July, no. 30, Johan Westerberg, Anna Westerberg.

95 JD, Cabinet-meeting document, 1916, 17 November, no. 32, Anders Lindh, Anna Svensson.

It is true that there was not a high incidence of applications for marriages between people who were related in the diagonal consanguinity degree, but nor does there seem to have been a principled aversion to such relationships. Relationships where it was made clear that the applicants had warm feelings for each other were supported by the community. In these cases, practical and economic circumstances as well as emotional attachments were perceived to be more important circumstances than the family relationship. In other words, couples, like the people who took up an active position in the case by submitting various certificates, felt that it was more important to defend the marital norm than to respect the formal incest prohibition. Marriage was described as the best solution for the individuals in question and for society at large. As in earlier periods, this marital norm was defended in principle by the authorities as well. The Act of 1915 established that from a societal perspective, marriage was 'the only desirable form of sexual relationship'. At the same time, it was noted that marriage also constituted an important prerequisite for 'the happiness and personal development of the individual'.[96]

In addition, it is clear that the right of an individual to personal happiness was a stronger argument than ever before. Apart from couples themselves emphasising their emotions, clergymen referred to the applicants' personal desires as legitimate reasons for their being allowed to marry. In a testimonial, vicar Vilhelm Larsson said that he had visited the couple in question and made sure that their desire for marriage was sincere. They were, according to his assessment, sincerely 'attached to each other' and had a 'heartfelt desire' to marry.[97] Another man and woman had taken a fancy to each other when in service at the same place. The perpetual curate commented that the couple should be allowed to marry for their 'own good'.[98] In what appears to be farm labourer Bror Johansson's personally formulated application, the same priorities were expressed with particular clarity:

> To His Royal Majesty! I wonder if Your Majesty would allow me to marry my father's half-sister we have fallen in love so *we cannot*

96 *Lag om äktenskapets ingående och upplösning*, p. 31.

97 JD, Cabinet-meeting document, 1917, 6 July, no. 34, Oskar Carlström, Helga Carlström.

98 JD, Cabinet-meeting document, 1916, 12 May, no. 40, Anders Andersson, Augusta Gustavsson.

> *be parted other than through death* so I thought I would ask Your Majesty if it is a hindrance that *we are a little bit related* I don't think it should make any difference if Your Majesty would be so kind as to let me know as soon as Your Majesty receives this letter I would be profoundly grateful. Yours faithfully B. G. Johansson[99]

Here both the handwriting and the wording indicate a limited education, but Bror's opinions cannot be doubted. His and his fiancée's feelings were too strong to be ignored. They loved each other and could not be separated other than by death, whereas the impediment to a legalisation of their relationship through marriage merely consisted of their being 'a little bit related'. This example, like previous ones, implies that it was far more important to defend an opportunity for personal happiness by forming a loving marriage than to respect the prohibition against marriage in the diagonal consanguinity degree.

In summary, it may be noted that although applications frequently began with an impersonal tone, love and future happiness were used as leverage when the applicants attempted to increase their chances of having their application for permission to marry approved. Several relationships had been going on for some time, which meant that two prohibitions were challenged simultaneously: the prohibition against sexual relations between unmarried people, and the prohibition against sexual relationships between relatives (*aunt*, *niece*). Here the marital norm was prioritised in favour of the incest prohibition not only by the applicants themselves but also by people around them. No one protested against medical arguments as potential impediments to marriage. While several couples had begun their sexual relationship long before they applied for permission to marry, all couples submitted to a personal medical examination without apparent protest and described their own and their respective families' medical history in detail. In other words, ideas on medical circumstances being legitimate impediments to marriage were reproduced by the decision-making authorities as well as by the general public. For this reason, it would be easy to assume that the applications that were rejected were commonly denied on medical grounds. When examining the outcome of the applications, however, this turns out not to be the case.

---

99 JD, Cabinet-meeting document, 1920, 26 November, no. 73, Bror Johansson, Ida Svensson. My italics.

Medical and social circumstances and age difference

The analysis of the applications for dispensation from the 1910s is made easier by the fact that the reasons that the authorities found decisive were often marked by underlinings in pencil or by a summarising note in the application itself.[100] These informal markings can be checked against the arguments that were presented in the official reports of the National Swedish Board of Health. The opinions of the National Swedish Board of Health were usually presented in two parts: a fairly long, detailed report (memo) and a very brief summary of the case along with the decision of the Board.

Both the Civil Code of 1734 and the Act of 1864 expressly stated that full and half relatives should be considered legally equivalent. In the marriage act of 1915, this formulation was removed; but the explanatory statements emphasised that full and half relatives should nevertheless be treated equally in future as well.[101] In spite of this, all the material shows that the authorities took account of whether a relationship was full or half, both in criminal and in dispensational cases, in the early twentieth century. Time and time again, decisions in the dispensational material were justified by using the family relationship as an argument. Rejections were considered justified 'in particular because the applicants are full relatives', while decisions on approvals were reinforced by the relevant case 'being only a matter of half-relatives'.[102] Around a third of the sixty-four applications came from people who were half-relatives.[103] All of them were approved.

The other assessments emphasised three factors: *medical impediments*, *social circumstances*, and *the age difference* between the

100 See, e.g., JD, Cabinet-meeting document, 1916, 28 April, no. 48, Johan Johansson, Elsa Olsson; JD, Cabinet-meeting document, 1916, 12 May, no. 36, Carl Johansson, Ester Johansson; JD, Cabinet-meeting document, 1916, 29 September, no. 36, Hjalmar Andersson, Anna Linder; JD, Cabinet-meeting document, 1916, 23 March, no. 32, Valfrid Andreasson, Ellen Karlsson; JD, Cabinet-meeting document, 1919, 28 May, no. 41, Salomon Karlsson, Olivia Mårtensson.

101 *Lag om äktenskapets ingående och upplösning*, p. 45.

102 See, e.g., JD, Cabinet-meeting document, 1916, 24 March, no. 41, Erik Ljungdahl, Astrid Johansson. A similar wording can be found in more or less all of the applications regarding half-relatives. For examples of full relatives, see JD, Cabinet-meeting document, 1917, 16 February, no. 39, Wilhelm Kaesen, Maria Kaesen.

103 Or, to be more precise, twenty-one out of sixty-four applications.

applicants. Surprisingly enough, it was most often the last-mentioned factor – the age difference – that was decisive for the outcome.

When an application was to be assessed, the medical circumstances were checked first and foremost. In order to gain knowledge of the appropriateness of the applicants getting married and potentially having children, the state required, via a medical examination and certificate, a confirmation of the applicants' being in full health and not at risk of passing on bad genes to the next generation. Any liabilities could lead to a swift rejection. Olof Tjärnlund and his *niece* Maria Johansson were, for instance, denied permission to marry because there was a brother and two cousins in their extended family who had been admitted to an asylum and two sisters who suffered from epilepsy.[104] But in spite of the sharp focus placed on a family's medical history, it was possible for people with known disorders in the family to be given permission to marry. In the application from Karl Muhr and Anna Sandelius, it was stated that Karl's father had become mentally ill in his old age and had died in an asylum. Even so, the couple were given permission to marry.[105] Oskar Nordström and his *half-niece* Johanna Blomkvist were also allowed to marry, although there were relatives on Oskar's side who showed signs of mental disorder and epilepsy. The National Swedish Board of Health said that because the disorder only existed on Oskar's side of the family, there were no medical impediments to the marriage. The Crown followed the recommendations of the National Swedish Board of Health and approved the couple's application.[106] Another man had a sister who was 'mentally deficient' while his fiancée and *niece* had a 'feeble-minded' aunt. The disorder of both the sister and the aunt was, however, said to have appeared after a childhood disease, and the couple were given permission to marry.[107] A mental disorder in the family hence did not automatically result in the rejection of a couple's application, if the risk of the disorder being passed on to the next generation was considered to be slight. Surprisingly enough, the proportion of applicants who

104 JD, Cabinet-meeting document, 1920, 26 March, no. 43; JD, R, 1920, 26 March, no. 42, Olof Tjärnlund, Maria Johansson.

105 JD, Cabinet-meeting document, 1916, 22 July, no. 31; JD, K, 1916, 22 July, no. 93, Karl Muhr, Anna Sandelius.

106 JD, Cabinet-meeting document, 1916, 22 December, no. 31; JD, R, K, 1916, 22 December, Oskar Nordström, Johanna Blomkvist.

107 JD, Cabinet-meeting document, 1916, 23 March, no. 32, Valfrid Andreasson, Ellen Karlsson.

were rejected because of their own disorders, or disorders in their families, was very small. Out of sixty-four applications, twenty-three were rejected. In only one case was the rejection based solely on medical grounds, namely the above-mentioned case of Olof Tjärnlund and Maria Johansson. In other cases, it was usually the age difference that put an end to the applicants' wedding plans.[108]

Age difference was the single most common justification for rejection, and its importance for the assessment of the applications for dispensation becomes apparent in several ways. The age of the applicants was mandatory information that had to be stated before the application was processed. The information should preferably be verified by way of a certificate from a clergyman who knew the family personally; alternatively, written information from the parish registers could be certified by the clergyman on duty. The ages of the applicants were very often underlined in pencil in the application documents, regardless of whether the application was rejected or approved. In addition, there were cases where the exact ages of – or the age difference between – the applicants were stated in the precise terms of years, months, and days.[109]

In their assessments, the National Swedish Board of Health thus always took the ages of the applicants into consideration. Indeed, information about ages seems to have overshadowed the medical circumstances in some cases. Karl Pettersson was sixty-eight years old and his *niece* Hilma Andersson was thirty-seven. Consequently, there were a little over thirty years between Karl and Hilma. Via medical certificates and testimonials about their families from acquaintances, it was noted that there were mental disorders in both Karl's and Hilma's families. They had three common relatives who either suffered from epilepsy or had been diagnosed as mentally ill. The medical liabilities were carefully stated in the report of the National Swedish Board of Health, but in the summary of the case these disorders were not mentioned at all. Conversely, the summary

108 Fifteen rejections were justified solely on the basis of a great age difference; two rejections were justified on the basis of a great age difference in combination with another impediment. One case was rejected because factual information was missing, and in some cases the reasons for rejection were not stated in detail but can be assumed to have had to do with the applicants' family positions relative to each other. See further discussion on pp. 251–3.

109 See, e.g., JD, Cabinet-meeting document, 1917, 9 November, no. 66, Frans Svenningsson, Ellen Svenningsson.

announced that the National Swedish Board of Health 'owing to the significant age difference between the applicants, cannot approve the submitted application'.[110] Karl and Hilma's application would probably have been rejected even if they had been closer in age; but it is very interesting that the National Swedish Board of Health chose to foreground age as being decisive for the outcome, and that the large age difference led to a rejection 'from a medical point of view'. Similar words were employed in a different case where there were no liabilities in the form of disorders in the applicants' family history. There was an age difference of thirty-five years between Johan Skog (sixty-one) and his niece Emilia Skog (twenty-six). Both Emilia and her father confirmed in separate certificates that they consented to the planned marriage and that there were no signs of disorders in the family. The application was rejected with the following wording: 'In view of the significant age difference, around thirty-five years, that exists between the applicants, the National Swedish Board of Health finds itself unable to recommend approval for the submitted application for medical reasons.'[111]

The National Swedish Board of Health thus described a significant age difference as a *medical* impediment. Professor Frej Svensson, who was chairman of the National Swedish Board of Health scientific council, presented his view of the matter in a written opinion dated 31 March 1917. He declared that the age difference between two spouses was of importance for the offspring from a hereditary perspective, because the gametes came from individuals at 'different stages of development'. This was, he argued, of particular significance when either of the individuals was outside his or her 'most potent age of procreation', that is to say, was not at the optimal age for producing children. If the man was under twenty-five years old or over fifty, or if the woman was under twenty or over forty, marriages should not be allowed between couples where the age difference was greater than twenty years. However, it was not made clear in concrete terms how this age difference might affect a child. Furthermore, Svensson stated that marriages between men and women with a greater age difference than twenty years were inappropriate from a social perspective as well. The man's age was

110 JD, Cabinet-meeting document, 1920, 16 January, no. 77, Karl Pettersson, Hilma Andersson.

111 JD, Cabinet-meeting document, 1919, 31 July, no. 46, Johan Skog, Emilia Skog.

especially important in this context, as the social reasons were connected to the man's ability to support and raise a child. A child was assumed to require support from its parents up until the age of fifteen. The recommended age limit for a man's parenthood was therefore set at the age of fifty-two, when he had fifteen years left to retirement.[112]

The legislation did not lay down any limitations for marriages on the basis of age difference between the man and the woman.[113] Neither was age difference, judging from the printed protocols from the joint preparatory legislative work, debated as a circumstance that impeded marriages in this arena.[114] Nor were there limitations preventing unrelated couples from marrying if there was a great age difference between the prospective spouses.

That spouses should preferably be fairly close to each other in age must instead be seen as an informal norm in society. There are early examples of a great age difference between a husband and wife being perceived as an unfavourable circumstance which should be avoided in order to increase the likelihood of a happy marriage.[115]

---

112 JD, Cabinet-meeting document, 1917, 27 April, no. 38, Knut Törnquist, Maria Törnquist.

113 *Nya äktenskapslagen med förklaringar*; *Lag om äktenskapets ingående och upplösning*.

114 In a little over one hundred typewritten pages, the legislators' motives for legitimising the marriage impediments are described. On one single occasion, it is noted in a subclause that diagonal consanguinity relationships were inappropriate 'especially because there is often a great age difference between the contracting parties'. *Lagberedningens förslag till revision av giftermålsbalken…I*, pp. 129–239, quotation on p. 199.

115 In 1711, a couple were advised against marrying because of an age difference of about forty years; but because both parties consented to the marriage, their wish was eventually granted by the Cathedral Chapter in Skara. SD, A1:30, 1711, 27 September, no. 17; SD, AI:30, 1711, 11 October, no. 175. In one case from the Strängnäs Cathedral Chapter, 'an old man of about a hundred years' wanted to marry a thirty-year-old maidservant. She was in service with him, and both his and her relatives consented to the marriage. The Cathedral Chapter approved their application in October 1676. StD, AI:II, 1686, 30 September, no. 3, p. 128; StD, AI:11, 1686, 6 October, no. 5, pp. 129f. Marklund refers to another case where the woman was almost forty years older than the man. After valiant attempts to prevent the union, the vicar married them. Marklund 2004, pp. 175, 192–94. Sandén also describes cases where odd couples have initially been dissuaded from getting married but eventually had their way. Sandén 2005, pp. 178f. See also Liliequist 2007, p. 180.

This norm is also indirectly expressed in dispensational cases where couples stated that they were close to each other in age as an argument for having their applications approved.[116] Although these are isolated cases, it is possible to conclude that certain ideals surrounding marital unions existed in which a great age difference between the spouses was seen as potentially detrimental. It is, however, uncertain how widespread or influential these notions were during earlier periods.

The pattern of marriages in Sweden corresponded to what has been called *the Western European marriage pattern*. This meant that men and women, unlike the situation in Eastern Europe, only married when they were able to form a household and support themselves. In the old agrarian society, that stage was often attained around the age of twenty-five. Among peasants, the age difference between husband and wife was relatively small at the time of the first marriage, whereas around ten years' difference between a man and his younger wife was more common in the higher estates.[117] Nevertheless, some studies indicate that the aversion to too great an age difference between spouses was more pronounced in the higher ranks than among the peasantry.[118] In a second and third marriage, the age difference between the spouses frequently widened with respect to the peasantry, too, because a widow or widower commonly remarried a previously unmarried younger person, rather than merging two established households. In cases where a widow remarried, it was thus not uncommon for the woman to be older than the man.[119] Besides, up until the second half of the eighteenth century, the custom of widow conservation was well established within both the clerical estate and the artisanal groups.[120]

Even though there have been certain norms regarding the ages of spouses during earlier periods, one can thus draw the conclusion

116 JR, BoA 1780, 25 February, Magnus Norling, Catharina Söderström; JR, BoA 1801, 28 October, Joseph Rautiain, Ulrika (cousin); JD, Cabinet-meeting document, 1920, 3 December, no. 56, Lars Wiberg, Herta Liljeroth.

117 On the Western European marriage pattern, see Coontz 2005, pp. 124–31; Gaunt 1996, pp. 14–19. On the age difference between spouses in the higher estates, see Davidoff, Doolittle, Fink, and Holden 1999, p. 126; Carlsson 1977, p. 109; Stadin 2004, p. 178.

118 Lennartsson 2012, pp. 105, 107f, 112; Sandén 2005, pp. 178, 180.

119 Gaunt 1996, pp. 178–80; Matović 1984, pp. 121, 130, 176; Göransson 1992, p. 119; Taussi Sjöberg 1988, pp. 72–4.

120 Widén 1988; Vainio-Korhonen 1997; Edgren 1983.

that these norms were not decisive for people's actions. If a marriage was considered advantageous for other reasons, the parties' ages relative to each other did not constitute an impediment to the alliance, neither among the peasants nor among the higher orders. The fact that information about a couple's respective ages was rarely recorded in connection with criminal trials and dispensational cases before the turn of the century in 1800 must also be taken to indicate that age was not regarded as relevant to the decisions. Over time, however, a change appears to have taken place.

Although the custom of widow conservation dwindled during the nineteenth century, historian Ulla Rosén, in a study on care of the elderly in the Swedish agrarian society, has shown that remarriage was used as a strategy for elderly care throughout the 1800s. Conversely, the number of marriages where there was a great age difference between the spouses declined at the beginning of the twentieth century, after various societal resources geared to supporting the elderly had been introduced.[121] According to the research of historian Margareta Matović, the general marriage pattern in Stockholm also changed during this time. In the 1860s and 1870s, it was relatively common for a woman to be older than a man in the lower social orders, even with respect to first marriages; but towards the end of the century, such alliances became increasingly rare.[122] Marja Taussi Sjöberg showed that there was a similar declining trend for older wives with younger husbands in northern Sweden during the same period.[123] Even though the proportion of older women did not decrease in the same way when it came to remarriages, the statistics can be interpreted as meaning that Sweden saw a cultural shift with regard to age differences between spouses during the second half of the nineteenth century. As a consequence of that shift, people in general were less prepared to accept great deviations in age, and nor would they approve of older wives and younger husbands. When the ages of couples applying for dispensation became decisive for the outcomes of cases at the beginning of the twentieth century, it may have been connected to this cultural shift.

Regardless of the general attitude to the ages of husbands and wives in earlier periods, ideas about the ages of spouses thus acquired a decisive importance in the assessment of applications for dispensation during the 1910s. All couples where the age difference was

121 Rosén 2004, pp. 145f.
122 Matović 1984, p. 184.
123 Taussi Sjöberg 1988, pp. 72–4.

greater than twenty years were initially denied permission to marry, and some couples were rejected even when the difference was just below twenty years.[124] Here, then, the National Swedish Board of Health seems to have been influenced by informal ideas about how an optimal marriage should be configured. The decisions, and the informal ideas on which those decisions were based, were justified internally by means of 'scientific' opinions submitted by experts, but those opinions did not present any support for the scientific arguments.

The fact that an application for marriage could be rejected because of a significant age difference appears to have come as a surprise to the applicants. In their first application from 1916, Hjalmar Andersson (fifty-three years old) and his *niece* Anna Linder (twenty-nine years old) stated that they, like all their relatives, were completely healthy, whereupon they invoked the new law and asked for permission to marry. All the submitted information was supported by enclosed certificates, and at the end of their formal letter the couple noted that they could not imagine that there could be any 'objections' to their marriage for 'medical reasons'.[125] There were twenty-four years between Hjalmar and Anna, and their application was rejected.[126] One year later they made a new attempt. From their second application, it transpires that Hjalmar and Anna had been encouraged in their desire to marry by doctors and lawyers, who had assumed that their application would be approved. Encouraged by this unofficial support, they had 'become formally engaged and exchanged rings' and planned to live together. The rejection had 'hit them hard', and they questioned the twenty-year limit, which was 'completely arbitrary'. In addition, they felt that they only exceeded the limit 'in an insignificant way'. What was more

124 JD, Cabinet-meeting document, 1917, 16 February, no. 39; JD, K, 1917, 16 February, Wilhelm Kaesen, Elisabeth Kaesen; JD, Cabinet-meeting document, 1919, 31 July, no. 46; JD, K, 1919, 31 July, Johan Skog, Emilia Skog; JD, Cabinet-meeting document, 1916, 29 September, no. 36; JD, K, 1916, 29 September, no. 245, Hjalmar Andersson, Anna Linder; JD, Cabinet-meeting document, 1917, 27 April, no. 38; JD, K, 27 April, no. 199, Knut Törnquist, Maria Törnquist; JD, Cabinet-meeting document, 1916, 12 May, no. 41; JD, K, 1916, 12 May, Erik Ljungdahl, Astrid Johansson; JD, Cabinet-meeting document, 1916, 12 May, no. 40; JD, K, 1916, 12 May, no. 86, Anders Andersson, Augusta Gustavsson.

125 JD, Cabinet-meeting document, 1916, 29 September, no. 36, Hjalmar Andersson, Anna Linder.

126 JD, K, 1916, 29 September, no. 245, Hjalmar Andersson, Anna Linder.

important was that they themselves and all their relatives were 'in the best of health'. They found it to be 'distressing' if their union and 'future happiness' were to be thwarted by medical objections.[127] By choosing the expressions they used, both Hjalmar and Anna recognised that the health issue was important and relevant in the context, but they did not accept that the age difference should be relevant to the decision. However, the couple did not succeed in convincing the authorities, and their second application was turned down as well.[128] A number of couples repeated their applications in a similar way after a rejection when age difference was stated as a reason.[129] I interpret this as a direct protest against the state's right to decide on these matters. In other words, a great difference in age was not accepted by the applicants as a legitimate impediment to marriage.

Although Hjalmar and Anna were unsuccessful, some couples managed to get decisions amended and their applications approved after repeated applications, in spite of there being a great age difference between them.[130] In these cases, it was social circumstances that caused the authorities to change their minds. In one application, a vicar entreated that the marriage between Oskar Carlström (forty-three years old) and his *niece* Helga Carlström (twenty-one years old) should be allowed to take place. The vicar did not understand why this marriage could not be approved now that the amended law had eliminated the 'fundamental' objections one might have had against such unions in the past. He did not mention the age difference between Oskar and Helga. Instead he emphasised that the applicants were well-behaved and hard-working. Though Helga and Oskar were already living together, their intimate relationship

127 JD, Cabinet-meeting document, 1917, 13 August, no. 28, Hjalmar Andersson, Anna Linder.

128 JD, K, 1917, 13 August, no. 89, Hjalmar Andersson, Anna Linder.

129 Examples of renewed applications where the rejection had been linked to the age difference: JD, Cabinet-meeting document, 1917, 16 February, no. 39, Wilhelm Kaesen, Elisabeth Kaesen; JD, Cabinet-meeting document, 1919, 31 July, no. 46, Johan Skog, Emilia Skog; JD, Cabinet-meeting document, 1916, 22 December, no. 32, Emanuel Carlsson, Anna Olsson; JD, Cabinet-meeting document, 1917, 23 June, no. 34, Oskar Carlström, Helga Carlström.

130 The applications of fourteen couples in total were rejected, of which half appealed against the decision at least once. Out of these, only four couples managed to have the decisions changed. Two of these four applied three and four times, respectively, before the decisions were amended.

had developed without their having endeavoured to make it happen. The couple had had one child together who had died, and the vicar felt that it would help them in their grief if they were allowed to marry. In conclusion, he noted that the couple were so devoted that it would be very difficult for them to be separated. Again, personal desires, practical circumstances, and economic relationships were foregrounded as arguments for approving a marriage. The National Swedish Board of Health allowed itself to be persuaded, their summary of the case stating that there were no reasons for rejection 'from a medical perspective', whereupon the Crown approved the application even though there were twenty-two years between Oskar and Helga.[131] Similarly, another couple had their application for permission to marry approved in spite of an age difference of a little over twenty years. In this case, the woman was said to have lived with and kept house for her intended husband for five years.[132]

After four applications, the previously mentioned couple Knut Törnquist (forty years old) and his *niece* Maria Törnquist (seventeen years old) also managed to be given permission to marry despite there being an age difference of more than twenty years between them. In the first opinion of the National Swedish Board of Health, a disorder in the family (one sister was said to be mentally ill after a childhood disease), Maria's youth, and the great age difference (twenty-two years) were stated as impeding circumstances. The second and third applications repeated the same arguments. References to Professor Svensson's opinions on the age difference between spouses were also made several times. When the three initial applications were submitted Maria was only seventeen years old, which was below the legal age for marriage, and she was said to be a full relative of Knut's. When the fourth and final application was submitted Maria had turned eighteen, and besides the couple claimed that they were only half-relatives. In line with this new information, Maria was thus only Knut's *half-niece*. The final opinion of the National Swedish Board of Health confirmed that this new information was decisive, and that in view of it, the Board no longer 'had any objections to make against an approval'. The fact that the age

131 JD, Cabinet-meeting document, 1917, 23 June, no. 34; JD, K, 1917, 6 July, no. 40, Oskar Carlström, Helga Carlström.

132 JD, Cabinet-meeting document, 1919, undated decision, received 18 January, no. 67, August Lundskog, Kristina Lindskog.

difference between Knut and Maria was over twenty years was not commented on in the final opinion.[133]

Initially, then, couples where the age difference was close to or exceeded twenty years had their applications rejected; but if a couple repeated their application and there were no other obstacles, the National Swedish Board of Health might reconsider their assessment. Often it was social or economic circumstances that decided these cases. Couples who lived and had children together stood a greater chance of having their applications approved than couples who had not yet initiated a sexual relationship. One application specifically mentioned that it would be desirable, especially for the woman and her children, if the relationship could be legalised, so that their 'mutual home [...] could continue'. The Crown subsequently approved the couple's application, though there was an age difference of nineteen years and seven months.[134] In one application, the Board summarised previous decisions. Without exception, the justification for all decisions had to do with social circumstances or the ages of the parties.[135]

Unlike the state of things in previous periods, when known immorality lessened the chances that a couple applying for dispensation would secure a favourable decision, information about living together and having mutual children could increase the chances of approval in the 1910s. Consequently, the absence of these factors could be a cause of rejection. On the front page of a rejected application, it is written in pencil: 'as far as is known no child and have not lived together'.[136]

The authorities hence took the social circumstances of the couple into consideration. There was reluctance to break up established relationships, especially if children were involved. The very circumstances which had previously been perceived as aggravating and

133 JD, Cabinet-meeting document, 1918, 13 December, no. 108; JD K, 1918, 13 December, Knut Törnquist, Maria Törnquist.

134 JD, Cabinet-meeting document, 1916, 14 July, no. 30; JD, K, 1916, 14 July, no. 56, Johan Westerberg, Anna Westerberg.

135 JD, Cabinet-meeting document, 1917, 9 November, no. 66, Frans Svenningsson, Ellen Svenningsson.

136 JD, Cabinet-meeting document, 1916, 12 May, no. 41, Erik Ljungdahl, Astrid Johansson. See also a case where the application was rejected because it could not be proved that the man was the child's father. JD, Cabinet-meeting document, 1917, 16 February, no. 39; JD R, K, 1917, 16 February, Wilhelm Kaesen, Elisabeth Kaesen.

which many applicants had attempted to keep secret from the state – that they were a loving couple, that they lived together, that they had children – were reasons promoting a favourable assessment. For some couples, this lack of knowledge may have led to their giving up their plans to marry after an initial rejection. Fredrik Engström (thirty-six years old) and his *aunt* Anna Holmgren (thirty-eight years old) barely managed to avoid such an outcome. The first two applications of this couple were, like those of many others, brief and to the point without revealing any detailed information about their personal lives. When these applications were rejected, two more years elapsed before a third application was drawn up. A personal letter from Anna, where she described her life and where she admitted to already having a relationship with Fredrik, was enclosed with the final application. She described how she, 'young and inexperienced', had come to Stockholm to live with her elder sister. Her sister's family was described as poor and socially dysfunctional. Anna was exploited as an unpaid household help and as a babysitter, and at the same time she found it difficult to protect herself from her brother-in-law's unwelcome advances. Regarding her sister's eldest child Fredrik, who was the same age as Anna, she wrote:

> The eldest boy saved me from his father many times. He was quiet and sad and different in character from both his father and his mother. For this reason he was never accepted in the home. The consequence was that he turned to me. I respected him and felt sorry for him. It continued in this way until I realised I loved him.[137]

A few years later, Anna and Fredrik moved to a home of their own and assumed responsibility for raising a girl who had been badly treated in her own home. In her letter, Anna emphasised that it would be considerably better for this child if Anna and Fredrik were allowed to marry, so that the girl would not be teased by her friends. These circumstances had not been mentioned in the previous applications, she admitted, because the couple had, in their 'great foolishness', believed 'that it would be better that way'. Anna's candid letter met with approval, and the couple were given permission to marry in September 1918.

It may be noted that Anna was Fredrik's *aunt*, which is likely to have been the reason why their previous applications had been

137 JD, Cabinet-meeting document, 1918, 18 September, no. 50, Fredrik Engström, Anna Holmgren.

rejected (there was only an age difference of two years between them, and there were no known disorders in the family). The National Swedish Board of Health did not find any medical impediments to their marriage in the first application rounds, but the Crown nevertheless chose to reject their application without any particular justification.[138] The material contains twenty-nine relationships between a man and his *niece*, but only two relationships between a man and his *aunt*.[139] There were thus only a few couples who applied for permission to marry when the woman's family position was in the generation above the man's. The numbers indicate that there were still ideas rife in society regarding the importance of the family position for romantic relationships. The acceptance of a relationship between a man and his niece had been greater than the acceptance of a relationship between a man and his aunt for a long time, and these notions were a probable reason for the rejections of Fredrik and Anna's previous applications.

The importance of family position in this context is also illustrated by the only application for marriage where the applicants were related in an affinity degree. The case involved a man and his *stepdaughter*. Lars Wiberg (thirty-five years old) wrote to the king during the autumn of 1920, asking for permission to marry his stepdaughter, Herta Liljeroth (twenty-eight years old). When Lars had married Herta's mother a few years earlier, Herta was already an adult and had moved away from home. In addition, she had been married herself and had three children of her own. After Lars's wife and Herta's husband had died, they now wanted to marry. Lars justified his application in the following way:

> Because no blood relationship thus exists between us, because furthermore Herta Liljeroth has never resided in my home, or in any other way perceived herself to be in the relationship of a child to me, the less so as we are approximately of the same age, and, in conclusion, because we have now grown extremely fond of each other ...[140]

138 The first application was rejected because of incomplete information, the second without any particular justification. JD, Cabinet-meeting document, 1916, 8 September, no. 49; JD, Cabinet-meeting document, 1916, 8 September, no. 34; JD, K, 1916, 8 September, no. 77, Fredrik Engström, Anna Holmgren.

139 Including *half-nieces* and *half-aunts*, the figures total forty-five and seven relationships, respectively.

140 JD, Cabinet-meeting document, 1920, 3 December, no. 56, Lars Wiberg, Herta Liljeroth.

The application was rejected with the brief justification that it was in opposition to existing law. Consequently, there was no scope for exceptions in this case. Lars's application stressed several circumstances which he felt distinguished their relationship from the relationship that the legislation had in view: that there was no biological kinship between them; that they had never lived together in the same household; that they had never been in a parent–child relationship with each other; that they were almost same age; and that they had 'taken a fancy' to each other. All these circumstances were ignored by the authorities. As in earlier periods, there were thus strong ethical objections in society against sexual relationships between family members in lineal kinship degrees. In this case, the objections were based entirely on the family positions of the applicants relative to each other. The fact that no other applications for marriage were submitted for similar relationship categories increases the likelihood that these ideas were also shared by the public.

Criminal cases

Although incest has always been a relatively uncommon crime, it became even rarer in Swedish courts around the turn of the century in 1900. In the 1910s, only about ten people per year were prosecuted for and convicted of incest in Sweden. The figures rose somewhat during the subsequent decades (approximately twenty to thirty) only to drop again after 1930. It is likely that the temporary increase may be ascribed to newly introduced laws on child welfare, which resulted in more crimes being discovered and reported.[141]

In the 1930s, two scientific studies were conducted concerning the prevalence of the crime of incest in the country. Torsten Sondén, a reader in psychiatry, investigated court material for incest crimes between 1913 and 1933, involving just over 150 convicts. His preliminary conclusions were presented in 1935, in connection with an official government inquiry about the ranges of punishment for particular crimes in Sweden.[142] Another contemporaneous study used material from one hundred Swedish incest cases between 1929

141 The number of prosecuted families is said to have been around ten per year in 1913–18, twenty per year in 1919–27, thirty per year in 1928–30, and twenty per year in 1931–3. *SOU 1935:68*, p. 47. Similar figures are given for the number of persons convicted during the same time. Kinberg, Inghe, and Riemer 1943, p. 45.

142 *SOU 1935:68*.

18 Olof Kinberg (1873–1960), physician, psychiatrist, and co-author of *Incestproblemet i Sverige* ('The incest problem in Sweden'), which was published in 1943.

and 1937. The authors of this study were Olof Kinberg, at that time a teacher of forensic psychiatry and psychiatrist at the central prison of Långholmen; Gunnar Inghe, active within social medicine and the editor of *Populär tidskrift för sexuell upplysning* ('Popular periodical for sexual information'); and Svend Riemer, a German academic and later a professor of sociology in the United States.[143]

In connection with these investigations, the phenomenon of incest was analysed from a number of perspectives. Quantitative studies were made concerning the prevalence of the phenomenon in the country, complemented by geographic studies where comparisons

143 Kinberg, Inghe, and Riemer 1943.

were made regarding the prevalence of the crime of incest in different counties, or in the city versus the countryside. On an individual level, those who had been prosecuted and convicted of incest were studied from medical, psychological, and social perspectives. Their occupations and ages were noted, as was their physical and psychological health. The convicts and their families answered questions about their living conditions and sleeping habits. They described their alcohol-consumption habits and how their family dynamics worked. They also gave an account of their religious faith and whether they led a moral or immoral life.

According to the statistical results of these two studies, incest crimes were largely distributed among three relationship categories. Roughly half or a little more than half of incest crimes occurred between *father and daughter*, while *stepfather/stepdaughter* and *sibling relationships* each made up one quarter of the total. Other relationship combinations were very unusual.[144] Furthermore, the investigations showed that the phenomenon of incest was over-represented in the lowest social groups in society; for example, among unskilled labourers in the city and unpropertied farm workers in the countryside.[145]

Like many others belonging to the same social stratum, these families often lived in dysfunctional relationships and had significant economic problems. In several cases one or both parents were alcoholics, and the children were exposed to neglect and abuse of various kinds.[146] In the Sondén study, the 'wide-spread objectionable custom' of family members sharing a bed was held up as a direct cause of incest crimes.[147] In the Kinberg/Inghe/Riemer study, however, it was argued that this connection could not be proven.[148] Even so, both investigations established that overcrowding in the social groups in question was problematic, that the 'typical incest offender' suffered from sexual abstinence, that certain psychological stresses might

144 Kinberg, Inghe, and Riemer 1943, p. 46; *SOU 1935:68*, p. 46.

145 Kinberg, Inghe, and Riemer 1943, p. 85; *SOU 1935:68*, p. 50.

146 In the Kinberg/Inghe/Riemer study, 'the inner disintegration of family life' was said to be characteristic of families where incest occurred. Fifty-five out of fifty-eight families lived in conditions that entailed a 'complete breakdown of family life' (Kinberg, Inghe, and Riemer 1943, pp. 105f). In the Sondén study, the misuse of alcohol in combination with other environmental factors (overcrowding) were presented as the major causes of the crime. *SOU 1935:68*, p. 51.

147 *SOU 1935:68*, p. 52.

148 Kinberg, Inghe, and Riemer 1943, p. 118.

occur (even if the crime could not be directly linked to psychological disorders), and that an incest offender was not particularly criminally inclined. In some isolated cases, it turned out that the offender was regretful and ashamed of his actions after the fact; but far too often, the 'proper' moral insight was lacking.[149]

The empirical results corresponded to an ideological notion about the 'typical' sex offender. German forensic psychiatry emphasised both internal factors (mental illness or an abnormal sexual drive) and external factors (bad social conditions) as the causes of various sexual crimes; and historian Åsa Bergenheim has shown that Swedish doctors and forensic psychiatrists were strongly influenced by the ideas from Germany.[150] According to these ideas, the crime of incest was more common among the lowest and most primitive citizens in society than among more cultured people. Similar ideas could be found among contemporaneous medical experts in Denmark and the United States.[151] In France, the image of the incest perpetrator as a monster, an unnatural person, was established towards the end of the nineteenth century. Here, too, connections were made between incestuous acts and economic and cultural poverty.[152]

Whether the crime of incest can in fact be linked to social class may be questioned, though, as the number of unrecorded incest crimes is sure to grow along with a family's rising position in society. But this was not discussed at the time.[153]

In summary, the Swedish investigators affirmed that a poor childhood environment with an inferior cultural and moral education constituted a basic risk factor for incest crimes, which, in combination with a 'triggering factor' (sexual abstinence or the influence of alcohol), could drive people to commit an incestuous act.[154] Alcohol was no longer a mitigating circumstance for the commission of criminal acts, a circumstance that may be linked to the fact that a temperance movement now had strong political support in Swedish society.[155]

149 *SOU 1935:68*, pp. 45, 51; Kinberg, Inghe, and Riemer 1943, pp. 126, 128, 181, 193, 195.

150 Bergenheim 1998, pp. 130f.

151 Seidelin 2014, pp. 86–8, and the literature referred to therein; Gordon 1986.

152 Formally speaking, incest was not defined as a criminal act in France. Giuliani 2008.

153 On hidden crimes of incest in the higher social classes in the United States, see Herman and Hirschman 1977.

154 *SOU 1935:68*, p. 51.

155 Nilsson 2008, pp. 138–42, 200f.

19 After the turn of the century in 1900, the majority of incest crimes discovered were committed in families from the lowest social strata. Incest hence came to be defined as a lower-class problem.

Violence and exploitation

When a number of affinity prohibitions were abolished at the end of the nineteenth century, the general picture of the crime of incest began to change. For centuries, the majority of these crimes had involved voluntary sexual relationships between adults. As the number of prohibitions decreased, the relationship categories that were dominated by voluntary relationships disappeared. Those relationships that tended to be the consequences of coercion and exploitation were still prohibited. Incest between members of a nuclear family had always provoked a particular revulsion, but those offences had constituted a minority of Swedish incest crimes, and these relationships were not the ones against which earlier laws had primarily been used. This fact might explain why it took so long before it became obvious to the authorities that incest between (step)parent and (step)child was often a matter of downright abuse.

Still, the above-mentioned investigations from the 1930s did draw attention to these circumstances. Kinberg, Inghe, and Riemer affirmed that voluntary incestuous relationships between adult individuals were 'very unusual'. Nor was it common for girls to behave seductively or provocatively, as had been claimed in other contemporaneous studies from abroad.[156] The official investigation from 1935, which included the Sondén study, established that incestuous relationships were to a high degree a matter of crimes against minors or abuse of paternal authority. Not enough attention had been paid to this fact in earlier discussions, the investigators said, and this could not be 'emphasised too much'.[157] Statistics showed that upwards of 75% of alleged incest crimes were committed by an older man and a younger girl. That the girls in these contexts were found to be accessories to the crime was regarded as extremely unfortunate, though the judges often allowed them to escape with a conditional sentence. The girls were, after all, sentenced for actions they had been forced to commit, and for this reason it was considered urgent for the legislation to be changed so that the protection for children and adolescents improved.[158] As a direct consequence of this investigation, the legislation was changed two years later. Those who had been enticed or intimidated into committing incestuous acts because of a position of dependency or youth were henceforth made completely exempt from punishment.[159]

Even so, the 'objective harm' suffered by the victimised girls was considered to be relatively limited. This conclusion was justified by the belief that the children were already traumatised by the conditions of the environment in which they grew up, where quarrels and violence were everyday occurrences, as well as by the belief that their deficient moral education meant that they neither realised nor were particularly harmed by the abuse to which they were subjected.[160] Following an analysis of incest crimes against Swedish children from 1850 to 1910, Bergenheim describes the existence of such beliefs. Even when a child claimed to be in pain, or when there was bruising, swelling, and discolouration of the genitals, the doctor would declare that there were no 'actual injuries'. The psychological condition of the child was not discussed at all.[161] The child was thus considered free of guilt with respect

156 Kinberg, Inghe, and Riemer 1943, pp. 41, 249, quotation on p. 41.
157 *SOU 1935:68*, pp. 49f, 59.
158 *SOU 1935:68*, pp. 37, 55f. On the court's treatment of the victimised girls, see also Bergenheim 1998, pp. 136f.
159 Semmler 2003, p. 10.
160 Kinberg, Inghe, and Riemer 1943, pp. 316, 331.
161 Bergenheim 1998, pp. 136f.

to the criminal act, but was not felt to suffer any real harm from the crime.

But it was not only the younger party who was perceived as a potential victim at this time. Environmental factors and other circumstances related to a person's upbringing were given such a prominent place as an explanatory basis for incest that not even the initiator of the crime could be held completely responsible for his actions. In cases where an individual had grown up in a bad environment and there was some triggering factor (alcohol or sexual abstinence), the individual in question was seen as virtually predestined to engage in incestuous behaviour. The study by Kinberg, Inghe, and Riemer found that incest might develop 'from a constellation of circumstances' where the incest offender was a 'victim' rather than a free agent.[162] The crime was described as the extreme effect of 'an advanced social and moral decay', against which society should have taken action long before. The strict legislation was regarded as being too severe towards these 'disadvantaged and pitiable people' who had grown up and lived in 'economic, social, and moral destitution'.[163]

Here the investigators were evidently influenced by contemporary eugenic as well as sexological ideas. Incest offenders were described as 'psychologically and socially underdeveloped in comparison to other people, who [were] born into a happier environment and were better equipped biologically'.[164] They were thought to exist in a parallel, culturally impoverished, proletarian stratum of society which had evolved as an unhappy consequence of industrialisation. They were also considered to be at the mercy of their own biology and their heightened male sexual drive, which might compel them to commit incestuous acts in the event of sexual abstinence. They were, in other words, victims of their environment, their culture, and their natural urges.

Paradoxically enough, the development outlined above amounted to a complete reversal in the basic attitude to incest offenders. Previously, both parties had been considered to be equally responsible for the crime, regardless of their ages or social circumstances; now they were both to a large extent regarded as victims of their culturally impoverished environment and their biology, which partly exempted them from responsibility for committing the acts. This

162 Kinberg, Inghe, and Riemer 1943, pp. 286f.
163 Kinberg, Inghe, and Riemer 1943, p. 289.
164 Kinberg, Inghe, and Riemer 1943, pp. 297f.

line of reasoning also led to a recommendation that the sentences be reduced. In order to prevent future incest crimes it was, among other things, recommended that the already ongoing sterilisations of 'oligophrenic' or psychologically inferior individuals should be made more efficient, while societal efforts should improve the environment in which children were brought up.[165] This view was completely in line with contemporary criminological explanatory models, where attention was paid to social circumstances as a cause of criminal behaviour.[166]

Voluntary relationships

Though relationships based on violence and exploitation dominated incest crimes during the early twentieth century, there were examples of couples who voluntarily initiated sexual relations in violation of the law. How did the authorities and the community react to these forbidden relationships?

In December 1915, Oskar Nordström (thirty-two years old) and his *half-niece* Johanna Blomqvist (twenty-one years old) were accused of incest. The relationship had been initiated three years earlier, when Johanna was employed as a housekeeper for Oskar, and the couple now had two children together. They claimed that they had not understood that they were acting in opposition to the law because Oskar was only the half-brother of Johanna's mother. The prosecutor petitioned for a mild punishment and the couple were sentenced to a fine. Seven months later they applied for a dispensation for marriage, which was granted.[167]

Under similar circumstances, Ester Johansson (twenty-four years old) moved in with her uncle, butcher Karl Johansson (forty-one years old), to help him with his housekeeping. After a year or so they began a sexual relationship which resulted in two children. Before Ester moved in, Karl was said to have led an 'intemperate

---

165 Kinberg, Inghe, and Riemer 1943, pp. 337–49.

166 Häthén 1990, p. 221; Bergenheim 1998, pp. 127–31. The trend within criminal policy that emphasised the importance of a criminal's predispositions in combination with his or her social environment was referred to as 'the positive school' and was primarily inspired by Italian professor of criminology Enrico Ferri. Inger 2011, pp. 293, 305, 308.

167 Råneå hundred, AIa:130 1915, 5 October, no. 39; 6 December, no. 69; JD, Cabinet-meeting document, 1915, 22 December, no. 31; JD, R, K, 1915, 22 December, Oskar Nordström, Johanna Blomqvist.

and disorderly life'; but she apparently had a good effect on him, and she had taken on the care of the home, the children, and Karl's invalid parents in a 'commendable manner'. In 1913, the couple applied for a dispensation for marriage but had their application rejected. In spite of the rejection, they continued to live together. About a year later, Ester's sister Ebba (seventeen years old) moved in with the family, and within a short period of time she too was enticed into having sexual relations with Karl. When Ester found out, she temporarily left the home but returned after a week or so. Shortly thereafter they were all arrested, accused of incest.[168]

The arrest was occasioned by a formal letter in which it was claimed that the butcher in the village had 'for a long time' lived with his niece and that they had children together. The relationship had not been openly admitted to, but according to the writer of the letter 'everyone' in the neighbourhood knew what was going on. The report was made in the hope that the 'chastisement prescribed by law' might be visited on the couple and that their 'deplorable relationship' might come to an end. The 'deplorable' aspect of the relationship seems only to refer to the family relationship. The fact that Ester's sister Ebba had also begun a sexual relationship with Karl is not mentioned in the letter, and whether this was known in the community is uncertain. All the people involved 'freely and without coercion' confessed their participation in the crime, whereupon Karl was sentenced to six months of hard labour for each crime of incest, that is to say a year in total. Ester and Ebba were given a conditional sentence of one month's imprisonment after their lawyer had pointed out that neither of them had been over the age of eighteen when the incestuous relationships began; that it might be questioned whether the family relationship could really be considered to be offensive, in that the new law permitted dispensations for marriage for the same kinship category; and that Ester's children risked faring badly if Ester was given a more severe punishment.[169] As in the previous case, Karl, Ester, and Ebba were thus sentenced to relatively mild punishments.

The man who reported the crime to the authorities was no doubt offended by the family relationship between Ester and Karl, but it had taken him a long time to act. Karl and Ester's first child was born in 1909, and after this event everybody ought to have realised

168 Västra Göinge hundred, AIb:32, 1915, 8 October, no. 16.

169 Västra Göinge hundred, AIb:32, 1915, 8 October, no. 16; HSoB, BIIc:236, 1915:2, 1 November, no. 301.

that Ester was more than simply his housekeeper. The couple lived together for over six years before they were reported to the authorities. Once more, then, the picture of a passive local community emerges – a community where people certainly gossiped in private, but took no active measures in order to remedy the situation. This passive attitude was, according to Kinberg, Inghe, and Riemer, common even when the younger party was obviously the victim of abuse. The authors point out that the public primarily reacted emotionally to incestuous relationships. People were horrified at the situation, and at the same time they felt a forbidden temptation to know more about the relationship in question. For this reason, it was common for prohibited relationships to go on for years while the community watched the actions of the persons involved from a distance, gossiping in whispers about what they had seen.[170] The community was in other words reluctant to 'interfere' in what they perceived to be private affairs.

This passivity can be recognised from previous periods. In the past, most incest crimes were brought to light when the woman became pregnant; but during the early twentieth century, it was only every fifth crime that was brought to the authorities' attention because of a pregnancy.[171] This change is probably due to the fact that sexuality was less strictly controlled and that it was considerably more common for women to bear children outside marriage – especially in the lower social strata, which is where the majority of incest crimes were discovered.

Incestuous relationships based on genuinely warm feelings between the accused parties seem always to have been supported by the immediate community, and from the nineteenth century onward they were also treated more leniently by the authorities. Reader of psychiatry Torsten Sondén, who was responsible for parts of the official inquiry of 1935, called these relationships 'the idyllic type'. He described situations where a 'truly mutually affectionate relationship' had developed between a man and a woman. This usually involved a stepfather and his stepdaughter after the man had been widowed. In a few such cases, the people in question had wanted to marry and had become engaged, believing that their relationship was completely legal because there were no biological ties between them. This misconception was, according to Sondén, 'fairly common [...] among the population in Sweden'. Some couples had also been

170 Kinberg, Inghe, and Riemer 1943, pp. 266–8.
171 Kinberg, Inghe, and Riemer 1943, p. 269.

supported in their relationship by a clergyman or a lawyer who recommended that they apply to the king for a dispensation for marriage. Their disappointment was great when they realised that the law regarded the family relationship as a marriage impediment 'for which a dispensation cannot be granted'.[172] The investigators argued that these individuals should not be punished as severely as those who had committed crimes of incest under other circumstances. Apart from safeguarding the legal rights of children and adolescents, the investigators therefore also wished to differentiate the penalties imposed so that it would be possible to distinguish 'aggravated' incest cases from 'less serious' ones.[173]

A certain differentiation among the legal penalties was conceded as early as the Act of 1864, and the cases previously referred to have shown that judges used the opportunity to reduce sentences in practice. In addition, the 1937 revision of the law introduced two separate ranges of punishment in order to distinguish between aggravated crimes of incest and those that were not so serious.

Sondén's claim that people in general thought that only biological family relationships were forbidden is supported by examples from the Kinberg/Inghe/Riemer study. One man expressly stated that he could not be defined as a sexual offender because he was not related to the woman in question, who was his *stepdaughter*.[174] Similarly, the preceding section showed that the absence of biological kinship ties was foregrounded as an argument for having applications for dispensation approved. Even though people occasionally claimed to be ignorant of other incest prohibitions too, the main dividing line seems to run between biological and non-biological family relationships.[175] Consequently, the definition of family and kinship had once more ended up at the centre of attention when the limits of incest prohibitions were negotiated. While some people felt that a stepfather and stepdaughter should definitely be regarded as relatives, other people argued that only people with biological kinship ties should be considered to be related to each other. The sharper focus on biological kinship was probably a result of the increased importance of medical science in society.

Just as in earlier periods, there was a grey zone between legal and illegal relationships where the legislation set a boundary that

172 *SOU 1935:68*, pp. 53f.
173 *SOU 1935:68*, pp. 37, 59f, quotation on p. 37.
174 Kinberg, Inghe, and Riemer 1943, p. 237. See also pp. 384, 391.
175 Kinberg, Inghe, and Riemer 1943, pp. 236, 262.

was not always known or accepted by the wider public. It is hence possible to distinguish a general trend over time, a trend according to which those prohibitions that were most distant from ordinary life at any one time were simply unknown to some people. In other words, the liberalisations that have been implemented were always preceded by increased cultural acceptance. It should, however, be added that the relationship in the diagonal consanguinity degree (*aunt*, *niece*) forms an exception. This kinship is biological; and although it was argued around 1900 that Sweden should abolish this incest prohibition, like Denmark, Norway, and Germany, there was both knowledge of and an acceptance of the fact that this family relationship constituted a potential impediment. Sexual relations between couples in the diagonal consanguinity degree were decriminalised in 1937, but the marriage prohibition remained until 1973.[176]

Partial summary and overview, 1840–1940

During the course of the nineteenth century, the importance of religion in the public sphere in Sweden continued to wane. One consequence of this development was that the penalties for incest crimes could be reduced. At the same time, the tolerance for horizontal and diagonal affinity relationships kept growing. The number of applications for dispensation rose steadily, and they were routinely approved. In addition, more and more people chose to live openly together in defiance of the law. Recurring discussions in the Riksdag finally led to several affinity prohibitions being abolished in 1872. The proportion of voluntary relationships hence declined among the incest crimes, and this made incest appear more of a crime of violence than a moral crime.

Around the turn of the century in 1900, race-biological ideas also came to be of great importance in the assessment of incest cases in Sweden. Medical science was gaining ground, and discussions on impediments to marriage would now include references to medical and genetic conditions. Besides, the debate contained hints of social-Darwinist notions which tied people's social positions to their biological inheritance. Those who had been equipped with 'good' genes were believed to manage better in society than those who had been saddled with 'inferior' ones. Since most of the incest crimes that

176 Kinberg, Inghe, and Riemer 1943, p. 278; Tottie 1974, pp. 25, 176.

were discovered around the turn of the century in 1900 were committed by individuals from the lowest social groups, the crime came to be perceived as a lower-class problem. Being children of 'unfit' parents, and lacking clear moral governance during their childhood and adolescence, incest criminals were described as victims of both their biology and their environment.

In order to harmonise Nordic legislation, an opportunity for people to apply for dispensation to marry in the diagonal consanguinity degree (*aunt*, *niece*) was introduced in 1915. In accordance with the new race-biological way of thinking, however, detailed medical examinations and descriptions of the family background were required for these applications to be approved. Even though it was the kinship in itself, and the health hazards that it was thought to entail, that dominated the theoretical incest debate in Sweden at this time, it was – surprisingly enough – not these issues that determined the decisions on permissions to marry. Instead, the authorities focused on the age relationship between the applicants, rejecting applications from couples where the age difference was greater than twenty years. Although there were no legal restrictions, the authorities thus chose to act in accordance with informal norms according to which spouses should be of the same age.

Once more, it becomes obvious that the handling of incest cases was to a great extent governed by informal norms in society. These norms were rarely specific to Sweden. Similar ideas could be found in several European countries. Developments in the other Nordic countries, in Germany, and in Austria were similar to those in Sweden, even though the countries on the continent were often a couple of decades ahead of the Nordic countries. In all areas, incest prohibitions were debated on the basis of secular ideas in which the view on the family and on social morality was crucial. Tolerance for marriages between related individuals increased while the number of prohibitions decreased. Incest crimes discovered at the turn of the century in 1900 were often linked to social problems in the lower social groups, to poverty and immorality.[177]

In Britain, marriages between biological cousins were permitted, but not between a man and his wife's sister. In spite of this prohibition, such marriages did occur; but they were vulnerable because the legitimacy of the relationship could be questioned after the fact. If the marriage was declared invalid, any children would lose their

177 Jarzebowski 2012; Saurer 1997.

right of inheritance. In 1835, the British Parliament passed a proposal for legislation which meant that all marriages that had been entered into between related individuals before 1835 should be considered legitimate. The aim of this proposed legislation, *Lord Lyndhurst's Act*, was to protect the legitimacy of previously contracted marriages. Instead, however, it launched an animated debate that lasted for a hundred years. Over time support for cousin marriages diminished, partly because of the race-biological ideas that were spreading all over Europe; and at the beginning of the twentieth century, these relationships exchanged status. The prohibition against marriages between brothers-in-law and sisters-in-law was abolished in 1907, and the following year cousin marriages were forbidden.[178] In turn-of-the-century Britain, too, race-biological debates led to incest being linked to poverty and immorality.[179]

In contrast to other countries, incestuous relationships were not illegal in France after 1791. As a consequence, incest became invisible during the greater part of the nineteenth century. The community did not interfere in what happened behind the family's closed doors. Not until towards the end of the century, when the race-biological debate had been going on for a couple of decades, did public opinion wake up. Now incestuous acts were condemned as being unnatural, and they came to be linked to poverty and immorality in the same way as in other European countries.[180] While the problem of incest was the subject of animated debate in Britain throughout the nineteenth century, the issue was all but suppressed in France. Even so, these countries ended up taking similar positions around the turn of the century in 1900.

The similarities across national borders were considerably greater than the differences. The position of religion changed everywhere, the proportion of marriages between related individuals rose, and medical science obtained increased influence. Everywhere, too, developments were variously affected by ideas of race biology. These ideas were partly connected to social circumstances, the crime of incest being singled out as a distinctly social problem among the poor, and partly to new definitions of the family: now there was a distinct dividing line between the biological and the non-biological.

---

178 Kuper 2009, pp. 66–92. Denbo 2001, pp. 182–7.
179 Kuper 2002, pp. 180–3.
180 Giuliani 2008.

The phenomenon of incest in Sweden over 250 years: a summary discussion

Incest is a topic that provokes strong feelings. From time to time, tragic stories about the abuse of minors are revealed, causing widespread horror and concern. As late as 2008, an incest case from Austria created headlines all over the world when it was discovered that a man had kept his biological daughter locked up in his basement and abused her for over twenty years.[1] But revelations of voluntary sexual relationships between relatives also cause powerful reactions among the general public. In the 1990s, Woody Allen created a scandal by marrying the daughter of his former partner, which is only one example of many where voluntary sexual relationships between relatives have attracted attention and created indignation in the community.[2]

What is it about these cases that affects people so much? Why do other people's sexual activities become interesting to the people around them?

In all societies, the sexual lives of citizens are limited in one way or another by formal or informal rules. Incest prohibitions may be said to be universal, because they have existed in some form in almost all known cultures. At the same time, the rules are variable and the boundaries negotiable, indicating that the prohibitions are to some degree socially constructed. There are simply no universal answers to the question of which marriage alliances may be considered legitimate. No one drawing of boundaries is more 'correct' than any other, and no universal definition of incest may be considered to be valid in all contexts. One comprehensive question which this study attempts to answer has to do with the values and cultural ideas that determine which relationships are accepted or defined as

1 Thorén 2009.

2 E.g., Sundholm 2005; Anonymous 2012; Anonymous 2014; Wallroth 2015.

forbidden and punishable in a society. In other words, on what norms are the rules actually based?

In Sweden the configuration of incest prohibitions has varied from the Middle Ages, when a man was forbidden to marry his deceased *wife's sixth cousin* according to the matrimonial laws of the Catholic Church, to today's incest prohibitions which only include sexual relationships between members of the same biological nuclear family (*parent/child*, *full siblings*). The penal consequences of incest crimes have varied significantly over time, too. For instance, a sexual relationship between a man and his deceased *wife's sister* led to a fine during the Middle Ages, to capital punishment in the seventeenth and eighteenth centuries, and to imprisonment in the nineteenth century, only to be completely decriminalised from 1872 onwards. Clearly, then, definitions of incest and the penal consequences of incest crimes have changed from one extreme to the other. Case law for incest was at its very strictest in Sweden around the turn of the century in 1700. Conversely, today the country stands out owing to its liberal legislation. Even though the situation in Sweden thus evinces exceptional characteristics, developments can always be put in relation to norms and values that have existed far outside the country's borders.

Since attitudes to incest may be so closely linked to general social phenomena, it is not strange that the changing position of incest prohibitions in society has gone through a similar transformational process in countries with similar cultures and histories. During the early modern period, Catholic countries were characterised by numerous incest prohibitions and mild penalties, whereas Protestant areas were characterised by fewer prohibitions but severe punishments. The latter was true of Sweden as well as of Denmark, Norway, Iceland, Holland, and the German-speaking areas. Subsequent centuries saw a development in the direction of fewer prohibitions and milder punishments all across Europe.

Circumstances in Britain differed from those in the rest of Protestant Europe in two ways: firstly, incest crimes were not transferred to secular jurisdiction after the Reformation, and as a result, incest crimes were relatively mildly punished. Secondly, cousin marriages were allowed after Henry VIII abolished the prohibition in the sixteenth century. In most other Protestant countries, cousin marriages were not legalised until the nineteenth century. In spite of the divergent characteristics of Britain with respect to the legal handling of incestuous acts, there were great similarities compared to other countries in how such relationships, in practice, ended up in conflict with ideas surrounding family life and social hierarchies.

Legal developments in France were also special because incest was completely abolished as a crime in 1791. From a moral point of view, incestuous acts nevertheless continued be considered deviant; and as in many other European countries, fears surfaced towards the end of the nineteenth century regarding degeneration and bad social conditions in relation to incestuous acts. Consequently, national differences did not prevent the emergence of significant similarities across national boundaries when it comes to the question of how incestuous acts have been perceived and discussed in society.

Previous research on this topic has focused either on crimes of incest and judgement-book material, or on marriage strategies and applications for dispensation. While the investigation of criminal cases has often dealt with the early modern period, when such crimes were punished most severely, studies of marriage patterns have concentrated on the nineteenth century, when marriages between related people were at their most popular. Earlier scholars hence focused on various aspects of the phenomenon of incest, but no one has specifically investigated the social practice of legal application and its long-term changes.

Here my investigation differs from what has been done before. By allowing it to cover a longer period of time, and to include different arenas in society, I have been able to extend the perspective, which has provided a better overview of the changes that took place. This has enabled me to identify ideological continuity as well as ideological change. That, in turn, made it possible to bring out those norms that formed the basis for formal legislation in Sweden during different periods.

My analysis was inspired by American sociologist Joel M. Charon's interpretation of the theory of symbolic interactionism. According to this theory, the common norms and life ideals in a society are the outcome of an ongoing negotiation between individual actors and groups. It is in the encounters between people – and in the symbolic interaction involved in these encounters – that an opportunity for change comes about. When single individuals or entire groups challenge social regulatory frameworks through speech or action, this leads to a questioning of the legitimacy of basic normative values, and the result of that is a renegotiation of the boundaries of the relevant norms. In the process of negotiation that ensues, cultural ideas and ideals which the actors take as their point of departure – and which they perceive to be relevant in the context

– are made visible. These negotiations can lead either to the re-establishing of the legitimacy of the norms or to an adjustment of the norms' boundaries.

By assuming that change occurs when people interact, I was able to steer the investigation to arenas where established norms and rules were challenged in different ways. Apart from incest crimes and applications for dispensation, where the legislation was variously tested through people's actions, the prevailing regulatory framework was challenged in open discussions between lawyers, theologians, and politicians in connection with debates in the Riksdag and legislative action. For this reason, the source material for the investigation has consisted of laws and preparatory legislative material, of criminal cases (approximately 230) and applications for dispensation (approximately 200), and of parliamentary records from twelve different debates.

Continuity and change

Society's attitudes to incest and incest prohibitions can usefully be discussed in terms of continuity and change. The long timelines in this study have helped in bringing out those ideas that have lived on more or less unchanged throughout the centuries, as well as the emergence of new ideals and values.

The legislation at the beginning of the investigated period was certainly strict and authoritarian; but in spite of everything there was a built-in flexibility in the system which left scope for interaction and negotiation. The investigation also shows that historical actors have been able to argue for diametrically opposed points of view even though they started out from a certain shared cultural framework. Throughout the period investigated in this book, there was a sense of insecurity surrounding the assessments of relationship categories that were in a kind of grey area between formal illegitimacy and informal acceptance. As the laws changed, so did the relationships that caused consternation; but this insecurity recurred time and again, indicating that there was always a reciprocal influence between legislation and the popular sense of justice.

Incest crimes: from religious crimes to moral crimes to crimes of violence

Ever since the Middle Ages and the introduction of Christianity in Sweden, the Bible provided the basic guiding principles for Swedish incest legislation. After the Reformation, the number of prohibitions was reduced and the range of punishments was made more severe; but incest continued to be defined and treated as primarily a religious crime.

When the legitimacy of the incest prohibitions was challenged during the latter part of the eighteenth century, religious arguments took up less space in the debate. Instead, the main reasons for the prohibitions tended to be connected with social morality. Loose living and general immorality were believed to threaten the social order, and incest prohibitions were needed in order to create balance and stability. Incest had thus become a moral crime.

A hundred years later, the prohibitions against cousin marriages and several affinity relationships had been abolished, which led to relationships between a father and his *(step)daughter* becoming the most common incest crime. These relationships were more often based on violence and exploitation, which is why incest was increasingly perceived to be a crime of violence. Consequently, the current association between incest and abuse is due to the reduction of the scope of incest prohibitions that occurred towards the end of the nineteenth century, when several of the voluntary incest relationships were legalised.

In very broad terms, society's idea of incest has thus shifted from a perception of the forbidden act as a religious crime to a moral crime and then to a crime of violence.

Economic circumstances

The general attitude towards and the existence of incestuous relationships have to a great extent been influenced by material factors, such as financial matters and inheritance. Economic circumstances have determined which relationships have been perceived as advantageous in different contexts. For instance, when cultural taboos surrounding cousin marriages diminished in society, the popularity of these alliances increased, especially among propertied groups. During the Middle Ages and also at the beginning of the early modern period, the possibility of dispensation was primarily used by the nobility; but during the nineteenth century, when several affinity relationships also became more culturally acceptable, the popularity of marriage alliances between related people increased in all social groups.

Both Swedish and international research has shown that there was a shift in emphasis during the second half of the eighteenth century as regards people's expectations concerning marriage, from a primary focus on marriage as a financial settlement between two families to a view of a matrimonial union as a loving alliance between two individuals. But for the individual, the emotional dimension of marriage was important both before and after the love match became an established ideal. At the same time, though, the individual in question had to bear his or her economic situation in mind. The fact that marriage between related people became immensely popular during the nineteenth century can definitely be linked to economic conditions. Economic and practical arguments were used as active means of exerting pressure when people applied for dispensations for marriage well into the 1910s; and although people from all social groups made use of marriage alliances within the family, this phenomenon was more common among propertied groups than among those who lacked wealth.

Even though the emotional aspects of marriage were valorised in society after the turn of the century in 1800, individuals have always acted on the basis of practical as well as emotional circumstances. In the course of the most recent hundred years, since the Swedish state assumed the role of social safety net for its citizens – through, among other things, organised care for the elderly, unemployment benefits, and income support – the ideals of mutual love and individual choice have acquired even greater significance.

The institution of marriage

For centuries, the conception of marriage as the only legal union between a man and a woman has been of decisive importance to the ways in which incest prohibitions have been formulated and challenged. During the eighteenth century, for instance, requirements for a virtuous relationship were introduced for those who wished to gain approval for a dispensation for marriage. At the same time, dispensation was in fact granted for certain marriages even when people did not live up to the requirement of virtue. Both these fundamentally contradictory attitudes on the part of decision-makers were geared to safeguarding and reinforcing the institution of marriage while counteracting extramarital relations.

The institution of marriage was also defended on a popular level. While the relevant relationship categories have varied over time, the arguments regarding the sanctity of marriage have remained the same. When couples attempted to legalise their relationships after the fact by applying for dispensation for marriage, the community was also forced to take up a position as to which norm was more important to defend, the *institution of marriage* or the *kinship prohibition*. As long as the cases concerned relationships in the border area between legal and illegal, both the general public and the authorities appear to have come down on the side of marriage.

Over the past century, marriage as an institution has lost its status as the only officially accepted form of cohabitation in Swedish society. The strong connection of marriage to religion has dissolved, and today it is considered completely natural for two people to choose to live together without first having gone through an official marriage ceremony. For those who nevertheless choose to marry, the phrase 'till death us do part' no longer carries any literal meaning, since the possibility of divorce is always present. It has become possible to opt out of marriage, or to choose marriage and then change one's mind, matrimonial law having been adapted to the personal desires of individuals. Ideas regarding equality and the right to make individual choices have consequently played a crucial role in discussions about the legal regulation of matrimony during the greater part of the twentieth century. Further back in history, however, these issues had little significance where matrimonial law was concerned. Marriage was perceived as all but indissoluble, and the debate dealt primarily with who was allowed to marry whom from a kinship perspective.

In other words, the absolutely most enduring and most important issue that has dominated the debate on marriage for almost a thousand years has had to do with the potential spouses' family relationship relative to each other and with the question of where the line should be drawn between acceptable family relationships and prohibited ones.

Views on love and passion

Ideas about love and passion in society have varied over time, in ways that have affected how incestuous relationships have been perceived and dealt with. In earlier times, love was an ambiguous concept. Conjugal love was described as a positive energy that strengthened the bond between spouses, whereas extramarital love was seen as a potentially dangerous force which should be suppressed by any means available. Extramarital sexuality symbolised uncontrolled, dangerous passions which could be exploited by the Devil in order to lead people to their ruin. As long as extramarital sexuality was saddled with such unfavourable connotations, love, tenderness, and passion could not be regarded as mitigating circumstances when an incest crime had been committed. While prosecuted couples might be reprieved for a single offence because of intoxication or youthful indiscretion around the turn of the century in 1700, couples whose relationships were described as loving and tender were executed without the court of appeal recommending a reprieve.

Towards the end of the eighteenth century, a gentler practice was established in connection with the assessment of incest crimes in Swedish courts. The death penalty was almost always reduced to a month's imprisonment on bread and water; and in several cases where the relationship appeared to be reciprocal, the punishment was reduced further. The lenient handling of convicted incest offenders is clearly connected to ideological changes that occurred in Europe, changes which brought demands for a humane and equal penal policy. But the mild punishments can also be linked to new ideas about romantic relationships. At the same time as the matrimonial ideal changed, love and the emotions generally were acquiring ever more favourable connotations. To act on the basis of personal emotions without allowing reason to govern one's actions had previously been seen as a weakness that could only be excused in children. With Romanticism, personal taste and mutual love between spouses were valorised and idealised. Emotionality became a virtue.

This cultural change, which has been demonstrated by Niklas Luhmann, Stephanie Coontz, and Ronny Ambjörnsson among others, had an impact on the handling of incest crimes in that mutual love was now treated as a mitigating circumstance. In several incest cases where the relationship was described as loving, the couples were sentenced to more lenient punishments than what was in fact prescribed by both law and practice. Even though the court of appeal never formally invoked a couple's love as a motive for reducing a sentence, the pattern indicates that at this time greater consideration was given to the nature of the relationships. The valorisation of the role of emotions from the end of the eighteenth century onwards also meant that love and mutual attraction were increasingly often used as leverage in order to have an application for dispensation approved.

Clearly, then, prevailing attitudes to love and passion affected assessments of different relationships. As long as love was not seen as a thoroughly positive and valuable force, it could not be invoked either to excuse a committed crime or to justify exceptions from the prohibitions; but when emotions came to be regarded as meritorious, the situation changed. Love became a common argument both for justifying applications for dispensation and for excusing crimes committed. True, people around prosecuted individuals had been more favourably disposed towards relationships that appeared to be reciprocal in earlier times as well; but it was not until love was valorised in society that mutual affection came to function as a mitigating circumstance in the official assessment of a case.

Kinship: from extended households to nuclear families

One of the most important results of this investigation is the insight into the extent to which views and definitions of kin and family have influenced ideas about incest and incest prohibitions.

David Herlihy claims that the incest prohibitions originally aimed to promote a healthy family life by preventing romantic relationships between members of the same household. He thus sees the household as the unit that was to be protected by the provisions. Because the household could include other members than the innermost nuclear family, it was logical that incest prohibitions also covered cousins or relatives by marriage living under the same roof. Any romantic relationships between different members of the household risked causing jealousy and sowing dissension among people who had an interest in sticking together and helping one another. Michael Mitterauer also thinks it likely that the composition of the family and the household structure constituted a more fundamental explanation than biological kinship for how incest prohibitions have been configured in various societies.

The positive influence of incest prohibitions on the stability of the household recurred as an argument on several occasions when incest prohibitions were debated in the nineteenth century, even though the family rather than the household was referred to in the Swedish material. However, similar ideas regarding the household may have influenced how relationships were perceived much earlier in history. At the beginning of the eighteenth century, the Skara Cathedral Chapter approved an application for marriage from a man and his *sister's stepdaughter* but rejected an application from a man and his *wife's stepdaughter*. On the basis of the theoretical division of incest degrees, the first of these family relationships is closer because only one marriage separates the people in question; but if one looks at the situation from the point of view of the household, it is more likely that the latter individuals have lived under the same roof – and that would make the decision of the cathedral chapter more logical.

Family life changed in the nineteenth century. Previously, the family had first and foremost constituted a work community living in close interaction with servants, neighbours, and friends. Alongside the nuclear family, a household usually consisted of more distant relatives and sometimes additional servants. Later on, the size of the household was reduced and the private life of the family was separated from the provision of their daily livelihood. Henceforth the nuclear family came to stand out as a separate and more intimate unit. Since the number of individuals that were included in a family/household had been reduced, it was seen to be reasonable that the boundaries of incest prohibitions should be adapted to the more modern family composition. Though the number of prohibitions was reduced, the family was therefore protected in the same way as before from jealousy and dissension due to love affairs between family members.

This change is apparent in debates conducted in the Swedish Riksdag during the first part of the nineteenth century. All political debaters supported and defended basic ideas regarding the importance of marriage, family, and social morality for the development of a good society. But there were different views about how the forms of social intercourse in a normal family functioned, which resulted in different positions being assumed with respect to the drawing of boundaries of incest prohibitions. The main dividing line thus had to do with how the family should be defined, that is to say, where to draw the lines between kin, family, and society. The changed forms of social intercourse within the family were a main argument for those politicians who promoted a reduction of Swedish incest prohibitions. For instance, since cousins and relatives by marriage did not live together or socialise as intimately as before, it was argued that it made sense for the boundaries of the prohibitions to be revised in accordance with contemporaneous patterns of social intercourse. Opponents claimed that the behavioural pattern of families had not changed that much, and that the prohibitions were needed in order to promote the solidarity of families and safeguard their opportunities for helping one another when somebody needed economic or social support. Similar arguments were presented by both sides throughout the period; but over time, more and more people came to support the ideas that pointed towards reform and change, and in 1872 several of the affinity prohibitions were finally abolished.

The definition of the family, and ideas about social intercourse within the family and the household, were hence obviously decisive for the formulation of incest prohibitions. At this time, incest prohibitions were justified by references to ethics and social morality linked to the composition of families. When new family patterns emerged, this development entailed direct consequences for the ways in which the prohibitions were formulated.

Kinship: family hierarchies

Ideas about kin and family have always affected assessments of incestuous relationships from another perspective as well. Early modern society had a hierarchical construction, and one of the most powerful guiding principles was filial deference and respect between the generations. Filial deference was understood to be a foundational principle which should be safeguarded in all contexts, so that society could continue to exist in balance and harmony. This notion was crucial to perceptions of incestuous relationships. A child should always – regardless of age – show respect for and obedience towards his or her elders, especially his or her parents or other people who might have a disciplinary function. Step-parents and parents-in-law as well as aunts and uncles were hence included in the principle of filial deference. Sexual relationships constituted an obvious threat against the natural respect and deference that was considered to exist between the generations, which is why the taboo against sexual relationships between the generations was particularly powerful.

Under the old legislation, incest crimes should be assessed according to the closeness of the family relationship, regardless of whether it was lineal or horizontal. In spite of this, people who were related in a lineal degree (*stepmother*, *stepdaughter*) were more severely dealt with when they had violated the moral norms than people who were related in a horizontal degree (*wife's sister*, *brother's widow*). While reprieves were rare around the turn of the century in 1700, people who were related in a horizontal degree were very occasionally reprieved from the death penalty if there were greatly mitigating circumstances. People related to each other in a lineal degree were hardly ever reprieved if they were found guilty of an incest crime. However, a woman might be reprieved if she was thought to have been forced to participate in the sexual act.

The same tendency to treat people related in a collateral degree with greater leniency can be noted in applications for dispensation from the whole of the eighteenth century. People who were related to each other in a vertical degree (*wife's stepdaughter*, *stepmother's aunt*, *aunt's husband's widow*) found it more difficult to have their application for dispensation approved than people who had a horizontal family relationship (*wife's ex-husband's sister*, *wife's brother's widow*). Here the safeguarding of filial deference, or the natural respect that was assumed to exist between children and parents, was explicitly mentioned. The same ideas influenced the legislation in that when the prohibitions were relaxed, it was the prohibitions against the horizontal relationship categories that were abolished first, followed by the diagonal ones and, finally, the lineal ones.

Ideas about a person's position in the family were especially important when the religious regulatory framework was unclear. With the aid of the dispensational system, cousin marriages were more or less routinely approved throughout the eighteenth century with the justification that this prohibition was secular, that is to say not included among the prohibitions in Leviticus. But no similar exceptions were made regarding other prohibitions where the parties came from different generations in the family (*stepfather's widow*, *wife's niece*). The Bible did not forbid these relationships either, and the Crown was entitled to grant dispensations for marriage in all these cases. Nevertheless, dispensations were only approved in cases involving cousins related in horizontal degrees.

Judging from the practical handling of applications for dispensation and criminal cases, people's family positions relative to each other hence had a very significant impact on how the relationships were perceived. Sexuality between people from different generations was regarded as a threat to the hierarchical order in society. In this context, family positions were defined solely in accordance with social circumstances, not according to the age relationship between the people in question. Ages were rarely stated, which indicates that this information was not thought to be relevant for the assessment of a case, regardless of whether it involved an application for dispensation or had to do with the examination of a suspected crime.

The lineal affinity prohibition remained until the middle of the twentieth century, but the prohibition against marriage persisted for yet another couple of decades. Sexual relationships were thus not punished following the amendment of the law; but in order to be able to marry, official permission was still required. As late as 1920, an application for dispensation between a man and his *stepdaughter* was rejected in spite of their being relatively close to each other in age (he was thirty-five, she twenty-eight), and in spite of their never having lived together in the same household. The directly lineal affinity relationship was still perceived to be so objectionable that the prohibition could not be revoked even though the applicants had never lived together in the relationship suggested by their family positions. The fact that lineal relationships were less common among criminal cases and applications for dispensation indicates that this attitude also had a certain degree of support among the population at large. Only in 1973 was the prohibition against marriages in the lineal affinity degree completely removed from Swedish legislation.

Clearly, then, there were informal norms that reinforced the taboo against sexual relationships across the generational divide in spite of the fact that the older legislation did not differentiate between horizontal and vertical kinship. Although the legislation became more lenient over time, these norms were active well into the modern era. Indeed, they have proved extremely persistent; and they probably affect us to this day.

Kinship: from family position to age relationship

During the early modern period, the position of an individual in society was determined by several power-creating factors such as sex, age, wealth, social position, and marital status. The individual's position was attended by certain expectations about his or her behaviour, expectations that were based on ideals and widely shared norms governing a person's conduct towards his or her fellow human beings. Among these power-creating factors, filial deference was, as we have seen, one of the most powerful. During the first half of the eighteenth century, the focus was solely on which family position the people in question had in relation to each other when an incest case was assessed, and this applied both to criminal cases and to applications for dispensation. The actual ages of the two persons were rarely stated. In these contexts, then, the family position appears to have been more important than the age relationship.

Towards the end of the century, the older generation's position of authority was challenged in Swedish society. David Gaunt and Birgitta Odén have shown that the number of conflicts between the generations increased, and at the same time the unconditional respect for older people dwindled. In international research, David Warren Sabean and several others have shown how family relationships, contacts, and networks as well as marriage alliances tended to shift from vertical to horizontal relationships in large parts of Europe at the same time.

Temporally speaking, these changes coincide with an increased interest in the ages of applicants in the Swedish dispensational material. Whether this is a consequence of an ongoing renegotiation of the relationships between generations is hard to tell with any certainty; but from this period onwards, information about the ages of applicants clearly mattered more in the practical assessment of incestuous relationships. Firstly, occasional couples invoked a small age difference as an argument in order to have their application for permission to marry approved. Secondly, the ages of the applicants were enquired after and noted by the authorities, which indicates that this information was now considered to be a relevant basis for decision-making. Thirdly, the first divergent decisions, where applications for marriage were granted in opposition to the previous practice, can be directly linked to the age relationship between the applicants. In other words, when the cases involved relationship categories that had acquired increased cultural acceptance, it was the age relationship between the parties that determined the outcome. If there was a small age difference between the applicants (*stepfather's widow*, *wife's niece*), or if the man was older than the woman (*uncle's widow*), a dispensation could be granted even though the parties' family positions crossed a generational divide.

The increased importance of the age relationship to the outcome of applications for dispensation can also be linked to informal norms that idealised marriages between couples of the same age. Even though the ideal marriage had always contained the notion that spouses should be about the same age, numerous examples show that the ideal could be set aside when a marriage alliance appeared to be advantageous for other reasons. One example is supplied by the so-called widow conservation, i.e., when a younger clergyman married the older widow of his predecessor in order to secure her continued support. In these cases, the difference in ages never constituted an insurmountable impediment to marriage. If the marriage was perceived to be advantageous from a practical or emotional perspective, that circumstance had consequently overshadowed any objections that might exist because of the age difference between the prospective spouses. As time passed, though, so did this kind of marriage.

Several indications suggest that the tolerance for marriages where the presumptive spouses failed to meet the ideal-age-relationship requirement decreased during the nineteenth century. The custom of widow conservation was significantly reduced in the clerical estate as well as in artisanal groups, and at the same time marriage patterns changed. In northern Sweden and in Stockholm, it has been shown that the number of marriages where there was a great age difference between the spouses, and where the woman was older than the man, decreased towards the end of the century. Taken altogether, the material indicates that there was less tolerance for deviations with regard to age difference between spouses in relation to the ideal. This cultural shift also entailed consequences for the assessment of dispensational cases at the beginning of the twentieth century.

Around the turn of the century in 1900, the Swedish incest debate had been medicalised, as it had been in the rest of Europe. The experts were no longer clergymen but doctors; and in connection with applications for dispensation, applicants were now required to submit several medical certificates. Although there was great interest in predispositions for disorders and health risks at this time, most of the rejections were in fact justified by 'too great an age difference' between the prospective spouses. Even though age did not constitute an official impediment to marriage according to the legislation, it was hence used as an active impediment to marriage by the authorities. Here the authorities probably acted in accordance with cultural ideas that connected spouses of the same age with happy marriages: ideas that seemingly gained strength during the second half of the nineteenth century.

In summary, it can thus be established that interest in age has changed radically over time. At the turn of the century in 1700, age was not recorded either in connection with the assessment of incest crimes or in the processing of applications for dispensation. A century later, around 1800, there was an increased interest in the age relationship, above all between couples applying for dispensation. When yet another century had passed, a great age difference between presumptive spouses came to be used as a decisive argument for rejecting a couple's application for permission to marry, even though this did not constitute an official impediment to marriage. By now, age – previously completely irrelevant to the assessment of incestuous relationships – had become the decisive factor.

The lower tolerance of a great age difference between spouses may be viewed in relation to two circumstances: firstly, economic changes in society which reduced an individual's dependence on kin and family for his or her support; secondly, the new ideals of love and reciprocity between husband and wife.

Incest offenders: from perpetrators to victims

Society's attitude to incest crimes and incest offenders may also be linked to various jurisprudential conceptions. During the early modern period, when incest was defined as a crime against God's law, it was essential that any criminals were brought to trial and punished. Regardless of the context in which the crime had been committed or the intention of the guilty parties, they had offended against God's law. If they were not punished, one risked invoking God's wrath in the form of crop failure, war, or disease. Lawyers assumed that both parties had participated voluntarily in the sexual act; their guilt was consequently judged to be the same, and they were sentenced to equivalent punishments. Though there were a few cases where the authorities deviated from this exclusively religious interpretation of the crime, these ideas constituted the basis for judicial policy.

At the turn of the century in 1800, the rhetoric regarding religion and God's law was toned down in favour of arguments concerning the preservation of morality and the promotion of shared social morals. The crime of incest was perceived to be a social hazard because it challenged general moral values and risked leading young people astray. As before, however, it was assumed that both parties had participated voluntarily in the sexual act. They were thus still considered equally guilty of the crime; and even though the set penalties had been reduced, men and women were still punished in an equivalent manner. Consequently, the idea that incest involved two offenders, and that both were equally guilty, did not change. There were no discussions about the uneven power relationship between, for instance, an older man and his younger relative, or between a master and a maid who was also his kinswoman. Since the responsibility for the crime was shared equally between the man and the woman, their punishments would be essentially the same.

In connection with the Penal Act of 1864, the penalties for incest distinguished between the older and the younger party for the first time. The younger party was described as having been seduced by the older, and would therefore receive a milder punishment; but both were still held partly responsible for the crime.

When several prohibitions against affinity relationships were abolished in 1872, relationships between a father and his (*step*)*daughter* came to be in the majority among Swedish incest crimes. Because most of these relationships were based on violence against or exploitation of a girl or a younger woman, the crime of incest came to be associated with violence, exploitation, and abuse for the first time. The woman, who was in a mentally and physically disadvantageous position relative to her (step)father, was described as the victim of his actions, which made her innocent of the incest crime.

But even the guilt of the father began to be questioned. In the 1930s, it was found that the crime was almost exclusively committed among the lower orders, especially in families with a difficult economic situation and a morally dubious way of life. Since the majority of discovered offences were committed by people from the lowest stratum in society, the crime of incest was linked to bad social conditions. The man in question was described as more poorly equipped biologically speaking, as his parents belonged to what was defined as an 'inferior citizenry' according to the race-biological viewpoints of the time. In addition, the man's strong sexual drive was foregrounded as a possible cause of the incest crime. Sexual abstinence might make a man lose control so that he committed unnatural sexual acts, such as incest. Besides, both the male offender and the female victim were regarded as victims of the environment in which they had grown up, in that they had not been provided with proper cultural education and moral discipline in their homes – a deficiency which, according to the authorities' way of thinking, resulted in their lacking 'proper' moral insights.

As a result of these developments, the view of incest offenders had, paradoxically enough, been turned upside down. Previously, both parties had been considered wholly responsible for the criminal act, and very little account had been taken of the environment in which the people in question grew up, or how the incestuous act had come about. Nor had the age relationship of the accused, or their family position relative to each other, been taken into serious consideration when the issue of guilt was determined. The authorities' point of departure had been that the crime had been committed by two active offenders, and therefore the burden of guilt and the penal consequences had been shared alike between the man and the woman. Now each of them was seen as something of a victim. She was considered to be a victim of his actions, whereas he was regarded as a victim of his biology, both because of his 'inferior genes' and his 'powerful sexual drive'. Furthermore, they were both described as victims of their impoverished cultural environment, in consequence of which neither could be held to be fully responsible for his or her actions.

And then what?

Incest and incest prohibitions did not cease to be debated in the middle of the twentieth century just because my investigation ends there. On the contrary, there was renewed interest in this issue in

Swedish society during the second half of the twentieth century, an interest which has led to more inquiries, new proposals for laws, and changed regulations.[3] In 1947, the lineal affinity prohibition (*mother-in-law*, *daughter-in-law*, *stepmother*, *stepdaughter*) was abolished, even though the prohibition against such marriages remained in force. The prohibitions against marriages in lineal affinity degrees (*stepmother*, *daughter-in-law*) as well as in diagonal consanguinity degrees (*aunt*, *niece*) were not abolished until 1973. In that same year, sexual relations between *half-siblings* were decriminalised, but for marriages between half-siblings a dispensation is still required.[4] In this way, the Swedish incest legislation became one of the most liberal in the world. Developments have thus continued in the direction of increasing liberalisation; indeed, a complete abolition of all incest prohibitions was discussed in the 1970s.[5] Those who advocated this idea wanted sexual relations between biological relatives where children had been exploited to be treated as *exploitation of a child in a position of dependency*, without taking special account of the family relationship.[6] The proposal was not realised, though, and the prohibition against sexual relations between members of a nuclear family still stands.[7]

These more recent negotiations have invoked genetic, ethical, and social arguments, as in earlier times, in order to legitimise everything from continued prohibitions to additional liberalisations.[8] Today there is an increased tolerance of deviant sexual behaviour in Swedish society, the well-being of the individual taking precedence in relation to the sexual act. The law is primarily intended to protect vulnerable people without moralising about voluntary acts performed by adult individuals.[9] Nevertheless, the topic continues to arouse strong emotion. Some people believe that incest prohibitions should only be discussed on the basis of the perspective of hereditary biology,

---

3 These more modern investigations have been studied in a practical application paper by Sara Semmler. Semmler primarily analyses public inquiries from 1976, 1982, and 2001. Semmler 2003.

4 *SOU 1976:9*, p. 31. The changes in the law occurred in connection with the legislation of 1973, which entered into force in 1974.

5 Semmler 2003, p. 17.

6 *SOU 1976:9*, proposal for a statute, pp. 12, 19.

7 *Justitieutskottets betänkande 1977/78:26*, pp. 5–8.

8 Inger 2011, p. 326; Tottie 1974, p. 35. See also *Proposition 1977/87:69* (Government bill 1977/87:69), where several arguments for and against a liberalisation of the incest prohibitions were discussed.

9 *SOU 1976:9*, proposal for a statute, p. 17.

whereas others also wish to incorporate ethical assessments. Regardless of which standpoint is chosen in these discussions, it is important to realise that all opinions bear the stamp of values that are present in the social context at the relevant point in time.

At the most fundamental level, incest prohibitions may be seen as examples of how people's sexuality has been circumscribed over time. The issue thus involves universal ideas that are as topical today as they were three hundred years ago. The varying status of incest relationships in society – where one and the same relationship has been assessed as natural or unnatural, legal or illegal, depending on the period in which a person happened to live – reflects not only the changing regulation of sexuality over time, but also shifts in more general norms and values in society. Whatever stance a person adopts in relation to the problem of incest, it must hence be regarded in the light of the norms and values that were current during that particular period.

Unlike earlier studies, my investigation has been able to demonstrate a close connection between cultural norms and the official legislation in a long-term perspective. Although the laws of different periods were justified with religious, moral, or biological arguments, many other cultural values have turned out to have been crucial to the implementation of the legislation, including the practical processing and assessment of various cases of incest. Ideas regarding kinship, the definition of the family, and the view of relationships within the family are examples of factors that have played a decisive role in the assessments of different cases. The occurrence of incestuous relationships has also been affected by economic conditions at a structural as well as an individual level. Furthermore, notions regarding marriage, sexuality, love, and passion have influenced the assessments of different cases in various ways. The prevailing view regarding the relevant persons' respective ages has also been important to assessments of incestuous relationships at different points in time. All of these varying norms and values in society have had a direct impact on how incest has been defined, how relationships have been assessed, and how any crimes have been handled; and they are likely to continue to do so.

Appendix: Tables

Appendix 1. Number of applications for dispensation directed to the Judiciary Inspection for the specified years

Relationship, a man and his …	1730	1750	1780	1801	1815	1850	1870	1920
Consanguinity, diagonal degree								
aunt	–	–	–	–	–	–	–	1 (1)
niece	–	–	–	5 (2)	2 (1)	1	–	9 (2)
Consanguinity, second degree	–	–	–	–	–	–	–	–
cousin	4 (3)	40 (4)	105 (1)	153	264	–	–	–
Affinity, first lineal degree								
stepdaughter	–	–	–	–	–	1	–	1
step-granddaughter	–	–	–	–	1	–	–	–
stepmother	–	–	–	–	–	–	1	–
Affinity, first collateral degree								
wife's sister	–	–	1	10	36	58 (8)	66 (3)	–
brother's widow	–	–	–	7	13	27 (2)	37 (3)	–

Affinity, diagonal degree								
wife's niece	1	–	5 (4)	11	8	10	9 (1)	–
wife's grandniece	–	–	–	–	–	1	–	–
wife's aunt	–	–	–	–	–	1	–	–
uncle's widow	–	–	1 (1)	5 (2)	18	8	5	–
Affinity, ≥ second degree								
wife's stepdaughter	–	–	–	1	–	–	–	–
wife's stepmother	–	–	–	–	–	1	–	–
stepfather's/stepson's widow	–	–	1	–	2	1	–	–
stepfather's/stepmother's sister	–	–	–	–	1	–	1	–
stepson's stepdaughter	–	–	–	–	1	–	–	–
stepdaughter-in-law's stepdaughter	1	–	–	–	–	–	–	–
Total	6	40	113	192	346	109	119	11
Total, not including cousins	2	0	8	39	82	109	119	11

Source: The diaries of the Judiciary Inspection for the year in question. The information for 1920 is taken from the database of Cabinet meeting documents after searching for 'äktenskap* hinder' ('marriage* impediment') at the Ministry of Justice. The figures include mirror relationships. Half-relatives are indicated within parenthesis.

Appendix 2. Numbers of applications for dispensation directed to the Skara Cathedral Chapter for the specified years

Kinship	**Closeness**	**Relationship, a man and (his) …**	**1710–34**	**1775–1806**
Consanguinity	Second degree	cousin	8	16
	Diagonally (2+3)	parent's cousin	8	–
		cousin's daughter	10	–
	Total		**26**	**16**
Affinity	First lineal degree	father and son	–	1
	First collateral degree	stepsister	–	2
	Diagonally (1+2)	wife's niece/ grandniece	6	3
		sibling's stepdaughter	3	3
		son-/daughter-in-law's sister	2	–
		step-parent's sister	2	8
		uncle's widow	–	1

≥ Second degree	wife's cousin	7	–
	cousin's widow	5	–
	two cousins	2	–
	stepfather's niece	1	1
	wife's brother's widow/wife's former husband's sister	6	2
	father-in-law's widow	1	–
	step(grand)father's widow	3	–
	wife's cousin's widow	2	–
	wife's nephew's stepdaughter	1	–
	wife's nephew's widow	1	–
	wife's uncle's widow	1	–
	uncle's widow's daughter	1	–
	aunt's husband's widow	3	–
	grandmother's brother's widow	1	1
	a woman and her uncle's widow	1	–
	wife's step-granddaughter	1	–
	step-uncle's widow	–	1
Total		50	23

Source: SD, series AI.

Appendix 3. Incest cases within the jurisdiction of the Göta Court of Appeal, 1694–1716, 1783–1800, 1810, 1840–58

Family relationship	Relationship, a man and (his) …	1694–1716 (22 years)	1783–1800, 1810 (19 years)	1840–58 (19 years)
Consanguinity, first lineal degree	mother	–	3	2
	daughter	2	3	7
Consanguinity, first collateral degree	sister	4 (1)	4	5 (2)
	niece	6 (3)	4 (2)	2
Consanguinity, diagonally	aunt	1	1	–
Consanguinity, ≤ second degree	cousin, other	5 (1)	–	–
Consanguinity per year		**0.8**	**0.8**	**0.8**
Affinity, first lineal degree	stepmother, mother-in-law, mother and daughter, father and son with the same woman, stepdaughter	10	2	1
	stepdaughter	21	12	10
Affinity, first collateral degree	wife's sister, two sisters with the same man, brother's widow, two brothers with the same woman	42 (2)	13 (1)	18 (5)
Affinity, diagonally	wife's aunt, uncle's widow	8 (5)	3 (1)	–
	wife's niece	22 (5)	6	5
Affinity, second degree	wife's cousin, two cousins, other	10	–	–
Affinity per year		**5.1**	**1.9**	**1.8**
Number of cases, total		**18+113=131**	**15+36=51**	**16+34=50**

Source:
1694–1716, GHA, series BIIA, material from 1715 is missing.
1783–1800, 1810, GHA, series BIIA.
1840–58, GHA, series BIIA, HSoB, series BIIb.
Within parenthesis = half-relatives

Appendix 4. Incest prohibitions and punishments in Sweden 1500–2000, a schematic overview

Relationship, e.g.,	<1500	1680	1727	1734	1810	1845	1864	1872	1915	1937	1947	1973
Consanguinity, first/ second lineal degree												
mother/grandmother	fine	death					labour/ gaol			young acq		
daughter/granddaughter	fine	death					labour/ gaol			young acq		
Consanguinity, first collateral degree												
sister	fine	death					labour/ gaol					
half-sister	fine	death					labour/ gaol					acq/ disp
Consanguinity, diagonal degree												
aunt	fine	death					labour/ gaol		disp	acq/disp		acq
niece	fine	death					labour/ gaol		disp	acq/disp		acq
Consanguinity, second collateral degree												
cousin	fine	disp				acq						

Appendix 4. Incest prohibitions and punishments in Sweden 1500–2000, a schematic overview (Continued)

Relationship, e.g.,	<1500	1680	1727	1734	1810	1845	1864	1872	1915	1937	1947	1973
Affinity, first lineal degree												
mother-in-law/daughter-in-law	fine	death					labour/gaol				acq/disp	acq
stepmother/stepdaughter	fine	death					labour/gaol				acq/disp	acq
a mother and her daughter/father and son with the same woman	fine	death					labour/gaol		acq			
Affinity, first collateral degree												
wife's sister/brother's widow	fine	death		corp/gaol	disp		fine	acq				
wife's half-sister	fine	death		corp/gaol	disp		fine	acq				
two sisters/two brothers with the same woman	fine	death		corp/gaol	disp		fine	acq				
Affinity, diagonal degree												
wife's aunt	fine	death		corp/fine	disp		fine	acq				
uncle's widow	fine	death		corp/fine	disp		fine	acq				
wife's niece	fine	death		corp/fine	disp		fine	acq				

Affinity, second degree							
wife's stepmother	fine				disp	fine	acq
stepson's/stepfather's widow	fine				disp	fine	acq
wife's cousin	fine	disp	acq				
two cousins	fine	disp	acq				
wife's brother's widow	fine	disp	acq				

The years usually but not always correspond exactly to amendments of the law.

Legend:
- disp = relationship prohibited and punishable but dispensation for marriage possible
- acq/disp = relationship decriminalised but marriage prohibited without a dispensation
- young = the younger party
- corp = corporal punishment
- labour/gaol = hard labour or gaol

Colour codes:
- death penalty
- corporal punishment/hard labour/gaol, possibly a fine
- fine/gaol/possibility for dispensation
- relationship prohibited but free of punishment; dispensation for marriage required
- ☐ acquitted

Appendix 5. People executed for incest in Sweden 1749–1802

Year	County	Man	Woman	Relationship
1751	Kronoberg	1	1	–
–	Värmland		1	–
1752	Kronoberg	1 (45)	2 (30/40)	–
–	Nerikes/Värmland	2	2 (15/35)	–
–	Västerås	1 (25)		stepmother
–	Västerås		1 (35)	–
1753	Östergötland	1 (30)		blind aunt
–	Kronoberg	1 (30)	1 (60)	–
1754	Stockholm	1	1	daughter
–	Kronoberg	1 (30)	1 (20)	–
–	Kalmar	1 (45)	1 (30)	stepdaughter
–	Nerikes/Värmland	1	1	sister
–	Österbotten	1		stepdaughter
1755	Stockholm	1		stepdaughter
–	Västernorrland	1 (65)		daughter
–	Österbotten	1 (25)	1 (20)	sister
–	Åbo/Björneborg	1 (55)	1 (25)	daughter
1756	Kronoberg	1 (25)		stepdaughter
–	Malmöhus	1 (60)	1 (25)	–
–	Savolax/Kymmenegård	1 (40)	1 (20)	daughter

1757	Jönköping	1	1	daughter
–	Västerbotten	1 (45)	1 (40)	–*
1758	Älvsborg	1 (55)		2 daughters
1763	Jönköping	1 (70)	1 (30)	married daughter
1764	Västermanland	1 (30)	1 (20)	–
1766	Östergötland		1 (25/50)	–
1767	Östergötland	1		–
1768	Älvsborg		1 (20)	–*
–	Västmanland	1 (25)	1 (45)	stepmother
1770	Göteborg/Bohuslän	1 (50)		stepdaughter
1771	Uppsala	1 (45)		–
1772	Uppsala	1 (35)		stepdaughter
–	Gotland	1 (35)	1 (30)	sister
1773	Österbotten	1 (20)		mother
–	Lovisa/Kymmenegård/Savola	1 (25)		–
1776	Skara	1	1	–*
1777	Skara	1	1	wife's sister*
1797	Kalmar	1	1	–*
Total		**32**	**26**	

Source: Olivecrona 1866.
* = accused of several crimes in addition to incest, e.g., infanticide. Figures within parentheses indicate the ages of the persons in question.

Appendix 6. Established punishments for incest criminals who risked the death penalty

Relationship	E.g., a man's relationship with (his) …, or equivalent	Number of cases	Number of accused men/women	The man				The woman			
				Absc.	Death	F/CP	Acq.	Absc.	Death	F/CP	Acq.
Consanguinity, first degree, lineal	daughter	1	1/1	-	1	-	-	-	-	-	1*
Consanguinity, first degree, horizontal	sister	4	3/4	1	3	-	-	-	3	1	-
Consanguinity, diagonal	niece, aunt	7	4/7	-	4	-	-	-	4	3	-
Affinity, first degree, lineal	stepmother, stepdaughter, mother-in-law, a mother and her daughter	23	12/21	10	9	3	-	-	14	7	-

Affinity, first degree, horizontal	wife's sister, brother's widow, two sisters	29	18/24	11	12	5	1	-	15	9	-
Affinity, diagonal	wife's niece, wife's aunt	21	19/21	2	-	19	-	-	1	19	1
Total		85	57/78	24	29	27	1	-	37	39	2
Total minus diagonal affinity		64	38/57	22	29	8	1	-	36	20	1

Source: Incest cases from the GHA, Criminal-case decisions, 1694–1716 (series BIIA)
Death = sentenced to death; F/CP = sentenced to a fine or corporal punishment; Aqc. = Acquitted, * = Acquitted from guilt, not from the deed itself.
The number of cases does not agree with the number of relationships.
Sentences in cases belonging to the relationship category 'diagonal affinity' were routinely commuted to a fine or to corporal punishment.
Number of men sentenced to death: 29/38 = 76% (if the 22 who absconded had been tried and sentenced to death: 51/60 = 85%).
Number of women sentenced to death: 36/57 = 63%.
Total number of persons sentenced to death: 65/95 = 68% (if the 22 who absconded had been tried and sentenced to death: 87/117 = 74%).

Bibliography

Unprinted sources

Regional State Archives in Göteborg (GLA)

Hundred-court archives[1]

Kind hundred, Ala:69, 1786, 24 October, no. 170; 26 October, no. 210; 6 December, no. 1. Giöthar Dahl (59), Annika Svensdotter (29)
Kind hundred, Ala:70, 1787, 23 January, no. 21; 25 January, no. 54; 1 February, no. 143; 2 February, no. 144. Giöthar Dahl (60), Annika Svensdotter (30)
Kinne hundred, AIa:38, 1795, 27 October, no. 85. Olof Mattsson (55), Brita Svensdotter (24)
Kinnefjärding hundred, AIa:28, 1791, 18 October, no. 1. Jan Skjön (25), Stina Olofsdotter (26)
Kullinge hundred, Ala:31, 1777, 2 October, no. 108. Anders Bengtsson (40), Kirstina Larsdotter (22)
Kullinge hundred, Ala:32, 1778, 24 January, no. 49; 27 January, no. 62. Anders Bengtsson (41), Kirstina Larsdotter (23)
Kullinge hundred, Ala:40, 1786, 4 May, no. 30. Anders Bengtsson (49), Kirstina Larsdotter (31)
Kåkind hundred, AIa:17, 1702, 23 June. Jon Larsson, Karin Jönsdotter
Kåkind hundred, AIa:20, 1710, 23 June. Johan Håkansson (25), Estrid Månsdotter (39)
Nordals hundred, AIa:7, 1714, 13 February. Jon Nilsson (40), Märta Jönsdotter (25–26)
Vilske hundred, AIa:5, 1693, 18 October. Lars i Spånbacka (20), Britta Andersdotter (26)
Vättle hundred, AIa:3, 1702. Ingeborg Andersdotter and Anders Torstensson

1 Numbers within parentheses following personal names denote the person's age as stated in the relevant document. Where ages are omitted, the records do not supply this information.

Archives of the Skara Cathedral Chapter (SD)

Records (series AI), 1710–34, 1776–1806, all (86+39 cases)

Regional State Archives in Härnösand (HLA)

Hundred-court archives

Råneå hundred, AIa:130, 1915, 5 October, no. 39; 6 December, no. 69. Oskar Nordström (32), Johanna Blomqvist (21)

Regional State Archives in Lund (LLA)

Archives of the Skåne and Blekinge Court of Appeal (HSoB)

Fiscal decisions and letters (series BIIb), 1840–58, all (18 cases)
Decisions and resolutions (series BIIc)
BIIc:236, 1915:2, no. 301. Carl Johansson (41), Ester Johansson (20), Ebba Johansson (17)

Hundred-court archives

Albo hundred, AIa:10, 1713, 22 May. Jäppa Andersson, Karin Pärsdotter
Gärds hundred, AIa:67, 1784, 28–29 April, no. 1; 12 June, no. 61; 15 June, no. 73; 18 June, no. 74. Mattias Larsson, Karna Olasdotter
Gjärd hundred, AIa:71, 1788, 28 February, no. 32; 2 March, no. 78; 7 March, no. 91. Nils Trulsson (32), Ingar Gisselsdotter (26)
Medelsta hundred, AIa:77, 1784, 6 December, no. 9; 8 December, no. 1; 15 December, no. 14. Mårten Pettersson (23), Ingjär Persdotter (17)
Medelsta hundred, AIa:85, 1792, 31 May, no. 58; 31 May, no. 5; 14 November, no. 131. Olof Ahlberg, Catharina Ahlberg
Medelsta hundred, AIa:133, 1840, 13 February, no. 429; 29 February, no. 445; 11 May, no. 249; 5 June, no. 462. Jöns Persson, Kierstin Mattisdotter
Medelsta hundred, AIa:142, 1849, 30 May, no. 376; 20 June, no. 462. Börje Hjelte (47), Maria Börjesdr (22)
Listers hundred, AIb:1, 1703, 15 April. Ingemar Olsson, Elna Mattsdotter
Listers hundred, AIb:1, 1704, 7 January. Per Svensson, Inga Persdotter
Tönnersjö hundred, AIa:100, 1848, 26 September, no. 17; 20 October, no. 122. Per Eriksson (42), Emilia Jönsdotter (24)
Västra Göinge hundred, AIb:32, 1915, 8 October, no. 16. Karl Johansson, 41, Ester Johansson (20), Ebba Johansson (17)
Östra Göinge hundred, AIa:32, 1711, 2 August. Torsten Nilsson, Tova Jönsdotter

Regional State Archives in Uppsala (ULA)

Archives of the Strängnäs Cathedral Chapter (StD)

Records and agendas (serie AI):
AI:8, 1676, 28 June
AI:9, 1679, 3 December, no. IV, p. 62
AI:9, 1677, 14 February, no. III, p. 12
AI:10, 17 October, no. 1, p. 37
AI:10, 1681, 3 August, no. 2, p. 17
AI:10, 1684, 3 December, no. 4, p. 337
AI:11, 1685, 3 August, no. 2, p. 17
AI:11, 1685, 2 February, no. 8, pp. 61f
AI:11, 1686, 28 April, p. 86
AI:11, 1686, 5 May, no. 12, p. 89
AI:11, 1686, 14 July, no. 6, p. 104
AI:11, 1686, 4 August, p. 112
AI:11, 30 September, no. 3, p. 128
AI:11, 1686, 5 October, no. 5, pp. 129f

Regional State Archives in Vadstena (VLA)

Archives of the Göta Court of Appeal (GHA)

Archives of the legal clerk
  Transcripts (series EVII AABA)
    EVII AABA:2621, 1785, no. 5, 118, 145. Lars Sundborg, Stina Sundborg
Main archives
  Criminal-case records (series AII), 1700–16, all (76 cases)
  Criminal-case decisions (series BIIA), 1694–1716, 1783–1800, 1810, 1840–1858, all (131+46+5+32 cases)
Documents pertaining to referred criminal cases (series EVAC)
  EVAC:52, 1785, no. 25. Per Olofsson, Margaretha Hansdotter
  EVAC:86, 1791, no. 26. Knut Ringsten (58), Märta Nilsdotter (30)
  EVAC:937, 1840, no. 27. Johannes Holm (44), Maja Lisa Petersdotter (37)
  EVAC:940, 1840, no. 100. Andreas Nilsson (48), Maria Andersdotter (22)
  EVAC:948, 1840, no. 29. Carl Andersson, Anna Jönsdotter
  EVAC:952, 1840, no. 23. Edela Nilsdotter (27)
  EVAC:971, 1841, no. 47. Jakob Larsson (44), Greta Andersdotter (29)
  EVAC:973, 1841, no. 105. Carl Jonasson (27), Anna Maria Carlsdotter
  EVAC:1003, 1843, no. 14. Börje Bengtsson (58), Inger Börjesdotter (19)
  EVAC:1013, 1843, no. 111. Sven Wall, Anna Nilsdotter
  EVAC:1021, 1844, no. 112. Peter Haraldsson Boman (52), Anna Nilsdotter (21)
  EVAC:1041, 1845, no. 103. Petter Dahl (63), Maria Samuelsdotter (27)
  EVAC:1046, 1845, no. 105. Per Hansson (49), Katarina Magnusdotter (32)

EVAC:1060, 1846, no. 27. Jonas Andersson, Stina Andersdotter
EVAC:1066, 1846, no. 31. Carl Johansson (33), Sofia Rehn (26)
EVAC:1083, 1847, no. 105. Jonas Nilsson (49), Fredrika Zeinvoldt (27)
EVAC:1235, 1855, no. 53. Nils Fagerström (27), Sofia Olsdotter (26)
Letters patent and royal ordinances regarding criminal cases (series EIAC)
EIAC:3, 1698, 11 April. Gunnar Sannesson, Annika Carlsdotter
EIAC:15, 1784, 10 August. Mattias Johansson, Brita Bengtsdotter
EIAC:25, 1785, 22 April. Per Olofsson, Margaretha Hansdotter
EIAC:15, 1787, 11 June. Giöthar Dahl (60), Annika Svensdotter (30)
EIAC:15, 1787, 29 October. Bengt Larsson Säf (60), Inga Bengtsdotter (32)
EIAC:15, 1788, 18 February. Bengt Larsson Säf (60), Inga Bengtsdotter (32)
EIAC:17, 1796. 7 November. Olof Nilsson (49), Cajsa Larsdotter (28)
EIAC:21, 1841, 20 April. Andreas Nilsson (48), Maria Andersdotter (22)
EIAC:22, 1845, 24 August. Johannes Svensson Heberg (30), Anna Svensdotter (20)
EIAC:22, 1845, 28 July. Johannes Nilsson (30), Maria Öberg (6)
EIAC:22, 1845, 19 August. Anders Olofsson (52), Anna Johansdotter (34)

Hundred-court archives

Bankekind hundred, AIa:7, 1705, 8 April. Per Jönsson (18), Kirstin Månsdotter (26)
Bråbo hundred, Ala:4, 1701, 1 August. Lars Böllia, Kirstin Olufsdotter
Hammarkind hundred, A1a:11, 1704, 30 April. Holsten Bengtsson (64), Anna Eriksdotter (24)
Hammarkind hundred, AIa:81, 1786, 3 March, no. 156. Olof Nyström (42), Rebecka Nilsdotter (28)
Hammarkind hundred, A1a:82, 1787, 11 May, no. 83. Olof Nyström (43), Rebecka Nilsdotter (29)
Hammarkind hundred, A1a:83, 1788, 13 March, no. 187. Olof Nyström (44), Rebecka Nilsdotter (30)
Hammarkind hundred, A1a:83, 1788, 13 March, no. 188. Nils Klippa (50), Ingeborg Nilsdotter (14)
Hammarkind hundred, A1a:85, 1790, 13 March, no. 87. Olof Nyström (46), Rebecka Nilsdotter (32)
Hanekind hundred, A1a:34, 1785, 10 February, no. 2. Hans Åhlfeldt, Maja Johansdotter
Norra Vedbo hundred, AIa:15, 1708, October. Erik Johansson, Britta Persdotter
Stranda hundred, A1a:128, 1850, 10 May, no. 149; 10 May, no. 150. Anders Larsson Röding, Stina Jönsdotter
Stranda hundred, A1a:129, 1850, 13 September, no. 146; 13 September, no. 147. Anders Larsson Röding, Stina Jönsdotter
Stranda hundred, A1a:130, 1851, 25 January, no. 188; 25 January, no. 189. Anders Larsson Röding, Stina Jönsdotter

Stranda hundred, A1a:132, 1851, 24 September, no. 239. Anders Larsson Röding, Stina Jönsdotter
Sunnerbo hundred, A1a:101, 1790, 21 May, no. 19. Gumme Persson, Ingeborg Gunnarsdotter
Vista hundred, Ala:12, 1694, 18 May. Anders Linnardsson, Anna Ambjörnsdotter
Västbo hundred, A1a:8, 1704, no. 30. Johan Simonsson, Anna Erlandsdotter
Västbo hundred, AIa:65, 1791, 3 May, no. 71. Knut Ringsten (68), Märta Nilsdotter (30+)
Västbo hundred, A1a:202, 1849, 19 June, no. 173; 20 June, no. 197. Johan Dahl (55), Brita Eriksdotter
Åkerbo hundred, AIa:23, 1783, 23 April, no. 2; 4 June, no. 51. Olof Nyström (39), Rebecka Nilsdotter (25)
Ölands Norra hundred, A1a:80, 1786, 21 March. Petter Sjöberg, Anna Ekbom
Ölands Norra hundred, A1a:196, 1849, 20 June, no. 309; 12 July, no. 383; 2 August, no. 399; 23 August, no. 403. Jonas Andersson, Maja Nilsdotter
Ölands Norra hundred, A1a:213, 1855, 7 February no. 3; 28 February, no. 1. Carl Carlsson (22), Karin Nilsdotter (29)
Ölands Södra hundred, AIa:90, 1795, 17 July, 13 August, 27 August, 9 October, 31 November, 1 December, 23 December. Olof Nilsson (48), Cajsa Larsdotter (27)
Ölands Södra hundred, AIa:91, 1796, 26 March. Olof Nilsson (49), Cajsa Larsdotter (28)
Östkinds hundred, Ala:4, 1713, 16 February. Catharina Olufsdotter, Abraham Andersson

Other archives

Gryt parish, C:3, birth records, 1756–1800. Olof Nyström, Rebecka Nilsdotter
Hammarkind hundred, death records, FII:23. Olof Nyström, Rebecka Nilsdotter
Hammarkind hundred, death records, FII:24. Olof Nyström, Rebecka Nilsdotter

Swedish National Archives (RA), Stockholm

Archives of the Ministry of Justice (JD)

Cabinet-meeting records 1915–20. SVAR digital: search terms: 'äktenskap* hinder' ('marriage* impediment'), all (64 cases with the available decision reports, records of the Council of the Realm, and drafts)

Archives of the Judiciary Inspection (JR): Diaries (D), Appellate and application cases (BoA), Records of the Council of the Realm/Council of the State (R), Drafts (K)

1697, 23 December, BoA; Petter Bilock, XX[2], *half-cousin*
1720, 25 April, BoA; Carl Christiernum, Agneta von Hyltén, *wife's cousin*
1722, 27 June, BoA; Nils Creutman, Anna Maria von Chérman, *wife's brother's widow*
1727, 8 March, BoA; Göran Borg, Adriana Fineman, *wife's half-cousin*
1729, 11 March, BoA; Sven Johansson, Johanna Persdotter, *cousin*
1730, 20 March, BoA, K; Rasmus Olofsson, Karin Mårtensdotter, *half-cousin*
1730, 21 April, BoA, K; Jöns Andersson, Ingeborg Andersdotter, *wife's brother's widow*
1730, 3 June, BoA, K; Nils Arvidsson, Ingeborg Bengtsdotter, *cousin*
1730, 3 June, K; Jöns Svensson, Anna Östensdotter, *two cousins*
1730, 3 June, BoA, K; Anders Nilsson, Ingeborg Olsdotter, *wife's niece*
1730, 9 June, K; Christian Månsson, Boel Svensdotter, *half-cousin*
1730, 26 November, K; Per Persson, Elin Andersdotter, *half-cousin*
1750, 28 November, R; Anders Ersson, Kierstin Hansdotter, *cousin*
1750, 31 January, D; Larsson, Larsdotter, *cousin*
1770, 20 June, BoA, R; Anders Clarquist, Britta Belin, *cousin*
1770, 23 August, BoA, K; Johan Hammarström, Stina Ros, *wife's half-niece*
1774, 8 August, BoA, K; Friedrich Schuberts, Margareta Lidman, *stepgrand-father's widow*
1775, 4 May, R, K; Per Ersson, Lisa Maria Persdotter, *wife's half-niece*
1775, 28 July, D; Jon Jönsson, XX, *cousin*
1775, 13 September, R, K; P. Ekberg, XX, *wife's grandniece*
1775, 28 October, BoA; Carl Zachrisson, Lena Jakobsdotter, *cousin*
1775, 22 November, R; Wilhelm Larsson, Marja Johansdotter, *cousin*
1775, 22 November, R; Per Kettunen, Karin Pic ..., *cousin*
1780, 14 January, BoA; Lars Liedman, Christina Maria Tysell, *cousin*
1780, 21 January, BoA, K; Bengt von Strokirsch (22), Eleonora von Strokirsch, *cousin*
1780, 21 January, BoA; E. Nordholm, Charlotta Nordenberg, *cousin*
1780, 28 January, BoA, K; Anders Svensson, Karna Åkesdotter, *wife's half-grandniece*
1780, 18 February, BoA; Olof Andersson, Kierstin Andersdotter, *cousin*
1780, 25 February, BoA; Nils Larsson, Ingrid Rasmusdotter, *cousin*
1780, 25 February, BoA, R, K; Magnus Norling (26), Catharina Söderström (28), *stepfather's widow*
1780, 10 March, BoA, K; Lars Boman, Christina Lindman, *wife's half-niece*
1780, 17 March, BoA; Nils Nilsson, Anna Olasdotter, *cousin*

2 'XX' in these lists stands for the unknown name of the other party.

1780, 17 March, BoA; Per Svensson, Anna Carlsdotter, *cousin*
1780, 29 March, BoA; Holsten Wernesson, Anna C. Rystrand, *wife's half-niece*
1780, 5 May, BoA; Daniel Björkman, Margaretha Björkman, *cousin*
1780, 9 May, BoA; Emanuel Stråhle, Elisabeth Stråhle, *cousin*
1790, 22 March, K; Per Jönsson, Kristina Bengtsdotter, *wife's niece*
1790, 22 March, D; Elias Ribbing, Lena XX, *wife's niece*
1790, 16 September, BoA, K; Emanuel Schagerström, Greta Stina Collin (24), *wife's sister*
1790, 16 September, BoA; Erik Larsson, Catharina Larsdotter, *wife's sister*
1790, 16 September, BoA, K; Olof Andersson (24), Britta Eriksdotter (27), *uncle's widow*
1790, 16 September, BoA, K; Anders Johansson (29), Anna Andersdotter (36), *uncle's widow*
1790, 23 September, K; Johan Lang (41), Magdalena Jönsdotter (33), *half-uncle's widow*
1790, 29 November, BoA; Jon Nilsson, Annika Persdotter, *wife's half-niece*
1792, 24 April, BoA; Johan Assarsson (25), Maria Jonasdotter (29), *uncle's widow*
1801, 19 January, BoA; Nils Nilsson, Maria Johansdotter, *wife's niece*
1801, 28 January, BoA; Johan M. Schmidt (47), Beata E. Sohlwig (52), *wife's half-sister*
1801, 28 January, BoA, K; Peter Brunström, Anna E. Holmström (33), *wife's sister*
1801, 4 February, BoA, K; Jon Månsson (45), Karna Månsdotter (20), *wife's niece*
1801, 7 March, K; Jöns Ivarsson, Kierstina Isaksdotter, *stepson's daughter*
1801, 7 March, BoA; Johan Ivarsson, Kierstina Isaksdotter, *stepson's daughter*
1801, 27 April, R; Johan Eliasson, Anna Jakobsdotter, *cousin*
1801, 27 April, R; Johan Börjesson, Christina Hansdotter, *cousin*
1801, 27 April, R; Jon Johansson, Nilla Larsdotter, *wife's sister*
1801, 27 April, R; Per Hansson, Bengta Andersdotter, *wife's half-sister*
1801, 13 May, BoA, R, K; Jonas Fredrik Brink, Botilla Kullenberg, *wife's sister*
1801, 13 May, BoA, K; B. N. Hanberg, Christina Elmgren, *wife's sister*
1801, 13 May, BoA; Johan Fredrik Martin, Lovisa Ulrika Hallberg, *wife's sister*
1801, 13 May, BoA, R, K; Johannes Håkansson (31), Brita Jakobsdotter (38), *uncle's widow*
1801, 13 May, BoA, R, K; Anders Eriksson, Maria Svensdotter, *half-uncle's widow*
1801, 14 May, BoA, K; Olof Ersson, Maria Andersdotter, *brother's widow*
1801, 3 June, BoA, K; Anders Nilsson (34), Brita Eriksdotter (33), *half-niece*
1801, 4 June, K; Olof Jönsson, Anna Olofsdotter, *cousin*
1801, 4 June, BoA, K; Per Wretman (24), Elisabeth Nyman (44), *uncle's widow*

1801, 10 June, K; Nils Wilhelmsson, Johanna Rasmusdotter, *cousin*
1801, 1 July, K; Robert M. Broman, Anna Elisabeth Broman, *cousin*
1801, 1 July, BoA; Johan A. Hedberg, Helena S. Hamisch (24), *cousin*
1801, 1 July, BoA; Anders Hansson (40), Catharina Ersdotter (34), *wife's niece*
1801, 8 August, BoA; Sven Jönsson, Stina Larsdotter, *wife's sister*
1801, 19 August, K; Carl Ehrenborg, Charlotta Wachschlager, *cousin*
1801, 7 October, BoA; Nils Berg Andersson, Anna Maria Schultz, *cousin*
1801, 7 October, BoA; Hans Knutsson, Pernilla Bengtsdotter, *cousin*
1801, 7 October, BoA, K; Per Persson, Catharina Jönsdotter, *wife's niece*
1801, 7 October, BoA; Erik Andersson, Anna Christina Jönsdotter, *wife's niece*
1801, 21 October, BoA, K; Adam Quist (32), Anna Elisabet Stark (26), *wife's niece*
1801, 28 October, BoA; Johannes Larsson (20), Greta Johansdotter (19), *cousin*
1801, 28 October, BoA; Joseph Rautiain, Ulrika XX, *cousin*
1801, 25 November, BoA, R, K; Gustaf Cronstedt, H. M. Fleetwood, *cousin*
1801, 25 November, R; XX Norberg, Carolina Swedelin, *cousin*
1801, 25 November, R; Åke Pålsson, Boll Svensdotter, *cousin*
1801, 25 November, R; Olof Andersson, Anna XX, *cousin*
1801, 25 November, R; Bonde Larsson, Kierstin Andersdotter, *cousin*
1801, 25 November, BoA, R, K; Simon Isaksson I. (58), Brita Johansdotter, *wife's sister*
1801, 21 December, D; Per Larsson, Greta Nilsdotter, *cousin*
1802, 12 January, BoA, K; Lars Jönsson (62), Bengta Nilsdotter (32), *wife's niece*
1802, 4 May, D; Johan Andersson, Anna Johansdotter, *uncle's widow*
1802, 4 May, D; Johan Petersson, XX, *granduncle's widow*
1802, 4 May, D; Simon Johansson, XX, *half-uncle's widow*
1802, 11 May, BoA, K; Olof Olsson (32), Karin Hansdotter (24), *wife's sister*
1803, 20 January, D; Måns Persson, Kerstin Håkansdotter, *half-niece*
1807, 28 January, BoA; C.A. Blomcreutz, Johanna Schröderheim, *wife's sister*
1807, 12 January, K; Jonas Werner, Maria Bengtsdotter, *wife's sister*
1807, 12 February, K; Gunnar Pehrsson, Brita Pehrsdotter, *wife's stepdaughter*
1807, 24 February, K; Jöns Persson, Kierstin Persdotter, *cousin*
1807, 24 February, K; Jöns Larsson, Karna Jönsdotter, *cousin*
1815, 8 May, BoA, K; Nils Petersson, Catharina Persdotter, *wife's niece*
1815, 17 May, BoA, K; Petrus Persson, Sara Jönsdotter, *wife's sister*
1815, 24 May, K; Lars Bygdén, Brita Åberg, *niece*
1815, 24 May, K; Thomas Friberg, Sara Hinter, *cousin*
1815, 24 May, K; Bengt Gunnarsson, Ella Gabrielsdotter, *cousin*
1815, 24 May, K; Rasmus Hansson, Maria Andersdotter, *cousin*
1815, 24 May, K; Jakob Hellberg, Sofia Tenger, *cousin*
1815, 24 May, K; Jan Jansson, Stina Pehrsdotter, *cousin*
1815, 24 May, K; Ola Larsson, Ingeborg Nilsdotter, *cousin*
1815, 24 May, K; Abraham Nensén, Anna Åhman, *cousin*

1815, 24 May, K; Adam Sjögren, Maria Fisselgren, *cousin*
1815, 24 May, K; Ernst Tengwall, Ingrid Möller, *cousin*
1815, 24 May, BoA, K; Daniel Dahlqvist, Eva Nyberg, *wife's half-sister*
1815, 24 May, BoA, K; Håkan Jönsson, Maja Nilsdotter, *half-uncle's widow*
1815, 24 May, BoA, K; Jakob Andersson, Anna Jönsdotter, *stepson's stepdaughter*
1815, 26 July, BoA, K; Johan Lundberg, Beata Lundberg, *stepfather's widow*
1807, 24 February, K; Erik Andersson, Brita Eriksdotter, *uncle's widow*
1850, 9 July, BoA, R, K; Carl Sporring, Sofia Elisabeth Åkerbladh, *stepdaughter*
1850, 1 February, BoA, K; Sven Åkesson (50), Bengta Nilsdotter (50), *wife's sister*
1850, 22 January, BoA, K; Thomas Nilsson (24), Brita Jonasdotter (33), *brother's widow*
1850, 22 January, BoA, K; Sven Börjesson (25), Stina Carlsdotter (35), *uncle's widow*
1850, 5 February, BoA, K; Anders Jönsson (24), Hedda Jönsdotter (32), *brother's widow*
1850, 5 February, BoA, K; Anders Nilsson (37), Anna B. Svensdotter (30), *wife's niece*
1850, 14 February, BoA, K; Johannes Jönsson (41), Johanna Johansdotter, *wife's sister*
1850, 19 February, BoA; Johannes Svensson (31), Elna Mårtensdotter (27), *wife's sister*
1850, 19 February, BoA; Jöns Larsson (57), Karin Olofsdotter (59), *wife's half-sister*
1850, 20 February, BoA, K; Erik Nilsson (47), Stina Cajsa Lindberg (22), *wife's niece*
1850, 25 February, BoA; Johannes Andersson (27), Maja Svensdotter (34), *brother's widow*
1850, 27 February, BoA, K; Olof Jönsson (57), Catharina Ersdotter (52), *wife's sister*
1850, 27 February, BoA, K; Hindrick Waern, Lena Cajsa Larsdotter (46), *wife's sister*
1850, 27 February, BoA, K; Israel Sundqvist (52), Brita S. Malmberg (52), *brother's widow*
1850, 6 March, BoA; Anders Larsson (27), Cajsa Olsdotter (28), *uncle's widow*
1850, 21 March, BoA; Isak Carlsson (44), Gustava Pettersdotter (33), *wife's sister*
1850, 3 April, BoA; Hans Larsson, Hanna Jönsdotter (41), *uncle's widow*
1850, 8 May, BoA, K; Per Andersson (45), Margret Henriksdotter (50), *uncle's widow*
1850, 15 May, BoA, K; Måns Persson (41), Elna Nilsdotter (31), *wife's niece*
1850, 5 June, BoA, K; Johan Hesling (47), Brita Andersdotter (37), *uncle's widow*

1850, 9 July, BoA; Anders Andersson (28), Gertrud Jönsdotter (37), *uncle's widow*
1850, 10 April, BoA; Anders Tjäll (65), Brita Maja Larsdotter (41), *wife's sister*
1850, 10 April, BoA; Anders C. Persson (44), Sara C. Svensdotter (33), *wife's half-sister*
1850, 10 April, BoA; Carl Hasselöv, Catharina Margaretha Åhlund, *wife's half-sister*
1850, 10 April, BoA; Sven Åkesson, Pernilla Åkesdotter, *brother's widow*
1850, 10 April, BoA; Erland Jönsson (35), Johanna Johansdotter (21), *wife's niece*
1850, 30 April, BoA; Lars Rasmusson (51), Kierstin Pehrsdotter (46), *wife's sister*
1850, 30 April, BoA; Anders Andreasson (33), Johanna Svensdotter (21), *wife's sister*
1850, 28 May, BoA, K; Sven Jönsson (25), Petronella Larsdotter (30), *brother's widow*
1850, 22 May, BoA, K; Anders Svensson (36), Gustava Christiansdotter (23), *wife's sister*
1850, 22 May, BoA, K; Anders Jönsson (35), Helena O. Wiström (29), *wife's sister*
1850, 9 July, BoA; Jan Jansson (23), Anna Andersdotter (24), *brother's widow*
1850, 21 November, BoA, R; Gustav Larsson (23), Cajsa Johansdotter (26), *wife's sister*
1850, 21 November, BoA, K; Nils Olsson (34), Lena Andreasdotter (32), *wife's half-sister*
1850, 21 November, BoA, R, K; Sven Pettersson (38), Cajsa Andersdotter (45), *wife's stepmother*
1850, 21 November, R; Anders Nilsson, Karna Thomasdotter, *wife's sister*
1850, 21 November, R; Anders Nilsson, Karna Thomasdotter, *wife's sister*
1870, 11 February, K; Carl Ulrick, Maria Florentina Wiklund, *wife's sister*
1870, 11 February, K; Per Persson, Carolina Abrahamsdotter, *wife's sister*
1870, 11 February, K; Jan Fredrik Carlsson, Sofia Tenngren, *wife's sister*
1870, 11 February, K; Tuve Persson, Kierstin Bengtsdotter, *wife's sister*
1870, 11 February, K; Johannes Johansson, Anna Katarina Nilsdotter, *brother's widow*
1870, 25 February, K; Nils Petter Nilsson, Johanna Andersdotter, *wife's sister*
1870, 25 February, K; Johan Axel Lagergren, Eugenia Isabella Robertsson, *wife's sister*
1870, 25 February, K; Hans Andersson, Anna Jönsdotter, *brother's widow*
1870, 20 May, K; Carl Ludvig Larsson, Anna Bernhardina Larsson, *stepmother*
1870, 20 May, K; August Engborg, Maria Mathilda Sjögren, *wife's sister*
1870, 20 May, K; Anders Johansson, Anna Johanna Johansdotter, *wife's sister*
1870, 20 May, K; Jonas Andersson, Anna Carolina Gabrielsdotter, *wife's sister*

1870, 20 May, K; Johan W. Johansson, Johanna Mathilda Pettersdotter, *brother's widow*
1870, 20 May, K; Erik Gustaf Djerf, Brita Maja Larsdotter, *half-brother's widow*
1870, 20 May, K; Christoffer Jansson, Märta Elisabeth Nätterlund, *uncle's widow*
1870, 23 December, K; Nils Jönsson, Botilla Persdotter, *wife's sister*
1870, 23 December, K; Jonas Germindsson, Christina Svensdotter, *wife's niece*
1870, 23 December, K; August Engman, Clara Svensson, *stepmother's sister*

Archives of the Lower Judiciary Inspection

Precedents, FII:3, 1785, 11 February. Jan Gustaf Hägerflykt, Helena Gertrud Theet

Printed sources

Almqvist, Jan Eric (ed.). 1933. *Förarbeten till Sveriges Rikes Lag 1666–1686 med bidrag av statsmedel* (Uppsala)
Anonymous. 1528. Statutes of the town of Västerås
——. 1611. Letters patent, 1 October. *Then Stormächtigste Högborne Konug; och herres/ Herr Carls then Nijondes medh Gudz Nåde. Swar uppå the Högmåhls Saker...*
——. 1611. Penal Act of Charles IX of Sweden, 1 October
——. 1678. Letters patent, 1 March. *Öpet Bref/ huru wida Skyldskap i Echtenskap förbiudes...*
——. 1680. Royal regulation, 3 December. *Förordning och Stadga/ Om the grader, som uthi Skyldskapen til ächthenskapsbyggiande skole wara förbudne*
——. 1689. Letters patent, 25 April. *Til Swea hofrätt at referera til kongl. Maj:t så ofta några Casus förefalla angående lägersmål i första och andra gradu lineae inaequalis...*
——. 1699. Royal regulation, 10 October. *Til alle Hof- och Öfwer-Rätter/ at the/ som bedrif-wa antingen Hor/ eller ock Lönskeläger uti then första Swågerskapsgraden skola beläggias med lifsstraf*
——. 1700. Letters patent, 28 March. *Til N.N. Hofrätt/ om Hor med ens Hustrus Broders Enkia*
——. 1703. Royal ordinance, 2 December. *Angående några förbudne grader i Ächtenskapsmål.*
——. 1714. Letters patent, 13 November. *Wi/ Kongl. Swea Hof-Räts Vice Præsident... Hälse... Hos Hans Kongl. Maj:t är uti underdånighet berättadt/ hurusom Under-domarne til Consistorium remitterat Ächtenskaps måhl/ angående Personer/ som begåt Lägersmåhl med deras aflidne Hustrurs Syskonebarn...*

——. 1725. Letters patent, 22 June. *Wi, Friherre Petter Scheffer, Præsident uti Kongl. Swe Hof-Rätt... Hälse... huruledes nu mera mångfaldige ansökningar, om tillåtande af Syskone Barns Äkchtenskap hos Kongl. Maj:t uti underdånighet inkomma...*

——. 1725. Letters patent, 26 June. *Wi, Germind Cederhielm..., Præsident uthi Kongl. Götha Rikes Hoff-Rätt... Hälse Såsom hoos Hans Kongl. Maj:t mångfaldige ansökningar inkomma... at med Syskonebarns Ächtenskap må förfaras...*

——. 1727. Royal regulation, 3 March. *Kongl. Maj:ts Nådige Förordning/ At de som wilja ingå Ächtenskap med sine afledne Makars Syskonebarn...*

——. 1732. Letters patent, 16 June. *Til Swea Hof-Rätt, om theras straff, som wid Executioner med gatulopp, spö och risslitande beträdas med efterlåtenhet i theras plikt...*

——. 1733. Letters patent, 6 October. *Wi, Hans von Fersen, Præsident uti Kongl.Maj:ts Swea Hoff-Rätt... Hälse... Ehuruwäl åtskillige tid efter annan utgångne Kongl. Bref och Förordningar utwisa/hwilcka Äcktenskap uti Swågerlag å sidone kunna tillåtelige finnas / eller ej...*

——. 1736. Royal regulation, 23 September. *Förordning angående Chartae-Sigillatae afgiften*

——. 1738. Letters patent, 15 February. *Til Consistorium i Lund, at bonden N. ej får träda i ächtenskap med thes afledna hustrus stjufdotter...*

——. 1738. Letters patent, 16 March. *Til Consistorium i Skara, at N ej får träda i ächtenskap med sin afledna halfbroders dotter...*

——. 1738. Letters patent, 23 November. *Transumt af Kongl. Majestets bref til Consistorium i Carlstad, at N får ingå giftermål med sin Sonahustrus syster...*

——. 1741. Letters patent, 10 June. *Transumt af Kongl.Majestets bref til Consistorium i Borgo, om en bonde, som sökt tilstånd at ingå ächtenskap med sin afledna hustrus broders enka...*

——. 1744. Letters patent, 12 June. *Wi, Grefwe Carl Frölich, Præsident uti Kongl.Maj:ts och Riksens Swea Hofrätt... Hälse... en af... Riksens Hofrätter, i anledning af et förekommit brott-mål, sig i underdånighet förfrågat om Lagens rätta förstånd, angående böter för en Husbonde, som lägrat sit Syskonebarn...*

——. 1744. Letters patent, 12 December. *Til Consistorium i Götheborg, angående giftermål med sin stjufsons stjufdotter...*

——. 1749. Letters patent, 22 February. *Til Consistorium i Calmar, angående tilstånd för en dreng, at bygga ächtenskap med sin afledna fästeqwinnas stjufdotter...*

——. 1752. Letters patent, 23 December. *Til Consistorium i Calmar, angående N. som sökt at få til äckta taga sin Moders Stiuffaders Enka...*

——. 1754. Letters patent, 7 November. *Til Consistorium i Calmar, angående äckten-skap emellan sin Stiufmoders half-syster...*

——. 1757. Royal regulation, 25 November. *Til Consistorierna i Riket, huru förhållas bör med dem, som äro behäftade med fallandesot och åstunda äktenskap...*

——. 1761. Letters patent, 2 April. *Til Consistorium i N. at enkling får träda i äktenskap med sin afledne hustrus halfbroders enka...*
——. 1761. Letters patent, 21 May. *Kongl. Maj:ts Utslag uppå enkans N. underdåniga ansökning, thet Kongl. Maj:t i anseende til anförde omständigheter och skäl, i nåder täcktes tillåta henne at ingå äktenskap med sin afledne mans systerson...*
——. 1761. Letters patent, 26 November. *Kongl. Maj:ts Utslag uppå Bondens N. underdåniga ansökning, at som Consistorium i N. genom Utslag then 14 October innewarande år nekat honom med sin afledne hustrus halfsysters sone dotter N. få bygga äktenskap...*
——. 1767. Letters patent, 2 June. *Kongl. Maj:ts Utslag uppå Qwinnfolkets N. N. underdåniga ansökning, at som hon, af enfaldighet, uti afsigt, at få bygga hionelag med sin moders afledne half-systers efterlemnade man...*
——. 1768. Letters patent, 19 June. *Kongl. Maj:ts Utslag på gamla Enklingens N. N. giorde underdåniga ansökning, at få träda i äktenskap med sin dotters stiufdotter N....*
——. 1768. Letters patent, 22 June. *Til Consistorium i N. Stad, at äktenskap ej kan wara tillåtit med Swärsons dotter af förra giftet...*
——. 1769. Letters patent, 22 November. *Til Consistorium i N. Stad, at äktenskap må wara tillåtit med Stiufmoders Syster...*
——. 1774. Letters patent, 8 August. *Kongl. Maj:ts Utslag uppå Sämskmakare-Gesällens N. N. och thes Faders Stiuf-Faders Enkas N. N. underdåniga ansökning, om Nådigt tilstånd, at med hwarannan träda i äktenskap...*
——. 1785. Letters patent, 11 February. *Kongl. Maj:ts Utslag uppå underdåniga ansökning, at få ingå äktenskap med sin afledna hustrus Syster N...*
——. 1809–71. Parliamentary publications for all estates with appendices, 1809/10, 1823, 1828, 1834, 1840, 1844, 1847, 1859/60, 1862/63, 1868, 1870, and 1871
——. 1810. Royal regulation, 10 April. *Angående ändring uti allmänna lagens stadgande i 5 och 6 §§ 2 kap. giftermålsbalken*
——. 1815. *Förslag till Giftermåls Balk* (Stockholm)
——. 1829. Royal regulation, 8 September. *Kongl. Maj:ts Nådiga Kungörelse, om hwad som bör iakttagas i affseende på underdånig anhållan om Kongl. Maj:ts Nådiga tillåtelse för Syskonebarn att med hwarandra ingå äktenskap...*
——. 1831/32. 'Om incestuösa giftermål m.m. i anledning af en i Lund år 1813 utgifven academisk afhandling: de connubiis inter cognatos & affines prohibitis', in *Juridiskt Arkif*, vol. 2 (Christianstad)
——. 1838. *Förslag till Allmän Civillag: Andra Upplagan, med de förändringar, som, wid utarbetande af Förslag till Criminal-Lag, blifwit gjorde, och tillökt med Register* (Stockholm)
——. 1839. *Kongl. Maj:ts och Rikets Svea Hofrätts Underdåniga Utlåtande öfver Lag-Committéens Förslag till Allmän Criminal-Lag* (Stockholm)
——. 1840. *Utlåtande, i anledning af Anmärkningar wid Förslaget till Allmän Criminallag, af Lagcommiteen, Andra Upplagan* (Stockholm)

——. 1841. *Lag-Commissionens förslag till Sweriges Rikes Lag af år 1734; jemte de wid samma Förslag gjorde anmärkningar, Lag-Commissionens derå afgifna swar, samt Riksens Ständers förhandlingar och Beslut wid Lagens granskning och antagande å Riksdagarne 1731 och 1734* (Stockholm)

——. 1872. Royal regulation, 24 May. *Kongl. Maj:ts Nådiga Förordning, angående upphäfwande af 2 kap. 5 och 6 §§ Giftermålsbalken...*

——. 1883. *Nytt juridiskt arkiv, afd. I. Tidskrift för lagstiftning* (Stockholm)

——. 1907. *Nytt juridiskt arkiv, afd. I. Tidskrift för lagstiftning* (Stockholm)

——. 1913. *Lagberedningens förslag till revision av giftermålsbalken och vissa delar av ärvdabalken I. Förslag till lag om äktenskapets ingående och upplösning m.m.* (Stockholm)

——. 1916. *Nya äktenskapslagen med förklaringar enligt lagberedningen av Valfrid Spångberg* (Stockholm)

——. 1921. *Svenska Prästeståndets protokoll från år 1719*, part 1 (Uppsala)

——. 1935. *Promemoria angående ändringar i strafflagen beträffande straffsatserna för särskilda brott m. m.* Official Government Reports (Statens offentliga utredningar) (*SOU 1935:68*)

——. 1962. *Penal Code (1962:700)*, Chapter 6, Section 7

——. 1976. *Sexuella övergrepp förslag till ny lydelse av brottsbalkens bestämmelser om sedlighetsbrott.* Official Government Reports (*SOU 1976:9*)

——. 1977–1978. Government bill 1977/78:69

——. 1977–1978. Report of the parliamentary committee on justice, 1977/78:26

——. 1982. *Prästeståndets riksdagsprotokoll 1723* (Stockholm)

——. 1984. *Sveriges Rikes Lag. Gillad och antagen på riksdagen år 1734. Till 250-årsdagen av lagens tillkomst efter den första i antikva tryckta upplagan av år 1780*, facsimile edition with an introduction by Stig Jägerskiöld (Lund)

——. 2001. *Sexualbrotten – Ett ökat skydd för den sexuella integriteten och angränsande frågor.* Official Government Reports (*SOU 2001:14*)

——. 2010. *Sexualbrottslagstiftningen – utvärdering och reformförslag.* Official Government Reports (*SOU 2010:71*)

——. 2012. 'German Incest Couple Lose European Court Case', *BBC NEWS*, 12 April (accessed 23 July 2015) www.bbc.com/news/world-europe-17690997?print=true

——. 2014. 'Frenchman Wins Legal Right to Marry his Ex-stepmother', *The Daily Telegraph*, 6 October (accessed 23 July 2015) www.telegraph.co.uk/news/worldnews/europe/france/11140937/Frenchman-wins-legal-right-to-marry-his-ex-stepmother.html

Biurman, Johan. 1767 [1729]. *En kårt dock tydelig bref-ställare* (Stockholm)

Flensburg, Ebbe Gustaf (ed.). 1916. *Lag om äktenskapets ingående och upplösning. Med förklarande anmärkningar, prejudikat och alfabetiskt register* (Stockholm)

Flintberg, Jacob Albrecht. 1803. *Lagfarenhets-Bibliothek, af Jacob Albrecht Flintberg. Lagmann. Femte Delen, innefattande Missgärnings-balken i Sweriges Allmänna Lag, …* (Stockholm)

Karlsson, Karl-Johan. 2010. 'S-politiker: Gör incest lagligt', *Expressen*, 15 March 2010 (accessed 23 May 2015) www.expressen.se/nyheter/s-politiker-gor-incest-lagligt/

Nehrman, David. 1729. *Inledning Til Then Swenska Iurisprudentiam Civilem, af Naturens Lagh och Sweriges Rikes Äldre och nyare Stadgar uthdragen och uppsatt af David Nehrman Juris Patrii & Rom. Prof. Ord. Med Hans Kongl. Maj:ts Nådigsta Privilegio* (Lund)

Nehrman, David. 1747. *Föreläsningar öfwer Giftermåls Balken, hålne wid Kongl. Academien i Lund af David Nehrman Juris Patrii et Rom. Prof.* (Stockholm)

Schlyter, Carl Johan. 1813. *De Connubiis inter cognatos aut adfines prohibitis, Dissertationem venia consult. fac. jur. Lund. die 11 Dec. 1813. h. l. q. a. m. s. P. P. Holmbergson, Johannes, J. U. D. Juris Patrii Professor & Carolus Johannes Schlyter, Blekingus* (Lund)

Schmedeman, Johan (ed.). 1706. *Kongl. stadgar, förordningar, bref och resolutioner, ifrån åhr 1528 in til 1701 angående justitiæ och executionsährender, med een förteckning på stadgarne främst, och ett fulkommeligit orda-register efterst wid wercket öfwer thes innehåld…* (Stockholm)

Schmidt, Carl (ed.). 1838–1839. *Juridiskt Arkif.* vol. 9 (Christianstad)

Sjögren, Wilhelm (ed.). 1901. *Förarbetena till Sveriges Rikes Lag 1686–1736*, vol. III, *Lagkommissionens protokoll 1712–1735* (Uppsala)

—— (ed.). 1901. *Förarbetena till Sveriges Rikes Lag 1686–1736*, vol. VI, *Lagkommissionens förslag 1719–1734* (Uppsala)

—— (ed.). 1903. *Förarbetena till Sveriges rikes lag 1686–1736*, vol. V, *Lagkommissionens förslag, 1698–1718* (Uppsala)

—— (ed.). 1908. *Förarbetena till Sveriges Rikes Lag 1686–1736*, vol. VII, *Utlåtanden öfver lagkommissionens förslag* (Uppsala)

Sundholm, Magnus. 2005. 'Pappa gifte sig med min syster', *Aftonbladet*, 30 January (accessed 28 April 2015) www.aftonbladet.se/nyheter/article10536765.ab

Thanner, Lennart (ed.). 1962. *Prästeståndets riksdagsprotokoll, 1680–1714*, vol. 4 (Norrköping)

Thorén, Caroline. 2009. 'Källarfångarna i Amstetten. Fallet Fritzl – det här har hänt', *Dagens Nyheter*, 15 March (accessed 23 July 2015) www.dn.se/nyheter/varlden/fallet-fritzl-det-har-har-hant/

Tottie, Lars. 1974. *Giftermål och skilsmässa. Kommentar till 1973 års ändringar i giftermålsbalken* (Stockholm)

Wahlberg, C. J. (ed.). 1878. *Åtgärder för lagförbättring 1633–1665*, documents collected by C. J. Wahlberg (Uppsala)

Wallroth, Emmelie. 2015. '18-åring kär i sin pappa – nu vill de ha barn', *Metro*, 17 January (accessed 23 July 2015) www.metro.se/nyheter/18-aringen-ar-kar-i-sin-pappa-nu-vill-de-ha-barn/EVHoap!uT1tNsEvsgP7c/

Literature

Almquist, Jan Eric. 1961. 'Straffet för incest i Sverige under reformationstiden', *Svensk Juristtidning*, 1, 31–40

Alström, Carl Henry. 1958. 'First-Cousin Marriages in Sweden 1750–1844 and a Study of the Population Movement in Some Swedish Subpopulations from the Genetic-Statistical Viewpoint: A Preliminary Report', *Acta Genetica*, 8, 295–369

Ambjörnsson, Ronny. 1978. *Familjeporträtt: Essäer om familjen, kvinnan, barnet och kärleken i historien* (Stockholm: Gidlund)

Arnhart, Larry. 2004. 'The Incest Taboo as Darwinian Natural Right', in *Inbreeding, Incest and the Incest Taboo: The State of Knowledge at the Turn of the Century*, ed. by Arthur P. Wolf and William H. Durham (Stanford: Stanford University Press), pp. 190–218

Baldwin, John W. 1994. *The Language of Sex: Five Voices of Northern France around 1200* (Chicago: University of Chicago Press)

Bergenheim, Åsa. 1998. 'Brottet, offret och förövaren: Om synen på incest och sexuella övergrepp mot barn 1850–1910', *Lychnos*, 121–59

Bergenlöv, Eva. 2002. 'Våldtäkt: Brott mot Gud, ordningen eller individen?', in *Offer för brott: Våldtäkt, incest och barnamord i Sveriges historia från reformationen till nutid*, ed. by Eva Bergenlöv, Marie Lindstedt Cronberg, and Eva Österberg (Lund: Nordic Academic Press), pp. 179–236

Bexell, Oloph. 2008. 'Uppbrottet ur enhetskyrkan', in *Signums svenska kulturhistoria: Det moderna genombrottet*, ed. by Jakob Christensson (Lund: Signum), pp. 55–93

Bittles, Alan H. 2012. *Consanguinity in Context* (Cambridge: Cambridge University Press)

Bjurman, Eva Lis. 1998. *Catrines intressanta blekhet: Unga kvinnors möten med de nya kärlekskraven 1750–1830* (Stockholm: Brutus Östlings bokförlag Symposion)

Blom, Ida. 2012. *Medicine, Morality, and Political Culture: Legislation on Venereal Disease in Five Northern European Countries, c. 1870–c. 1995* (Lund: Nordic Academic Press)

Blumer, Herbert. 1969. *Symbolic Interactionism: Perspective and Method* (Englewood Cliffs, N.J.: Prentice-Hall)

Braun, Christina von. 1989. *Die schamlose Schönheit des Vergangenen: Zum Verhältnis von Geschlecht und Geschichte* (Frankfurt/M: Neue Kritik)

Broberg, Gunnar, and Mattias Tydén. 1991. *Oönskade i folkhemmet: Rashygien och sterilisering i Sverige* (Stockholm: Gidlund)

Brown, Callum, G. 2001. *The Death of Christian Britain: Understanding Secularization 1800–2000* (London: Routledge)

Brundage, James A. 1987. *Law, Sex and Christian Society in Medieval Europe* (Chicago: University of Chicago Press)

Carlsson, Sten. 1977. *Fröknar, mamseller, jungfrur och pigor: Ogifta kvinnor i det svenska ståndssamhället* (Uppsala: Studia historica Upsaliensa)

Carmichael, Calum M. 1997. *Law, Legend, and Incest in the Bible: Leviticus 18–20* (Ithaca and London: Cornell University Press)

Chammas, Jaqueline. 2011. *L'Inceste romanesque au siècle des Lumières: De la Régence à la Révolution (1715–1789)* (Paris: Champion)

Charon, Joel M. 2007. *Symbolic Interactionism: An Introduction, An Interpretation, An Integration* (Upper Saddle River, N.J.: Pearson Education)

Christensen-Nugues, Charlotte. 2004. 'Äktenskap och familj', in *Signums svenska kulturhistoria: Medeltiden*, ed. by Jakob Christensson (Lund: Signum), pp. 295–334

Coontz, Stephanie. 2005. *Marriage, a History: From Obedience to Intimacy or How Love Conquered Marriage* (New York: Viking)

Corbett, Mary Jean. 2008. *Family Likeness: Sex, Marriage, and Incest from Jane Austen to Virginia Woolf* (Ithaca: Cornell University Press)

Darrow, Margaret H. 1985. 'Popular Concepts of Marital Choice in Eighteenth Century France', *Journal of Social History*, 19:2, 261–72

Davidoff, Leonore, and Catherine Hall. 1987. *Family Fortunes: Men and Women of the English Middleclass 1780–1850* (Chicago: University of Chicago Press)

Davidoff, Leonore, Megan Doolittle, Janet Fink, and Katherine Holden. 1999. *The Family Story: Blood, Contract and Intimacy 1830–1960* (London: Longman)

Davidson, Denise Z. 2012. '"Happy" Marriages in Early Nineteenth-Century France', *Journal of Family History*, 37:1, 23–35

Denbo, Seth, J. 2001. 'Speaking Relatively: A History of Incest and the Family in Eighteenth-Century England'. Unpublished PhD dissertation, University of Warwick

Donahue, Charles, Jr. 2016. 'The Legal Background: European Marriage Law from the Sixteenth to the Nineteenth Century', in *Marriage in Europe, 1400–1800*, ed. by Silvana Seidel Menchi (Toronto: University of Toronto Press), pp. 31–60

Durham, William, H. 2004. 'Assessing the Gaps in Westermarck's Theory', in *Inbreeding, Incest and the Incest Taboo: The State of Knowledge at the Turn of the Century*, ed. by Arthur P. Wolf and William H. Durham (Stanford: Stanford University Press), pp. 121–38

Edgren, Lars. 1983. 'Hantverkaränkor på äktenskapsmarknaden: "Änkekonservering" inom malmöhantverket 1816–1840', *Ale*, 4, 1–17

Egerbladh, I. and A. H. Bittles. 2011. 'Socioeconomic, Demographic and Legal Influences on Consanguinity and Kinship in Northern Coastal Sweden 1780–1899', *Journal of Biosocial Science*, 43:4, 413–35

Egmond, Florike. 2001. 'Incestuous Relations and their Punishment in the Dutch Republic', *Eighteenth-Century Life*, 25:3, 20–42

Ekenstam, Claes. 1993. *Kroppens idéhistoria: Disciplinering och karaktärsdaning i Sverige 1700–1950* (Hedemora: Gidlund)

Erickson, Mark T. 2004. 'Evolutionary Thought and the Current Clinical Understanding of Incest', in *Inbreeding, Incest, and the Incest Taboo: The State of Knowledge at the Turn of the Century*, ed. by Arthur P. Wolf and William H. Durham (Stanford: Stanford University Press), pp. 161–89

Eriksson, Gunnar. 1983. *Västerlandets idéhistoria 1800–1950* (Stockholm: Gidlund)

Frances, Catherine. 2005. 'Making Marriages in Early Modern England: Rethinking the Role of Family and Friends', in *The Marital Economy in Scandinavia and Britain 1400–1900*, ed. by Maria Ågren and Amy Louise Erickson (Aldershot and Burlington: Ashgate), pp. 39–56

Frandsen, Paul John. 2009. *Incestuous and Close-Kin Marriage in Ancient Egypt and Persia: An Examination of the Evidence* (Copenhagen: Museum Tusculanum Press)

Gaunt, David. 1996. *Familjeliv i Norden* (Södertälje: Gidlund)

Giddens, Anthony, and Philip W. Sutton. 2014. *Sociologi* (Lund: Studentlitteratur)

Goody, Jack. 1983. *The Development of the Family and Marriage in Europe* (Cambridge: Cambridge University Press)

Gordon, Linda. 1986. 'Incest and Resistance: Patterns of Father-Daughter Incest, 1880–1930', *Social Problems*, 33:4, 253–67

Giuliani, Fabienne. 2009a. 'Monsters in the Village? Incest in Nineteenth Century France', *Journal of Social History*, 42:4, 919–32

——. 2009b. 'L'écriture du crime: l'inceste dans les archives judiciaires francaises (1791–1898)', *L'atelier du centre de recherches historiques*, 5, 1–25

——. 2014. *Les liasions interdites: Histoire de l'inceste au XIXe siècle* (Sorbonne: Sorbonne publications)

Gunnlaugsson, Gísli Ágúst. 1994. 'Sedlighetsbrott i Norden 1550–1850', in *Den 22. Nordiske historikermöte, Oslo 13–18 augusti 1994: Rapport II: Normer og sosial kontroll i Norden ca. 1550–1850: Domstolene i samspill med lokalsamfunnet*, ed. by Kåre Tönnesson (Oslo: University of Oslo, Department of History), pp. 103–22

Göransson, Anita. 1990. 'Kön, släkt och ägande: Borgerliga maktstrategier 1800–1850', *Historisk tidskrift*, 4, 525–44

——. 1992. 'Från släkt till marknad: Ägande, arbete och äktenskap på 1800-talet', in *Kvinnohistoria: Om kvinnors villkor från antiken till våra dagar* (Stockholm: Utbildningsradion), pp. 104–21

Hammar, K. G. 2012. 'Lydnad, lyhördhet och olydnad', in *Dygdernas renässans*, ed. by Eva Österberg, Marie Lindstedt Cronberg, and Catharina Stenqvist (Stockholm: Atlantis), pp. 103–24

Hansen, Anna. 2006. *Ordnade hushåll: Genus och kontroll i Jämtland under 1600-talet* (Uppsala: Acta Universitas Upsaliensis)

——. 2010. 'Att välja den rätta', in *Det politiska äktenskapet: 400 års historia om familj och reproduktion*, ed. by Bente Rosenbeck and Hanne Sanders (Göteborg: Makadam), pp. 41–65

Hansen, Torleif. 1993. *Bergen lagting som straffedomstol i appellsaker 1702–1737* (Bergen: Alma mater)

Hastrup, Kirsten. 1990. *Nature and Policy in Iceland 1400–1800: An Anthropological Analysis of History and Mentality* (Oxford: Clarendon Press)

Hehenberger, Susanne. 2003. 'Inzest oder "Hurerey"? Inzest in der gerichtlichen Praxis des 18. Jahrhunderts: Eine Untersuchung am Beispiel

Oberösterreichs', in *Historische Inzestdiskurse: Interdisziplinäre Zugänge*, ed. by Jutta Eming, Claudia Jarzebowski, and Claudia Ulbrich (Königstein: Ulrike Helmer Verlag), pp. 189–213

Herlihy, David. 1995. 'Making Sense of Incest: Women and the Marriage Rules of the Early Middle Ages', in *Women, Family and Society in Medieval Europe: Historical Essays 1978–1991*, ed. by A. Mohlo (Oxford: Berghahn), pp. 96–109

Herman, Judith, and Lisa Hirschman. 1977. 'Father-Daughter Incest', *Signs*, 2:4, 735–56

Hofsten, Erland. 2001. *Svensk befolkningshistoria: Några grunddrag i utvecklingen från 1750* (Stockholm: Norstedts; first published in 1986)

Holberg, Ludvig. 1974. *Latinske Smaaskrifter*. 2 vols. Introduction, translation, and commentary by A. Kragelund (Copenhagen: Gad)

Hull, Isabel V. 1996. *Sexuality, State, and Civil Society in Germany, 1700–1815* (Ithaca: Cornell University Press)

Hunt, Lynn. 1992. *The Family Romance of the French Revolution* (Berkeley and Los Angeles: University of California Press)

Häthén, Christian. 1990. *Straffrättsvetenskap och kriminalpolitik: De europeiska straffteorierna och deras betydelse för svensk strafflagstiftning 1906–1931* (Lund: Studentlitteratur)

Inger, Göran. 2011. *Svensk rättshistoria* (Malmö: Liber)

Jansson, Arne. 1994. 'Mörda för att få dö', in *Människovärdet och makten: Om civiliseringsprocessen i Stockholm 1600–1850*, ed. by Arne Jarrick and Johan Söderberg (Stockholm: Stockholmia), pp. 21–52

Jansson, Karin Hassan. 2000. 'Bakom normen: Kvinnofrid och genuskonstruktion i det tidigmoderna Sverige', in *Bedrägliga begrepp: Kön och genus i humanistisk forskning*, ed. by Gudrun Andersson (Uppsala: University of Uppsala, Department of History), pp. 157–75

——. 2002. *Kvinnofrid: Synen på våldtäkt och konstruktion av kön i Sverige 1600–1800* (Uppsala: Acta Universitatis Upsaliensis)

——. 2006. 'Våldsgärning, illgärning, ogärning: Könskodat språkbruk och föreställningar om våld i den medeltida landslagen', in *Våld: Representation och verklighet*, ed. by Eva Österberg and Marie Lindstedt Cronberg (Falun: Nordic Academic Press), pp. 145–65

——. 2010. 'Ära och oro: Sexuella närmanden och föräktenskapliga relationer i 1700-talets Sverige', *Scandia*, 75:1, 29–56

Jarlert, Anders. 2001. *Sveriges kyrkohistoria, 6: Romantikens och liberalismens tid* (Stockholm: Verbum)

Jarzebowski, Claudia. 2003. 'Eindeutig uneindeutig: Verhandlungen über Inzest im 18. Jahrhundert' in *Historische Inzestdiskurse: Interdisziplinäre Zugänge*, ed. by Jutta Eming, Claudia Jarzebowski, and Claudia Ulbrich (Königstein: Ulrike Helmer Verlag)

——. 2006. *Inzest: Verwandtschaft und Sexualität im 18. Jahrhundert* (Cologne: Böhlau)

——. 2012. 'Kulturhistorische Aspekte', in *Inzestverbot*, published lecture from Öffentliche Anhörung des Ethikrat, Berlin, 22 November, downloaded from the author's academic webpage. www.geschkult.fu-berlin.de/e/fmi/institut/mitglieder/Professorinnen_und_Professoren/jarzebowski.html#Publikationen (accessed 23 July 2015)

——. 2014. 'The Meaning of Love: Emotion and Kinship in Sixteenth-Century Incest Discourses', in *Mixed Matches: Transgressive Unions in Germany from the Reformation to the Enlightenment*, ed. by David M. Luebke and Mary Lindemann (New York and Oxford: Berghahn), 166–83

Johnson, Christopher, H. 2011. 'Siblinghood and Emotional Dimensions of the New Kinship System, 1800–1850', in *Sibling Relations and the Transformations of European Kinship, 1300–1900*, ed. by Christopher H. Johnson and David Warren Sabean (New York: Berghahn), pp. 189–220

Johnson, Christopher, H. and David Warren Sabean (eds). 2011. *Sibling Relations and the Transformation of European Kinship, 1300–1900* (New York and Oxford: Berghahn)

Jónsson, Mar. 1994. 'Defining Incest by the Word of God: Northern Europe 1520–1740', *History of European Ideas*, 18:6, 853–67

——. 1998. 'Incest on Iceland, 1500–1800', published lecture from University of Winnipeg, 19 March, http://web.uvic.ca/~becktrus/assets/text/jonsson_01.php (accessed 15 May 2015)

——. 2003. 'Guds ord og døden: Danske teologer og blodskam 1680–1770', *Kirkehistoriske samlinger*, 101–122

Joris, Elisabeth. 2007. 'Kinship and Gender: Property, Enterprise, and Politics', in *Kinship in Europe: Approaches to Long-Term Development, 1300–1900*, ed. by David Warren Sabean, Simon Teuscher, and Jon Mathieu (New York: Berghahn), pp. 231–57

Kerchner, Brigitte. 2003. 'Ein öffentliches Geheimnis: Blutschande im 19. Jahrhundert', in *Historische Inzestdiskurse: Interdisziplinäre Zugänge*, ed. by Jutta Eming, Claudia Jarzebowski, and Claudia Ulbrich (Königstein: Ulrike Helmer Verlag)

Kinberg, Olof, Gunnar Inghe, and Svend Riemer. 1943. *Incestproblemet i Sverige* (Stockholm: Natur och Kultur)

Koefoed, Nina. 1999. 'Forandringer i normer for ægteskap og lovgivning mellem 1770–1800', unpublished dissertation, Aarhus University

Korpiola, Mia. 2005. 'Rethinking Incest and Heinous Sexual Crime: Changing Boundaries of Secular and Ecclesiastical Jurisdiction in Late Medieval Sweden', in *Boundaries of the Law: Geography, Gender and Jurisdiction in Medieval and Early Modern Europe*, ed. by Anthony Musson (Burlington: Ashgate), pp. 102–17

——. 2006. 'Lutheran Marriage Norms in Action: The Example of Post-Reformation Sweden, 1520–1600', in *Lutheran Reformation and the Law*, ed. by Virpi Mäkinen (Leiden: Brill), pp. 131–69

Krogh, Tyge. 2000. *Oplysningstiden og det magiske: Henrettelser og korporlige straffe i 1700-talets förste halvdel* (Copenhagen: Samleren, University of Copenhagen)

Kuper, Adam. 2002. 'Incest, Cousin Marriage, and the Origin of the Human Sciences in Nineteenth-Century England', *Past and Present*, 174, 158–83

——. 2009. *Incest and Influence: The Private Life of Bourgeois England* (Cambridge MA: Harvard University Press)

Lagerqvist, Lars O. and Ernst Nathorst-Böös. 1999. *Vad kostade det? Priser och löner från medeltid till våra dagar* (Stockholm: Natur och Kultur/LT)

Lanzinger, Margareth. 2015. *Verwaltete Verwandtschaft: Eheverbote, kirchliche und staatliche Dispenspraxis im 18. und 19. Jahrhundert* (Cologne: Böhlau)

Lennartsson, Malin. 1999. *I säng och säte: Relationer mellan kvinnor och män i 1600-talets Småland* (Lund: Biblioteca historica lundensis, 92)

——. 2009. 'Hävdande och hustrubröst: Sexualitet, kropp och identitet i det tidigmoderna Sverige', *Historisk tidskrift*, 129:3, 361–80

——. 2012. 'Barnhustrur eller mogna brudar? Nya perspektiv på giftermålsmönstret i svensk stormaktstid', *Scandia*, 78:2, 86–127

Lennartsson, Rebecka. 2001. *Malaria Urbana: Om byråflickan Anna Johannesdotter och prostitutionen i Stockholm kring 1900* (Stockholm: Östlings förlag)

Lennerhed, Lena. 1994. *Frihet att njuta: Sexualdebatten i Sverige på 1960-talet* (Stockholm: Norstedts)

Levin, Hjördis. 1994. *Masken uti rosen: Nymalthusianism och födelsekontroll i Sverige 1880–1910: Propaganda och motstånd* (Stockholm: Brutus Östlings bokförlag Symposion)

Liliequist, Jonas. 1988. 'Bekännelsen, döden och makten: En studie i social kontroll med utgångspunkt från tidelagsbrottet i 1600- och 1700-talets Sverige', in *Historia nu: 18 Umeåforskare om det förflutna*, ed. by Anders Brändström (Umeå: Umeå University)

——. 1992. *Brott, synd och straff: Tidelagsbrottet i Sverige under 1600- och 1700- talet* (Umeå: Umeå University)

——. 2007. 'Kärlek, kön och sexualitet', in *Signums svenska kulturhistoria: Gustavianska tiden*, ed. by Jakob Christiansson (Stockholm: Signum)

Lindberg, Bo. 1976. *Naturrätten i Uppsala 1655–1720* (Uppsala: University of Uppsala)

Lindberg, Bo. 1992. *Praemia et Poenae: Etik och straffrätt i Sverige i tidig ny tid* (Uppsala: University of Uppsala)

Lindstedt Cronberg, Marie. 1997. *Synd och skam: Ogifta mödrar på svensk landsbygd 1680–1880* (Lund: Cronberg Publications)

——. 2002. 'Incest: Från brott mot Gud till brott mot barn inom familjen', in *Offer för brott: Våldtäkt, incest och barnamord i Sveriges historia från reformationen till nutid*, ed. by Eva Bergenlöv, Marie Lindstedt Cronberg, and Eva Österberg (Lund: Nordic Academic Press), pp. 105–78

Luhmann, Niklas. 2003. *Kärlek som passion: Om kodifieringen av intimitet* (Malmö: Liber). Translation by Ole Agevall of Luhmann's *Liebe als Passion: Zur Codierung von Intimität*, first published by Suhrkamp (Frankfurt) in 1982

Lundquist, Tommie. 1982. *Den disciplinerade dubbelmoralen: Studier i den reglementerade prostitutionens historia i Sverige 1859–1918* (Göteborg: University of Gothenburg, Department of History)

Lövkrona, Inger. 1999. *Annika Larsdotter – barnamörderska: Kön, makt och sexualitet i 1700-talets Sverige* (Lund: Historiska Media)
Malmstedt, Göran. 1994. *Helgdagsreduktionen: Övergång från ett medeltida till ett modernt år i Sverige 1500–1800* (Göteborg: University of Gothenburg, Department of History)
Marklund, Andreas. 2000. 'Gossen och husbonden: Ideal, individer och äktenskap i 1700-talets Sverige', in *Bedrägliga begrepp: Kön och genus i humanistisk forskning*, ed. by Gudrun Andersson (Uppsala: University of Uppsala, Department of History)
——. 2004. *I hans hus: Svensk manlighet i historisk belysning* (Umeå: Boréa)
Mathieu, Jon. 2007. 'Kin Marriages: Trends and Interpretations from the Swiss Example', in *Kinship in Europe: Approaches to Long-Term Development, 1300–1900*, ed. by David Warren Sabean, Simon Teuscher, and Jon Mathieu (New York: Berghahn), pp. 211–30
Matović, Margareta R. 1984. *Stockholmsäktenskap: Familjebildning och partnerval i Stockholm 1850–1890* (Stockholm: Liber)
Mcleod, Hugh. 2000a. 'New Perspectives on the Religious History of Western and Northern Europe', *Kyrkohistorisk årsskrift*, 135–45
——. 2000b. *Secularisation in Western Europe, 1848–1914* (London: Macmillan)
Melby, Kari, Anu Pylkkänen, Bente Rosenbeck, and Christina Carlsson Wetterberg. 2006. *Inte ett ord om kärlek: Äktenskap och politik i Norden ca 1850–1930* (Göteborg: Makadam)
Meyer-Renschhausen, Elisabeth von. 1997. 'Zur Rechtsgeschichte der Prostitution: Die gesellschaftliche "Doppelmoral" vor Gericht', in *Frauen in der Geschichte des Rechts: Von der Frühen Neuzeit bis zur Gegenwart*, ed. by Ute Gerhard (Munich: C. H. Beck), pp. 772–89
Mitterauer, Michel. 1994. 'The Customs of the Magians: The Problem of Incest in Historical Societies', in *Sexual Knowledge, Sexual Science: The History of Attitudes to Sexuality*, ed. by Roy Porter and Mikulás Teich (Cambridge: Cambridge University Press)
Morris, Polly. 1992. 'Incest or Survival Strategy?', in *Forbidden History: The State, Society, and the Regulation of Sexuality in Modern Europe*, ed. by John C. Fout (Chicago: University of Chicago Press)
Nilsson [Hammar], Anna. 2012. *Lyckans betydelse: Sekularisering, sensibilisering och individualisering 1750–1850* (Höör: Agering)
Nilsson, Roddy. 2008. 'Den sociala frågan', in *Signums svenska kulturhistoria: Det moderna genombrottet*, ed. by Jakob Christensson (Lund: Signum), pp. 139–73
——. 2011. *Kontroll, makt och omsorg: Sociala problem och socialpolitik i Sverige 1780–1940* (Lund: Studentlitteratur)
Odén, Birgitta. 1991. 'Relationer mellan generationerna: Rättsläget 1300–1900', in *Maktpolitik och husfrid: studier i internationell och svensk historia tillägnade Göran Rystad*, ed. by Bengt Ankarloo (Lund: Lund University Press, pre-2000 imprint), pp. 85–116

——. 2001. 'Kyrkan och relationen mellan generationerna', in *Svensk kyrkohistoria, 6: Romantiken och liberalismens tid*, main author Anders Jarlert (Stockholm: Verbum), pp. 251–60

Oja, Linda. 1999. *Varken Gud eller natur: Synen på magi i 1600- och 1700-talets Sverige* (Stockholm: Brutus Östlings bokförlag Symposion)

Olivecrona, Knut. 1866. *Om dödsstraffet* (Uppsala: W. Schultz)

Persson, Bodil E. B. 2001. *Pestens gåta: Farsoter i det tidiga 1700-talets Skåne* (Lund: Nordic Academic Press)

Petersson, Birgit. 1983. *'Den farliga underklassen': Studier i fattigdom och brottslighet i 1800-talets Sverige* (Stockholm: Almqvist & Wiksell International)

Pulman, Bertrand. 2012. 'Contribution à l'histoire des débats sociologie/psychoanalyse: Westermarck, Durkheim et Freud face à "l'horreur de l'inceste"', in *Revue française de sociologie*, 53:4, 623–49

Rosén, Ulla. 2004. *Gamla plikter och nya krav: En studie om egendom, kvinnosyn och äldreomsorg i det svenska agrarsamhället 1815–1939* (Växjö: Växjö University Press)

Rublack, Ulinka. 1999. *The Crimes of Women in Early Modern Germany* (Oxford: Clarendon Press)

Rundquist, Angela. 1989. *Blått blod och liljevita händer* (Stockholm: Carlsson)

Sabean, David Warren. 1998. *Kinship in Neckerhausen, 1700–1870* (Cambridge: Cambridge University Press)

——. 2011a. 'German International Families in the Nineteenth Century: The Siemens Family as a Thought Experiment', in *Transregional Families in Europe and Beyond: Experiences Since the Middle Ages*, ed. by Christopher H. Johnson, David Warren Sabean, Simon Teuscher, and Francesca Trivellato (New York and Oxford: Berghahn), pp. 229–53

——. 2011b. 'Kinship and Issues of the Self in Europe Around 1800', in *Sibling Relations and the Transformations of European Kinship, 1300–1900*, ed. by Christopher H. Johnson and David Warren Sabean (New York: Berghahn), pp. 221–39

Sabean, David Warren, and Simon Teuscher. 2007. 'A New Approach to Long-Term Development', in *Kinship in Europe: Approaches to Long-Term Development, 1300–1900*, ed. by David Warren Sabean, Simon Teuscher, and Jon Mathieu (New York: Berghahn), pp. 1–32

Sabean, David Warren, Simon Teuscher, and Jon Mathieu (eds). 2007a. *Kinship in Europe: Approaches to Long-Term Development, 1300–1900* (New York: Berghahn)

——. 2007b. 'Outline and Summaries', in *Kinship in Europe: Approaches to Long-Term Development, 1300–1900* (New York: Berghahn)

Salonen, Kirsi. 2001. *The Penitentiary as a Well of Grace in the Late Middle Ages: The Example of the Province of Uppsala 1448–1527* (Saarijärvi: Academia Scientiarum Fennica)

Sandén, Annika. 2005. *Stadsgemenskapens resurser och villkor: Samhällssyn och välfärdsstrategier i Linköping 1600–1620* (Linköping: University of Linköping)

Sanders, Hanne. 2001. 'På rejse mellem Gud och Djævelen: En introduktion', in *Mellem Gud og Djævelen: Religiøse og magiske verdensbilleder i Norden 1500–1800*, ed. by Hanne Sanders (Copenhagen: Nordic Council of Ministers), pp. 7–16

Saurer, Edith von. 1997. 'Stiefmütter und Stiefsöhne: Endogamieverbote zwischen kanonischem und zivilem Recht am Beispiel Österreichs (1790–1850)', in *Frauen in der Geschichtes des Rechts: Von der Frühen Neuzeit bis zur Gegenwart*, ed. by Ute Gerhard (Munich: C. H. Beck), pp. 345–66

Savin, Kristiina. 2011. *Fortunas klädnader: Lycka, olycka och risk i det tidigmoderna Sverige* (Lund: Sekel)

Seidelin, Mette. 2014. 'En nem og ikke alltid uvillig partner? Opfattelsen af børns rolle i incestsager 1930–1967', unpublished PhD dissertation, University of Southern Denmark

Semmler, Sara. 2003. 'Motiv bakom kriminaliseringen av vuxenincest enligt BrB 6:6§', unpublished practical application paper (Göteborg)

Serrano, Alberto C., and David W. Gunzburger. 1983. 'An Historical Perspective of Incest', *International Journal of Family Therapy*, 5:2, 70–80

Sjöberg, Maria. 1996. 'Hade jorden ett kön? Något om genuskonstruktion i det tidigmoderna Sverige', in *Historisk tidskrift*, 3, 362–96

——. 2001. *Kvinnors jord, manlig rätt: äktenskap, egendom och makt i äldre tid* (Hedemora: Gidlund)

Sjögren, Mikael. 1997. *Fattigvård och folkuppfostran: Liberal fattigvårdspolitik 1903–1918* (Stockholm: Carlsson)

Spang-Hanssen, E. 1963. *Fra Ludvig Holbergs unge dage: Hans strid med Andreas Hojer* (Copenhagen: Gad)

Stadin, Kekke. 2004. *Stånd och genus i stormaktstidens Sverige* (Lund: Nordic Academic Press)

——. 2005. 'De starkaste banden', in *Signums svenska kulturhistoria: Stormaktstiden*, ed. by Jakob Christensson (Lund: Verbum), pp. 375–407

Strong, Anise K. 2005. 'Incest Laws and Absent Taboos in Roman Egypt', in *Ancient History Bulletin*, 19:1, 31–41

Sundin, Jan. 1982. 'Kontroll, straff och försoning: Kyrklig rättvisa på sockennivå före 1850', in *Kontroll och kontrollerade: Formell och informell kontroll i ett historiskt perspektiv*, ed. by Jan Sundin (Umeå: University of Umeå, Department of History), pp. 39–85

——. 1992. *För Gud, staten och folket: Brott och rättskipning i Sverige 1600–1840* (Stockholm: Institutet för rättshistorisk forskning)

Taussi Sjöberg, Marja. 1988. *Skiljas: Trolovning, äktenskap och skilsmässa i Norrland på 1800-talet* (Stockholm: Författarförlaget)

——. 1994. 'Mellan far och make: Ägandet, arvet och kvinnorna', in *Bryta, bygga, bo: Svensk historia underifrån*, ed. by Gunnar Broberg, Ulla Wikander, and Klas Åmark (Stockholm: Ordfront), pp. 50–71

——. 1996. *Rätten och kvinnorna: Från släktmakt till statsmakt i Sverige på 1500- och 1600-talet* (Stockholm: Atlantis)

Telste, Kari. 1993. *Mellom liv og lov: Kontroll av seksualitet i Ringerike og Hallingdal 1652–1710* (Oslo: University of Oslo, Department of History IKS)

——. 1997. '"Piger! Troe ei Elskers Ord": Ekteskapslöfter i norsk rett fra reformasjonen til 1900', in *Seklernas Sex: bidrag till sexualitetens historia*, ed. by Åsa Bergenheim and Lena Lennerhed (Stockholm: Carlsson), pp. 113–26

——. 1999. *Brutte löfter: En kulturhistorisk studie av kjønn og aere 1700–1900* (Oslo: Acta humaniora, Unipub. forlag)

Terjesen, Harriet Marie. 1994. *Blodskam og Leiermål i Forbudne Ledd: En studie med utgangspunkt i kilder fra Rogaland i tidsperioden 1602–1659/61*, Tingbokprosjektet [The judgement-book project] (Oslo)

Thomas, Keith. 1984. *Man and the Natural World: Changing Attitudes in England, 1500–1800* (Harmondsworth: Penguin. Originally published by Allen Lane in 1983)

Thunander, Rudolf. 1992. *Förbjuden kärlek: Sexualbrott, kärleksmagi och kärleksbrev i 1600-talets Sverige* (Stockholm: Atlantis)

——. 1993. *Hovrätt i funktion: Göta hovrätt och brottmålen, 1635–1699* (Stockholm: Institutet för rättshistorisk forskning)

——. 1995. 'Den svenska hovrätten i 1600-talets rättsliga system', *Scandia*, 61:1, 21–8

Turner, Jonathan and Alexandra Maryanski. 2005. *Incest: Origins of the Taboo* (London: Paradigm)

Tydén, Mattias. 2002. *Från politik till praktik: De svenska steriliseringslagarna 1935–1975* (Stockholm: Almqvist & Wiksell International)

Ubl, Karl. 2008. *Inzestverbot und Gesetzgebung: Die Konstruktion eines Verbrechens (300–1100)* (Berlin: De Gruyter)

Vainio-Korhonen, Kirsi. 1997. 'Yrket i arv? Släkt- och äktenskapets betydelse i rekryteringen av nya hantverkare', in *Fundera tar längsta tiden, sa skräddarn, då han sydde byxor: Frågeställningar och problem kring hantverksforskningen från medeltiden till skråväsendets upplösning*, ed. by Ulla Heino and Kirsi Vaiono-Korhonen (Åbo/Turku: Turun yliopiston historian laitoksen julkaisuja), pp. 169–78

Walkowitz, Judith R. 1982. *Prostitution and Victorian Society: Women, Class, and the State* (Cambridge: Cambridge University Press)

Widén, Solveig. 1988. *Änkeomsorg i ståndssamhället: Försörjnings- och understödsformer för prästänkor i Åbo stift 1723–1807* (Åbo/Turku: Åbo Akademi)

Winberg, Christer. 1985. *Grenverket: Studier rörande jord, släktskapssystem och ståndsprivilegier* (Stockholm: Institutet för rättshistorisk forskning)

Witte, John, Jr. 2002. *Law and Protestantism: The Legal Teachings of the Lutheran Reformation* (Cambridge: Cambridge University Press)

Wolf, Arthur P. 2004. 'Introduction', in *Inbreeding, Incest, and the Incest Taboo: The State of Knowledge at the Turn of the Century*, ed. by Arthur P. Wolf and William H. Durham (Stanford: Stanford University Press), pp. 1–23

Wolf, Arthur P. and William H. Durham (eds). 2004. *Inbreeding, Incest, and the Incest Taboo: The State of Knowledge at the Turn of the Century* (Stanford: Stanford University Press)

Ågren, Maria. 1997. *Att hävda sin rätt: Synen på jordägande i 1600-talets Sverige speglad i institutet urminnes hävd* (Stockholm: Institutet för rättshistorisk forskning)

Österberg, Eva, Malin Lennartsson, and Hans Eyvind Naess. 2000. 'Social Control Outside or Combined with the Secular Judicial Arena', in *People Meet the Law: Control and Conflict-Handling in the Post-Reformation and Pre-Industrial Period*, ed. by Eva Österberg and Sölvi Sogner (Oslo: Scandinavian University Press), pp. 237–66

Index

When names and concepts that occur in the running text also appear in footnotes, references to the latter have been omitted.

abuse, sexual *see* coercion
affinity 21–3, 35–6, 41–2, 51–2, 57–61, 63–5, 68–70, 74–5, 78–80, 96–8, 107, 110–11, 113, 119, 124–5, 130–1, 134–5, 138, 141, 157, 159–60, 164, 166–9, 170n, 173, 189–90, 192, 196–7, 206, 208, 210–14, 217–18, 221, 224–5, 230, 231n, 232, 252, 257, 264, 271, 276, 278–9, 282, 284
age
  difference 62, 110, 156, 162, 180, 240–50, 252, 265, 280–1
  relationship 113, 118, 133, 152, 163–5, 265, 279–81
alliance 4n, 29, 35n, 46–9, 57, 141, 200, 203, 215, 246, 267, 271–2, 279–80
Almquist, Jan Eric 35n, 40n
Alström, Carl Henry 140n, 215n
Ambjörnsson, Ronny 47n, 86n, 103n, 274
aristocracy 11, 17n, 28n, 29, 37, 41, 48–50, 115n, 140n, 142, 144–5, 190, 198–200, 202, 215, 271
Arnhart, Larry 4n
Augustine of Hippo (354–430) 46n
Austria 23, 29, 41, 68n, 135, 149, 205–6, 265, 267

Baldwin, John W. 86n, 182n
Bergenheim, Åsa 210n, 226–7n, 256, 258, 260n
Bergenlöv, Eva 91n, 94–5
Bexell, Oloph 208n
Bittles, Alan H. 3n, 5n, 34n, 141n, 144n, 215n
Biurman, Johan 18n
Bjurman, Eva Lis 47n
Blom, Ida 227n
Blumer, Herbert 9n
bourgeoisie 13n, 29, 115n, 142, 145, 190, 194, 215
Braun, Christina von 47n, 143–4n
Broberg, Gunnar 226n, 228n
Brown, Callum G. 208n
Brundage, James A. 86n, 182n

canon law 37, 39n, 81
Carlsson, Sten 19n, 114n, 140n, 223n, 245
Carmichael, Calum M. 36n
cathedral chapter 13, 19, 33–4, 37n, 40n, 48, 50n, 51–2, 54–63, 65–6, 67n, 113–14, 116–17, 130, 155–6, 158, 244n, 275, 288
Chammas, Jacqueline 27n, 134–5n
Charon, Joel M. 8n, 9–10, 269
Christensen-Nugues, Charlotte 35n, 37n
coercion 2, 24, 27, 69n, 88–98, 102, 108, 110n, 111, 113, 127, 181–3, 187, 205, 210, 255, 257–8, 260–2, 264, 267, 270–1, 282
consanguinity 21–3, 35–6, 51–2, 57–9, 63–4, 65n, 69–70, 75, 78, 97, 107–8, 110, 124–5, 135, 138, 167, 169, 170n,

192–3, 197, 210–12, 229–30, 231n, 232, 235, 239, 244n, 264
consistory *see* cathedral chapter
Coontz, Stephanie 46, 47n, 114n, 194n, 245n, 274
Corbett, Mary Jean 143n
court of appeal 1, 12–17, 32–4, 59, 61n, 65–6, 69, 73–4, 76–8, 81n, 83, 86, 92, 95, 98, 102, 106–8, 110–11, 113–14, 116, 120, 124, 126, 129, 168n, 173n, 179, 189, 216n, 274

Darrow, Margaret H. 149, 205n
Darwin, Charles (1809–82) 4, 226–8, 264
Davidoff, Leonore 47n, 143–4n, 182n, 194n, 245n
Davidson, Denise Z. 47–8n, 144n, 151
Denbo, Seth 25, 26n, 47n, 134–5n, 165n, 205n, 266n
Denmark 27, 41, 75, 132–3, 138, 163, 186–7, 191, 202, 205, 229, 256, 264, 268
diocese *see* cathedral chapter
dispensation *see under* incest
Donahue, Charles, Jr. 35n, 39n
Doolittle, Megan 143n, 194n, 245n
Durham, William H. 4n
Dutch *see* Holland

economic factors 4, 25, 28, 46–9, 98, 110, 118–19, 126, 136, 142, 144–6, 149–51, 157, 164–5, 194, 199–203, 207–9, 215, 222n, 234, 238, 249–50, 255–6, 259, 271–2, 276, 281, 283, 285
Edgren, Lars 165n, 245n
Egerbladh, I. 141n, 215n
Egmond, Florike 25, 38n, 68n, 75n, 97n, 134n
Ekenstam, Claes 226n
endogamy 28, 48–9, 143
England 25–9, 38, 41, 47n, 68n, 135, 143–4n, 165, 205, 227, 265–6, 268
Erickson, Mark T. 3n
Eriksson, Gunnar 228n
eugenics 202, 226n, 228, 230, 233, 259, 264–6, 283
exogamy 35, 48

false fathers 122–4
family
position 113–18, 128, 133, 152–3, 157–60, 163–5, 242n, 252–3, 279–80, 283
relationship 16, 22–3, 37, 55, 57, 59–63, 65, 67–8, 75, 78–80, 91–2, 94–5, 100, 107–8, 110, 116–18, 124, 127–8, 133, 142, 152, 160, 167, 169, 179, 186, 188, 194–5, 197–8, 205, 211, 220, 223–5, 230, 231n, 232–3, 235, 238, 240, 261, 263–4, 273, 275, 277–9, 284
Ferri, Enrico 260n
filial deference 43–4, 63–4, 153, 155–7, 159, 161–2, 165, 197, 204, 206, 258, 277–9
Fink, Janet 143n, 182n, 194n, 245n
Fox, Robin 4n
France 27, 29, 135, 138, 142, 144n, 149, 151, 165, 186, 205, 227, 256, 266, 269
Frances, Catherine 48n
Frandsen, Paul John 3–4n, 23n
Freud, Sigmund (1856–1939) 3

Gaunt, David 7n, 35n, 37n, 39n, 46n, 49n, 107n, 114n, 155n, 164, 165n, 245n, 279
generation 5, 21, 35, 48, 63, 115–16, 127, 153, 156–61, 163–5, 186, 197–8, 202, 204, 228–9, 241, 252, 269, 277–80
genetics 4–5, 264, 284
Germany, including Prussia 22, 24–6, 29, 38, 41, 47, 55n, 74n, 75, 97–8, 108, 134–5, 139, 142–3, 183, 186, 205, 209, 227–8, 229n, 254, 256, 264–5, 268
Giddens, Anthony 8–9n
Giuliani, Fabienne 27, 186n, 205n, 256n, 266n
Goody, Jack 46n
Gordon, Linda 256n
Great Britain *see* England
Grotius, Hugo (1583–1645) 42
Gunnlaugsson, Gísli Ágúst 6n
Gunzburger, David W. 3n
Gustav III (1746—1792), king of Sweden 138

Göransson, Anita 24n, 29, 47–8n, 145n, 215, 245n

Hall, Catherine 47n, 143–4n
Hammar, K. G. 44n
Hansen, Anna 10–11n, 47n, 115, 116n, 155n
Hansen, Torleif 26, 27n, 123n
Hartmansdorff, August von (1792—1856) 198
Hastrup, Kirsten 38n
Hehenberger, Susanne 37n, 68n, 75n, 134–5n
Henry VIII (1491-1547), king of England 28n, 268
Héritier, Françoise 4n
Herlihy, David 3n, 35n, 46n, 64, 275
Herman, Judith 256n
hierarchy 17, 25, 43–4, 47, 92, 114–17, 133, 153, 157, 198, 202, 204, 269, 277–8
Hirschman, Lisa 256n
Hofsten, Erland 142n
Hojer, Andreas 132, 187, 191
Holberg, Ludvig (1684–1754) 132
Holden, Katherine 143n, 182n, 194n, 245n
Holland 25, 38, 68n, 75, 97, 134, 268
household 39, 54, 64, 94, 100, 109, 115–16, 127, 145, 149, 153, 159, 171, 182, 194-5, 199, 217–18, 223, 245, 251, 253, 275–6, 278
Hull, Isabel V. 6n, 24n, 38n, 74–5n
hundred (court) 1n, 11–12, 15–16, 19, 30, 32–3, 56, 59, 63, 66–7, 72–4, 77, 80, 82n, 83, 86, 93, 95, 96n, 100–2, 104–5, 110–11n, 119, 121–3n, 124, 126–9, 138, 170n, 171–2, 173–4n, 177–9n, 181, 184n, 185, 189n, 191, 199, 216–17, 220n, 221, 224, 234, 244n, 253, 260–1n, 266, 271–2, 285
Hunt, Lynn 143n, 165n, 205n
Häthén, Christian 137–9n, 209–10n, 260n

Iceland 6, 27, 75, 133, 268
incest
  collateral (degree) 21–3, 28, 36, 41, 57–61, 64–5, 70, 78–80, 97, 110–4, 116, 119, 124, 130–1, 133–5, 141–2, 144, 146, 167–9, 170n, 180, 190, 192, 204, 206, 208, 210–14, 217–18, 221, 224–5, 227, 264, 277–9
  diagonal (degree) 23, 36, 42, 52, 57–8, 64, 68, 70, 74, 78–80, 97, 117n, 124–5, 131, 134, 146, 157, 159, 160, 164, 167–70, 180, 190, 192n, 208, 210–14, 224–5, 229–30, 232, 235, 238–9, 244n, 264–5, 278, 284
  dispensation 12, 14, 17–20, 28–9, 31, 37–8, 41–2, 45–6, 48–59, 63, 65–6, 68–9, 114, 116, 130, 133–4, 139–42, 146–9, 151–3, 157–61, 163–6, 168, 175, 180, 188–9, 193, 200n, 201–4, 206, 213–15, 218, 224, 229–35, 237, 240, 242, 245–6, 260–1, 263–5, 269–72, 274–5, 277–81, 284
  horizontal (degree) *see* incest, collateral
  lineal (degree) 21–3, 28, 36, 70, 75, 78–80, 97, 110–12, 114, 116, 117n, 124, 130, 133, 135, 141–2, 146, 158n, 160, 162, 167–9, 170n, 180, 192, 194, 197, 204, 206, 211–12, 214, 230, 232, 253, 277–9, 284
  prohibition 2–7, 12–14, 18, 20, 23–4, 26–7, 28n, 29–30, 34–9, 41–2, 44–5, 46n, 48–50, 57, 59, 62–5, 67–70, 75, 84, 88, 98, 103, 107, 112, 117, 130, 132–4, 141, 151, 155, 157, 163, 166, 169, 186–206, 208, 210–13, 216, 218, 225, 229–30, 236, 238–9, 257, 263–8, 270–9, 282–5, 291
  taboo *see* incest, prohibition
  vertical (degree) *see* incest, lineal
incestuous relations: a man and (his)…
  a mother and her daughter 23, 36, 39, 79–80
  a woman and her niece *see* wife's niece
  aunt 23, 36, 42, 50n, 70, 78, 97, 167, 169, 211, 229–30, 232, 235, 238–9, 251–2, 264–5, 284

aunt's husband's widow 61, 67, 114, 117, 277
brother's wife/widow 23, 36, 70, 79, 97, 111–12, 131, 134, 146, 147n, 163n, 167, 169, 189–90, 192, 201, 210–11, 214, 217–18, 277
cousin 3, 5n, 18, 22–3, 28–9, 36, 41–2, 49–59, 64, 70, 78, 140n, 141, 143, 146–7, 148n, 152, 157–8, 161n, 167, 169, 189n, 190, 192–3, 195–6, 198–202, 210, 214–15, 245n, 265–6, 268, 271, 275–6, 278
cousin's daughter 57, 78
cousin's widow *see* wife's cousin
daughter 23–4, 36, 70, 78, 97, 107–8, 167, 169, 181, 185, 211, 221, 255, 267, 282
daughter-in-law 23, 70, 79–80, 97, 110–11, 112n, 169, 180, 211, 284
daughter-in-law's niece 67
daughter's stepdaughter 159n, 164n
grandmother/daughter 5, 22–3, 36, 70, 78, 169, 211
mother 22–3, 36, 39, 70, 125, 167, 169, 211
mother-in-law 23, 70, 79, 167, 169, 211, 230, 284
niece 3, 5, 23, 26, 36, 41–2, 44, 50, 64n, 69–70, 78, 93, 97, 109, 125, 129, 146, 157, 161n, 167, 169, 179, 185, 192, 211, 217, 219n, 220, 229–30, 232, 235–6, 239, 241–3, 247–9, 252, 260–1, 264–5, 284
parent's cousin 52, 57, 65
sibling's stepdaughter 52, 58, 63–4, 275
sister 108–9, 255, 284
son-in-law's daughter 78n, 153
stepdaughter 23, 26, 36, 70, 78–80, 83, 97, 107–8, 110–11, 122–3, 125, 127, 141, 167, 168n, 169, 171–3, 177, 181, 185–6, 206, 211, 230, 232, 252, 255, 262–3, 277–8, 282, 284
stepfather's/son's widow 63, 66–7n, 79, 117n, 157–8, 160, 162, 169, 188–90, 211, 214, 278, 280
stepgrandfather's widow 158–9
stepmother 23, 36, 39, 70, 79, 97, 110–11, 116, 167, 169, 187, 206, 211, 230, 277, 284
stepmother's aunt 62, 65, 114, 117, 277
stepmother's stepmother 63, 117n, 153
stepson's stepdaughter 153, 160
two cousins *see* wife's cousin
two sisters 3, 21, 23, 36n, 39, 61, 70, 78–9, 84, 97, 111–12, 125, 167, 169, 217
uncle's wife/widow/concubine 22–3, 36, 50n, 67, 70, 74, 79–80, 97, 117, 146, 148n, 150, 151n, 153, 156–7, 160, 161n, 162–4, 167, 169, 190, 192n, 211, 214, 280
wife's aunt 23, 79, 134, 167, 169, 189n, 211, 253n
wife's brother's widow/concubine 23, 52, 57, 60–1, 64, 70, 79, 278
wife's cousin 22–3, 28n, 51–2, 56–7, 59, 64–5, 70, 79, 130, 141, 143, 166–7, 169
wife's cousin's widow 51–2
wife's former husband's sister 52, 60
wife's grandmother/daughter 22–3, 70
wife's nephew's widow 52, 58
wife's niece 23, 41, 44, 52, 58, 60, 64, 67, 69–70, 74, 78–80, 97, 117, 125, 131, 134, 147–8n, 150, 151n, 152–3, 157, 159–60, 163, 167, 169, 188–90, 210–11, 214, 278, 280
wife's sister 26, 87n, 93–4, 100–2, 112–13, 128, 131, 134, 143–4, 187, 196–7, 205, 266
wife's stepmother/daughter 22, 23, 42, 63–4, 70, 130, 153, 157, 160, 169, 190, 196, 210–11, 214, 275, 277
incestuous relations: a woman and...
a father and his son 21, 23, 79, 112n, 167
two brothers 21n, 97, 167, 290
Inger, Göran 14n, 35, 40n, 49n, 73n, 81–2n, 132n, 138n, 207–9n, 212n, 223, 260n, 284n

Inghe, Gunnar 14n, 253n, 254–5, 256n, 257, 258n, 259, 260n, 262–3, 264n
Italy 29, 149, 227, 260n

Jansson, Arne 171
Jansson, Karin Hassan 10, 17, 55n, 85n, 87n, 90, 91n, 93–4, 118n, 123n, 183n
Jarlert, Anders 136n
Jarzebowski, Claudia 24, 35n, 37, 38n, 48n, 54n, 64n, 85n, 89, 90n, 103–4n, 107n, 134–5n, 183n, 187, 205n, 265n
Johnson, Christopher H. 28–9n, 143n, 205n, 215n
Jónsson, Már 6, 7n, 27, 38–9n, 75, 138n
Joris, Elisabeth 144–5, 146n

Kerchner, Brigitte 187n, 205n
Kinberg, Olof 14n, 253n, 254–5, 256n, 257, 258n, 259, 260n, 262–3, 264n
Koefoed, Nina 163n, 187, 205n
Korpiola, Mia 7n, 37–8n
Krogh, Tyge 27, 75, 132–3n, 187
Kuper, Adam 24–6n, 28–9, 38n, 47–8n, 143n, 205n, 215, 266n

Lagerqvist, Lars O. 51n, 200n
Lanzinger, Margareth 29n, 37n, 149n
legislation 2, 5, 7, 13, 20, 26–7, 35n, 39–40, 58, 61, 63, 66, 74, 83, 87, 91, 118, 125, 129–30, 132–5, 138–9, 145, 151, 155, 168, 186, 189–91, 196–7, 199, 202–3, 213, 217, 222, 228–9, 244, 253, 258–9, 263, 265–6, 268–71, 277–9, 281, 284–5
- 1571 Swedish Church Ordinance 40n
- 1608 Statute Book of Sweden 40–1, 69, 133
- 1686 Swedish Church Law 40n
- 1734 Statute Book of Sweden 13, 44, 81n, 130–2, 139, 155, 168–9, 210, 240
- 1864 Statute Book of Sweden 13, 209–12, 240, 263, 282
- 1915 Marriage Code 13, 228, 230, 238, 240, 265
- *see also* canon law

Lennartsson, Malin 11n, 16n, 21n, 34n, 40n, 48–9n, 55n, 85–7n, 103n, 113–14n, 116n, 245n
Lennartsson, Rebecka 226n
Lennerhed, Lena 226n
Lévi-Strauss, Claude 4n
Levin, Hjördis 207n, 227n
Leviticus 36, 40, 88, 133, 278
Liliequist, Jonas 11n, 70n, 82, 83n, 108n, 118n, 120, 170–1, 182n, 244n
Lindberg, Bo 74n, 85n, 138n, 191n
Lindstedt Cronberg, Marie 11n, 24n, 46n, 55n, 73n, 81n, 89, 90–1n, 101n, 106n, 108n, 118n, 123n, 127n, 181n, 210n, 222, 223n
local (court) *see* hundred (court)
Lord Lyndhurst's Act (1835) 26n, 266
love 47, 51, 53–4, 56, 98–9, 102–3, 105–6, 127, 134, 143–4, 146–9, 151, 156, 158, 165, 171, 175, 177, 179–80, 194–5, 204, 219, 227, 236, 238–9, 251, 272–6, 281, 285
Luhmann, Niklas 47, 103–4n, 144n, 274
Lundquist, Tommie 226–7n
Luther, Martin (1483–1546)/ Lutheran 29, 37–9, 42, 115n, 153–4, 198, 207, 226
Lövkrona, Inger 107n, 123n, 171n

McLeod, Hugh 208n
Maimonides, Moses (1138–1204) 42
Malmstedt, Göran 19n, 120–1n, 136n
Marklund, Andreas 10n, 21n, 34n, 47n, 85n, 153n, 182n, 186n, 244n
Maryanski, Alexandra 3–4n, 48n
Mathieu, Jon 28n, 143–4n, 215n
Matović, Margareta R. 47n, 245n, 246
Mead, George Herbert 9n
Melby, Kari 46n
Meyer-Renschhausen, Elisabeth von 227n
Mitterauer, Michel 3–4n, 23, 34n, 64n, 107, 275
Morris, Polly 26, 38n, 68n, 205n
Månsson, Ola (1821–95) 213
Mörner, Oscar (1816–88) 213

Naess, Hans Eyvind 11n, 16n
Nathorst-Böös, Ernst 51n, 200n
natural law 41–2, 132, 134, 137, 191
Nehrman, David (1695–1769) 21n, 130n
Netherlands *see* Holland
Nilsson [Hammar], Anna 54n, 86n, 103n, 149n, 186n
Nilsson, Roddy 207n, 223n, 227n, 256n
nobility *see* aristocracy
Norway 26, 55n, 68n, 75, 93n, 125, 132–3, 138, 229, 264, 268

Odén, Birgitta 44n, 153n, 164, 165n, 279
Oja, Linda 137n
Olivecrona, Knut 138n, 168n

paternal authority *see* filial deference
Petri, Olaus (1493–1552) 73
Persson, Bodil E. B. 120n
Petersson, Birgit 207n
Pufendorf, Samuel (1632–94) 138
Pulman, Bertrand 4n

race biology *see* eugenics
Ribbing, Arvid (1794–1865) 199
Riemer, Svend 14n, 253n, 254–5, 256n, 257, 258n, 259, 260n, 262–3, 264n
Rosén, Ulla 246
Rublack, Ulinka 6n, 25, 38n, 55n, 75n, 87n, 90n, 98, 108, 118n, 134n
Rundquist, Angela 47n, 199n

Sabean, David Warren 28–9n, 143, 144n, 205n, 215n, 279
Salonen, Kirsi 35n, 37n
Sandén, Annika 21n, 111n, 244n
Sanders, Hanne 104n
Saurer, Edith von 29n, 205n, 206n, 265n
Savin, Kristiina 104n, 121n
Schlyter, Carl Johan (1795–1888) 14n, 190, 191n, 192, 195, 196n, 198n, 202n
Seidelin, Mette 256n
Semmler, Sara 5n, 258n, 284n
Serrano, Alberto C. 3n
Sjöberg, Maria 47n, 118n, 144–5
Sjöberg, Marja Taussi *see* Taussi Sjöberg
Sjögren, Mikael 207n
social
  construction 4, 6, 10, 92, 137, 277
  control 8, 10, 11n
  Darwinism *see* Darwin
  interaction 7–10, 269, 276
  intercourse *see* social interaction
  practice *see* social interaction
Sondén, Torsten 253, 255n, 258, 262–3
Spang-Hanssen, E. 132n
Sparre, Erik (1816–86) 213
Stadin, Kekke 54n, 103n, 115n, 245n
Stiernhöök, Johan (1596–1675) 40–4, 153, 157n
Strokirch, Henning Adolf von (1757–1826) 189
Strong, Anise K. 3n
suicide by execution (following self-denunciation) 170–1
Sundholm, Magnus 267n
Sundin, Jan 24n, 32n, 77, 78n, 81n, 118n, 136n
Sutton, Philip W. 8–9n
Svensson, Frej 243, 249
Switzerland 29, 142, 144, 149
symbolic interactionism 9, 269

Table of Duties 115n, 153, 198
Taussi Sjöberg, Marja 55n, 81n, 145n, 245n, 246
Telste, Kari 26, 47n, 55n, 87n, 90n, 118n, 123n, 125, 127n
Terjesen, Harriet Marie 24n, 26, 68n, 75n
Teuscher, Simon 28n, 143n, 215n
Thomas, Keith 85n, 104n
Thorén, Caroline 267n
Thunander, Rudolf 6n, 15n, 24n, 33–4n, 39n, 60n, 66n, 69n, 72n, 74n, 77, 92n, 104n, 106n, 118n
Tottie, Lars 5n, 264n, 284n
Turner, Jonathan 3–4n, 48n
Tydén, Mattias 226n, 228n

Ubl, Karl 35n

Vainio-Korhonen, Kirsi 165, 245n
violence *see* coercion

virtue 53–4, 56, 69, 85, 108, 148–9, 152, 186, 192–3, 272, 274

Walkowitz, Judith R. 227n
Wallroth, Emelie 267n
Westermarck, Edvard (1862–1939) 3–4
Western European marriage pattern 114n, 245
Widén, Solveig 165, 245n
widow conservation 165, 245–6, 280
Winberg, Christer 49n, 144n
Witte, John, Jr. 39n
Wolf, Arthur P. 3–4n

Ågren, Maria 144n

Österberg, Eva 11n, 16n

EU authorised representative for GPSR:
Easy Access System Europe, Mustamäe tee 50,
10621 Tallinn, Estonia
gpsr.requests@easproject.com

www.ingramcontent.com/pod-product-compliance
Ingram Content Group UK Ltd.
Pitfield, Milton Keynes, MK11 3LW, UK
UKHW021824140426
5217IPUK00004B/81

* 9 7 8 9 1 9 8 4 6 9 9 0 5 *